Media and Development

Richard Vokes

LONDON AND NEW YORK

First published 2018
by Routledge
2 Park Square, Milton Park, Abingdon, Oxon OX14 4RN

and by Routledge
711 Third Avenue, New York, NY 10017

Routledge is an imprint of the Taylor & Francis Group, an informa business

© 2018 Richard Vokes

The right of Richard Vokes to be identified as author of this work has been asserted by him in accordance with sections 77 and 78 of the Copyright, Designs and Patents Act 1988.

All rights reserved. No part of this book may be reprinted or reproduced or utilised in any form or by any electronic, mechanical, or other means, now known or hereafter invented, including photocopying and recording, or in any information storage or retrieval system, without permission in writing from the publishers.

Trademark notice: Product or corporate names may be trademarks or registered trademarks, and are used only for identification and explanation without intent to infringe.

British Library Cataloguing-in-Publication Data
A catalogue record for this book is available from the British Library

Library of Congress Cataloging-in-Publication Data
A catalog record has been requested for this book

ISBN: 978-0-415-74553-6 (hbk)
ISBN: 978-0-415-74554-3 (pbk)
ISBN: 978-1-315-79782-3 (ebk)

Typeset in Times New Roman
by Saxon Graphics Ltd, Derby

 Printed in the United Kingdom by Henry Ling Limited

Media and Development

At the start of the twenty-first century, the relationship between media and development has never felt more important. Following a series of 'media revolutions' throughout the developing world – beginning with the advent of cheap transistor radio sets in the late 1960s, followed by the rapid expansion of satellite television networks in the 1990s, and the more recent explosion of mobile telephony, social media, and the internet – a majority of people living in the Global South now have access to a wide variety of Information and Communications Technologies (ICTs), and live in media-saturated environments.

Yet how can radio, television, and mobile phones be most effectively harnessed towards the goals of purposive economic, social, and political change? Should they be seen as primarily a provider of channels through which 'useful information' can be delivered to target populations – in the hope that such information will alter those populations' existing behaviours? Or should they be seen as a tool for facilitating 'two-way communication' between development providers and their recipients (i.e. as technologies for improving 'participatory development')? Or should new media environments be approached simply as spaces in which people living in the developing world can define 'development' on their own terms?

This timely and original book – which is based on a critical reading of the relevant literatures, and on the author's own extensive primary research – introduces readers to all of these questions, helping them to reach their own informed positions on each. Drawing on case studies from all over the world – including 'hate radio' in Rwanda; theatre for development in India; telenovelas in Latin America; mobile banking and money in Africa; and GIS and humanitarianism in Haiti – it will be of interest to undergraduate and postgraduate students of media and development, international development professionals, and to anyone with an interest in how media does, can, or should change the world.

Richard Vokes is a Senior Lecturer in Anthropology and Development Studies at the University of Adelaide. He has long-standing research interests in the Great Lakes region of East Africa, especially in the areas of visual and media anthropology.

Routledge Perspectives on Development

Series Editor: Professor Tony Binns, *University of Otago*
www.routledge.com/Routledge-Perspectives-on-Development/book-series/SE0684

Since it was established in 2000, the same year as the Millennium Development Goals were set by the United Nations, the *Routledge Perspectives on Development* series has become the pre-eminent international textbook series on key development issues. Written by leading authors in their fields, the books have been popular with academics and students working in disciplines such as anthropology, economics, geography, international relations, politics and sociology. The series has also proved to be of particular interest to those working in interdisciplinary fields, such as area studies (African, Asian and Latin American studies), development studies, environmental studies, peace and conflict studies, rural and urban studies, travel and tourism.

If you would like to submit a book proposal for the series, please contact the Series Editor, Tony Binns, on: jab@geography.otago.ac.nz

For a complete list of titles, please visit www.routledge.com/series/SE0684

Global Finance and Development
David Hudson

Population and Development, 2nd Edition
W.T.S. Gould

Conservation and Development
Andrew Newsham and Shonil Bhagwat

Tourism and Development in the Developing World, 2nd Edition
David J. Telfer and Richard Sharpley

Conflict and Development, 2nd Edition
Andrew Williams and Roger MacGinty

Cities and Development, 2nd Edition
Sean Fox and Tom Goodfellow

Children, Youth and Development, 2nd Edition
Nicola Ansell

Information and Communication Technology for Development (ICT4D)
Richard Heeks

Media and Development
Richard Vokes

To David James Vokes

and

To all the Atukundas, Nshekanabos, Tumwesigyes, and Busingyes, big and small

Contents

List of figures   *xi*
List of boxes   *xiii*
Acknowledgements   *xiv*

    Introduction: media and development, a complicated relationship   1

1 The rise and rise of media for development   33

2 Development in the news: from iconographies of disaster to post-humanitarian communication   64

3 Media, empowerment, and agency: the promises of participatory communication   112

4 Structural-adjustment and media globalization   157

5 ICT4D in new media worlds   192

6 Development and celebrity   233

Bibliography   *261*
Index   *282*

Figures

1.1	Poster for a family planning campaign in Uganda	44
1.2	A maternity health campaign in Uganda	46
1.3	Front cover image of 'The Baby Killer' leaflet	50
1.4	Promotional image for *Hum Log*	58
2.1	'The Abolition of the Slave Trade': image of Captain Kimber	68
2.2	1876–1879 famine in India, by Willoughby Wallace Hooper	69
2.3	'Indigenous man, Nsala, pictured with the severed hand and foot of his dead daughter' by Alice Harris	70
2.4	Biafra War protests	74
2.5	'The Slave Mother'	79
2.6	The suffering mother and child	81
2.7	An image from the aftermath of the Nazi Holocaust: SS troops are forced to carry concentration camp victims to burial sites, 1945	82
2.8	In the aftermath of the Haiti earthquake, 2010	83
2.9	Concentration camp survivors, 1945	84
2.10	Refugees of the Syrian Civil War	85
2.11	The Syrian refugee crisis	87
2.12	'Madonna and Child' by Orazio Gentileschi	89
2.13	Pietà by Michelangelo	90
2.14	Expulsion of Adam and Eve from Eden by Masaccio	92
2.15	Crossing of the Red Sea by Ghirlandaio (although the artist is disputed)	93
2.16	Oxfam's GROW campaign	104
2.17	The Death of Aylan Kurdi	106

3.1	Participatory methods in development	135
3.2	A TFD group, the Kigezi Rugo Actors	141
3.3	The Chiapas Media Project	147
3.4	A CMP cameraman at work	148
4.1	Image of Radio Venceremos	176
4.2	Community radio in Kinshasa, the Democratic Republic of Congo	177
4.3	Shop selling mobile phone services, south-western Uganda	181
4.4	Worldwide internet access	184
5.1	Agbogbloshie e-waste dump in Ghana	221
5.2	A scene from the play 'Hate Radio' (a South African play that reconstructed hate radio in the Rwandan genocide of 1994)	225
6.1	Poster of Millennium Development Goals	242
6.2	Drop the Debt campaign, 'Haven't we taken enough?'	245
6.3	Product Red poster (GAP)	249
6.4	Julien Clerc, UNHCR Goodwill Ambassador for Francophone Countries in Chad	251
6.5	David Beckham working as a UNICEF Goodwill Ambassador in Sierra Leone	252
6.6	Bono and Africa	253
6.7	Matt Damon with Zimbabwean refugees in South Africa	254

Boxes

1.1	Social marketing and infant mortality in Honduras	47
1.2	Telenovelas	54
1.3	Soul City, South Africa	55
1.4	Tinka Tinka Sukh ('Happiness Lies in Small Things'), India	57
2.1	Band Aid and Live Aid	76
2.2	Africa is a country	100
2.3	Post-humanitarian communication	102
2.4	Oxfam's GROW campaign	103
2.5	The death of Aylan Kurdi	105
3.1	Jana Sanskriti, India	139
3.2	Wan Smolbag, Vanuatu	140
3.3	Chiapas Media Project, Mexico	147
4.1	Freedom of the Press Report	174
4.2	Miners' radio in Bolivia	176
4.3	The 'digital divide'	184
4.4	Global internet access	186
4.5	Global Bollywood	188
5.1	The Telecentre cookbook	201
5.2	Media and the 'Arab Spring'	207
5.3	GIS and the Haiti earthquake disaster, 2010	212
5.4	KONY 2012	213
5.5	Map Kibera, Kenya	214
5.6	Guiyu, China	220
5.7	Internet scams	229

Acknowledgements

My knowledge of media and development has evolved over nearly twenty years of working in the Great Lakes region of East Africa. Over this period, I have conducted a wide range of ethnographic research projects – especially in the societies of south-western Uganda, close to the three-way border between Uganda, Rwanda, and the Democratic Republic of Congo – all of which have focused on questions of media and social change.

Collectively, these projects have examined: media and the growth of Global Pentecostalism; the rise of 'hate radio' in Rwanda in 1993–1994; the politics and sociology of satellite television broadcasting in the developing world; the effects of Africa's mobile phone 'revolution'; and, most recently, the spread of smartphones, the internet, and social media (for more on my research, see https://adelaide.academia.edu/RVokes).

My work in the Great Lakes has been funded by a range of agencies and institutions, including: the British Institute in East Africa; the British Library; the Economic and Social Research Council (UK); the Radcliffe Brown Fund of the Royal Anthropological Institute; the Royal Society of New Zealand's Marsden Fund; the Vice-Chancellors' Fund of Oxford University; UNICEF; and the Wenner-Gren Foundation (USA). I would like to thank all of these organizations for their generous support.

However, my biggest debt of gratitude in Africa is to the family of the late Onasmus Bwire, 'my' family in Uganda. I am eternally grateful for everything they have done for me, and I extend my thanks especially to Gertrude Atukunda Kobirunga, to Gladys Mushabe and her husband Herbert Muhumuza, to Grays Nomuhangi and his wife Lilian Tumuramye, and to all of their children. A special debt of gratitude is reserved for the head of that family, Grace Bwire, and his partner Lydia Kabahenda. I thank Grace for welcoming me into his home and for having been such a wise teacher – and loyal friend.

At Routledge, I would like to thank Tony Binns and Andrew Mould for having commissioned this book, Egle Zigaite for her assistance with its production, and the three anonymous reviewers who provided such helpful comments on an earlier draft.

I am also extremely grateful to all those individuals and organizations who allowed me to reproduce their images in this book, including: Alex Halkin, Andrew McConnell, Anti-Slavery International, the Bodleian Library, Chiapas Media Project/Promedios, Daniel Seiffert, Francisco Vazquez, Harry Tanous, the Jubilee Debt Campaign, Katrien Pype, OptionDee, Oxfam GB, UNDP Brazil, and War on Want.

As ever, my biggest debt of gratitude is to my lovely wife Zheela, and to my children Elisabeh Atukunda, (Joe) Yusuf Nshekanabo, David Tumwesigye, and Michael Busingye.

Introduction

Media and development, a complicated relationship

- **The growing interest in 'all things media'.**
- **Definitions of media.**
- **Theories of development.**
- **Media *for* development vs. media development.**
- **Representations of development.**

Recent years have seen an explosion of interest in the ways in which media might advance the goals of international development. There has been growing interest in how all forms of media might be used to improve the lives of the world's most disadvantaged people living in the developing world (sometimes called the 'Third World' or the 'Global South'): a phrase which refers especially to the poorest nations in Africa, Asia, and Latin America, and also includes parts of the Middle East and Oceania. The result has been an ever-widening exploration by donor governments, multi-lateral aid agencies, and non-governmental organizations (NGOs) of the ways in which everything from print media to photography, radio, television, film, mobile phones, the internet, and social media might be used to advance their goals of poverty reduction, health programming, good-governance agendas, disaster reduction, and conflict transformation. At the same time, there has been an increasing engagement by developing world governments, and by citizens in the developing world themselves, with the possibilities afforded by new media, especially by social media, for achieving their own visions of economic, political, and social change.

This is not to say that the relationship between media and development is itself new. On the contrary, one could argue that ever since the invention of the first form of mass communication – the printing press – in fifteenth-century Germany, official institutions have *always* used media as a means for assisting disadvantaged populations to improve their economic activities, their health outcomes, and their general wellbeing (Kovarik, 2011). Certainly, following the invention of photography, film, and early radio technologies in the nineteenth century, governments throughout the world have regularly employed all kinds of media as part of their wider plans to transform the lives of their populations (Anderson, 1983). From the late 1940s onwards, mass communications also played a central role in the efforts of the newly independent governments of Africa, Asia, and Latin America to 'build' their new nations – and in the efforts of citizens of those same countries to forge and project alternative visions of those same countries' possible futures (Bajorek, 2012). Nevertheless, even against this background, there is still something qualitatively new about the current historical moment, in terms both of the volume and of the variety of media that are now being used by development agencies, African, Asian, and Latin American governments, and developing world citizens, to an increasingly wide variety of ends.

There have been three separate, albeit interrelated, trends that have generated the current situation. The first dates back to the 1980s and early 1990s, when the International Monetary Fund (IMF) and the World Bank imposed so-called structural-adjustment programmes (SAPs) on countries throughout the developing world. Amongst other things, these programmes required the governments of those nations to deregulate their media environments by dissolving state-owned publishing, broadcasting, and telecommunications monopolies, and by 'opening up' their economies to increased imports of manufactured goods, including electronic goods (many countries had previously restricted such imports). Within a short time, these moves had resulted in an explosion in the number of commercial, rural, and community newspapers and magazines, and radio and television stations, operating in countries across the developing world, and in local markets becoming saturated with new radios and televisions. In this context, development agencies, national governments, and ordinary citizens across the developing world all began to explore ways in which these new and expanded media environments could be used to forward their economic, political, and social goals.

The second trend can also be traced to the 1990s, when a number of major international agencies, led by several United Nations (UN) agencies, began to explore ways in which the then recent explosion of the internet across the developed world might also be used to advance the goals of international development. At first, these initiatives looked mainly at how the spread of these digital media might be used to improve communications between development agencies themselves, with a view to improving the quality of their interventions through increased data sharing, joint policy formation, and coordinated service delivery (Unwin, 2008). However, very quickly such programmes became equally focused upon how internet access might be expanded across the developing world, to provide a tool through which ordinary people might try to improve their economic, political, and social positions and outlooks. In other words, the focus became upon how to bridge the 'digital divide' between the wealthier and the poorer parts of the world, with a view to extending the benefits of the new 'Information Society' to the peoples of the developing world as well (Heeks, 2008). These initiatives culminated in two UN-sponsored World Summits on the Information Society (WSIS), held in Geneva, Switzerland, and Tunis, Tunisia, in 2003 and 2005, respectively, the latter of which set ten targets for improved access to information-communication technologies (ICTs) worldwide by 2015, and also established the Information Economy Report series. These reports are still published annually by the United Nations Conference on Trade and Development (UNCTAD).

The third, and final, major trend began in the early 2000s, and is often referred to as the 'mobile phone revolution'. This was the process – really, set of processes – through which mobile phone ownership and access grew exponentially over a short period of time, as a result of which these devices became a routine part of everyday life. Although this revolution occurred throughout the world, it was most rapid in the developing world. For example, between 2000 and 2004, mobile phone ownership grew faster in Africa – the poorest continent in the world – than anywhere else on earth. Over this period, the number of mobile phone users grew by almost 60% per year in Africa, compared with around 20% per annum in America and approximately 25% per annum in Europe (GSMA Intelligence, 2014a). In addition, it could be argued that the spread of mobile phones had a more profound effect in the developing world than in the Global North, given that for many people living in Africa, Asia, and Latin America, mobile phones provided them with their first, and only, access to any form of telecommunications (GSMA Intelligence, 2014b, 2014c). It was through mobile phones that a majority of people in the developing world also gained their first access to the internet and social media, given the general paucity of fixed-line telephones and internet-enabled computers that has always existed in many developing countries.

In hindsight, it is tempting to see the mobile phone revolution in the developing world as simply a combined outcome of the previous two trends identified above. After all, it is certainly true that had SAPs not forced African, Asian, and Latin American governments to deregulate their telecommunications sectors, then the various multi-national companies who went on to build mobile phone infrastructures and to deliver mobile phone services across the developing world, would not have been allowed to operate in those countries in anything like the way that they did (Nielinger, 2004). Throughout Africa, Asia, and Latin America, the mobile revolution was in fact driven by a relatively small number of companies. In addition, it is also tempting to draw a direct correlation between development agencies' attempts to boost ICT in the developing world and the subsequent explosion of mobile phones throughout those same regions. However, a degree of caution must be exercised on both counts, in that the deregulation of media environments by no means made the mobile revolution that was soon to follow an inevitable outcome (Kovarik, 2011; Gershon and Bell, 2013). As we shall see, a range of other causal factors also played an important part. In addition, although most agencies have today conveniently forgotten the fact, the initial emphasis of Information Society initiatives was upon widening access to computers, *not* to mobile phones (Kenny, 2006). Some development agencies even actively discouraged attempts to promote the growth of mobile phones in the developing world. For example, as late as 2001, I personally heard a senior official from a major development agency publicly state that his organization didn't support initiatives aimed at promoting mobile phone use in Uganda, because its policy-makers were of the view that a country like Uganda '[wasn't] ready for mobile phones yet'. His comments may have been made with reference to a then widely held view within some development organizations that countries like Uganda needed to first develop their woefully inadequate fixed-line phone systems before they could even start to think about *mobile* phones: we now know, of course, that fixed-line infrastructures were soon to be superseded by digital telephony not only throughout the developing world, but across the globe. However, the point is that whatever the exact origins of the mobile phone revolution were, its genesis certainly did radically transform media environments throughout the developing world. The result was that – even though a digital divide does still exist between the developed and the developing worlds – today, even the most remote of African villages may have become 'media-saturated' environments. Thus, extraordinary new possibilities have been afforded to development agencies, African, Asian, and Latin American governments, and ordinary citizens throughout the developing world to harness these new media landscapes towards their desired ends.

The scholarly community has also shown a renewed interest in the study of these issues in recent years. Again, such study is not in itself new. On the contrary, from the time academics first began to take the study of media seriously – a development that is commonly credited to sociologists of the 'Chicago School' in the 1920s – scholars have always documented the diverse and profound ways in which different sorts of media can: (1) change the experience, opinions, and identities of the persons who engage with them (i.e. 'media-users'); (2) effect both the nature, and the range, of interpersonal relations; and (3) sometimes even bring about wider social transformations (for a critical introduction to media studies, see Ott and Mack, 2014). Later, the study of 'development communication' emerged as a distinct field in its own right, especially following the work of theorists such as Daniel Lerner, Everett Rogers, and Wilbur Schramm in the late 1950s and early 1960s. From the outset, development communication was primarily interested in how and why access to different sorts of media might improve people's economic, political, and social situations. In the decades following, this academic field has seen lively debate, and has been subjected to a series of sustained critiques, as a result of which it has experienced a number of major 'paradigm shifts' – as we shall see. However, across all of this, its central focus – how media use might positively benefit people in the developing world – has remained unchanged. Yet even against this historical background, there is still something new in scholars' current enthusiasm for the study of these subjects. Therefore, and reflecting the 'real-world' developments described above, the past decade has also witnessed an explosion in the number of academic research projects looking at media in poverty reduction, health programming, and disaster relief, as well as in the number of scholarly publications devoted to these subjects (for references, see the section 'Further Reading' below). The period has also seen the establishment of more than a dozen academic journals dedicated to the study of what is now called 'Media for Development' ('M4D') or 'Information and Communication Technologies for Development' ('ICT4D').

Yet despite all of this renewed engagement with M4D/ICT4D by development agencies, by developing world governments and their citizens, and by academics – and despite the long history of practice and theory upon which all of these groups may now draw – there remains remarkably little consensus upon even some of the most fundamental questions relating to what part media can, or should, play within international development, and within other processes of planned social change. In other words, as even the most cursory survey of current development policies and/or academic writings on the subject soon reveals, debate continues to rage – and in some senses is more vexed than ever before – on some of the most fundamental questions: which are the best types of media, or combinations of media, to use in different contexts, and to achieve different sorts of development outcomes? Are some forms of media better suited than others for poverty reduction programmes, or for political projects, or for health programmes? Do some kinds of media messages have a positive effect on planned social change, whilst others have a more negative influence? How can we measure the impacts of different sorts of development-related media messages amongst their target audiences? In what ways does media use 'empower' people in the developing world? What contribution could different sorts of 'media communities' make towards development goals? How important are ongoing efforts to improve media access in the developing world, and/or to breach the 'digital divide' between the developed world and Africa, Asia, and Latin America? How might media revolutions, such as the recent mobile phone revolution and the rise of the internet and social media, be effectively harnessed by ordinary people in pursuit of their own visions of purposive social change?

Through an historical overview of the key developments in M4D/ICT4D from the end of the Second World War until the present day, the main aim of this book is to provide readers with a sense of why these questions continue to remain so vexed, to provide them with a sense of the complexities of the issues involved here, and to help them develop their own perspectives on how these questions might best be answered.

What is 'media'?

Given how much work has been done on media for development, it may seem extraordinary that there are still ongoing disagreements over even these most fundamental of questions. What is the source of these ongoing controversies? To begin with, at least part of the problem lies in the very nature of 'media' itself, a category that at the outset must be defined as including both the physical technologies of communication and their associated infrastructures (for example, newspapers, radio, television, computers, and smartphones, together with printing presses, radio stations, television satellites, broadband cables, and transmission masts), *and* the content that is transmitted through these (including text, sound, and still and moving images). On the one hand, media technologies and infrastructures have always presented a range of challenges within development. Historically, these difficulties stemmed mostly from the cost of media devices, and from the logistical challenges posed by their associated infrastructures. For example, early attempts to introduce radio as a tool for development in British colonial Africa, from the late 1930s onwards, were initially hampered by the cost and size of the radio sets themselves – given that, at that time, the expensive and bulky crystal set was the most common type of radio receiver – and by the technical difficulties of siting transmitters capable of broadcasting over such vast and variegated terrain (Vokes, 2007a). Even today, costs may still present a problem, even for radio-based development projects, given that the cost of batteries is still a significant issue for many people living in the developing world (Vokes, 2016a).

Media technologies also pose problems of uptake, or 'adoption': the fact that simply because a new media device or platform has become available is no guarantee that many people will go on to actually *use it*. Scholarly research has long highlighted that in all times and places, the rate at which people take up new media technologies is highly variable (beginning with Rogers, 1962), with most people tending to eschew them for an extended period of time. More recent work has also emphasized how most people tend to make sense of new communications technologies in relation to formats that they have used in the past (Gershon and Bell, 2013). In other words, people everywhere are less likely to take up entirely new media than to replace, or to 'upgrade', their previously used formats. The most detailed framework for understanding the processes through which new media technologies become established within all social contexts remains Roger Fidler's (1997) model of 'mediamorphosis'. In the present period, the challenges of media technologies within processes of development are more likely to be of a different order, and to relate instead to the recent proliferation of so many different kinds of 'new', and reconfigured, media devices across the developing world. The period since the mobile phone revolution has witnessed not only a rapid proliferation of new technologies, but also an increasing blurring of the boundaries between distinct technologies, such that people may now watch 'television' not only on 'traditional' television sets, but also on their computers, smartphones, and tablet devices. In media studies, this blurring of the boundaries between different media technologies – and of the wider communications environments within which they exist – is known as 'convergence' (Jensen, 2010). In these contexts, even the most remote of African villages may be now 'media-saturated' (Hjarvard, 2008). As a result, any development agency, national government or community group that is planning to use media to further its goals must first make a series of choices as to precisely which media platform, or set of platforms, will be most likely to reach their target audiences – and/or create those audiences – and to engage them in the desired manner. The challenge, of course, is that if the wrong choices are made here, then the intended communications they wish to achieve will be simply lost among the mass of other media platforms and content.

On the other hand, media *content* may also generate a range of complexities of its own. These relate to the fact that there is *always* a potential for difference, or slippage, between what the person who creates the media content intends for it to convey, and what the person, or 'media-user', who consumes, or 'receives', that same content actually takes from it. As first observed by Schramm (1954), and as elaborated by cultural studies theorist Stuart Hall in his now famous article *Encoding and Decoding in the Television Discourse*, published in 1973 – in what is now usually referred to as just 'Hall's Theory' – this is because the meanings which attach to any piece of media content may become altered at each of the four stages of its 'circuit of communication'. According to Hall, these include: (1) the point of *production* – during which there is an inevitable tendency for the creator to cast the content, to 'code' it, in ways which conform to the dominant ideologies, values, and assumptions of the society of which he or she is a part; (2) the processes of *circulation* – which have the potential to shape not only *who* will receive a given item of content, but also *how* they will engage with it. All manner of factors, from what form the content is in (e.g. text or image) to which venues it circulates through (e.g. public or private), having the potential to alter its meaning; (3) the point of *consumption*, or 'reception' – at which point individual items of content may be understood, or interpreted, 'received', quite differently by different media users, depending on their age, gender, cultural or religious background, and/or just their own personal memories and experiences; and finally, (4) the processes of *reproduction* – through which users, having previously interpreted the media content in their own way, then pass it on in this altered form. Certainly, these changes do not alter all circuits of communication in quite the same way, and may be more or less subtle in different cases. Yet in some cases the four stages of Hall's model may generate quite profound differences between what is intended and what is received. Moreover, for any development agency, national government, or community group operating a media project, these slippages may be especially problematic, in that they may result in those groups' initially positive intentions – and it is fair to say that most processes of purposive social change begin with positive intentions (even if these are sometimes misconceived) – becoming at best diluted, and therefore less effective, and at worst distorted, and therefore counter-productive.

Historically, one of the major issues relating to encoding-decoding with which development agencies had to grapple related to the way in which all media content, at the point of production (stage 1 in Hall's model), tends to be organized, or 'encoded', according to distinct styles or categories of representation, usually referred to as *genres*. As a minimum list, these genres may include news reporting/ documentary, educational content, advertising, fictionalized drama, and other types of entertainment (e.g. art, music, dancing). At the time development communication first emerged as a field in its own right, at least some agencies continued to assume that only certain kinds of generic styles were suitable for encoding development-related content. Indeed, the output of the British Colonial Film Unit (BCFU) – which was housed within the British government's Colonial Office, and which between 1939 and 1955 produced over 200 development-educational films mostly for African audiences, on everything from agriculture to healthcare to legal affairs – was characterized by just *one* generic style. Informed by the frankly racist ideas of the then influential film-maker and film-theorist William Sellers – which held that Africans had only limited cognitive capabilities, and therefore needed to be presented with material in a 'child-like' fashion – practically all of the BCFU's films were overly slow and didactic, and were characterized by a technique that 'precluded the use of close-ups, cross-cutting, short scenes and excessive movement within the frame' (Rice, 2010). Looking back at the BCFU's archives – a large part of which is now online (see www.colonialfilm.org.uk) – we now realize that these films tell us much more about the colonial mindset than they reveal about any relationship between media genres and development outcomes. We can only imagine (or examine through secondary research) what African audiences of the 1930s to 1950s might have made of these kinds of patrimonial, and *patronizing*, films. Later development communication projects rejected the kind of racist assumptions that had informed the BCFU's films. However, until the 1970s, much of the field's output continued to make extensive use of various kinds of factual and educational genres, as we shall see below (Waisbord, 2001).

From the late 1970s onwards, a growing number of development organizations began to experiment also with delivering their messages – even their most serious, health-related messages – through other sorts of genres instead, including through more entertainment-oriented genres (McPhail, 2009). Initially, this move was particularly associated with Latin America, where both official agencies and international organizations increasingly used the telenovela format – a style of television programme that has some similarities with the American genre of the 'soap opera' – as a means for delivering development messages on everything from agricultural change to domestic violence. The thinking was that by replicating genres that were already popular, these agencies would be better able both to reach wider audiences and to keep those audiences more effectively engaged, and the approach did meet with a good degree of success, in both respects, as we shall see. However, the challenges of genre have still not gone away. On the contrary, within our current technological moment, in which all media content can be quickly and easily broken down into its smallest units of meaningful size – units that are now commonly referred to as 'memes' – and then equally quickly and easily recombined in a limitless number of ways (think: 'mash-up'), the very idea of what a 'genre' is today is more contested than ever. As a result, development organizations are now experimenting with a much wider range of content styles than ever before.

Yet it is not only the genre that may affect the way in which media content is received and interpreted. All content may raise other complicated issues of reception. Specifically, we now realize that in addition to genre, all media users do habitually make sense of, or 'interpret', all content differently, according to their age, gender, cultural and/or religious background. In short, all media messages may be received and interpreted very differently by different individuals and audiences. One implication is that it is impossible to understand, and to predict, how media content will be received by some or other user group, without knowing more about the wider social worlds and communication contexts in which its members live (Ginsburg, 1993; Ginsburg *et al.*, 2002; Abu-Lughod, 2004). It also means that media messages may be received in ways that are very different to the media creator's intentions. One early, and very famous, example of this happening was Ernest Friedrich's book *Krieg dem Kriege!* (*lit.* 'War against War!'), which was first published in 1924, and which contained over 200 photographs that documented the various, hideous injuries that had been suffered by soldiers in the trenches of the First World War. Even today, when images of what we would now call 'body horror' have become much more common, the images in Friedrich's book remain quite shocking to view. An anti-war campaigner, Friedrich intended for the book to document the realities of the Great War and, in so doing, to serve as an antithesis to the kind of jingoistic propaganda that European publics had been exposed to during the conflict itself – the majority of which had represented the fighting as an entirely noble pursuit. He also intended for this to be a *universalist* message – that is, one that appealed not to any one or other side in the war, but to a common humanity shared by all – and in pursuit of this, within the original publication, each of the photographs was captioned in four languages: German, English, French, and Dutch (the book was later also translated into more than 40 other languages as well). Yet if these were Friedrich's intentions, they became very badly distorted in the way the book was received. This is because all of the images that Friedrich had used in the book happened to have been taken from German Army archives only and, as a result, they showed only injuries that had been suffered by *German* soldiers. Even though similar injuries had been suffered by soldiers fighting on all sides in the Great War, of course, this allowed the Nazi propaganda machine in the 1930s to interpret the book not as a universalist statement on the general suffering experienced during the war, but as evidence of the injustice that the conflict had wrought upon the German people *only* – and this was later used to justify German rearmament in preparation for what became the Second World War. In effect, then, an intended pacifist, anti-propaganda, and humanist publication became reinterpreted as a justification for future conflict within the – highly toxic – propaganda of a far-right nationalist regime. Although this is an extreme example, it highlights the potential challenges that all media producers face when trying to encode media messages in ways that might bring about any intended social change.

Today, other issues of reception may make things more complicated still. Indeed, the complexities of reception have become the very stuff of contemporary media studies, as a result of which it is beyond my scope here to give an overview of the entire field (again, the best introduction is Ott and Mack, 2014). However, one issue that is of particular relevance for development for communication relates to how media scholars now recognize that in our current 'mediatized' (i.e. media-saturated) environments, media users are constantly exposed to, even 'bombarded' with, far more media content than they could ever hope to process. In this context, it has been argued that users may tend to actively focus upon only those messages that are likely to 'gratify' them – that is, to help them meet their own personal needs and goals. These needs and goals vary from user to user, based on a plethora of factors, including age, gender, cultural and religious background, and personal biography. This model of reception is usually referred to as 'Uses and Gratification Theory' (UGT; McQuail, 1994; Ruggiero, 2000). The logical implication of these insights into mediatization and UGT is that, today, all development agencies, developing world governments, and community broadcasters face especially difficult challenges in their uses of media. Because all of these organizations' media content is, by definition, always focused upon bringing about social change, it may be the *least* likely to simply gratify media users' existing outlooks and behaviours – and may be therefore the most likely to be simply 'filtered out' by them.

What is 'development'?

Ongoing disagreements over the kind of fundamental questions outlined above are not only shaped by our changing understandings of 'media', but also by our shifting ideas about what 'development' itself is: about who can most effectively carry it out, about what it should be trying to achieve, and about how its outcomes can best be measured. It is certainly true that, for a long time, our definitions of all of these things were entirely clear and, at times, appeared even to be self-evident. The story really begins here with the 'Age of Enlightenment', from roughly 1650 to 1780, during which a movement of highly influential philosophers and other intellectuals sought to promote scientific rationalism, reason, and logic as a means for dislodging superstitious – and religious – explanations of the world (Berlin, 1984). In so doing, this movement aimed to also promote a new notion of the 'rational self' – a concept that lies at the root of our contemporary ideas of 'individualism' – as a means for challenging the edicts of certain traditional authorities, and especially those of ecclesiastical institutions such as the Catholic Church (which was then extremely powerful throughout the world). As part of this wider movement, these same intellectuals also introduced the idea of what we now call 'development' – although at the time it was more commonly referred to as the 'Idea of Progress' – or the notion that the application of science and technology to the practical problems that all societies inevitably face has the potential also, by dislodging people's 'traditional' explanations of, and behaviours towards, those same problems, to generally 'improve' those societies (Rist, 2014). This process, through which science and technology replaced religious/traditional/cultural ideas and practices to the assumed betterment of a whole society, later became known as 'modernization' (see also Leys, 1996).

By the early nineteenth century, the idea that something called progress/development could be achieved through (what we now call) modernization had become a dominant idea within 'western' (i.e. Euro-American) thought. However, it must also be noted that throughout much of that century, the vast majority of policy-makers and academics still regarded progress/development as a goal for only Euro-American nations themselves and for a limited number of other 'civilized' societies around the world. No serious scholar or commentator would today use the term 'civilized' to distinguish the contemporary western world from other nations. However, during the nineteenth century, it was common to do so. By this view, social change could not be forced upon, or accelerated within, any of the other, 'non-civilized' societies of the world – a category which included the vast majority of the hunter-gatherer, pastoralist, and agriculturalist societies of the colonized parts of Africa, Asia, and Latin America – which instead had to be left to change at their own, 'natural' pace. In other words, it was believed that social transformation through technological innovation could not be achieved in these societies because they were simply not capable of coping with it. In the latter part of the nineteenth century, this sort of thinking became elaborated within the theories of 'social evolutionism', which, although they differed from each other in certain key respects, all assumed that all non-civilized societies would either organically 'evolve' into more sophisticated forms (read: Euro-American societies) or else die out (for the best introductions to nineteenth-century ideas about social evolution, see Ingold, 1986; Kuper, 1988).

It was not until the early twentieth century – by which time social evolutionism had begun to be widely rejected as too general, as well as both explicitly and implicitly racist – that a notion of 'development through modernization' even began to be applied to a majority of societies of Africa, Asia, and Latin America. And, in fact, it wasn't until after the Second World War, and the era of major *de*colonization that followed it, that this became a defining objective for all of the nations of (what we have come to know as) 'the *developing* world'. Indeed, it is for this reason that 'development as modernization' is today most associated, in many scholars' and other commentators' minds, with the period between 1949 and roughly the mid-1970s (Peet and Hartwick, 2015). Throughout this period, the way in which development was conceived – by international development organizations, by developing world governments, and by NGOs – bore a striking resemblance to the way in which it had been originally defined by Enlightenment thinkers. Therefore, throughout this time, development was consistently thought of as a process of progressive transformation, whereby whole societies would be shifted away from their 'traditional' modes of production towards 'modern' industrial ones – which by boosting economic growth, would also facilitate increased spending on health and education. This sort of transformation was primarily to be achieved through technology transfers, including transfers both from western nations to the developing world and from developing nations' own metropoles to their peripheral regions. It also required people to change their traditional/cultural values, attitudes, and practices – which were taken to be rooted in the past and, therefore, to be a hindrance to progress – and to adopt new, modern 'worldviews' (Rist, 2014). The key point here is that all of this also implied a relatively obvious, and straightforward, role for media. This is because, on the one hand, the spread of media devices and platforms was itself a form of technology transfer, which would address the perceived 'deficit' of those media technologies in Africa, Asia, and Latin America. And, on the other hand, it was assumed that media messages, by providing people with more 'useful information', could be easily used to change people's existing values, attitudes, and behaviours. This latter perception was informed by a simple 'sender–receiver' model of communication – sometimes called the 'hypodermic needle model' or 'magic bullet theory' – or the idea that media messages, irrespective of how they are interpreted, could directly '"effect" or guide people's thinking' and behaviour (Rennie, 2006: 141). As we shall see, we now know that the relationship between media messages and people's behaviour is in fact much more complicated than that.

From around the mid-1960s onwards, modernization theory became subject to a growing number of critiques. In particular, academics influenced by 'dependency theory' – many of whom were from Latin America or Africa – argued that modernization was simply too Eurocentric and paternalistic (see especially Frank, 1966, 1967). For dependency theorists, modernization was fundamentally flawed because it cast *only* the Euro-American world as 'modern' – and thus implied the rest of the world must be 'backwards' (Evans, 1979). It also implied that progress could only be achieved in Africa, Asia, and Latin America if the countries of those continents followed the same path to prosperity that the Euro-American world itself had since the industrial revolution from *c.* 1750 onwards (Leys, 1996). In short, modernization required all of the nations of the developing world to simply become more 'European-like'. For critics, these features of modernization were not only derogatory in their own right, but they also failed to capture the fact that the expansion of the Euro-American world during colonialism, and the ongoing legacies of that expansion, were in fact the source of many of the developing world's current problems (Rodney, 1972). From the early 1980s onwards, a further group of scholars, many of whom were also from the developing world, began to argue that development as modernization itself, precisely because this *was* predicated on various kinds of 'transfers' from the wealthier to the poorer parts of the world, could even be seen as a continuation of those very same processes of colonial expansion (Rahnema and Bawtree, 1997; Young, 2016). In other words, development itself could be thought of as *neo*-colonial. In this view, which came to be known as 'post-colonial development theory', all of the concepts and practices of 'development', as these had been conceived in relation to modernization, should simply be done away with altogether (Sachs, 1992). Instead, processes of positive social change in the developing world should be more effectively achieved not by forcing changes onto the societies of Africa, Asia, and Latin America according to any kind of western-defined models, but instead by allowing the governments and citizens of those nations to set and define their own goals, and to pursue their own agendas for achieving those goals.

These ideas had a greater influence over some donor governments, multi-lateral development agencies, and NGOs than others. However, in general terms, they forged a greater awareness, across all of these different kinds of organizations, of the potential value of, for example, traditional knowledge, or 'indigenous knowledge'. Whereas previously, in line with modernization theory, donors and development agencies would have simply dismissed indigenous knowledge as a barrier to progress, and as anyway 'backward', they now tried to identify ways in which they might facilitate its use in development programmes and projects, and for simply preserving and protecting it in its own right (Sillitoe, 2009). To begin with, these efforts focused especially upon forms of indigenous environmental – or ecological – knowledge (IEK). This involved an exploration of how knowledge about local environments contained in things such as traditional stories, myths, rituals, and so on, could be used to improve environmental management (Pottier *et al.*, 2003). Related projects also examined how ownership of certain elements of IEK – for example, knowledge about the healing properties of some or other plant – might be protected using legal instruments such as international intellectual property (IP) laws (Drahos, 2014). Meanwhile, in response to the criticisms that development as modernization had represented, at best, an imposition of western ideas upon the developing world and, at worst, a continuation of Euro-American colonial domination of Africa, Asia, and Latin America, donor governments, multi-lateral agencies, and especially NGOs also began to explore ways in which the development enterprise could be made more collaborative or 'participatory' in nature (Slocum, 2003). At first, these efforts focused upon how individual projects could be made more effective through the inclusion of local perspectives – especially those of certain marginalized groups, such as women – in all stages of the project management cycle. As a minimum list, there are at least four stages to any project cycle, namely: (1) background research; (2) project design; (3) project implementation; and (4) monitoring and evaluation of results (Chambers, 1983). However, over time, the notion of participation expanded further, to also include the ways in which international development agencies might try to better tailor macro-level policies to the specific needs and desires of individual developing world countries, through broader dialogue with the governments of those countries. For example, these processes became fundamental to the formation of country-specific Poverty Reduction Strategy Papers (PRSPs). These are policy instruments that the IMF and World Bank require developing world countries to adopt in order to become eligible for debt-relief programmes.

The key point here is that all of these shifts also radically changed the way in which donors, multi-lateral agencies, and NGOs conceived of the potential contribution that media could make to the development enterprise (Melkote and Steeves, 2015). Thus, against their earlier view of media as simply a vehicle through which to deliver their own developmental messages – that is, as a 'one-way' mode of communication – they now began to focus on the ways in which media might be used to facilitate two-way, even multi-directional, dialogue between themselves and ordinary people living in the developing world and, more importantly, within and between community groups themselves (Beltran, 1976, 1980). From the outset, there was never one agreed set of approaches for how this kind of 'participatory communication' might be achieved. As we shall see, it involved everything from the facilitation of indigenous Theatre for Development (TFD) groups to address social issues (Kamlongera, 2005), to the creation of radio phone-in shows around particular political and health issues (Otim, 2009), to simply providing funding and/or training, or some other kinds of support, to independent community media projects to pursue their own interests (Halkin, 2008). In recent years, following the advent of mobile phones, the internet, and social media, participatory communication has increasingly involved participatory geographic information systems (GIS) as well. These typically involve a combination of geo-spatial data and software, with 'crowdsourced' content – as might be collected from large numbers of people via email, Twitter, or SMS – to create dynamic (i.e. 'real-time') participatory websites relating to some or other emerging situation. Participatory GIS has proved especially effective for rapidly mapping people's experiences of, and for designing relevant responses to, various kinds of fast-changing and large-scale events, such as wars or natural disasters (Gao *et al.*, 2011). However, it has been used in a range of other contexts as well.

The third major shift in thinking about what development is, about how it should be carried out, and about what it should be trying to achieve, with which we are interested here is the emergence of the so-called 'Washington Consensus'. The term 'Washington Consensus' – which was coined by a British economist, John Williamson in 1989 – refers to a set of economic and legal policies that developing world governments, beginning with those in Latin America, had adopted in response to the financial crises of the 1970s (Naim, 1994). These later came to be seen, by most western donor governments and all multi-lateral development organizations, as a favoured approach to development. Throughout the late 1980s and early 1990s, these policies formed the basis of the so-called 'structural-adjustment' programmes (SAPs) that the IMF and World Bank imposed on countries throughout the developing world (Bello *et al.*, 1993; Sahn *et al.*, 1999). At the heart of the Washington Consensus was the idea that progress was most likely to be achieved when it was driven not by national government agendas (i.e. state-led planning), but by economic markets. In this regard, it was particularly informed by 'neo-liberal' economic theories, which have long postulated that unfettered markets will always tend towards growth (Dixon and Drakakis-Smith, 1993).

By this logic, donor governments and multi-lateral development organizations encouraged and/or compelled developing world governments to undertake economic and legal reforms aimed at reducing their interventions into their national economies, and in other ways to create more 'market-friendly' conditions within their countries. In practice, this involved requiring developing world governments to: (1) stop providing subsidies to national industry; (2) privatize state enterprises; (3) improve their fiscal discipline – in order to reduce the size of their deficits; (4) undertake tax reform – to increase their tax income, again with a view to reducing deficits; (5) set interest rate targets that reflected actual, or 'real', market activity – as opposed to a government's aspirations on trade targets; (6) allow exchange rates for currencies to be similarly market-determined; (7) remove tariffs on imports – thereby allowing the free movement of goods into the country; (8) remove legal barriers on foreign direct investment (FDI) – thereby allowing the free movement of capital into the country; (9) recognize international property rights – in order to build confidence among international companies and investors who may wish to 'do business' in that country; and (10) generally 'deregulate' – that is, generally remove any other regulations, across all sectors, which might unreasonably deter international companies or investors from entering those markets, or which might restrict their competitiveness once they had entered them. The reader may be wondering why on earth any developing world country would ever agree to such measures – measures that significantly *reduced* the degree of control that it had previously had over its own national economy? However, the truth is that, in most instances, the governments involved had very little choice but to acquiesce. As a result of a complicated series of factors, which are discussed at length in Chapter 4, by the time the SAPs were introduced, many countries throughout the developing world were experiencing insurmountable problems of national debt. They were, in effect, bankrupt (World Bank, 1989; Danso, 1990). In this context, the IMF and World Bank, in particular, were able to use developing states' existing financial problems as a lever with which to impose the 'bitter-pill' of SAPs/neo-liberal reforms. Moreover, following their implementation, these policies proved to have great longevity. Thus, although some of the more 'market fundamentalist' tendencies of the original Washington Consensus have become tempered in recent years – to such a degree, in fact, that some theorists are talking about a 'post-Washington Consensus' (e.g. Khan and Christiansen, 2011) – in practice, most of the states of Africa, Asia, and Latin America have continued to pursue some versions of neo-liberalism, up until the present time (Serra and Stiglitz, 2008).

Once again, these changing notions of what development is, and how it should be carried out, altered the ways in which donor governments, multi-lateral organizations, NGOs, developing world governments, and the citizens of developing countries themselves thought about, and engaged with, the media. For development agencies, development conceived primarily in terms of an expansion of global markets meant that they were generally welcoming of the rapid proliferation of new radio and television stations, and of media devices, that followed – which was a sign, of course, that those markets were working (Vokes, 2010). In addition, development agencies perceived that in a context of increasing globalization, access to a greater range of media would provide ordinary people living in the developing world with new economic benefits, by allowing them to access new kinds of 'useful information' (Coyne and Leeson, 2004). For example, it was thought that exposure to real-time information about international coffee prices and markets would enable coffee farmers in the developing world to make better informed choices about the optimal time to sell their crops, in order to maximize their profits. Finally, development agencies hoped that deepening global networks and connections would also allow for new kinds of transnational political mobilization, including ones that might eventually form a new kind of 'civic structure' capable of holding national governments in Africa, Asia, and Latin America to account (Minderhoud, 2009). As we shall see, all of these things did come to pass. Yet the rapid expansion of global media infrastructures and content that occurred after structural-adjustment also produced a range of other, less desirable outcomes as well. Meanwhile, for developing world governments and their citizens, neo-liberalism – and the globalization of media that followed it – similarly presented a range of opportunities, but also some challenges. Most importantly of all, the new media environments that emerged from structural-adjustment provided ordinary people, throughout the developing world, with access to more media technologies and exponentially more content than ever before. This in turn resulted in their being able to participate in development projects in entirely new ways. It also afforded them new means for articulating, and for disseminating, their own perspectives on what 'development' itself is, and/or should be (see, for example, Bart Barendregt's work on how mobile phones have been used to forge distinct visions of development in Indonesia; Barendregt, 2006). It has also resulted in ordinary people throughout Africa, Asia, and Latin America developing new ways to engage with media, in processes of self-making, in projects of community engagement, and in forms of political and social activism. The effects of these emergent mediated practices will be explored in detail in Chapters 4 and 5.

The key point, then, is that when we try to understand the nature of media for development, our task is more complicated that trying to hit a 'moving target', or even trying to hit two moving targets. Rather, it involves trying to bring two moving targets into line with each other in ways that will help us to reach informed positions in relation to the kinds of questions outlined above.

Media development

To complicate matters still further, when we talk about media *and* development, we are today no longer referring to only media *for* development – that is, to the ways in which donor governments, multi-lateral aid agencies, NGOs, and developing world governments and their citizens may use media in order to advance their economic, political, and social goals. Instead, we are also talking about a further domain, which is today commonly referred to – somewhat confusingly, perhaps – as *media development*. This is the separate albeit overlapping set of processes and initiatives through which development agencies and NGOs might try to engage with a developing world country in an attempt to strengthen its media sector, and to improve the socio-legal environment in which that sector operates. In other words, it refers to those processes and initiatives that are focused upon improving 'press freedoms'. In practice, these processes have typically had a wide and somewhat disparate range of goals, and have included: increasing the number of media producers, especially news outlets, that operate in a country; assisting new outlets to achieve financial viability; improving the professional standards of journalists – in particular, through more in-country media training and better networking of local journalists with their international counterparts; increasing the amount of locally produced content that is broadcast *vis-à-vis* foreign-produced material; developing more robust media regulations and laws, and assisting media support groups that are capable of advocating for their enforcement (see Prahalad and Hammond, 2002; Mottaz, 2010; Scott, 2014a).

The emergence of media development as a distinct field in its own right in fact pre-dates the current burgeoning interest in media for development with which we opened. Indeed, the ideas which animate it even pre-date the modern idea of progress/development itself, tracing as they ultimately do to the seventeenth-century philosophy of John Milton. According to Milton, a strong and a 'free' press played a vital role in stabilizing democracy, both by facilitating a plurality of political perspectives and platforms to emerge and by providing a mechanism for holding governments to account. Later, following the end of the Second World War, Milton's ideas – which were further elaborated in the nineteenth century by other liberal philosophers such as John Stuart Mill – informed the allies' focus upon media development as a means for replacing the former dictatorships of Germany, Italy, and Japan, all of which had used monopolistic media regimes as a means for disseminating propaganda, with more stable, democratic governments. As part of the allies' efforts here, in 1948 freedom of expression and the right to 'seek, receive and impart information and ideas through any media' became enshrined as Article 19 of the nascent United Nations (UN) Organization's Universal Declaration of Human Rights (UNGA, 1948). However, it was not until 1980 that media development began to emerge as a distinct field within international development (i.e. as a particular concern for those designing interventions in the Global South). In that year, the UN's Educational, Scientific, and Cultural Organization (UNESCO) set up an International Bureau for the Development of Communication (IBDC), which was specifically tasked with developing a pluralistic and free media throughout the world. This was followed, shortly afterwards, by US think-tank Freedom House's publication of (what became) its annual Freedom of the Press Report. This publication ranked all countries of the world, on a scale of 1 to 100, according to their levels of 'media freedom', in what became the first of many similar indexes. Later examples include the International Research and Exchanges Board's Media Sustainability Index (MSI) and Reporters Sans Frontières' Press Freedom Index (PFI). Although all of these initiatives were global in scope, they all tended to place developing world countries at the bottom of their respective ranking scales. As a result, within a short period of time, they had all become heavily focused upon the Global South.

Yet, if all of these organizations *did* highlight the issues of press constraints in the developing world, there was little that they could do about these prior to the advent of structural-adjustment. As described above, before that time the media sectors of many countries in Africa, Asia, and Latin America were characterized by a single, state-owned media broadcaster with a legal monopoly over output (Myers, 2008). Thus, it was not until SAPs began to dissolve these monopolies, and to bring about wider deregulation of national media environments, that interventions aimed at increasing pluralism and strengthening press freedom began to be made in earnest. Thus, it was not really until the mid- to late 1990s that media development started to emerge as a major field within international development. However, more or less continuously from that time onwards, those engaged in media development have had to grapple with many of the same complexities, and to respond to at least some of the same criticisms, as were faced earlier by practitioners of media *for* development. For example, the field as a whole has been accused of paying too little attention to issues relating to the material infrastructures of media in the developing world, and therefore focusing too heavily upon approaches for improving media content (Berger, 2010) – although this criticism may be at least partly misplaced, as it could be argued that a broader definition of 'media infrastructure' might include not only physical receivers, transmitters, and wires, but also the legal environments within and through which these are made active. In addition, media development has been also frequently criticized for focusing too heavily upon media *producers*, to the neglect of media *consumers*. In other words, it has been argued that whilst programmes to establish more broadcasters, and to improve training for journalists, may be valid in their own right, their effects will ultimately be futile if a similar effort is not also put into questions of audiences' 'media literacy' (Hobbs, 1998) – and as we have already seen, issues of reception are amongst the most complicated elements of any media environment.

Most significantly, over the past 20 years, media development has also been attacked for being Eurocentric (Wasserman, 2013). This is largely an outcome of the field's general emphasis upon the various country ranking scales, which, although they are each constructed according to different criteria and using different methodologies, all tend to place more developed countries towards the 'top of the table' and less developed nations towards the bottom. For example, in Reporters Sans Frontières' PFI for 2014, western countries make up the entire top ten (nine European countries plus New Zealand), while developing nations account for the bottom ten. The problem is that once again this implies not only a general superiority of the Global North over Africa, Asia, and Latin America, but also a sense in which the best course of action is for the Euro-American world to 'transfer' elements of its own supposedly better media industries to the developing world, in order that the latter might try to 'catch up'. As a result, the field as a whole has tended to fixate upon only those forms of media development that result from some sort of intervention by western agencies and organizations into the developing world, as opposed to those produced by innovations made *in the developing world itself* – which today might include anything from a new media technology developed by a Chinese company, to a new kind of content produced by an African blogger. More significantly, in recent years, a general assumption of the superiority of western media environments has been increasingly challenged by things like the Leveson Inquiry, a wide-ranging judicial inquiry that was set up in the UK in 2011 to examine the politics and ethics of the British press in the light of a scandal in which one of the country's largest newspapers, the *News of the World*, had hacked into the mobile phone of a murdered schoolgirl, Millie Dowler. The resulting Leveson Report (2012) challenged one of the core tenets of media development, that increased media pluralism automatically checks the power of governments, by documenting how, in the UK at least, greater media diversity had instead increased both the range and the depth of relations that exist between the press and those in power (for a good discussion of the aftermath of the Leveson Inquiry, see Barnett, 2013). In this context, a 'western' model of media organization and practice may not be the best one to follow after all. Yet experience has also shown that it is not only in western countries that greater media plurality may have unintended, and undesirable, political consequences. For instance, in what has become the most infamous example, the growth in media providers that resulted from Rwanda's liberalization programmes of the early 1990s generated not a more balanced media landscape capable of limiting the powers of the government, but instead a proliferation of ethnic 'hate' media, which, it is widely agreed, helped to propel a small network of Hutu extremists called the *akazu* to power. It was this group that both designed and implemented the Rwandan genocide of 1994 (Vokes, 2007a).

Thus, just as media *for* development has had to grapple with complex questions relating to issues such as the relationship between media technologies vs. content, the balance between external engagements vs. internally generated change, and the potential pitfalls of unintended – and sometimes highly negative – effects, so too those working in media development have faced many of the same issues. Once again, then, this book will help readers to understand the complexities and stakes of what is involved here.

Media representations of development

Finally, no examination of the relationship between media *and* development would be complete without an exploration of one additional area as well, that of *representations of development*. By this is meant the ways in which the issues and problems facing the developing world, as well as the development interventions which attempt to address them, are communicated to global media audiences in newspapers, on radio and TV, and via the internet, as well as in novels, on film, and in art (Lewis *et al.*, 2014). It is a commonly held perception that such representations fall into two distinct categories: the first being constituted of those still and moving images which are made by independent media producers – such as an impartial news broadcaster – with a view to simply informing their audiences about what is happening in the developing world; and the second being constituted of those images which are produced by international development organizations themselves as part of their fund-raising campaigns (Clark, 2004). However, this distinction is in many ways misleading, given that from the time representations of the problems facing Africa, Asia, and Latin America first began circulating in the Euro-American world, the line between informing about, and advocating for, those same issues has always been extremely blurred. For example, in what is often taken to be the first example of 'humanitarian photography', Captain Willoughby Wallace Hooper's images of India's 'Great Famine' of 1876–1878, photos that were apparently taken simply to document the event – with a view to informing British and Australian audiences about what was happening – soon became central to the fund-raising efforts of the Indian Famine Relief Committees that sprang up to respond to the crisis (Twomey, 2012a, 2012b). Similarly with the Biafra Crisis in the late 1960s, when media coverage of a war-induced famine in Eastern Nigeria played a crucial role in garnering financial support for the humanitarian airlift that was to follow – which was overseen by the International Committee of the Red Cross (ICRC; de Waal, 1997). And so too with the Ethiopian Famine of 1983–1985, when one now famous segment by a BBC television news crew – including cameraman Mohamed Amin and reporter Michael Buerk – became the catalyst for what was then the world's largest ever fundraising campaign, which included the Live Aid concerts of 1985 (Philo, 1993). Today, the relationship between information and advocacy has become even more complex still, given a contemporary media environment in which: (1) it is now quite common for news crews to be 'embedded' within humanitarian and development organizations as a means for gaining access to the issues they are covering, especially when they are working in some of the more troubled parts of the world (Pfau *et al.*, 2005); (2) practically all aid agencies have their own press centres, which, in addition to putting out daily press releases, are capable of producing their own documentary films and 'broadcast-ready' news segments – which can be played over the internet or distributed to external broadcasters to be 'dropped into' their own programming (for example, see UNICEF's Press Centre: www.unicef.org/media); and (3) a development organization might typically begin a new campaign by first deciding which celebrity, or even celebrity reporter, to approach to be its spokesperson – the rule of thumb now being that the higher the profile of the celebrity who attaches to a campaign, the more news coverage that campaign will ultimately receive (Richey, 2015).

The realization that even the apparently most independent of media images of the developing world have always been intrinsically implicated in processes of advocacy is important for a number of reasons. In particular, it helps us to understand how and why, in the period between roughly the mid-1960s and early 1990s, media representations of Africa, Asia, and Latin America, but especially those of Africa, came to be dominated by *humanitarian* imagery – that is, imagery depicting war, famine or disaster, and characterized by images of atrocity (Lissner, 1981). This repetition of atrocity imagery from the developing world can be partly understood in terms of a wider fascination across *all* global media coverage with the extremes of human experience. This fascination led news producer Bill Applegate to coin his now famous phrase: 'if it bleeds, it leads'.

However, it also reflects a longer history of humanitarian practice, in which images of suffering from 'distant places' have long been used as a tool for advocacy and fundraising (Fehrenbach and Rodongo, 2015). From the advent of modern humanitarianism onwards – which can be traced to the anti-slavery campaigns of the late eighteenth and early nineteenth centuries – such images of suffering were circulated with a view to generating a 'shock effect' among their viewers, in an attempt to galvanize those same viewers to action – by, for example, making a donation, or engaging in fundraising or advocacy. From the second half of the 1960s onwards, these already well-established humanitarian practices became combined with the circuits of the then rapidly expanding global media networks, to powerful effect (Nissinen, 2012). However, by the late 1980s, humanitarian and development organizations' constant use of atrocity imagery, even where this was effective for fundraising, was coming in for increasing criticism. On the one hand, its use was criticized for demeaning the people represented and for reproducing – and reinforcing – some of the more problematic elements of modernization theory: especially the perceptions that Africa, Asia, and Latin America were essentially 'backwards' and therefore needed 'saving' (Lousley, 2014). Some theorists have even interpreted such images, and the associated media coverage within which they were typically embedded, as reinforcing of the wider global political economy – one in which western nations remained by and large dominant over those of the developing world in economic, political, and military terms (Hattori, 2003; Vestergaard, 2013). On the other hand, from the early 1990s onwards, a growing number of media scholars, and even development workers themselves, began to also query whether a constant repetition of negative images really *was* the most effective means for motivating their audiences to action. It was argued that such images may be just as likely to induce so-called 'compassion fatigue', whereby viewing publics become 'turned off' to images of some crisis or disaster, simply because they have seen so many similar images of other crises or disasters in the past (Sontag, 1977; Moeller, 1999). The argument was that a repetition of only negative images for purposes of advocacy may in fact be counter-productive for fundraising and awareness-building purposes (although not all scholars agreed with this argument, as we shall see).

In response to these critiques in recent years, advocates for humanitarian and development causes have increasingly tried to reduce the amount of negative imagery they circulate, and to instead engage in 'strategic positivism' – sometimes called 'deliberate positivism' (Chouliaraki, 2010). This involves focusing media coverage and advocacy campaigns upon the positive effects and solutions that development interventions achieve, rather than upon the problems which caused them to intervene in the first place. For example, rather than focusing media coverage upon the effects of a famine, a development agency might instead try to focus upon individuals who they have helped to avoid the potential malnutrition which that same famine might otherwise have caused, through, for example, a food distribution programme. The hope is that this sort of coverage might still motivate viewers to action – although not so much by trying to convince them of the *need* for fundraising, etc., but by focusing viewers' attention upon the positive *outcomes* that their actions could potentially achieve. Alternatively, advocates and agencies might today try to engage also in strategies of 'post-humanitarianism' (Chouliaraki, 2013), which involve shifting the focus of media coverage away from *any* aspects of any specific crises and events, and more towards a *general* understanding of developmental issues and problems. A good example of the kind of post-humanitarian campaign to which Chouliaraki refers here is Oxfam's recently launched GROW campaign, which began in 2013. GROW doesn't refer to any specific famines or food-insecurity events, but instead seeks to focus media users' minds upon issues of global food distribution, and global patterns of food shortages, in general. In so doing, the campaign – as all examples of post-humanitarianism – does still aim to motivate its viewers to action. However, rather than trying to motivate them to simply make a donation, the GROW campaign encourages its viewers to undertake more general kinds of activities, such as reflecting upon how their own food consumption practices may contribute to global patterns of food inequality, planning for how to reduce their own household food waste, and thinking about how to eat less meat and dairy, how to change their buying practices in ways that support small-scale farmers, and so on. It is also noteworthy that post-humanitarian campaigns are typically also characterized by experimentation with genres and styles (Scott, 2014a). In other words, they are less likely to be framed in news/educational genres and to use 'realist' imagery – that is, cast in ways that seek to didactically 'inform' their viewers about some or other situation in another part of the world – than to make use of alternative, interactive genres and more 'evocative' images – as might instead invite viewers to imagine how they would react if their own lives were to be negatively impacted by famine, war, or disaster

(Chouliaraki, 2013). Examples of this kind of approach can be found in the humanitarian campaigns that have emerged in response to the unfolding Syrian refugee crisis in Europe (Vandevoordt, 2016). The literature for almost all of these campaigns has been characterized less by any attempt to educate donor audiences about the origins of this refugee crisis, or to show them images of what is happening back in Syria itself – although both of these things are easily accessible via other sources, of course – than by an attempt to encourage viewers to think about the 'refugee experience' in general, and to imagine how they would fare if placed in a similar situation themselves.

Yet how effective these newer, post-humanitarian approaches currently are, or are likely to be in the future, is also caught in the complexity of new media environments, and in the ever-greater proliferation of platforms and increased convergence between platforms. In these contexts, there is a risk that humanitarian and development organizations may fall back upon atrocity imagery to maintain their 'impact' (Palecanda, 2015). Yet even if they do not, they still face difficult challenges over precisely which kinds of platform or platforms to use in their campaigns, even before they have begun to consider the complex issues of content. One recent example that highlighted how new media environments have afforded humanitarian and development organizations enormous opportunities, yet have also presented them with new kinds of challenges, is that of the KONY 2012 campaign. This was a campaign by a US-based advocacy group called Invisible Children that was output on Vimeo, YouTube, and social media with phenomenal success. It eventually reached a worldwide audience of over 100 million people. However, Invisible Children's use of a 'viral' campaign also later came in for a range of criticisms, whilst aspects of the campaign's content also drew negative reactions (for an introduction to all of these, see Vokes, http://bit.ly/H6giiY). Another strategy that new media environments have given renewed impetus to is for humanitarian and development organizations to make increasing use of celebrities to 'front' their campaigns, again with a view to increasing the impact of those campaigns among international media audiences (Richey, 2015).

More generally, and more significantly, new media environments have also eroded any control that humanitarian and development organizations may have previously had over the kinds of images of 'distant suffering' that are reproduced in the media. In other words, in the age of mobile phones, the internet, and social media, it is not only humanitarian and development organizations that have the ability to circulate imagery from wars, famines, and disasters to global audiences. Ordinary people living in those contexts are just as capable of doing so as well, not only by way of participatory GIS, but also through the internet and social media – which may then be picked up, and reproduced, by 'traditional' news outlets (for an excellent account of the 'infrastructures of representation' and circulation in contemporary international media, see Gursel, 2016). To date, the implications of these shifts have been most apparent in relation to the ongoing Syrian Civil War. Thus, if the Syrian crisis has become associated with experiments in post-humanitarian communication (see above), it is probably much better known as the most 'socially mediated' war and humanitarian situation in history (Lynch *et al.*, 2014), in which everyone from the Syrian government to rebel groups such as ISIS (Rodenbeck, 2014) and ordinary Syrian citizens have made frequent use of mobile phones, the internet, and social media to project their own representations of the situation out into the world (for interesting examples of how ordinary Syrians have used social media to broadcast their own representations of the war, see the Facebook page that emerged out of the community media project 'The Syrian People Know Their Way', available online at www.facebook.com/Syrian.Intifada). The key point, then, is that as a result of these multiple factors, media representations of development have recently become *much* more complicated – and more contested – than ever before.

Structure of the book

Chapter 1 examines the modern history of international development and shows how, from the very beginning, media has occupied a central role within development thinking and practice. It outlines the theories that first animated the core paradigm of media *for* development (M4D) – today known as 'ICT4D' – and looks at three ways in which this paradigm is still commonly applied within international development programmes and projects: as part of social marketing campaigns, as part of health promotion campaigns, and in the form of entertainment-education. Chapter 2 also explores the modern history of development, this time relating it to representations of development. It looks at how and why, from the late 1960s onwards, media portrayals of international development in Africa, Asia, and Latin America came to be dominated not only by images of atrocity, but by a relatively small number of 'types' of pictures of suffering. The chapter goes on to evaluate opposing arguments that have been made about these kinds of images, which range from claims that they have always galvanized international media audiences to action, to the alternative view that repeated exposure to these sorts of images may induce a kind of compassion fatigue.

Chapter 3 introduces several critiques of 'modernization theory' – including 'dependency theory', feminist critiques, and environmental critiques – and examines how these gained increasing traction within international development, and eventually gave rise to 'post-development' perspectives. The chapter looks in detail at what implications each of these critiques had for our understanding of the role of media for development and shows how, in combination, they led to the emergence of an entirely new paradigm for media for development: 'participatory communication'. The chapter examines the history of participatory communication and various related fields such as 'indigenous media', and it looks at how participatory approaches continue to be used today. It also evaluates the advantages and disadvantages of these approaches.

Chapters 4 and 5 examine the origins of the 'neo-liberal turn' in development, the effects it had in generating new media environments, including the ways it shaped the mobile phone revolution and the spread of the internet and social media across the developing world, and the implications it has had for media for development. These chapters find that although this massive expansion of media access across the developing world has produced a range of undoubtedly positive outcomes, the initial euphoria it generated amongst donor governments and development agencies has also been tempered in part by the emergence of some more negative consequences as well. It has also resulted in media for development being carried out on much more uncertain grounds than was ever the case beforehand. These chapters also look at the implications of new media environments for media development and the community media sector. Chapter 6 then focuses upon one particular outcome of new media environments: the way in which they have cemented, and made inexorable, a link between celebrity and development. It looks at how and why this link came about, what implications it has for international development in general, and how it has forever blurred any prior distinctions between development agencies, developing world governments and their citizens, and the audiences for media representations of development.

In these ways, the book provides a detailed overview of the shifting – and multifaceted – relationship between media and development. In so doing, it will help readers to understand the complexities of the issues involved and, ultimately, allow them to reach their own conclusion on the central questions for all of this: what does media contribute to the goals of international development, and of other kinds of planned social change? Which are the best types of media, or combinations of types, to use for different sorts of development projects? In what ways do different kinds of media 'empower' people in the developing world? How might media revolutions, such as the mobile phone revolution and the rise of the internet and social media, be more effectively harnessed towards purposive social change? And, how will emergent media platforms change processes for development in the future?

Summary

- In recent years, there has been a renewed interest in the relationship between media and international development. There are various reasons for this.
- However, there is a general lack of consensus, amongst both practitioners and scholars, over precisely what role media should play in development.
- Part of this problem stems from a lack of agreement over precisely what 'media' even is, or does. This reflects changes within theories of media.
- Another part stems from shifting paradigms of development. For a long time, the field was dominated by 'modernization theory'. However, today, it is instead characterized by various kinds of 'neo-liberal' theories (which have been to the fore ever since the emergence of the 'Washington Consensus').
- A renewed interest in media development also emerged out of the neo-liberal turn.
- Media representations of development have also undergone significant change in recent years, reflecting the much more complex media environments from which they emerge and into which they are broadcast.

Discussion questions

1. Do you think that the current excitement around media for development is justified?
2. What effects have the arrival of one or other new media technology had upon your own life, and/or upon the lives of people around you?
3. Can you think of any ways in which the introduction of new media might have *negative* impacts upon a society? What steps might be taken to minimize these effects?
4. Does a 'free press' always produce a more democratic society?
5. What impressions of international development have you derived from watching television news and other media sources?

Further reading

There is an enormous literature on the history of international development, and on the various 'paradigm shifts' that have defined it. Good starting points include: Leys, C. (1996) *The Rise and Fall of Development Theory*, Bloomington, IN: Indiana University Press; Peet, R. and Hartwick, E. (2015) *Theories of Development: Contentions, Arguments, Alternatives*, 3rd Edition. New York: Guilford Press; and Rist, G. (2014) *The History of Development: From Western Origins to Global Faith*, 4th Edition, London: Zed Books. Similarly, there are a huge number of publications that introduce the history of mass media, and the key concepts in media studies. A recommended starting point is: Ott, B. and Mack, R. (2014) *Critical Media Studies: An Introduction*, 2nd Edition, Malden, MA: Wiley-Blackwell. There is a growing literature focused specifically on 'media development'. One very important recent contribution to this is: Wasserman, H., ed. (2011) *Popular Media, Democracy and Development in Africa*, New York: Routledge (although this book is focused on African case studies, it raises key questions for the study of media development in other parts of the developing world as well). On representations of development, see: Dogra, N. (2014) *Representations of Global Poverty: Aid, Development and International NGOs*, London: I.B. Tauris; and Lewis, D., Rodgers, D. and Woolcock, M., eds. (2014) *Popular Representations of Development: Insights from Novels, Films, Television and Social Media*, New York: Routledge.

1 The rise and rise of media for development

- The origins of 'international development'.
- The place of media within modernization.
- Three models for development communication.
- Social marketing and its applications.
- Experiments with different genres.

The genesis of media for development

Conveniently, the modern history of both international development and 'media for development' can be traced to the very same event: US President Harry S. Truman's Inaugural Address of 20 January 1949. Truman's speech was made at an extraordinary moment in world history, coming as it did just a few years after the world had emerged from the nightmare that was the Second World War, yet as it had already begun to enter into a new era of global struggle (albeit one of a very different order) – that which would become known as the Cold War. In this context, Truman was keen to restate the United States' commitment to post-war reconstruction efforts and also to position his nation for the challenges ahead. Thus, the first three points of his speech referred to (in order): (1) the United States' commitment to the United Nations as the foundational authority of the new, post-war, international order; (2) a continuation of the European Recovery Programme (ERP, better known as the 'Marshall Plan') through which the US financed the reconstruction of the European economies that had been devastated by the war (the Plan eventually ran until 1952, at a total cost to the US of around US$120 billion in today's money); and (3) the United States' intention to create a military alliance with its North Atlantic allies – the North Atlantic Treaty Organization, or NATO – as a counter to the rising Soviet threat (NATO formally came into existence a mere two months later).

In its first draft, Truman's speech stopped there. However, at the last minute (or at least, so the story goes) an aide to the incoming president suggested inserting a fourth point, promising to extend the benefits of America's scientific and industrial progress to *all* of the poorer nations of the world (such assistance from the US had previously focused upon the countries of Latin America only). The decision – whoever did actually take it – was hugely significant because, at a stroke, it vastly elevated the importance of international development by effectively enshrining it as a key priority for US foreign policy (and by implication, for all of its international allies as well) – one akin to, and interconnected with, rebuilding the international system, reconstructing the major European economies after the war, and defending against the then rising Soviet threat. Reflecting this, soon after the speech was delivered, the US Congress created a new Technical Cooperation Program Unit (TCPU, which was eventually housed within the State Department, although became the forerunner to the contemporary US Agency for International Development, USAID). This was shortly followed by the UN's creation of an Expanded Programme of Technical Assistance (which later became the UN Development Programme, UNDP), and the World Bank's formation of the International Finance Corporation (IFC, to encourage private investment in the developing world) and the International Development Association (IDA, to provide concessionary loans to the world's poorest nations). For all of these reasons, then, Truman's speech is often seen as ushering in the 'Age of Development' (for a detailed discussion of Truman's speech and its implications, see Rist, 2014: 69–79).

Truman's speech also played a crucial role in defining precisely how development would be understood over the following decades. The wording of Point 4 emphasized the problems faced by people in Africa, Asia, and Latin America – for example, 'their food is inadequate. They are the victims of disease. Their economic life is primitive and stagnant' – stemmed from their relative 'lack' *vis-à-vis* populations in Europe and North America. Indeed, Truman's speech was one of the first major documents to use the term '*under*development'. The speech also stressed – as a corollary to this notion of 'lack' – that the most effective solutions for Southern problems surely lay, therefore, in the transfer of capital and knowledge, especially technical and scientific knowledge, from the North to the South (which might allow the latter to move from 'underdeveloped' to 'developed'; or in other words, to 'catch up' with the rich world, or simply to 'modernize'). In so doing, the speech also brought about a subtle shift in the meaning of the word 'development' itself, in that the term now came to have a transitive meaning – to refer to an action which is done *by* one entity *to* another (i.e. by a wealthier country to a poorer one). Amongst other things, this did away with any last remaining vestiges of evolutionary thought, in which non-European development was usually taken to be intransitive – that is, as something that occurred *within* those societies themselves, as an outcome of processes that unfolded 'under their own steam'. It also naturalized the need for overseas development assistance (ODA), or 'aid', through which wealthier countries provide financial assistance to countries in Africa, Asia, and Latin America.

Of greatest interest here, Truman's speech also implied a central role for media – and in so doing, it also inaugurated the field of what became known as 'Media for Development' (M4D). More recently, and especially following the advent of the internet, the field is now called 'Information and Communication Technologies for Development' ('ICT4D'). However, to avoid confusion, I will simply use M4D throughout this chapter. On the one hand, Point 4's emphasis upon knowledge transfers already implied the need for vastly expanded media infrastructures (after all, precisely how might *any* type of knowledge be transferred anywhere in the absence of physical media capable of actually transmitting it?). On the other, the speech's privileging of the transformative potential of new forms of technical and scientific knowledge, specifically, conveyed an implicit criticism of pre-existing forms of knowledge (i.e. cultural, or 'traditional', knowledge) as a kind of 'bottleneck' or 'barrier' to progress. And at that time, it was already widely believed that the very best way to weaken people's commitment to these sorts of cultural – or traditional – knowledge was through increasing their exposure to all kinds of modern education and information, as could be most effectively communicated through mass media.

For these reasons, many of the TCPU's early development projects and programmes placed a great emphasis upon expanding media infrastructures and access, and by the mid-1950s a range of other development organizations – in particular the UN's Educational, Scientific, and Cultural Organization (UNESCO) – had developed a similar focus. Initially, many of these efforts centred upon radio, as a result of which the period from the mid-1950s onwards saw a proliferation both of radio transmitters and of radio receivers across the developing world. For example, one estimate has suggested that between 1955 and 1970, the number of radio sets in sub-Saharan Africa increased from 460,000 to 33 million (this expansion was greatly assisted by the invention of the cheap and portable transistor radio in the 1950s; Mytton, 2000: 24). However, already by the 1960s, and certainly by the 1970s, these interventions increasingly involved television as well. This was more marked in some parts of the developing world than others – for example, in Central America and in South and Southeast Asia, where the US and Japan, respectively, used 'aid-for-trade' programmes as a means both for boosting television coverage, and for creating effective monopolies for their own television manufacturing companies. For instance, one such programme from Japan's International Cooperation Agency (JICA) to Sri Lanka provided free TV transmission equipment, and free training for staff working in educational television, in return for exclusive import rights for Japanese television makers such as Sony (Paul, 1996). Later, following advances in computing and the advent of the internet, a key focus instead became the expansion of telecentres (facilities which today are more commonly known as 'internet cafes'). More generally, levels of 'media saturation' came to be seen as 'indexes of development' in their own right. In other words, ratios of radios and televisions to the number of people in a given location came to be seen as markers of 'how developed' that place was. Already by the early 1960s, UNESCO had published a set of minimum targets on this score, which were initially set at: ten daily newspapers, five radio receivers, two television sets, and two cinema seats per 100 people. In other words, media came to be seen as both a means and an end for international development. (Subsequently, UNESCO has overseen a number of other initiatives aimed at monitoring media density in the developing world. Most recently, in 2004, the organization launched the umbrella Partnership on Measuring ICT for Development, which brings together a wide range of other agencies working on this issue.)

Three models for development communication

At the time Truman made his famous speech, the dual notions that international development should be conceived as a transitive process for modernization, and that media had a key role to play in facilitating this process, were both relatively novel – which is to say *untested* – ideas. Certainly, by then, at least some colonial powers had carried out various experiments for educating their subject populations in Africa, Asia, and Latin America through mass communications. For example, following the publication of the Plymouth Report in 1937, the British had undertaken a series of pilot projects across their African colonies with the aim of delivering mass education by radio (at that time, personal radio sets were still too expensive for most people to purchase, and so these pilots were mostly delivered over communal listening posts) (Vokes, 2007a). However, by the late 1940s, it was still not clear precisely what effects these experiments had had – or even, for that matter, whether they could be deemed 'successful' or not. Certainly, no general models existed to explain precisely how and why modernization might be achieved through mass media. Thus, it was not until some time *after* Truman's speech, and well into the 1950s, that both development agencies and academic observers began to build the evidential base necessary to support the assumptions made in the address, and to develop more general theoretical models for understanding the relationship between modernization and media.

In 1958, a Professor of International Communication at the Massachusetts Institute of Technology (MIT), Daniel Lerner, published what would become the seminal early work in M4D, in terms both of the empirical evidence that it documented and the theoretical model that it derived from this. The book, called *The Passing of Traditional Society: Modernizing the Middle East*, was a detailed, comparative study of the processes of modernization, and of the place that media had played within these, in six countries: Egypt, Iran, Jordan, Lebanon, Syria, and Turkey. Based on this wealth of comparative data, Lerner argued that a general pattern existed, whereby western countries' attempts to 'modernize' developing nations invariably began with attempts to build up the latter's manufacturing industries and education systems. These efforts in turn produced rising urbanization and increased literacy rates, which, over time, generated a desire for new forms of mass media (as the new urban educated classes sought out more news and other information programming). Later, as these individuals' exposure to media increased, it caused them to become more empathetic to modern values, and eventually to change their worldview altogether and to develop a 'mobile personality' (i.e. one that is generally accepting of change and is open to new ideas of economic practice and political organization). According to Lerner, the key trigger here – for any developing country – was 25% urbanization, at which point literacy rates were invariably high enough to generate the necessary demand for new media. Once introduced, the media themselves then effectively took on a life of their own, becoming what Lerner called a 'mobility multiplier' for the rest of the way.

Four years after Lerner's publication, a sociologist based at Ohio State University, Everett Rogers, published another key contribution to the emerging field of development communication, or M4D: *Diffusion of Innovations* (1962). Indeed, so important did Everett's book become, that it has continued to be widely read ever since (the fifth edition of the book, which was published in 2003, was recently classified as one of the most widely cited texts in all of the social sciences). Rogers' work had a similar aim to Lerner's, in that he too was interested in exploring how a comparison of different cases – in Rogers' case, he compared more than 500 examples – might be used to develop a more general model of innovations and their effects upon social change, including in developing world contexts. (However, Rogers didn't limit this study to an examination of 'modern' innovations only, such as manufacturing industries and modern education systems. Instead, he was interested in all kinds of innovations, which he defined in the broadest possible terms, as any 'idea, practice or object that is perceived as new' by its recipient(s). In addition, Rogers was also interested in what part mass media played in these processes. Finally, the Diffusion model, like Lerner's, also emphasized the importance of individual attitudes in shaping social change. According to Rogers, all individuals pass through a series of five subjective stages in their adoption of any innovation, in which: (1) they first become aware of its existence (Rogers terms this the 'knowledge stage'); (2) they develop a growing interest in it (the 'persuasion stage'); (3) they decide whether or not to try it out (the 'decision stage'); (4) they start to use it, evaluating its effectiveness as they do so ('implementation'); before (5) finalizing their decision, based on experience ('confirmation').

However, of crucial significance – and this is really the key insight of Rogers' book – individuals do not pass through these five stages at the same speed. Instead, people's different character-types, which also correlate with their different levels of socio-economic status, determine how quickly they will go from 'knowledge' to 'confirmation'. Thus, high risk-taking individuals, who are usually also of high status (and therefore wealthy enough to absorb a loss if things go wrong), move most quickly; they are followed by 'early adopters', who are open to some risk and are also key opinion leaders in their communities (they are generally also of high status); early adopters are followed by individuals who exhibit varying degrees of scepticism, and who are of varying status (Rogers divides this group into the two categories of 'early majority' and 'late majority'); finally come the 'laggards', who are markedly change-averse, display little or no opinion leadership, are of the lowest socio-economic status, and are the last to take up any innovation.

A key question for international development, therefore, became to what extent the introduction of mass media might help to speed up these rates of adoption, especially amongst the laggards? However, on this question, Rogers was more sceptical than Lerner, and found that mass communications do *not* always take on a 'life of their own' within processes of social change (as Lerner suggested). Rather, Rogers argued that although media could play a crucial role in raising initial awareness of an innovation – and therefore in accelerating individuals' transition from the 'knowledge stage' to the 'persuasion stage' – after that, and especially during the 'decision stage', the role of interpersonal communication was much more important. In other words, beyond risk-takers, most people would be more likely to try out an innovation not if they had heard about it on the radio or the television, but if they heard about it from somebody that they already knew. This drew attention to the key role played by 'opinion leaders' (who, by definition, know the most people within any given social setting). The logical conclusion was that in any developing context, media messages should be targeted not at the entire population, but instead at opinion leaders only (who would then communicate these same messages, face-to-face, to the population at large). Rogers later elaborated on this 'two-step' model for development communication – an idea which also drew heavily on the earlier work of sociologists Paul Lazarsfeld and Elihu Katz (who had previously proposed a 'two-step flow' model for *all* forms of mass communication) – in a joint publication with Lynne Svenning, called *Modernization Among Peasants: The Impact of Communication* (Rogers and Svenning, 1969).

Finally here, in 1964, a communications scholar based at Stanford University, Wilbur Schramm, published what was to become another key text in the emerging field of M4D, *Mass Media and National Development: The Role of Information in the Developing Countries*. Schramm's book was again highly influential, in part because of who he was – even today, he is widely regarded as one of the founders of the discipline of 'mass communication' – but also because it was funded by UNESCO, and so went on to directly inform that organization's emerging policies for M4D (mentioned above). In terms of content, Schramm's work – which, again, tried to extrapolate from a wide range of empirical cases to reach some more general conclusions – drew heavily on Lerner's study and, as such, repeated many of that book's key ideas. Schramm also argued that the path to modernization – what he famously called the 'terrible ascent' from tradition to modernity – could only be achieved through the interaction of industrialization, urbanization, and literacy, and that mass media had a key role to play in facilitating this interplay. In addition, he accepted Lerner's findings that media was crucial for changing individuals' attitudes and outlooks, and for encouraging them to develop more modern, mobile personalities. However, Schramm also extended Lerner's model by arguing that, in addition to changing perceptions, mass media could accelerate modernization in other, more 'structural' ways. In particular, he proposed that mass communications might help to speed up the transfer of modern techniques and ideas from the developed to the developing world – that is, they could form a key 'bridge' between the Global North and the Global South – and, as such, would eventually help to reduce the overall 'gap' between the two. In addition, he argued that media could help to make developing world governments both more accountable and more efficient, by broadening the 'policy dialogue' that informed their decision-making processes. In so doing, Schramm also became one of the first people to draw a direct connection between media and (what we would now call) 'good governance'.

The combined effect of the publication of these three models was that, by the mid-1960s, a consensus had emerged that if international development is best conceived as a transitive process for modernization – one that requires attitudinal and behavioural changes (including the adoption of modern innovations) across large parts of the developing world – then an expansion of mass media would always have both a direct and an overwhelmingly positive effect upon this, through its perceived ability to facilitate modernization, by changing individuals' attitudes and behaviours (Golding, 1974). To put it simply, modernization in the developing world would always occur more easily – and more quickly – if accompanied by an expansion of mass media. Or more simply still: in any developing world context, the more media the better. In addition, once these ideas had become established, they continued to dominate the field for several decades to come. Indeed, they have in many ways continued to shape the field up until the present day.

Social marketing

Since the mid-1960s, this general consensus over the role, the methods, and the potential benefits of development communication (or the 'dominant paradigm' as it is sometimes called) has remained hugely influential within both the media and international development fields (Waisbord, 2001). Even today, there are numerous examples of M4D programmes and projects that continue to reproduce its key ideas in a direct way. However, over recent decades, the dominant paradigm has become particularly associated with three different (albeit heavily overlapping) areas of M4D practice: (1) social marketing, (2) public health campaigns, and (3) entertainment-education (*ibid.*). It is in relation to these three domains that the dominant paradigm has had the greatest influence, but also has been extended – and altered – in key ways. Probably the most central of these three is social marketing. Social marketing began with the premise that if the aim of international development was to bring about attitudinal and behavioural changes through the media, then this could be more effectively achieved if the media messages were better tailored towards their target audiences (something that could only be achieved, of course, if one had first developed sufficient knowledge of the nature of those audiences) (McKee, 1999). In so doing, it drew on insights from the academic discipline of marketing, as well as from commercial sales practice, both of which, by the mid-1960s, were increasingly shifting away from an emphasis upon a 'selling approach' (whereby a firm puts most of its energy and resources into promoting the benefits of its existing products) towards a 'marketing approach' (in which the firm instead focuses upon researching its customers' desires, for which new products can later be developed; the process is today typically known as 'R&D') (Fox and Kotler, 1980; French *et al.*, 2009). In addition, social marketing also drew on insights from within media studies itself, which, by the late 1960s, was beginning to develop a greater understanding of the complexities of audience decoding and *reception* (issues that were eventually elaborated upon in a systematic way by Stuart Hall, in the early 1970s; see Chapter 1).

Whilst not directly challenging the main conclusions of Lerner and Rogers' work – for one thing, it generally conformed to Rogers' five-stage model for the adoption of innovations – social marketing did suggest that both men's reliance upon a series of 'ideal-types' (i.e. abstract categories) as a means for conceiving of the audience for development communication was inadequate. Instead, social marketing recognized that all audiences are made up of real people, who, in different social settings, will always have different sorts of attitudes and behaviours (and different sorts of needs and desires as well). These can only be properly understood through direct research *with those audiences themselves* (Kotler, 1979). Moreover, it is only through understanding the nature of these 'real-world' attitudes that one can ever hope to design appropriate media messages that are capable of engaging with them. In other words, one must first understand what a given community's (diverse) beliefs and practices actually are, before one can try to change them. Amongst other things, the social marketing approach did call into question Rogers' 'two-step' approach to development communication, by suggesting that media messages could in fact be effectively targeted at everyone within a population – but only if the specific attitudes and desires of all members of that population had been first properly mapped out and the development project's media content had been tailored accordingly.

More than anything else, social marketing introduced a battery of new methods (and related concepts) to the field of development communication, the majority of which continue to be widely used within the field today (Lee and Kotler, 2015). Thus, as part of its emphasis upon the value of thorough *market research*, social marketing introduced some of the more rigorous marketing methods used in the commercial world to international development practice. These included, in particular: (1) *audience segmentation* (sometimes also referred to as 'audience grouping'), a method whereby the researcher/social marketeer divides up her potential audience along various demographic lines, in an attempt to identify different 'lifestyle clusters' (which might form 'niche markets' for her products); and (2) *target group mapping*, whereby the researcher, having identified the particular lifestyle cluster (or clusters) of interest, then tries to 'map out' its members' habits and routines, especially as these relate to their media usage. The aim is to build up a detailed picture of when and where these people are most likely to engage with different types of (physical) media, and what sorts of media content they are most likely to pay attention to within those times and places.

These two stages of market research later feed into the methods for *product development*, which are constituted of: (1) *product placement*, whereby the researcher attempts to design not only one product, but several – each of which might be aimed at a different 'segment' within the overall target audience – and to identify both the

best locations, and the most effective media messages and media channels (or mixes thereof), through which each of these products could be presented to the relevant groups (it should also be noted that the term 'product' here may refer either to a physical object or to some kind of intangible, such as an idea or a behaviour);
(2) *facilitation and incentivization*, in which the researcher also looks for ways to increase the uptake of the new products, by making it both easier and more attractive for people to take them up. The methods here may involve anything from making the products more widely available in particular places, to providing people with some sort of psychological, or even monetary, incentive for trying the products. Finally, (3) *persistence* is also a key element of social marketing. Indeed, from the very beginning, social marketeers always stressed the importance of long-term engagement as being crucial to the success of any of the other methods outlined above (Lee and Kotler, 2015; Waisbord, 2001; Walsh *et al.*, 1993).

From the late 1960s onwards, social marketing was championed by USAID and by a small but influential group of development-focused NGOs that specialized in the approach (which included the Academy for Educational Development, DKT International, the Futures Group, and Population Services International). Through the efforts of these agencies, social marketing gained huge prominence within media for development, and was used in everything from women's education projects to environmental management programmes to agricultural extension (for an excellent overview of the sheer range of areas within which social marketing was applied during this time, see Kotler, 1979). However, it soon came to be seen as *particularly* effective for family planning (cf. Roberto, 1975).

Key here is to understand that prior to the advent of social marketing, family planning programmes – which, throughout the history of international development, had always revolved around attempts to *reduce* the number of children that families in the developing world produce – had generally relied upon a 'clinic approach'. This involved setting up specific sites ('clinics') in which a general set of tools and knowledge for reducing fertility (such as contraceptive devices and related educational services) could be made available, and then using general media advertising to raise awareness of these clinics' existence. However, by the late 1960s, it had become clear that this sort of approach was having little effect in reducing fertility rates among many developing world populations, not least because it was simply too 'passive' (Potts, 1996; Sai, 1986).

Figure 1.1 *Poster for a family planning campaign in Uganda*

Source: Author

Against this, then, a social marketing approach drew immediate attention to the ways in which, within any given population, different groupings – for example, men/women, unmarried/married, less educated/more educated, employed/subsistence-labourers, town dwellers/rural populations – invariably had quite different attitudes both towards fertility itself and towards the tools and techniques for controlling it. In addition, it highlighted how such groupings were likely to engage with different sorts of media in different places, at different times (Fox and Kotler, 1980). Thus, a more effective approach to family planning involved developing a range of 'products' for controlling fertility (which might include not only different contraceptive devices, but also such ideas as delaying marriage, reducing polygamy, and increasing birth spacing), which could be differentially targeted, through a range of media (including leaflets, billboard posters, radio adverts), to the different audience groupings (in all cases, the exact type of media, or 'media mix', used would depend on the existing habits of the particular target group) (Flora *et al.*, cited in Waisbord, 2001). In addition, the new social marketing programmes also placed a particular emphasis upon facilitation, which included everything from making the contraceptive pill more easily available to young women, to providing financial incentives for older men to undergo vasectomies (Andreasen, 1994).

Public health campaigns

Over the course of the 1970s, the perceived success of social marketing methods in relation to family planning resulted in these same methods being applied within an ever wider range of other 'health and wellbeing' campaigns, including improved nutrition projects, vaccination programmes, anti-smoking and alcohol awareness campaigns, as well as sexual health and hygiene programmes (French et al., 2009). A majority of these campaigns involved an extension of the basic assumptions – and models – that had earlier been used in family planning campaigns to these additional areas of public health as well. Thus, it was recognized that just as earlier approaches to family planning had relied on a 'clinic approach', so too health programmes related to these other areas had also generally relied on the creation of 'sites' (some of which were permanent, others temporary) through which positive health messages and interventions could be delivered (Sai, 1986). For example, by the early 1970s, the most common approach to rural health and nutrition projects still involved government and development agents travelling out to villages where they would hold one-day or one-week clinics and workshops (usually in the grounds of a local hospital, or in a school or some other public venue), during which they would deliver nutrition education and hand out healthy food samples, as well as technologies for improving food storage and hygiene. Again, the timing and location of these sessions was usually broadcast over the radio in advance (Rice and Paisley, 1981).

However, over time, there was growing recognition that these clinics were incredibly expensive to run (in addition to their extensive labour requirements, they also involved huge transport and fuel costs, a large amount of additional equipment, and so on), and were therefore difficult for developing world governments or even international donors – both of which have limited resources – to establish in sufficient numbers to meet the health needs of entire rural populations (Potts, 1996). Against this, then, it was recognized that a social marketing approach could be used to target more effectively only certain key actors, and in particular mothers (who, in most rural

Figure 1.2 A maternity health campaign in Uganda

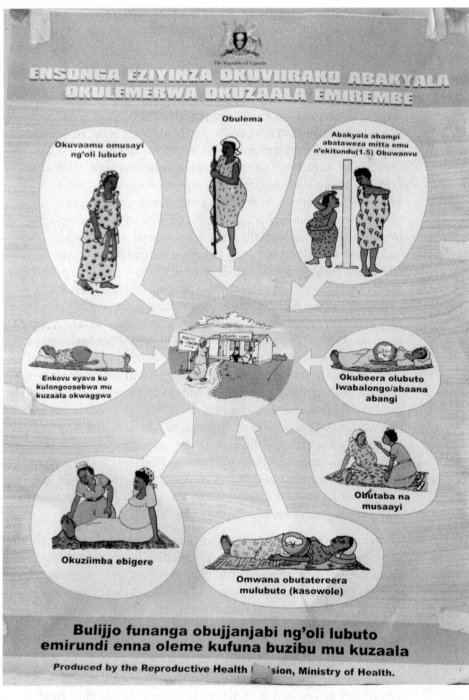

Source: Author

households, control not only their own nutrition but also that of their husbands and children), with a view to understanding their needs and desires and developing products that were appropriate to meeting these (*ibid.*). Yet during the 1970s, it was clear that the greatest threats to public health in the developing world – especially in rural areas and in tropical zones – were those that stemmed from acute (i.e. quick-onset) infectious diseases, such as diarrhoea, malaria, and tuberculosis (this consensus continued to hold until the discovery of the HIV/AIDS pandemic in the early 1980s). In this context, it was again felt that social marketing might be the best approach, given its potential to bring about a range of rapid behavioural changes among different audience segments (which might help to more effectively stem the transmission of those infectious diseases in the first place; Smith, 2009).

Box 1.1 Social marketing and infant mortality in Honduras

In 1978, a consortium involving USAID, the WHO, and UNICEF embarked on a major drive to improve infant mortality across the developing world. At the time, infant mortality in the Global South averaged an enormous 200+ deaths per 1000 live births – the vast majority of them from easily preventable diseases such as diarrhoea, measles, and respiratory tract infections. The consortium's first project in pursuit of this new drive was called the Mass Media and Health Practices Project, and initially involved Honduras in Central America and The Gambia in West Africa. The project adopted a social marketing approach and thus began by gathering a huge amount of market research, from both countries, into the feeding habits of new mothers and their preferences for the introduction of food supplements. Based on this data, two separate products were developed to combat diarrhoea-related dehydration: a pre-package set of salts and a home-mix of sugar, salt, and water. The former was deemed more appropriate for new mothers in Honduras, the latter for their equivalents in The Gambia. In both countries, the media mix focused upon educational radio programming, leaflets, and face-to-face contacts. However, in Honduras, it was quickly realized that the pre-packaged salts had a major design flaw, in that the instructions that were printed on them were illegible, to the point that most women using the product didn't even recognize that they were instructions. As a result, women tended to mix them in the same way that they would a headache cure with which they were familiar – that is, in a glass of water, rather than in the requisite 1 litre of water. This resulted in salt-to-water concentrations that were enough to kill a baby! In addition, it was also realized that even when the women did mix the salts correctly, they did not end up giving the entire 1 litre of solution to the baby, as is required, because they thought that this was simply too much medicine for any child to consume. Therefore, the social marketeers refined their media messaging to focus not only on the need for the salts but, more importantly, upon *how to administer them* as well. This resulted in a 'second round' of marketing, which again used educational radio programming (presented by a well-known radio personality called Dr. Salustiano), leaflets, and face-to-face contacts, but also some rather catchy radio songs and jingles, and public billboard advertising. The success of the programme in Honduras is highlighted by the fact that just one year into the programme, a study by Stanford University found that 93% of mothers across 20 sample rural communities knew about the campaign, 71% could sing one of the songs that had been used in its radio advertising, and 49% had used the product involved. Most importantly of all, the project also had had a direct effect in significantly reducing infant mortality rates. Between 1981 and 1982, these fell for children under 5 years of age from 47.5% to 25%. As such, the Honduras experiment formed a model for the rest of the consortium's drive, which over the next decade saw infant mortality rates fall sharply across the developing world.

Sources: Rice and Paisley (1981), Kendall et al. (1983), Smith (2009)

As the range of applications expanded, however, the perceived limitations of social marketing also came into sharper focus. Indeed, by around the late 1970s, a growing number of theorists and practitioners had begun to articulate a series of distinct criticisms of the approach (for more on the history of these emerging criticisms, see especially Fox and Kotler, 1980). The first of these criticisms was that they were all ultimately underpinned by the logic that public health problems were an aggregate outcome of individual behaviours – from which it followed that the only real way to improve the overall health of a population was to find ways to encourage people to change their behaviours (i.e. to get people to give up unhealthy practices by providing them with more healthy 'choices' instead). This view had long dominated western governments' thinking about their own public health problems and their responses to these – as it still does – and it seemed that in the context of international development, they were now simply projecting this same thinking onto the developing world as well (Waisbord, 2001). Yet there was a very real danger that this amounted to 'blaming the victims' – that is, suggesting that people's illnesses were effectively 'their own fault' (*ibid.*). More importantly, however, it was not at all clear which kinds of major health problems that existed in developing world countries *were* the outcome of individuals' poor 'choices'. On the contrary, the spread of infectious diseases such as diarrhoea through any population were much more likely to be an outcome of more 'structural' factors, such as poor infrastructure, poor sanitation, and malnutrition, all of which make the body more susceptible to infection (Pande et al., 2008). These were all things over which individuals living in those contexts had very little influence or control. The implication was that no amount of social marketing, no matter how effective this was on its own terms, could ever truly address the root causes of public health challenges – which instead required greater investment from governments (to improve infrastructure), greater engagement from social networks, such as family groups, neighbourhood or 'community' groups (to improve local sanitary conditions).

Secondly, it was also argued that despite their many sophisticated elements, the methods of social marketing ultimately remained 'top-down' – in that throughout all of the stages of both market research and product development, all decision making was ultimately taken by the researcher/social marketeer alone, rather than by the recipients of the programmes (Lee and Kotler, 2015). In this way, social marketing appeared to include no element of 'participation', and in so doing it tended to cast people in the developing world as simply consumers of, rather than as protagonists within, development interventions. In other words, it ran the risk of denying them any agency within their own affairs. Moreover, if this argument suggested that social marketing could be seen as ultimately manipulative, this perception was further reinforced by a third major critique that emerged at around this same time.

According to this third line of argument, social marketing's overall emphasis upon the techniques of 'western' advertising – which are themselves born, of course, out of a desire to *sell* things – also ran the risk of blurring the distinction between *developmental* goals and *commercial* ones. At best, this might result in social marketeers favouring the promotion of certain kinds of products over others, in line with the commercial interests of those funding their products. At worst, it might result in cynical – even sinister – attempts to use development projects as a 'smoke-screen' for the pursuit of purely commercial goals. And, unfortunately, there are concrete examples of this having actually happened in practice. The most notorious example of a social marketing based health campaign 'gone wrong' relates to the 'baby food scandal' that engulfed the multinational food and beverage giant Nestlé from 1973 onwards. This scandal related to a series of allegations that were made by the social activist magazine *New Internationalist* (Geach, 1973); by the British NGO War on Want, in a leaflet called 'The Baby Killer' (written by Mike Muller, in 1974); and by German director Peter Krieg's documentary *Bottle Babies* (released in 1975).

Figure 1.3 Front cover image of 'The Baby Killer' leaflet

Source: War on Want

Between them, these three publications argued that Nestlé's own social marketing practices for infant nutrition across the developing world, as well as those of developing world governments that were directly supported by Nestlé, were little more than a sham for enabling the food giant to massively expand the markets for its – hugely lucrative – powdered baby milk products across Africa, Asia, and Latin America. Based on case material drawn from Nigeria, Bangladesh, Chile, and elsewhere, the three publications jointly alleged that these programmes typically involved social marketeers framing new mothers' issues and concerns in ways that could be addressed by their giving up breastfeeding and going over to powdered-milk formula instead. They would then design advertising campaigns that were specifically targeted at these issues, and would also employ 'sales girls in nurses' uniforms' (Muller, 1974: 5) to deliver these same messages by direct word of mouth, and to provide incentives for new mothers to take them up (especially free samples). As a result, a significant proportion of women across the developing world either stopped breastfeeding completely or undertook it for a significantly reduced period of time. For example, in Nigeria, Muller found that more than 70% were bottle-feeding their babies when they were less than four months old – in a context in which breastfeeding had historically continued for up to four years (1974: 4–5).

From a developmental point of view, the effects of these campaigns were utterly disastrous. Given that baby formula is of significantly lower nutritional value than breast milk anyway, and does not contain any of the natural antibodies against infections that are contained in breast milk, combined with the fact that many women in the developing world often could not read the instructions on how to properly sterilize the bottles (in contexts of low literacy rates) and, even if they could, lacked the necessary equipment and conditions to do so safely, these campaigns in fact resulted *in significantly worse health outcomes for babies*. As Muller's leaflet pointed out, already by the mid-1970s, the link between early weaning onto baby formula and disease had been documented in India, Jamaica, Jordan, and elsewhere. Across the developing world, it had been linked to increased malnutrition, which in turn greatly increased incidence rates of infectious diseases such as diarrhoea. Meanwhile, in Chile, it had been directly linked with a threefold increase in rates of infant mortality (1974: 3) – and a massive body of subsequent research has in general confirmed all of these findings. However, from a commercial point of view, these same campaigns were highly effective. Indeed, already by 1980, the market in baby formula products across the developing world was worth an estimated US$1.5 billion per annum (Lorber and Cornelius, 1982). Today, it is worth many times that figure.

In response both to the allegations made in these three publications, and to Nestlé's subsequent attempts to sue some of their publishers for libel, a US-based group called the 'Infant Formula Action Coalition' (INFACT) launched a boycott of all Nestlé products among western consumers, which soon spread worldwide. Despite ongoing attempts by Nestlé to show that it is in full compliance with relevant international codes on responsible marketing, this boycott continues to this day. As of 2016, it continues to be organized by a British group 'Baby Milk Action', which has links to over 200 other organizations and networks across more than 100 countries (see www.babymilkaction.org).

Entertainment-education

By the early 1980s, therefore, the general premise that the process of modernization could be greatly sped up if it involved media – especially given media content's potential to change individuals' attitudes and behaviour (in ways that made both of these more 'modern') – had become something of a given within international development circles. Moreover, M4D practitioners and theorists working within this dominant paradigm had also reached a consensus that this could be made even more efficient – and effective – when it involved not a selling approach, but a marketing one. In particular, this latter approach drew attention to the benefits of audience segmentation and the use of different media channels for reaching different target audiences. Nevertheless, throughout the late 1960s and the 1970s, some social marketing programmes and projects *in practice* continued to deliver their content in the form of more didactic, educational genres (of the kind used by the British Colonial Film Unit, described in the Introduction). Yet, by the late 1970s, and especially following the seminal work of Stuart Hall on 'encoding and decoding' – and the wave of scholarship that followed in its wake – there was a growing recognition that by presenting the content in these genres, practitioners might be in fact appealing to only some audience segments (for example, men or the elderly), and may even be *reducing* the impact of their media messages among other segments (for example, women or the young).

The logical conclusion was that M4D programmes and projects might need to experiment with other genres as well, if they wanted to be more effective in delivering their messages to specific target audiences. This, in turn, gave birth to what is now commonly referred to as 'entertainment-education' (or sometimes just 'edutainment') (Singhal and Rogers, 1999; Singhal *et al.*, 2003). The basic premise of entertainment-education is that whilst the social marketeer is carrying out her initial market research, at the same time that she is trying to identify different 'lifestyle clusters' and map out the habits of these, as well as looking at the different kinds of physical media that alternative audience segments engage with during their daily routines, she must also document the different genres of content with which they most frequently engage – which in many cases will be primarily entertainment genres. The idea is that development messages can then be encoded within these same genres in order to ensure the most effective kind of product placement. Moreover, it was soon realized that the placement of these messages into specifically entertainment genres might also confer other potential advantages as well.

In 1977, a Professor of Psychology at Stanford University, Albert Bandura, published what was to become another foundational text for entertainment-education, *Social Learning Theory*. The book, which expanded upon the ideas that Bandura and his collaborators had been developing since the early 1960s, argued very strongly that all human beings learn new behaviours primarily through observing the actions of role models – and evaluating the consequences of those actions (i.e. whether they are rewarded or punished, to use psychologists' parlance) – and then trying to emulate those actions which they perceive to be the most successful ones. Crucially, though, the book also argued that people learn such behaviours by observing not only direct role models (i.e. people that they actually know and physically engage with), but also their *media role models*. Indeed, Bandura argued that with the latter, perceptions of which behaviours produced the greatest reward or punishment, and which should therefore be emulated, were even amplified. In so doing, Bandura introduced a series of key questions about mediation, about celebrity role models, and about media effects that have remained current in media studies, and in wider society, to the present day. More importantly, for our present purposes, his work also suggested that where development messages were encoded into dramatic entertainment genres (which invariably require their audiences to identify with some or other role model), these were much more likely to bring about the desired behavioural changes among those same audiences.

The earliest examples of social marketeers putting all of this into practice occurred in Latin America in the late 1970s. As part of their market research into different audience segments, these marketeers observed that various audience segments – including not only women, but also some men of lower socio-economic status, and a majority of youth – spent most of their television viewing time watching telenovelas (which are a distinctive kind of Latin American drama, in some ways similar to US 'soap operas'; see Box 1.2). Having identified this, the social marketeers, in collaboration with commercial television production companies, began to design ways in which development messages could be incorporated within the dramatic storylines of these telenovelas. The Mexican producer-director Miguel Sabido was the first to use this approach. However, so effective did it prove to be, both for delivering developmental messages to the widest possible target audiences and for then motivating those same audiences to action – indeed, in many cases, the effects proved to be nothing short of dramatic – that the approach was soon being incorporated into telenovelas across Latin America. In 1984, Sadibo was invited to India to reproduce his approach there, which resulted in the creation of South Asia's first ever television soap opera, *Hum Log* (*lit.* 'Us People'). The programme, which was produced by India's state-owned national broadcaster Doordarshan, and eventually ran for 154 episodes over a 17-month period, incorporated a wide range of social developmental issues (including ones related to family planning, alcoholism, women's rights, India's caste system, and nationalism) into multiple storylines that revolved around the trials and tribulations of one extended family in India's capital, New Delhi.

Box 1.2 Telenovelas

'Telenovelas' are a kind of television soap opera that emerged in Latin America (Brazil, Cuba, and Mexico) in the late 1950s, and became one of the most popular genres of television programming across Latin America, as well as among Spanish-speaking people in the US. By the mid-1980s, most Latin American broadcasters were showing 9–14 telenovelas per day, mostly during evening 'prime time'. Telenovelas have some features in common with US television soap operas. However, they tend to focus on quite different themes (especially issues of class conflict and social mobility), have highly convoluted and melodramatic plots, and usually have a limited run (most last for less than one year). They also have a more obvious commercial dimension, and were one of the first genres to introduce what we now call 'product placement'. As a result, they often generate huge revenues. Of greatest significance here, though, is the fact that from the late 1970s, they have also frequently been used, both by national governments and international donors, to deliver all kinds of educational messages – embedded within their entertaining and commercial style – to huge audiences. Among the first examples of this were Mexican Producer-Director Miguel Sabido's telenovelas 'Ven Conmigo' ('Come With Me'), 'Accompaname' ('Accompany Me'), and 'Vamos Juntos' ('Let's Go Together'), which delivered messages relating to adult literacy, family planning, and child abuse, respectively, within their plot lines. In all of these examples, the requisite message was embedded in a subtle way, in the form of a struggle between multiple characters who represented different points of view on the subject at hand. However, the audience was not left in any doubt as to what conclusions they should draw, and as to how they should change their own behaviours as a result. For example, it has been estimated that the telenovela 'Ven Conmigo' resulted in approximately one million Mexicans enrolling in adult literacy classes, and later examples have had even more dramatic effects. By the mid-1980s, the use of telenovelas to relay 'developmental' messages was being copied throughout Latin America. Today, Latin American television companies export Spanish- and Portuguese-language telenovelas to countries throughout the developing world, to the US, and to other developed nations. In addition, both the genre, and its use as a form of 'entertainment-education', has since been copied by broadcasters in other parts of the world (especially in South Asia, Southeast Asia, and the Middle East).

Sources: Rogers and Antola (1985), La Pastina et al. (2003), Lizarzaburu (2006).

Later, social marketeers' use of telenovelas was extended to a wide range of other developing world countries as well, and even to a number of developed nations. In 1994, the South African NGO the Soul City Institute introduced what was to become one of the most famous examples of the approach, in the form of a television and radio soap opera *Soul City, It's Real*. The programme, which was still running in 2014 – by which time it had reached a cumulative audience of 50 million people – examines issues relating to the AIDS epidemic, through storylines set in the fictional township of Soul City (see Box 1.3).

Box 1.3 Soul City, South Africa

In 1983, the first two cases of HIV/AIDS were discovered in South Africa. In the years that followed, the sheer scale of the epidemic in this country became increasingly clear. As of 2015, the disease continues to kill more than 160,000 South Africans per year, while a further 6.19 million people (or 11.2% of the country's entire population) are infected with the virus. In 1992, as one response to the growing crisis, an NGO called the Soul City Institute for Health and Development Communication was set up in one of South Africa's largest cities, Johannesburg, to explore ways in which M4D could be used to respond to the emergency. From early on, the institute focused in particular upon entertainment-education, developing a wide range of radio and television shows aimed at exploring relationships and sexuality in the time of HIV/AIDS (they have subsequently gone on to develop shows looking at other public health and social problems, such as alcoholism and child abuse). However, Soul City's best known series is its flagship soap opera, called *Soul City, It's Real*, which follows the lives of a group of fictional households in the imagined urban township of Soul City. The first series, which began in 1994, was spread across a range of media channels, and was constituted of 13 primetime television episodes, 60 radio programmes, an accompanying booklet, as well as a major poster advertising campaign and accompanying workshops. All of these materials were also dubbed, or translated, into each of South Africa's six main languages: Afrikaans, English, Setswana, Sotho, Xhosa, and Zulu. Later series – Soul City's twelfth series was broadcast in 2014 – have followed the same model. From the outset, *Soul City, It's Real* proved hugely popular, especially amongst women and young men, with one estimate suggesting that more than 80% of South Africa's entire population have watched or listened to it. Following a social marketing approach, the Soul City Institute has also conducted large-scale evaluations of its impacts, which have found that the soap opera has significantly changed people's perceptions of, and behaviours towards, some of the programme's main themes, which over the years have included: treatment of HIV+ babies, high-risk sexual practices, multiple and concurrent sexual partnerships (MCPs), male circumcision, and anti-retroviral drug therapies.

Sources: Tufte (2001), Wakefield (2015), www.soulcity.org.za.

Across large parts of the developing world, however – and especially in rural areas and in poorer urban areas – social marketeers found that these same target audience segments (i.e. women, men of lower social-economic status, and youth), given the different patterns of media ownership in those places, were less likely to watch television than to listen to radio entertainment. As a result, in these regions, researchers and their media partners concentrated on incorporating development messages into radio dramas instead. In 1993, an American social marketing organization, PCI Media Impact – which had been founded by David Poindexter, who had previously worked with Sabido on *Hum Log* – launched what was to become one of the most famous examples of an entertainment-education radio programme, a Tanzanian serial drama called *Twende na Wakati* (*lit.* 'Let's Go With the Times'). The drama, which was targeted particularly at women and young men, incorporated key messages about family planning and safe sex – the latter of which was a particularly pressing issue in the context of Tanzania's emergent AIDS epidemic – into its multiple storylines about a truck driver called Mkwaju (who in the course of his work engages in a wide range of extramarital sexual relations), Mkwaju's son Kibuyu (who is starting to follow in his father's footsteps), and

Mkwaju's long-suffering wife Tunu (who remains at home while the truck driver is away on the road). Over the course of its run, *Twende* invited its audiences to reflect on a wide range of issues regarding fertility and the reduction of risky sexual practices, through their identification with the everyday situations and dilemmas that faced these three main characters – but in particular that of Kibuyu, who was in many ways the main role model, especially for listeners who were young men (McPhail, 2009: 38–40). Once again, it was hugely successful in these aims. Indeed, a follow-up study by PCI Media Impact found that 82% of listeners reported that the drama had caused them to reduce risky sexual behaviours, while condom distribution in Tanzania rose by 153% during the first year of *Twende*'s broadcast (see www.comminit.com/edutain-africa/content/twende-na-wakati). Later, Everett Rogers with collaborator Peter Vaughan did an even more in-depth piece of research on the impact of *Twende*, and used this both to confirm and to update his now famous ideas about the *Diffusion of Innovations* (Vaughan and Rogers, 2000). As a result, social marketeers also took up entertainment-education for radio in a range of other developing world countries. Another of PCI Media Impact's best-known series is *Tinka Tinka Sukh* in India (Box 1.4), and other important examples were found in Afghanistan (Skuse, 2011), Mozambique (Karlyn, 2001), Nepal (Myers, 2002), and elsewhere.

Box 1.4 *Tinka Tinka Sukh* ('Happiness Lies in Small Things'), India

In 1984, a researcher at the Population Institute in Washington, DC, David Poindexter, took part in Miguel Sabido's project with the Indian government that developed the television series *Hum Log*. The following year, Poindexter set up an NGO called Population Communications International (PCI) Media Impact as a dedicated entertainment-education provider. The organization – which is today housed in the UN Headquarters in New York – has gone on to become the largest such organization in the world. Today, PCI Media Impact estimates than in the 30 years of its existence, it has produced more than 100 television and radio serial dramas, in over 45 countries (mostly in the developing world, but also in North America), which have had a combined audience of more than one billion people. The organization became particularly well known within the wider development community following the success of their 1993 Swahili-language radio serial drama *Twende na Wakati*, in Tanzania. However, another of PCI Media's best-known productions was the 1996–97 Hindi-language radio drama *Tinka Tinka Sukh* ('Happiness Lies in Small Things'), in India. The drama, which was targeted in particular at rural farmers (i.e. at lower socio-economic audiences) and atwomen, incorporated key messages about conservation, women's rights (especially in relation to marriage and dowry), patriarchy and inter-generational conflict, and HIV/AIDS into its multiple storylines about two extended families in a fictional North

Indian rural village. Reflecting the general style of media entertainment genres in South Asia (which may be best known to readers of this book from Bollywood films), *Tinka Tinka Sukh* was highly musical in nature. In fact, many of its songs were written by one of Bollywood's leading composers. The show was broadcast by India's main radio station, All India Radio (which was a partner on the project), and eventually ran for 104 episodes, regularly attracting audiences of more than 30 million people. In terms of its impact, a later study led by Professor of Media Studies at Ohio University, Arvind Singhal, found that the programme had had generally positive effects upon listeners, and in the most profound example had resulted in all of the residents of one rural Indian village, called Lutsaan, agreeing to end systems of dowry and to start a new school.

Sources: Singhal and Rogers (1999), Entertainment-Education Network Africa (2001).

Figure 1.4 *Promotional image for* **Hum Log**

However, as with earlier uses of social marketing for public health campaigns, the increasing wave of entertainment-education also resulted in growing criticisms being levelled against the approach. Once again, these included concerns that entertainment-education again assumed that development problems were primarily caused by individual behaviours, rather than structural factors (and we now know, for example, that it is not only risky sexual behaviours, but also a wide range of structural factors, which shape the prevalence and incidence rates of HIV/AIDS; Allen, 2006). Similarly, entertainment-education was criticized for lacking any kind of more 'participatory' elements. This was not always the case, however. For example, the Soul City Institute ran a series of radio phone-in shows alongside the television series, enabling viewers to reflect back upon that they had seen on TV. In addition, over time, PCI Media Impact's productions increasingly included participatory elements as well, especially following the launch of their 2006 'My Community' approach, which tried to incorporate local people's own personal stories into the process of scripting the entertainment-education dramas. And, once again, entertainment-education was accused of blurring the boundaries between development and commercial goals (Lizarzaburu, 2006). Indeed, within the telenovela genre, commercial interests were often much more obvious than they were in public health campaigns generally. In addition to the format being highly lucrative for the production companies that produced them (and who then sold them for broadcast in other countries), telenovelas are today generally credited with having first introduced the concept of what we now call 'product placement' (*ibid.*).

Conclusion

From the end of the Second World War onwards, international development became dominated by modernization theory. Central to this theory was the notion that the societies of the developing world were fundamentally lacking, or *under*developed *vis-à-vis* those of the North, primarily because they remained technologically backward and socially and culturally 'traditional'. Therefore, an urgent need existed for the societies of Africa, Asia, and Latin America to be 'brought up', something that was to be achieved through western intervention, in the form of technology transfers and the inculcation of a more 'modern outlook' among local populations. In relation to both, media appeared to have a central role to play. On the one hand, the spread of media technologies and their associated infrastructures constituted a form of technology transfer in its own right. On the other, media content had the potential to spread the kinds of information that might bring about the desired attitudinal changes. As a result, both western governments and multi-lateral development agencies, as well as developing world governments (many of whom also subscribed to modernization theory) put a great deal of money and time into developing media access and into designing media-based information campaigns (relating to everything from education programmes to economic interventions to health campaigns). And, over time, their efforts to do so became increasingly refined, as both academics and practitioners developed better models for how best to introduce new media technologies and to use these to change behaviours. They became even better with the advent of social marketing approaches to M4D.

Numerous programmes and projects which conform to this modernization approach to M4D – that is, which focus primarily upon changing individuals' attitudes and behaviours, with a view to making both things more 'modern' – can still be found throughout the developing world today. However, from quite early on, a number of critiques, both of modernization itself and of a modernization approach to M4D, began to take hold. In particular, these critiques questioned the focus upon individuals as the locus for development interventions in general, and for M4D interventions in particular, they problematized the 'top-down' nature of many M4D programmes, and they attacked the blurring of development goals and commercial interests within specific M4D programmes.

In addition, they also raised significant questions as to precisely how one can isolate – and measure – the effects of media messages, in 'real-world' contexts in which people are likely to be receiving the same or similar messages, via a range of non-mediated communication channels. In other words, how can we test whether the introduction of *Twende* really was the main cause (or even *a* cause) of the 153% rise of condom distribution in Tanzania between 1993 and 1994 (as PCI Media Impact claim), when people would have been receiving very similar messages about condom use from a range of other sources at the same time (including from, for example, school health programmes, NGO workshops, and even just 'word of mouth')? In addition, even if we could establish that *Twende was* the main cause there, how do we know that these effects were not just *ephemeral*, but had long-lasting consequences? For example, is there a danger that media messages are less likely than other kinds of communication (such as the 'messages' one receives from a doctor, a teacher, or a parent) to bring about more lasting changes to people's behaviour? We are here returning to some of the concerns that were first articulated by Rogers in his model of the 'stages' of behavioural change, and of the role of 'opinion leaders'. (Interestingly, Rogers devoted much of the latter part of his professional life – before his death in 2004 – to trying to develop even more accurate tools for addressing precisely these questions. More recently, the development of increasingly 'scientific' methods for measuring the effects of media messages, including their long-term impact, has become a central concern for organizations such as the NGO Development Media International, DMI.)

Moreover, and as we shall see in Chapter 3, these criticisms of modernization theory in general, and of a modernization approach to M4D in particular, were to proliferate and to become even more damaging over time. Nevertheless, the 'classic era' of international development, which began in 1949 and which helped to establish the 'Age of Development', also created an intrinsic connection between development and media that remains intact to the present day.

Summary

- From the very beginning of the modern history of international development, there has been an intrinsic link between development and media.
- Initial assumptions about the ways in which modernization might be 'sped up' using media were later supported by a large body of academic work.
- The theory and methods of M4D became increasingly refined, especially following the advent of a social marketing approach.
- Social marketing drove M4D programmes for several decades, and remain influential today.
- However, they have also come in for increasing criticism, in particular for their focus upon individual behaviours, and for their blurring of development and commercial goals.

Discussion questions

1. Critically assess the assumptions of 'modernization theory'. Are any of these assumptions valid today?
2. How useful are Lerner's, Rogers', and Schramm's models of media spread, and of its transformative effects? Do they tally with your own experiences of the ways in which people adopt new technologies and ideas, and of the consequences of this?
3. What are the pros and cons of a clinical approach vs. a social marketing approach?
4. Would you consider participating in the Nestlé boycott? How difficult would this be for you to observe?
5. Extreme cases aside, is there anything intrinsically wrong with a commercial company pursuing development goals and profits at the same time?

Further reading

There are huge literatures on all of the subjects covered in this chapter. Good introductions to the early history of M4D are provided by: McPhail, T. (2009) *Development Communication: Reframing the Role of the Media*, Malden, MA: Wiley; Melkote, S. and Steeves, H. (2015) *Communication for Development: Theory and Practice for Empowerment and Social Justice*, 3rd Edition, New York: Sage; and Waisbord, S. (2001) *Family Tree of Theories, Methodologies and Strategies in Development Communication*, New York: Rockefeller Foundation.

For an excellent, 'problem-solving' approach to the complexities of M4D in practice, see: Scott, M. (2014a) *Media and Development*, London: Zed Books.

For a lively introduction to social marketing in general, see: Lee, N. and Kotler, P. (2015) *Social Marketing: Changing Behaviours for Good*, 5th Edition, New York: Sage.

For more on social marketing and public health campaigns specifically, start with the comprehensive: French, J., Blair-Stevens, C., McVey, D. and Merritt, R. (2009) *Social Marketing and Public Health: Theory and Practice*, Oxford: Oxford University Press. See also: Atkin, C. and Wallack, L. (1990) *Mass Communication and Public Health: Complexities and Conflicts*, New York: Sage; and Hornik, R. (2002) *Public Health Communication: Evidence for Behaviour Change*, New Jersey: Lawrence Erlbaum.

For entertainment-education, see the now classic: Singhal, A., Cody, M., Rogers, E. and Sabido, M. (2003) *Entertainment-Education and Social Change: History, Research and Practice*, New York: Routledge.

Multimedia sources

Online portal: The Communication Initiative Network [Contains a huge amount of multimedia content, which is relevant for all of the topics covered in this book]

Available online at: www.comminit.com/global/spaces-frontpage

Online guide: Social Marketing: Expanding Access to Essential Products and Services to Prevent HIV/AIDS and to Limit the Impact of the Epidemic (UNAIDS, 2010)

Available online at: http://data.unaids.org/publications/irc-pub04/social_marketing_en.pdf

Documentary: *Bottle Babies* (dir. Peter Krieg, 1975) [The 'baby food scandal' that engulfed the multinational food and beverage giant Nestlé in the 1970s]

Documentary: *Formula for Disaster* (dir. Joseph Fortin/UNICEF, 2007) [Social marketing of a baby formula] Available online at: www.youtube.com/watch?v=3PBtb-UDhEc&t=1s

Documentary: *Miss HIV* (dir. Jim Hanon, 2008) [Media health campaigns and HIV/AIDS in Botswana and Uganda]

Documentary: *The Banake Initiative* (dir. Nicole Safter/DKT South Africa, 2010) [Social marketing and HIV/AIDS in South Africa] Available online at: https://vimeo.com/15199686

Television series: *Hum Log* (dir. Miguel Sabido, 1984) [Social developmental issues in New Delhi]

Television series: *Soul City, It's Real* (Soul City Institute, 1994–2014) [Entertainment-education in South Africa] Excerpts from the series, and related material, are available online at: www.soulcity.org.za/projects/soul-city-series

Development in the news

From iconographies of disaster to post-humanitarian communication

- The rise of humanitarian imagery.
- Global media between the Biafra Emergency (1967–1970) and the Ethiopian Famine (1983–1985).
- Elements of disaster iconography.
- The concept of 'compassion fatigue', and its critics.
- The future of humanitarian and development imagery.

Introduction

The period between the end of the Second World War and roughly the early 1990s – that is, the classic era of 'development as modernization' – saw a major trend develop in the way in which the issues and problems facing the developing world were represented via global media outlets: in newspapers and magazines, on the radio and on television. In particular, the period saw a rise to dominance of *humanitarian* imagery – that is, images of war, famine, and/or other disasters – as the predominant genre through which all interventions into the developing world were represented to media audiences. One consequence was that humanitarian imagery came to 'stand in for' all kinds of interventions into the developing world, including those that involved only *development* agencies – and it should be stressed that although humanitarian assistance and international development do have certain features in common, and do overlap in certain ways, they are also in several key respects quite distinct from each other.

This general elision of humanitarianism and international development within media imagery had a number of consequences. For one thing, it meant that international media audiences were effectively 'invited' to perceive all kinds of interventions into the developing world as focused upon *only* war, famine, or disaster – when, in fact, the vast majority of international development interventions were not during this period (and in fact, never have been focused upon these kinds of emergency contexts at all). As a corollary to this, such imagery also effectively cast *all* recipients of international aid as humanitarian subjects. In other words, by consistently representing people from Africa, Asia, and Latin America as either sick or as in some other way pathetic, abject, or passive, it generated a dominant 'visual narrative' that the developing world as a whole existed in a *constant* state of crisis and catastrophe. Above all, this played to a stereotype that Africans, Asians, and Latin Americans were essentially (i.e. always and inevitably) *victims*, and that the developing world as a whole was essentially needy, politically unstable, and dangerous.

The first aim of this chapter, then, is to examine how and why, especially in the period between roughly the mid-1960s and the early 1990s, humanitarian imagery came to dominate media representations of the developing world in this way. I will argue that this situation in fact reflects a much deeper history of humanitarian practice, in which images of suffering from 'distant places' have for a long time been used as a tool for advocacy and fundraising. From the second half of the 1960s onwards, these already well-established humanitarian practices were simply combined with the circuits of then rapidly expanding global media networks, to powerful effect. Yet it is equally important to recognize the kinds of images of suffering that were historically circulated by humanitarian organizations. These never included just any kinds of pictures of affliction, but instead only ones that conformed to a quite narrow range of visual conventions and tropes. As I will go on to show, these conventions and tropes were not random, but in fact drew upon a very long-established Christian 'iconography of disaster'. Once again, from the mid-1960s onwards, these highly conventionalized images were widely circulated through global media networks, and in this way became amplified exponentially. Indeed, so widely disseminated did they become, that they themselves even became *iconographic* – that is, they came to 'stand in for' the things that they represented (such that, for example, *any* picture of a malnourished child in Africa came to signify 'famine' in general).

Yet the observation that, between the mid-1960s and the early 1990s, media representations of the developing world did become dominated by humanitarian imagery only raises further questions about how these representations might have been received by global media audiences. After all, as we have already seen, even where media messages are dominated by a particularly strong narrative, there is no guarantee that their audiences will interpret them in any given way (see Introduction, above). Certainly, throughout this period, there is evidence that at least some of these pictures did have their intended effects on media audiences, such as on those occasions when they stimulated major fundraising drives. However, from the late 1960s onwards, a number of scholars raised concerns that the constant use of atrocity images might also draw other kinds of responses from their audiences besides. In particular, it was argued that such frequent exposure might also generate 'compassion fatigue' among media audiences, whereby they became 'numbed' to the suffering of 'distant others', and therefore disengaged from any efforts to help those same people.

More generally, over time, an increasing number of international development agencies began to realize that even where atrocity images did have a beneficial effect upon fundraising, this was not always an unambiguously positive thing. In particular, they realized that if the reason why audiences were giving money in this way stemmed from their perception that people in the developing world were essentially victims – and were therefore in need of 'saving' – then there was a danger that this was a patrimonial, sentimental, and uncritical response. In other words, there was a growing concern that even if humanitarian imagery might boost donations within a given campaign, it might still undermine some of international development's longer-term goals, such as deepening cooperation, empathy, and understanding across different contexts. In response, from the late 1990s onwards, and especially into the 2000s, a growing number of development organizations began to employ other kinds of images and media strategies within their campaigns, in an attempt to draw alternative, more constructive, responses from their media audiences. As a result, and although images of atrocity from the developing world still abound on global media outlets, it can be said that we have now entered an era of 'post-humanitarian communication', to borrow Lilie Chouliaraki's (2010) phrase.

Histories of humanitarianism

To understand how and why, between roughly the mid-1960s and the early 1990s, humanitarian imagery came to dominate international media representations of the developing world, it is necessary to first know something about the longer history of humanitarianism itself, and of humanitarian 'visual economies'. A crucial point to begin with is that humanitarianism is in fact *much* older than international development. The concept of humanitarianism, defined as the act of providing assistance to 'distant others', with whom one has no personal connections, can be traced back to Classical Greece, and it has remained a significant force within Euro-American philosophical and legal traditions since then. Moreover, humanitarian organizations – that is, agencies which exist only, or primarily, to further humanitarian goals – have existed continuously since the late eighteenth and early nineteenth centuries, when they proliferated as part of international attempts to abolish the slave trade: the Society for Effecting the Abolition of the Slave Trade (SAST), which was formed in London in 1787, is often taken to be the first purely humanitarian organization. However, the modern history of humanitarianism is more often traced to the late nineteenth and early twentieth centuries, and to two campaigns that occurred around that time: the Relief Campaign for the Indian Famine (1876–1878) and the campaign of the Congo Reform Association (CRA, 1904–1913). The CRA emerged in response to the gross human rights abuses that were being inflicted upon indigenous peoples as part of the labour regimes of the Belgian King Leopold's Congo Free State, in Central Africa.

From the anti-slavery campaigns onwards, the general *modus operandi* of humanitarian organizations remained more or less the same: (1) to create a network of committees and sub-committees in their home countries around the issue or incident at hand; (2) to present evidence at meetings of those committees that documented the ways in which that issue or incident was harming 'distant others'; and (3) to 'channel' the moral indignation and anger that ordinary committee members might feel in response to that evidence towards constructive ends, such as fundraising, recruitment drives, and political advocacy – in other words, to use the evidence presented at committee meetings to motivate its audience to action. Crucially, a significant portion of the evidence that was presented to the committees always consisted of 'atrocity' imagery (Twomey, 2012a). This was even true during the era of Abolitionism, when committees would be shown – in addition to material artefacts of the slave trade itself (such as the neck-chains and leg irons worn by slaves), and pictures of the layout of slave ships and Caribbean plantations – illustrations of the tortures that were frequently meted out to slaves, and that were sometimes based on eyewitness accounts.

For example, in early 1792, the SAST and other abolitionist organizations widely circulated an engraving that had been made by political satirist Isaac Cruickshank, following a parliamentary speech on the subject by William Wilberforce, that depicted an alleged incident that had occurred on board a slave ship called *The Recovery*. The incident involved the ship's captain, Captain Kimber, stringing up a young slave girl by one leg – in such a manner that she was placed 'in a situation indecent to her sex', as Wilberforce put it – and then repeatedly dropping her onto the deck until she was dead. Among SAST committee members, and among the public at large, the picture of this incident generated widespread disgust and anger, and this reaction later influenced the UK Admiralty's decision to prosecute Kimber for the crime. Although the captain was later acquitted, the case became a key event in the story of abolitionism, because it established the legal precedent that captains could be tried for the murder of slaves on their vessels (for more on the image, and its role in the trial of Kimber, see Sliwinski, 2011: 1–3).

It was following the emergence of photography – from the late 1830s onwards – that the evidence presented to humanitarian committees

Figure 2.1 'The Abolition of the Slave Trade': Image of Captain Kimber

Source: Published by S.W Fores, London (10 April 1792)

came to be made up primarily of atrocity imagery. For example, the evidence that circulated within the network of Indian Famine Relief Committees that emerged in the late 1870s was dominated by a series of photographs that had been taken by a British officer based in India, Captain Willoughby Wallace Hooper, during a tour he had made of famine relief camps in Madras. The photographs included portraits of highly emaciated (i.e. starving) men, women, and children, of a kind with which western media audiences would soon become familiar.

Later, the evidence that was presented to committees of the Congo Reform Association included a predominance of photographs taken by the British missionaries Alice and John Harris during their time at the Baringa Mission Station, Congo (where the husband and wife team were based between 1901 and 1905). The Harris' photographs included numerous harrowing examples of Congolese people, including children, whose hands had been apparently cut off for failure to meet the state-imposed quota for wild rubber collection.

Figure 2.2 1876–1879 famine in India, by Willoughby Wallace Hooper (photo taken between 1876 and 1879)

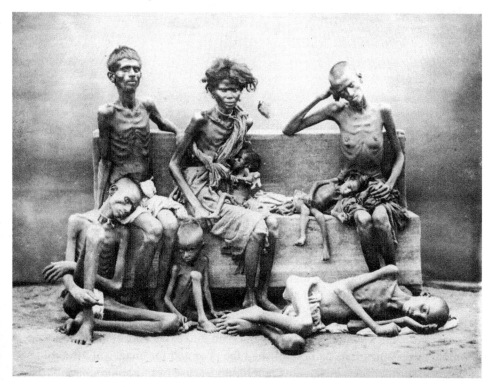

Figure 2.3 *'Indigenous man, Nsala, pictured with the severed hand and foot of his dead daughter' by Alice Harris*

Source: Anti-Slavery International

One of their photographs shows an indigenous man, Nsala, pictured with the severed hand and foot of his dead daughter, who had been killed for this offence.

In both of these cases – the Relief Campaign for the Indian Famine and the Congo Reform Association – the atrocity photographs taken by Captain Hooper and the Harris', respectively, were displayed at committee meetings (both as wall-hangings and in lantern-slide presentation), reproduced in the organizations' campaign literature, and generally circulated amongst members and potential members, for fundraising and advocacy purposes (Twomey, 2012a, 2012b).

Thus, by the early 1900s, almost half a century before international development *per se* had even come into existence, humanitarian organizations had established the potential for images of atrocity to further their goals – by generating a sense of moral indignation among viewers, which could then be mobilized towards constructive ends. Equally importantly, these organizations had also established rudimentary global 'media circuits', as we now call them, for transmitting such images 'from the field' – that is, from the places in the developing world in which the humanitarian organizations were working – to their specified target audiences 'back home'. Nevertheless, even in this context, it was still by no means inevitable that during the post-Second World War period, humanitarian imagery would come to dominate media coverage of the developing world, or that other (i.e. non-humanitarian) international development agencies would increasingly align themselves with it as a means for furthering their own agendas as well. In fact, throughout the first decade or so of modernization, most international development organizations did *not* take this approach. Instead, throughout the 1950s and into the 1960s, many of these agencies in fact tended to eschew photography, and relied instead upon tables, graphs, and charts as a means for communicating their activities to wider publics. According to the 'worldview' of modernization, these sorts of technical images were more in keeping with what was perceived to be the specialized and scientific nature of development work. Where development agencies did use photographs, these tended to be very 'technical' in nature, often focused upon the introduction of new technologies (such as manufacturing equipment, modern transport, and new media) to developing countries – again with a view to emphasizing the transformative potential of technical and scientific interventions (see Vokes, unpublished). As such, most of these pictures tended to be entirely positive in tone, in that they tended to show, for example, Indian construction workers posing on a dam construction site, or Brazilian workers standing proudly beside some new piece of industrial machinery, or African schoolchildren smiling as they watched television for the first time.

Between 1967 and 1970, however, a key event occurred in West Africa that was to establish humanitarian images of atrocity as the *dominant* means for communicating all kinds of interventions into the developing world to global media audiences: the Biafra Emergency. In May 1967, following a series of coups and counter-coups in the newly independent country of Nigeria, the eastern state of Biafra, which is home to a majority of Nigeria's Igbo ethnic group, declared independence. This began a three-year civil war, during which the Nigerian Army attempted to overthrow the separatist movement and to reincorporate Biafra into the Federal Republic of Nigeria, which they eventually did in early 1970. As part of their campaign during the war, government forces imposed a land and sea blockade of Biafra, in an attempt to 'starve Biafra into submission'. This generated a major famine that eventually killed at least one million civilians (although the exact figure remains disputed, with estimates ranging from 500,000 to three million). With both the UN and international governments reluctant to assist Biafra – not least because both the UK and the USSR actively supported the Nigerian government, including providing them with arms – the relief effort for the famine was led entirely by church groups and humanitarian non-governmental organizations (NGOs), working under the umbrella of Joint Church Aid (JCA). It is also noteworthy that some of the now largest humanitarian organizations in the world, such as Médecins sans Frontières (MSF), were in fact created during the Biafra crisis. However, without significant governmental funding for their operations, to begin with at least, JCA had to rely on money raised from western donor publics to fund these operations (Goetz, 2001). Yet, initially, it proved difficult for JCA to reach these audiences, given that many western news organizations regarded Biafra – which was, after all, a 'faraway' place in Africa – as simply not 'newsworthy' enough to cover.

In mid-1968, however, things changed dramatically, when one humanitarian worker, an Irish priest named Fr. Kevin Doheny, took two western journalists on a tour of a Biafran hospital filled with malnourished children. The resulting photographs were quickly circulated via global news networks and, almost overnight, made Biafra front-page news around the world. Over the following months, the humanitarian organizations, and the secessionist administration of Biafra itself, continued to assist journalists to produce large numbers of images of starving children, and other highly emotive images of the atrocities from the Biafra Famine, for distribution to western news stations (de Waal, 1997: 73–75). The public response to these images, which became a nightly feature of American and European television news programmes, generated an unprecedented volume of donations for the cause, and also resulted in huge fundraising drives, marches, and a surge in volunteering. It is even claimed that US President Lyndon Johnson's later decision for America to support the humanitarian operations – although the US remained officially neutral throughout the Nigerian civil war, by 1969 it was quietly funding almost half of the food aid involved – was a response to these same media images. In an oft-cited quote, it is said that Johnson once instructed his officials to 'just get those nigger [*sic*] babies off my TV set' (Gourevitch, 2010). Using the monies raised via these means, the humanitarian organizations began what became the biggest civilian airlift in history: having bought a number of old military cargo planes, they were used to fly food aid into Biafra from neighbouring countries. At its peak, in late 1969, it is estimated that the JCA operation – or 'Jesus Christ Airlines' as it became affectionately known – was delivering 250 metric tonnes of food aid into Biafra every day, enough to feed more than 1.5 million people.

It could be argued that the humanitarian agencies' actions during the Biafra Emergency were simply a continuation of humanitarians' long-established *modus operandi*, as I have described it above. In other words, it could be said that JCA once again simply deployed images of faraway suffering as a means of mobilizing support for their cause. However, it is also important to recognize that the humanitarian organizations involved in Biafra also did something radically new in this theatre, in that rather than simply producing images themselves and then circulating them to pre-existing committees and networks of their own sympathizers, they instead facilitated and encouraged professional journalists to take pictures and then circulate them through global print and television news channels (which in the late 1960s were still somewhat in their infancy). In this way, the members of JCA demonstrated the power of atrocity images, when reproduced and transmitted through mass communications channels, not only to motivate small numbers of people who were 'already committed to the cause', but also to galvanize potentially limitless numbers of media viewers, of all outlooks and backgrounds. As one famous commentator, Frederick Forsyth – who was posted to Biafra as a journalist during the crisis – put it at the time, the most striking thing about the response to the media imagery of the famine was that it mobilized donors who 'are known to have ranged from old-age pensioners to the boys at Eton College' (cited in Gourevitch, 2010).

So successful was the 'Biafra model', and so broad-based was the response to it, that it was soon being replicated by all kinds of organizations working in the developing world, across a wide range of campaigns, as a means both for advocacy and for fundraising. By around the mid-1970s, it had been adopted not only by humanitarian organizations but also by a wide range of international development agencies. As a result, by this time, it had become commonplace for all of these different kinds of agencies to have: established mechanisms

74 • Development in the news

Figure 2.4 *Biafra War protests*

Source: Getty Images

for facilitating the visits of western journalists to the sites of their operations; begun directing this 'media gaze' onto the most extreme examples of hardship within those contexts (as a result of which, the kind of imagery that was produced, even in non-disaster situations, ended up focusing upon death, malnutrition, and disaster, and to thus conform to 'atrocity imagery'); and set up public-relations departments and/or media offices whose job it was to ensure that the resulting imagery received the maximum possible 'news coverage' (for a famous – and stinging – critique of development agencies' use of atrocity imagery during this period, see Lissner, 1981). All of these elements were well established, and were therefore seen in action, in what became one of the biggest – and certainly the most famous – humanitarian and development operations of the late twentieth century: the response to the Ethiopian Famine of 1984 and its aftermath. This operation, which involved both humanitarian and development agencies in equal measure, is often taken as a key turning point in the history of media representations of development. However, important though the event certainly was, in many respects the way in which it was mediated was really also just a continuation of the Biafra model, as described above.

The Ethiopian Famine, like the Biafra crisis before it, was an outcome both of civil war, in this case the ongoing conflict between the communist government of President Mengistu Haile Mariam, known as 'the Derg', and a number of separatist groups across the country, and of failed rains (the 1984 *meher* rains). The event was first brought to international media audiences' attention when the aid agency Oxfam facilitated a Kenya-based cameraman, Mohamed Amin, and the BBC's South Africa correspondent, Michael Buerk, to visit a camp in which the organization was working on the outskirts of Korem Town, in Northern Ethiopia. Amin and Buerk's report on the camp, which was first broadcast on 23 October 1984 on the BBC, and soon syndicated to news broadcasters throughout the world, was saturated with images of atrocity, as it documented the daily lives of the thousands of starving men, women, and children who had gathered there. In the most harrowing sequence, which occurred around the middle of the original news broadcast, the report documented the death by starvation of a three-year-old girl. Equally disturbing was its final sequence, which showed a column of people leaving the camp, to return to their villages of origin, carrying the bodies of their dead relatives for burial. So powerful was the film that, by the evening of 23 October, it had already been watched by 7.4 million viewers on the BBC alone (Franks, 2014: 1). It was later syndicated to 425 other television broadcast stations around the world, to eventually achieve a combined global audience of an estimated 470 million people (Philo, 1993). In making the Ethiopian Famine so newsworthy, Amin and Buerk's report also generated a wider media interest in the East Africa country, which over the following months was carefully directed by the aid agencies themselves into an unprecedented fundraising effort. As one senior journalist who worked on the crisis, Peter Gill, later recalled, throughout this period 'the relief agencies provided most of the reference points: up-to-date information, places to visit, interviewees in the field and at home, and a means of response for concerned viewers' (cited in de Waal, 1997: 122). Yet by seeking to maximize media coverage of the crisis, both humanitarian agencies and development organizations also increased the circulation of images of atrocity. In other words, and as a study led by the UN's Food and Agriculture Organization (FAO) later confirmed (1987), the agencies' own actions resulted in the kind of images that had been broadcast in the Amin and Buerk report being repeated in international news reports of the Ethiopian crisis for several months to come (van der Gaag and Nash, 1987). This in turn further established these sorts of pictures as a dominant genre for media representations of humanitarian and development interventions in Africa, and in other parts of the developing world.

Finally, Amin and Buerk's film also directly motivated a number of celebrities, led by Bob Geldof, to respond to the crisis. In late November 1984, Geldof arranged for more than 40 of the UK's most famous musicians to form a charity supergroup called Band Aid, and to record a fundraising single for Ethiopia called 'Do They Know It's Christmas?' (Box 2.1). The single, which eventually sold more than two million copies, and raised more than US$20 million, led to a similar initiative among US musicians – who in March 1985 formed a supergroup called USA for Africa, and recorded the fundraising single: 'We Are the World' – and later also to the famous Live Aid concerts/media events on 13 July 1985. In inspiring all of these things, Amin and Buerk's reports also inaugurated a new era of celebrity involvement in international development, which has continued to shape the field ever since (to which we will return in Chapter 6).

Box 2.1 Band Aid and Live Aid

Michael Buerk's famous report from the Korem camp in Ethiopia was originally broadcast by the BBC on 23 October, and by the end of that same evening had already been viewed by 7.4 million people. Among these viewers was Bob Geldof, the lead singer of an Irish punk-rock group called the Boomtown Rats. Moved by the report, Geldof decided to produce a fundraising record to contribute to the Ethiopian famine relief effort. Over the following few weeks, Geldof – and his co-producer Midge Ure from the band Ultravox – gathered together 46 of the UK's best-known pop stars under the banner of 'Band Aid', and on 25 November the majority of these stars met at the SARM Studios in London to record the single 'Do They Know It's Christmas?' The record was released just eight days later and sold more than one million copies in the first week alone, which at the time made it the fastest selling record in UK history. Following the success of Band Aid, Geldof and Ure began planning for a follow-up fundraising concert, which became the Live Aid concerts. The concerts were held on 13 July 1995 and were staged simultaneously in Wembley Stadium, London and the

JFK Stadium, Philadelphia. The concerts were also a major global media event, aided by the BBC's decision to dedicate 16 hours of continuous coverage to the concerts (which was the full length of the concerts) and to a simultaneous telethon, across both its television and radio channels. In total, the concerts were broadcast live to 120 nations, with a combined audience of an estimated 1.5 billion people. It was largely as a result of this, at that time unprecedented, media coverage that the concerts eventually raised more than £150 million for the famine relief campaign. The entire Band Aid/Live Aid movement has since been criticized for amplifying humanitarian atrocity imagery across global media circuits, not least given that such images were interspersed with musical performances throughout the coverage of the concerts, for cementing the concept of the rock star humanitarian entrepreneur, and for generally heralding a new era in the connection between celebrity and international development, which we are still living in today. As media events, both Band Aid and Live Aid also relied primarily upon an appeal to audience 'sentimentality', and in so doing made little attempt to convey anything at all about the complex political context which had caused the Ethiopian famine in the first place, or about the difficulties which this posed for the development agencies that were trying to respond to it. Nevertheless, it remains a landmark moment in the evolution of media representations of development.

Sources: Philo (1993), de Waal (2008), Lousley (2014).

Iconographies of disaster

The period between the Biafra Emergency of the late 1960s and the Ethiopian Famine in the mid-1980s was therefore crucial in establishing a *modus operandi* for humanitarian organizations, and latterly for development agencies as well, through which images of atrocity were circulated via global media networks as a means to generate public support for all manner of humanitarian and development work in the developing world. However, a more detailed analysis of the voluminous atrocity imagery that was circulated during this period reveals that this material was not, in fact, made up of just *any* sorts of images of suffering. Instead, it was highly conventionalized, and was made up of only *certain kinds* of pictures of atrocity. Across this huge body of material, one in fact finds just four kinds of images being constantly reproduced, in relation to all manner of humanitarian and development contexts and campaigns: (1) the image of a mother cradling her child; (2) the picture of a relative carrying the dead body of his or her loved one; (3) the figure of a soldier (or some other person in authority) trying to protect a group of civilians in their time of need; and (4) the image of a mass of humanity attempting to carry on with 'everyday' tasks in the context of a hostile environment. So frequently were these same pictures reused that they even became iconic, in that they came to 'stand in for' the things that they represented. In other words, any media image of a mother cradling her distressed child immediately signalled 'famine', before any further information had been given about where the event was taking place, which combination of environmental and social-political circumstances had caused it, or how difficult the situation was.

The use of an image of a mother trying to protect her child in pursuit of a humanitarian cause can in fact be traced back to the anti-slavery movement. In this case, it traces not to the British-led campaigns of the early nineteenth century, but to the later anti-slavery campaigns in the United States (the campaigns which went on to become one of the major causes of the American Civil War of 1861–1865). In 1852, the American author and anti-slavery campaigner Harriet Beecher Stowe published a novel called *Uncle Tom's Cabin*, which attempted to communicate the inhumanity of slavery in the southern United States through the story of a fictional slave called Eliza. In the story, Eliza was forced to run away from the home of her masters in order to stop them from selling her infant son. The novel became a key text for the US abolitionist movement, and was later rendered pictorially by a range of anti-slavery artists and in a variety of media: from ceramics to postcards to the covers of sheet music. In one of the best-known examples, the cover of a contemporary piece of music called 'The Slave Mother' was adorned with the image of Eliza trying to shield her small child in her arms as she crossed the frozen Ohio River, with her evil slave master, brandishing his whip, in hot pursuit (for more on *Uncle Tom's Cabin*, and its contribution to the emergence of a 'sentimental economy' among western media consumers, see Lousley, 2014).

It was following the invention of photography, however, that the image of a mother cradling her baby became most widely used within humanitarian campaigns, after which time it became particularly associated with images of famine. This began with Captain Hooper's photos of the Indian famine in the 1870s, which contained several shots of starving mothers holding their severely malnourished children, including one in which two women cradle babies who are clearly on the point of death. Later, several of the most widely circulated images of the Biafra emergency, the Cambodian Famine of the late 1970s, and the Ethiopian famine, were all constituted of mothers holding their severely malnourished infants. For example,

Figure 2.5 *'The Slave Mother'*

Source: Alamy

Time Magazine – which was founded in 1923 as America's first news weekly, and has since remained one of the world's most widely circulated news publications – used the image as its cover illustration for its coverage of both the Cambodian and Ethiopian famines (*Time*'s cover of the Ethiopian famine can be viewed online at http://img.timeinc.net/time/magazine/archive/covers/1987/1101871221_400.jpg). A multitude of similar examples, of news publications using the picture of a starving mother holding her malnourished child as their front covers for stories on food emergencies, can also be found. In 2004, world famous photojournalist Sebastiao Salgado's seminal collection *Sahel: The End of the Road* – which was based on work that the Brazilian photographer had done for Médecins sans Frontières during the interconnected famines of Ethiopia, Sudan, Chad, and Mali between 1984 and 1986 – also contained several images of parents cradling their severely malnourished infants. As a result of humanitarian organizations' media strategies, then, the image of a mother holding her starving child became one of the quintessential media images of famine – wherever in the world the famine was actually taking place.

Humanitarian images of a relative carrying the dead body of his or her loved one have a somewhat different history, yet by the end of the twentieth century had become equally iconic – and powerful – as symbols for intervention into the developing world. At least some early examples exist of anti-slavery campaigners having circulated images depicting dead slaves. However, it was in the context of the images that emerged from the Holocaust, from the 1940s onwards, that the image of someone carrying a dead body became most profoundly burned into a collective 'visual memory' (as it were), as a key symbol of atrocity (Buettner, 2011). In particular, the images that photojournalists produced following the liberation of the Nazi concentration camps – such as the pictures that Lee Miller took of the US Army's liberation of Buchwenwald and Dachau concentration camps, or the footage that Sidney Bernstein produced for the UK film *German Concentration Camps Factual Survey* (which documented the aftermath of the British Army's liberation of various camps, especially Bergen-Belsen) – served to established a connection whereby any image of someone carrying one dead body could be used to stand in for the wider atrocity in which that person had been killed (Sliwinski, 2011: 83–110).

Figure 2.6 *The suffering mother and child*

Figure 2.7 *An image from the aftermath of the Nazi Holocaust: SS troops are forced to carry concentration camp victims to burial sites, 1945*

Source: PA Images

As a result, over the decades that followed, this same image was deployed again and again across all manner of humanitarian, political, and development campaigners, as a means for stimulating wider public engagement with all sorts of crises and emergencies. To cite just a few of the best-known examples here, a picture of a young man holding the dead body of his young son, in front of a set of burning buildings, from which multiple plumes of smoke are rising to the sky, was another of the most widely circulated early pictures from Biafra. In 1976, South African photojournalist Sam Nzima's picture of a student running with the dying body of Hector Pieterson in his arms was widely circulated by anti-apartheid campaigners, and soon became iconic of efforts to mobilize international public support for political intervention into that struggle (Nzima's was taken during the Soweto Uprising, and showed Pieterson in his final moments after he had been shot by the police). In 1994, the picture of a man carrying his dying child into a field hospital became one of the most widely used images from the Goma refugee camps – which were formed as civilians crossed the border into what was then Zaire, as they fled in the aftermath of the Rwandan Genocide, yet which were later hit by a cholera outbreak that killed an estimated 50,000 people (the image can be viewed online at https://reportdigital.files.wordpress.com/2014/01/hdafr0231.jpg?w=580). Later, the picture of a young man carrying the dead body of a young girl over his shoulder was widely circulated by development agencies seeking to raise awareness of the dire circumstances in which Haitians found themselves following the 7.0 magnitude earthquake that struck near to the capital of Port-au-Prince, on 12 January 2010.

In relation to the images of the 'soldier-protector', and of the mass of people trying to carry on quotidian tasks in the face of extreme adversity, it could be also argued that the modern history of these images as key symbols of mass atrocity again stems from photographs that were taken in the aftermath of the Holocaust. The pictures that photojournalists produced of the liberated concentration camps in the 1940s tended to include, within their frames, in addition

Figure 2.8 *In the aftermath of the Haiti earthquake, 2010*

Source: Getty Images

to the dead bodies of the Nazis' victims, and/or the emaciated figures of camp survivors, the figure of a liberating American, British, or Russian soldier. These figures were frequently positioned off to the side or at the back of the shot, but always stood in some sort of benevolent pose – that is, they were pictured in a way that implied that they were somehow 'helping out' (Struk, 2004; see, for example, Figure 2.7). In addition, as and when this liberation photography focused on the camp survivors, it tended to picture these people as they attempted to carry on with mundane, everyday activities, such as cooking. As a result, many of these photographs included elements or symbols of domesticity, such as pots and pans. These elements can be interpreted as the photographers' attempts to emphasize not only the horror of ordinary people having been caught up in such appalling

Figure 2.9 *Concentration camp survivors, 1945*

Source: Alamy

circumstances, but also the resilience of those same individuals as they nevertheless tried to maintain some semblance of 'normal' life even in those conditions. The focus upon victims' everyday items was also foregrounded in photographs of the mounds of shoes, spectacles, and suitcases that had been confiscated from civilians on their way to the gas chambers.

Images of a soldier-protector figure, and of people carrying out everyday tasks in the face of adversity, were also foregrounded within humanitarian and development agencies' media circuits. Therefore, from the Biafra emergency onwards, it became commonplace for these images to include, for example, a United Nations', NATO, or African Union peacekeeper, or even just a uniformed humanitarian or development worker – again, irrespective of where in the world the intervention was taking place.

Figure 2.10 *Refugees of the Syrian Civil War*

Source: Wikimedia Commons/Dragan Tatic

Similarly, another of the earliest pictures from Biafra – one which was taken, in fact, during Fr. Doheny's initial tour of the hospital in which he was based – showed several hundred children sitting in uneven rows at long tables as they ate from metal plates and cups. Later, Salgado's collection on the Sahelian famines included pictures showing masses of people gathered against the elements, several of which included symbols of domesticity, such as traditional cooking pots, milk gourds, and walking sticks. In what became the most iconic image of the whole series, Salgado invoked the mass of humanity gathered at Korem – the same camp from which Amin and Buerk had sent their famous report – through a picture of hundreds of tents, around which groups of people are huddled, and from which clothes and other items are seen hanging. Ominously, the picture also shows a vulture flying overhead, symbolizing that death is all around here (the picture can be viewed online at www.artvalue.com/image.aspx?PHOTO_ID=2344508). In 1994, photojournalist Howard Davies' pictures of several hundred Rwandan refugees crossing a bridge over the River Ruzizi, which is the border between Rwanda and the then Zaire (now the Democratic Republic of Congo), became *the* iconic image of that particular emergency. The picture, which was again produced while Davies was on assignment for aid agencies involved in managing the crisis, is saturated with symbols of domesticity, as the refugees carry everything from mattresses to jerry-cans to sacks of charcoal on their heads (one of the images from Davis' sequence can be viewed online at https://reportdigital.files.wordpress.com/2014/01/hdafr015.jpg?w=580&h=404). Most recently, in 2015, images of columns of people walking along roads and railway lines across Central Europe became iconic of the unfolding Syrian refugee crisis. Again, many of these pictures included symbols of domesticity, as the refugees were pictured carrying everything from sleeping bags to blankets to bags of groceries as they went.

Finally here, we might also note in passing that Amin and Buerk's famous film from the Korem camp in Ethiopia, as I have described it above, contained all four of these visual tropes, in that: its central sequence showed a mother trying (and failing) to save her starving daughter; it contained various images of people carrying the dead bodies of their relatives, including the closing sequence of a column of people leaving the camp with the bodies of their loved ones; it pictured various camp officials and aid agency workers throughout (in one sequence, a camp official tries to help those deemed most in need

Figure 2.11 *The Syrian refugee crisis*

Source: Getty Images

of food with 'a pen stroke on the forehead' – presumably as a means for prioritizing their access to any food aid that is available); and it also showed various signs and symbols of people nevertheless trying to carry on some semblance of 'normal' domestic life – by trying on clothes, building makeshift shelters, wrapping their families in blankets, etc. – even in these most dire of circumstances. One might even argue that the extraordinary impact that this particular news report went on to have stemmed, at least in part, from precisely the fact that it did combine all of these most iconic images of disaster and atrocity into just one news item.

Biblical crises

If from the mid-1960s until the early 1990s both humanitarian and development agencies did increasingly rely on images of atrocity as a means for generating wider support for their interventions into the developing world, it is important to recognize that they didn't use just any sorts of images of suffering to do this, but instead typically only four kinds of pictures of suffering, as noted above: the mother and child, the relative carrying the dead body, the soldier-protector, and the mass of humanity carrying on with quotidian tasks. Yet why these four shots in particular? It could be argued that each of these four kinds of pictures might be understood in purely instrumental terms. In other words, we could surmise that given humanitarian and development organizations' aims, these four conventionalized images simply turned out to be the most effective at galvanizing viewers to action, again and again, across repeated campaigns. It is easy to understand how each of these four kinds of images might have been successful in this way, given the degree of empathy that each of them invites in their viewers. In other words, the picture of the mother holding her starving child surely invites its observers to imagine how they would feel if forced to cradle their own broken child. Similarly, the picture of a person carrying their deceased relative undoubtedly invites its viewers to envisage how they would respond if placed in similar circumstances (for extended discussions on the relationship between atrocity imagery and empathy, see Sontag, 1977, 2003). Meanwhile, the image of the soldier-protector invites its viewers to imagine themselves in the position of someone trying to help out in a disaster context (and here, the viewer is invited to identify not with the victim, but with the intervention, i.e. with the humanitarian or development organization itself). Finally, the image of the mass of humanity trying to carry out quotidian tasks in a disaster setting again invites its viewers to imagine how they, too, would fare faced with such adversity. In all four cases, then, the image makes an appeal to empathy by inviting the viewer to identify with persons within that image. The first, second, and fourth conventions, by inviting the viewer to identify with the *victim*, specifically, may produce what the economist Thomas Schelling calls an 'identifiable victim effect' (1968). In so doing, they may draw an especially strong emotional response, one that is primarily characterized by what Lousley, following Berlant, calls 'sentimentality' (Lousley, 2014). This, in turn, may make it more likely that those same viewers would then go on to support a campaign aimed at helping the people shown in the pictures.

There is more to it than that, however. It is no coincidence that each of these four conventionalized images corresponds directly to a generic biblical scene of divinely induced – which is to say 'heaven sent' – suffering. Thus: (1) the humanitarian picture of the mother and child directly reproduces the scene of the 'Madonna and Child';

Figure 2.12 *'Madonna and Child' by Orazio Gentileschi*

(2) the picture of the relative holding the dead body mirrors the 'Deposition from the Cross' and/or the 'Pietà'; (3) the photograph of the soldier-protector invokes the 'Fall of Adam and Eve from the Garden of Eden' (usually called just 'The Fall'); and (4) the photo of humanity attempting to carry on with 'everyday' tasks in the context of a hostile environment directly reproduces the 'Crossing of the Red Sea'. Throughout the history of western art – that is, throughout practically all western artistic movements, periods, and styles (from Renaissance Art to the Baroque to Modern Art) – each of these biblical scenes has been pictured over and over again by artists and sculptors who have used them as a means for picturing, and thereby contemplating, the nature of suffering as an element of Christian faith. Thus, the picture of the Madonna and Child, by focusing on the maternal love that the Virgin Mary has for her infant son, invites the

Figure 2.13 *Pietà by Michelangelo*

Source: Stanislav Traykov/Wikimedia

viewer to contemplate the sacrifice that, for Christian believers, she later made by allowing Jesus to die for mankind's sins (for an example of this scene, see Orazio Gentileschi's painting of 1563).

The images of the Deposition from the Cross and the Pietà, which show the companions of Jesus and Mary holding his dead body as it is taken down from the cross, then extend this sentiment further (the most famous example of the Pietà is Michelangelo's sculpture of the scene made between 1498 and 1499, which still stands in St. Peter's Basilica in the Vatican City, in Rome).

Meanwhile, the image of the Fall of Adam and Eve, by representing what is for Christians the original misfortune of mankind – that is, its expulsion from the utopian Garden of Eden – invites viewers to reflect upon the very nature of suffering itself. Yet this picture also signifies God's mercy towards this suffering, and his ongoing attempts to try to protect mankind. This mercy is symbolized in the figure of the 'soldier-protector' angel, which is invariably pictured somewhere in the scene, usually in the background, and which in later interpretations of the picture is taken to be 'watching over' Adam and Eve. The implication is that having decided to banish men and women to the torments of earth, God nevertheless showed mercy to them by providing a soldier-angel to protect them on their way (see, for example, Tommaso Masaccio's fresco of the scene, which was painted in 1427).

Finally, the picture of the Crossing of the Red Sea represented the Old Testament story of the Israelites' divinely inspired exodus from slavery in Egypt to the land of their birthright, Canaan (which is roughly co-terminus with the present-day countries of Israel and Lebanon). The scene, which frequently pictures the Israelites carrying domestic items such as cooking pots, blankets, and musical instruments as they go, has long served, in both the Judaic and Christian traditions, as a way of emphasizing the need for trust in God – especially trust in his intention, and in his ability, to deliver the believers from adversity (see, for example, Cosimo Rosselli's fresco of the scene, of 1481, which can be still seen on the wall of the Sistine Chapel in the Apostolic Palace in the Vatican City, in Rome).

Thus, if after the mid-1960s humanitarian and development organizations did increasingly rely upon images of atrocity as a means for generating engagement with their causes among international media audiences, they did so by circulating not just *any*

Figure 2.14 *Expulsion of Adam and Eve from Eden by Masaccio*

Figure 2.15 *Crossing of the Red Sea by Ghirlandaio (although the artist is disputed)*

images of atrocity, but instead only ones that conformed very directly to a long-established Christian 'Iconography of Suffering' (Vestergaard, 2013). In this way, these images – which were first circulated, of course, by a distinctly faith-based group of humanitarian organizations, such as the SAST – reaffirmed, but also in a sense 'updated' (and certainly, greatly expanded the circulations of), a series of generic biblical images, all of which were already deeply embedded in a European collective 'visual memory' (as it were), as contemplations upon divinely induced suffering and upon religious faith as a response to this. It is also noteworthy that many of these images, both throughout the western art canon and in their reversioning within humanitarian and development imagery, also made great play of contrasts between light and dark, which is another key element of Christian iconography.

A number of previous commentators have discussed this Christian iconography of suffering and its visual elements of light/dark in relation to the humanitarian photography of Sebastiao Salgado (see, for example, Shawcross and Hodgson, 1987; Campbell, 2002). However, I am here extending these arguments to the analysis of a much wider range of the humanitarian and development imagery that was produced between the mid-1960s and early 1990s. The key point is that in reproducing all of these elements of Christian iconography, the humanitarian and development images that I am describing sent a series of unconscious messages to their viewing audiences, in relation to each of the crises in the developing world with which they were engaged. These messages were that: (1) this is a misfortune of *biblical proportions*; (2) its causes are ultimately 'heaven sent'; and (3) the people caught up in it are nevertheless trying to summon up the 'God-given' strength to carry on with some semblance of their normal lives, regardless. In other words, if the initial intention of humanitarian agencies and development organizations in circulating such pictures was to motivate their audiences to action, then they ultimately ended up achieving this by presenting those same audiences with images of 'fire and brimstone'. And I finish here by noting Michael Buerk's opening words in his famous film from Korem, which were: 'Dawn. And as the sun breaks through the piercing chill of night on the plain outside of Korem, it lights up a biblical famine. Now. In the twentieth century. This place, say workers here, is the closest thing to hell on earth.'

Compassion fatigue

If the period between the Biafra Emergency and the Ethiopian Famine did witness humanitarian atrocity imagery become a dominant genre through which all kinds of development-related interventions into the Global South were represented through global media outlets, then this same era also saw a growing range of criticisms being levelled against this genre. Primary amongst these was the argument that an overreliance on atrocity imagery, specifically, even if this was effective in the short term, had the potential to undermine humanitarian and development organizations' goals in the longer term, by inducing 'compassion fatigue' among its viewers. By this was meant that a constant exposure to more or less the same kinds of images of suffering had the potential to eventually induce a kind of 'numbing effect' upon their audiences, as a result of which those audiences would likely become more apathetic, or indifferent, to the suffering of people in the developing world – and therefore ultimately *less* likely to support programmes aimed at ending that suffering (for the best introduction to the concept of compassion fatigue, see Campbell, 2012). The idea that overexposure to humanitarian imagery might produce compassion fatigue in this way in fact traces to a 1968 report into media coverage of the Biafra Emergency by the

World Lutheran Federation (which went on to become one of the main humanitarian organizations involved in the JCA operation; Campbell, 2012: 4). However, the concept was later greatly expanded upon by, and therefore is today most closely associated with, the photographic theorist Susan Sontag, especially in her book *On Photography* (1977) – a collection of essays that had first been published in the *New York Review of Books* between 1973 and 1977, shortly after the Biafra Emergency had ended.

According to Sontag, the inherent power of photographs of atrocity stemmed, ultimately, from the emotional 'jolt' that they gave their audience upon first viewing them. As a result, their impact was diminished by repeated viewings, and was effectively reduced to nought in any context in which the visual space is saturated with shots of a similar nature (1977: 19–21). Sontag's arguments here proved highly influential and they were subsequently taken up by a variety of other academic and popular writers; perhaps the best known later example is media studies theorist Susan Moeller's book, *Compassion Fatigue: How the Media Sell Disease, Famine, War, and Death* (1999). Equally importantly, Sontag's thesis also proved highly influential among media professionals themselves, as a result of which discussions about 'compassion fatigue' soon became incorporated into the very news coverage to which the concept referred (see, for example, Campbell's discussion of media coverage of the Haiti Earthquake in 2010, in which images of atrocity effectively appeared alongside comments about the kind of compassion fatigue that such images were likely to induce; Campbell, 2012: 4, 26 n9). One consequence of this is that the phrase has even entered popular parlance. However, for a number of more recent critics, led by David Campbell, the whole idea of 'compassion fatigue' is in fact inherently flawed. As Campbell points out, both Sontag and Moeller developed their arguments based on very little evidence. For Sontag, her claims were based almost entirely on her own personal reactions to photographs (2012: 8–9), whilst for Moeller, they were based on interviews with media professionals, rather than on research with viewers themselves – that is, *not* with the very people who, it is claimed, are affected by compassion fatigue (*ibid.*: 13). Against this, a growing body of new empirical studies has found that repeated exposure to atrocity images tends to have different effects upon different viewers, which are shaped both by the viewers' own pre-existing dispositions and attitudes and their own personal histories, *and* by the inherent qualities of the images themselves – including whether the people in the pictures look particularly sad or distressed, or not. However, such exposure *rarely* induces a kind of general apathy and disengagement with the subjects being shown (*ibid.*: 17–22). Moreover, Campbell also points out that Sontag's thesis was published just a few years before Amin and Buerk's famous report, and the wider media coverage of the Ethiopian Famine, all of which induced in its viewers anything *but* compassion fatigue (*ibid.*: 9).

Yet even if the charge about 'compassion fatigue' doesn't quite stick, the emergence of humanitarian images of atrocity as a dominant genre for representing all kinds of development interventions into the Global South also raised other – and in some cases more compelling – concerns as well. For example, growing concerns were expressed that these kinds of pictures were simply unethical, especially to the subjects of the pictures themselves, given that they demeaned their subjects by picturing them at their lowest possible point, and often in circumstances in which they may not have been in a position to give their consent to be photographed in such ways (Nissinen, 2012; Fehrenbach and Rodogno, 2015). A number of more recent studies have also drawn attention to how, in certain ongoing, long-term humanitarian and development contexts, local people may sometimes also develop a growing familiarity with the genre of atrocity imagery, either when they are frequently requested or compelled to 'pose' for it, or later as they see its products on global media channels (to which they themselves may also have access, of course). For example, Nazia Parvez (2011) has documented how, in Kroo Bay, a 'slum' area in Freetown, Sierra Leone and that was badly affected by the country's civil war (1991–2002), atrocity and poverty imagery have become effectively a part of the locality's 'social fabric', to such a degree that they now negatively impact people's perceptions of the everyday world around them, and of their own life chances within it. Aubrey Graham (2014) has similarly highlighted how in parts of North Kivu Province, a region of the Eastern Democratic Republic of Congo (DRC) that was especially impacted by the Second Congo War (1997–2003), similar processes and effects can also be observed. Intriguingly, though, Graham also documents various tactics and strategies that local people use to negotiate the photographic encounter – through which they are rendered as 'humanitarian subjects' – in order to give themselves at least some degree of agency over the process and thus, ultimately, over how they are represented.

Yet the ethical implications of such negative imagery extend not only to the *subjects* of the pictures – they extend also to the photographers who are required to produce these kinds of pictures as well. In relation to the latter, it is important to note that in most instances, and following the 'Biafra model' described above, humanitarian agencies and development organizations generally did not take atrocity pictures themselves, but instead facilitated photojournalists to do so. Moreover, over time, as the global markets for these kinds of images grew and grew, an increasing proportion of these photojournalists were made up not of international photojournalists who had flown in to cover the crisis at hand, but instead of local photographers who were trying to make a living from producing such pictures (Clark, 2004). Yet, there was a danger here that humanitarian and development organizations might be putting these local photographers into ethically compromising situations, in which they were being invited to make a living by pictures of their fellow countrymen at their 'lowest point', by selling them into global media networks over which they had no control whatsoever. Another key point for this chapter is that, in most instances, once pictures had been handed over to news-syndication services, and to picture-editors, no one outside of those services and networks – neither the agencies themselves nor the photographers who took them – had any control over by whom, or how, they were subsequently published.

In 2008, a Dutch artist called Renzo Martens explored many of these areas of concern in a deeply sardonic, at times satirical, documentary art film called *Enjoy Poverty, Episode III* (which as the name suggests, is the latest instalment of his wider Enjoy Poverty Project; see www.enjoypoverty.com). The film examines how humanitarian imagery has become a dominant genre through which the Global North perceives the developing world, how such pictures have become an element of everyday social life in some parts of the Global South, and how it may have a corrupting influence upon local photographers. Set in the Eastern DRC, it begins by following a number of development projects in action. The film focuses upon the projects' European and North American employees' frequent use of personal cameras to photograph 'suffering' Africans as a metaphor for the way in which 'poverty' has become a global industry, which is sustained by atrocity imagery. The documentary then advances the thesis that these international employees have become the primary beneficiaries of the now vast sums of money that attach to this poverty industry (in that it is they who take the lion's share of wages, vehicle expenses, and hotel expenses), precisely because *they control the way in which it is pictured and therefore imagined*. It follows that poverty could also be a major resource for Congolese people themselves – one that is potentially more lucrative than their other sources of income, such as agricultural produce – if only they could gain some control over *how it is represented*.

The documentary changes gear: Martens throws a party for local people to 'celebrate poverty' (i.e. to draw their attention to just how potentially lucrative the poverty industry is) and then begins to implement his own, idiosyncratic development intervention. His aim is to 'emancipate' Congolese, by giving them a greater share of the 'poverty resource', by assisting them to 'monetize' their own images of their own suffering. In order to do this, Martens recruits local commercial photographers, whose work usually focuses upon recording wedding ceremonies and other uplifting life-cycle events, and 're-training' them to take atrocity imagery instead. His stated aim is to teach them how to take pictures that are suitably appalling that they will be commercially successful in global media markets, thus leading to great riches. The point is that these photographers' typical wedding photographs are worth next to nothing, whereas if they can produce even one 'good' picture of a starving child, then it could be sold to a global picture agency for US$50. However, towards the end of the film, the viewer realizes that the filmmaker's intervention here has been ultimately unsuccessful, as the photographers he has trained have failed to secure the press accreditation they need to enter conflict-affected zones (i.e. to enter the very places in which they would be able to take the 'most appalling', and therefore the most saleable, atrocity images). The film thus underscores just how entrenched the structures of the 'poverty industry', and of its modes of representation, still are. It also highlights just how difficult it is not only for ordinary people, but also for commercial photographers in the developing world, to challenge those ways of seeing (for a further discussion of the complex ethical engagements of Marten's film, see De Mul, 2011). Martens' film was later criticized on a number of counts, including the charge that it presented a rather stereotypical view of the work of humanitarian and development agencies themselves (Nielsen, 2009). However, as an examination of the nature of poverty, and the effects of its representations, it is an extremely thought-provoking piece.

Post-humanitarian communication

Between roughly the mid-1960s and the early 1990s, atrocity imagery came to dominate the way in which all kinds of humanitarian and development interventions into Africa, Asia, and Latin America were represented through global media outlets. This is not to say that during this time such images were the *only* kinds of images of the developing world that appeared in global media. For example, this same era also saw a renaissance of an imagery of the 'African pastoral', especially in fiction films. This imagery cast Africa not as a place of war and suffering, but as an untamed wilderness, even as an idyllic 'Garden of Eden', and it typically represented African people not as quintessential victims, but instead in relation to an albeit just as stereotypical set of conventions relating to 'noble savages' (Heffelfinger and Wright, 2005). The highest-grossing example of this African pastoral genre was the major Hollywood film *Out of Africa* (Pollack, 1985), which starred Robert Redford and Meryl Streep. More importantly, this period also witnessed an increasing number of initiatives led by African visual artists, academics, and photojournalists, which explicitly focused upon producing and circulating entirely different (i.e. *non*-stereotypical) imagery of African peoples (at least some of these were self-consciously designed as a 'corrective' to the general representation of the continent that emerged from atrocity imagery). For example, the 1970s and 1980s were a very important period for African cinema, during which seminal films such as *Xala* (Sembène, 1975), *Yeelen* (Cissé, 1987), and *Yaaba* (Ouedraogo, 1989) were released. The late 1980s onwards saw a renewed interest in African photography – that is, in photographs taken by photographers born in and/or resident in Africa or the diasporas – among historians, art theorists, and anthropologists (Vokes, 2012). The late 1980s and early 1990s also saw the launch of major international publications that significantly increased the circulation of, and therefore the profile of, African imagery, including the journal *African Arts* and the magazine *Revue Noire*. For a more recent example of an African-initiated project aimed at countering negative media stereotypes of the continent, see Box 2.2.

Nevertheless, throughout this period, atrocity imagery was still dominant – as a means for representing humanitarian and international development interventions, at least. And over time, this increasingly worried the humanitarian agencies and development

> ### Box 2.2 Africa is a country
>
> The frequent repetition by global media outlets of images of Africa that depict the continent as predominantly a place of war, famine, and disaster, and of African people as essentially passive victims, also drew a strong response from African journalists, writers, photographers, artists, and academics. From the 1960s onwards, attempts were made to counter these dominant stereotypes through the dissemination of alternative images of the continent and its people, which were output across all kinds of African newspapers, magazines, literary journals, art exhibitions, and academic venues. In recent years, these efforts have increasingly moved online, especially into the realm of the 'blogosphere'. Today, one of the best-known blogs challenging dominant perceptions of, and ideas about, Africa is 'Africa is a Country' (whose very name is an ironic reference to a popular misconception of the continent being a singular, uniform place). Founded by South African-born academic Sean Jacobs, the first version of Africa is a Country was set up in 2005, as a direct attempt to 'correct ... falsehoods/misrepresentations' about the continent and its peoples, and in response to the fact that at the time a majority of blogs about Africa were run by international development agencies and other official organizations. From the outset, the general model for the blog was for one contributor (from an eclectic mix of journalists, writers, and academics) to take a news story about Africa that was being circulated in mainstream media outlets and to write a kind of 'response' to it in the form of an extended blog post in order to correct any falsehoods or misrepresentations that it might contain. From early on, the blog developed a distinctive writing style of its own, one that I would describe as a blend of informed analysis with a satirical edge (in which authors of the blog's posts would often adopt a kind of 'faux incredulity', as if truly aghast that such stereotypes of Africa could still exist, in the present age). In addition, the blog's posts constantly emphasized the sheer depth and variety of the continent's social and cultural life. This format proved highly popular in its own right. More importantly, though, it meant that Africa is a Country was well placed to respond quickly – with informed commentary and withering criticism – to major news stories about the continent as and when these broke in mainstream news outlets. Moreover, in our current era of 'flat earth news' (to borrow Nick Davies' phrase from 2009), in which online news sources frequently (endlessly) re-version each others' content, Africa is a Country's better informed and more analytical content often ended up becoming inserted into, or in other ways shaping, mainstream news outlets' stories about Africa, especially where these ran on over a period of time. For example, the blog's content had a significant impact upon the long-running stories of the post-election violence that engulfed Kenya after December 2007, the Anti-Homosexuality Bill controversy in Uganda from 2009 onwards, and the 'Rhodes Must Fall' campaign which began in 2015.
>
> Sources: Davies (2009), Jacobs (2016), http://africasacountry.com.

organizations themselves. Specifically, the concern grew that by allowing people in the developing world to be constantly represented through such images, the agencies and organizations themselves might also be reinforcing wider negative perceptions of the developing world being a place that is essentially backwards, helpless, and infantile. This might in turn invite global media audiences to imagine that, in response, development operations must be dynamic, interventionist, and patrimonial. However, while most development agencies would have been happy to go along with such an imaginary during the early period of modernization theory – when, as we have seen, most international organizations generally *did* conceive of the societies of the developing world as backwards, and of development itself as a transitive process for 'bringing these societies up' into the 'modern world' – as confidence in modernization theory began to fade, these same assumptions came to be seen as increasingly problematic, as patrimonial, and as simply patronizing. Indeed, some theorists even argued that, in these ways, this kind of imagery – and the associated media coverage within which it is embedded – can even be seen as an intrinsic component of a contemporary global political-economy, in which wealthier nations remain by and large dominant over those of the developing world in economic, political, and military terms (Hattori, 2003).

There was also another more general problem here, which was that by relying on atrocity imagery that was increasingly iconographic, and which therefore invited audiences to think of famines, wars, and other disasters not as the outcome of real-world political, economic, and social processes, but instead as the effects of 'divine judgements', humanitarian and development organizations were effectively decontextualizing the very contexts in which they were working. In other words, by relying on such imagery, there was a danger that the agencies might effectively be failing to educate their own audiences about what was, in fact, going on in places such as Biafra, Ethiopia, and Haiti. Indeed, an overreliance on iconographic images may have even resulted in an extraordinary contradiction, whereby the more viewers were exposed to humanitarian and development organizations' coverage of crisis x, y, or z, the *more* impressionistic their understanding of those crises became and, therefore, the *less* they actually knew about what happening in those places. Interestingly, this problem was first recognized by humanitarian and development agencies themselves, in their own study of their campaign literature from, and the media coverage of, the Ethiopian famine. The study, which was called the 'Image of Africa Project', was led by the FAO (see above), but also involved a number of other European and African NGOs that had been involved in the crisis response. The contradiction outlined above was discussed at length in one of the final reports from the Image of Africa project, published by the British NGO Oxfam (van der Gaag and Nash, 1987).

In recent years, many humanitarian and development agencies have responded to these critiques by steadily reducing the amount of atrocity imagery they are involved in circulating, and instead engaging in 'strategic positivism' – sometimes called 'deliberate positivism' (Chouliaraki, 2010). Interestingly, in most cases, this still doesn't involve exposing the actual real-world political, economic, and social *causes* of particular crises or situations with which they are engaged. Rather, it involves moving away from *any* focus upon causes at all – be these actual causes or implied 'divine' ones – and instead focusing attention upon agencies' own interventions, and upon the positive effects and solutions that these have produced. In other words, the emphasis has shifted from causes to solutions. As part of this shift, there has also been a growing trend towards what Chouliaraki has called 'post-humanitarian' communication strategies (2010), which tend to focus not on aid agencies' responses to one or other famine, war, or disaster, but instead on their attempts to address malnutrition in general, or conflict-induced trauma in general, or some other general challenge (Box 2.3).

Box 2.3 Post-humanitarian communication

In a seminal article published in the *International Journal of Cultural Studies* in 2010, Professor of Media Studies at the London School of Economics, Lilie Chouliaraki, identified a growing trend among humanitarian agencies and development organizations to frame their campaigns in terms of what she calls 'post-humanitarian' media communication strategies. By this, she refers to those campaigns which break not only with the kind of generic images discussed in this chapter, but also with the kind of 'grand emotions' (e.g. pity, empathy, guilt) which these images invoke, and with the 'grand moral claims' they make (for example, the claim that western audiences have a duty to relieve the suffering of people in Africa, Asia, and Latin America given that we are all part of a 'common humanity'). Against all of this, post-humanitarian campaigns tend to rely upon entirely different aesthetic registers, to appeal to only 'low-intensity emotional regimes', and to make only very limited claims (or even no moral claims at all) of its viewers. One of the main case studies Chouliaraki uses to illustrate this argument is the World Food Programme's (WFP) *No Food Diet* appeal, which was launched in 2006. Although this campaign was focused specifically upon malnutrition in Africa, it did not include any images whatsoever of underfed or starving people. Instead, it pictured only a 'typical' African homestead, in which a mother prepared a meal before putting her children to bed. The media message, then, was not in the images at all, but in the accompanying commentary, in which the audience were told that the mother had prepared a meal here from the 'no food diet'. The commentary went on to say that this was even more effective than the (then popular) 'Atkins diet', because whereas Atkins could only make you thinner, the 'no food diet' was likely to kill you! In this way, the campaign appealed not to its audience's sense of pity or guilt, but to their sense of irony and absurdity. In addition, it didn't invite its audience to try to 'save' African children in the name of a shared humanity, so much as to reflect on their own dietary practices (as exemplified by things like the Atkins diet), and to compare these with the experiences of those distant others who are forced to follow the 'no food diet'. In all of these ways, campaigns such as this one have 'cleansed' humanitarian communication of its sentimentality, and have also foregrounded individual judgement – and personal action – over collective responses. And they have reduced the demands being made of their audiences, from 'give money' to 'think about your own life, and compare it to those of others'. In so doing, they may have also done much to inaugurate the age of what we now call (although Chouliaraki herself doesn't use the term) 'slackivism'.

Source: Chouliaraki (2010).

These kinds of approaches, which are also associated with experiments in new media platforms and in 'cross-platform' approaches, still aim to motivate their viewers to some sort of action, just not in ways that may induce the kind of patrimony described above. For example, a post-humanitarian campaign typically would not invite a viewer to give money in order to feed a starving person in Africa, but would instead invite them to reflect upon, and to change, their own consumption habits, in ways that might improve the food supply for all human beings on the planet. A good example is Oxfam's GROW campaign, which began in 2011 (Box 2.4).

Box 2.4 Oxfam's GROW campaign

Oxfam's GROW campaign is another good example of an appeal that used a post-humanitarian communication strategy. GROW, a four-year 'mega-campaign', was launched in 2011 across multiple media channels (i.e. it involved a 'cross-platform' approach), including a range of printed materials, radio and television advertising, and an extensive website. Once again, the campaign focused on patterns of malnutrition in the developing world. However, it located these within global structures of food production and distribution in general, and it also looked at the growing obesity epidemic in the developing world as another outcome of these same structures. Following the general pattern for post-humanitarian communication outlined above, GROW did not use any images of malnutrition. Instead, almost all of its shots of people from the developing world pictured them either actively engaged in agricultural activities or holding food they had grown, or were selling. Instead, the key media message was contained in the accompanying text and tables/graphs, which described how people in the developing world, as both food producers and food consumers, are made vulnerable to either malnutrition or obesity by the same global structures of production and consumption which effect us all. Moreover, they are being made more vulnerable by the ways in which these structures are being changed by the growing power of major transnational agri-businesses, by western governments' inaction, by climate change, and so on (see, for example, the campaign's main report, *Growing a Better Future: Food Justice in a Resource-Constrained World*, 2011). In this way, the campaign didn't appeal to any 'grand emotions', but instead to its audiences' general sense of anxiety over global capitalism, government inertia, and climate change. It also didn't invite its audiences to save people in the developing world, but instead to reflect upon their own food production and consumption habits and to think about growing at least some of their own food, to interrogate the supply chains of the food brands they buy at the supermarket, to increase the amount of fair-trade products they buy, to try to source more local produce, and so on. At the heart of this was the 'GROW method', which included a cookbook and various online toolkits for achieving this kind of more 'ethical consumption'.

Source: www.oxfam.org/en/campaigns/grow.

Figure 2.16 *Oxfam's GROW campaign*

Source: Oxfam GB

Yet even if these trends have at least partly shifted the emphasis of humanitarian and development problems away from causes to solutions, nevertheless they may still end up representing the aid agencies themselves as the primary agents for change in the developing world, rather than African, Asian, or Latin American people themselves. In other words, even with these newer approaches, aid agencies never quite solved their earlier problem of representing people in the developing world as essentially 'needy' or passive. Recently, these problems have been amplified by the growing nexus between international development and celebrity, a nexus that in many ways defines the current era (see Chapter 6). Finally, at least some humanitarian and development campaigns do continue to rely upon atrocity imagery: for example, Save the Children recently ran a television campaign in the UK, as a fundraiser for their development work in Africa, that continued to repeat the tropes of the mother in need, the malnourished child, and the 'soldier-protector' humanitarian figure (the ad can be viewed online at www.youtube.com/watch?v= 99pQ0KJfdoE). Therefore, despite humanitarian and development agencies having been aware of the issues and problems associated with atrocity imagery since the late 1980s, the issues involved in finding alternatives to it remain pertinent, even today. Therefore, in 2015, the Overseas Development Institute (ODI) hosted a major, high-profile Twitter chat, titled #DevPix, in which agencies themselves, as well photographers, other media professionals, and academics debated these very issues (available online at https://storify.com/odi_webmaster/devpix-improving-how-development-organisations-use).

Box 2.5 The death of Aylan Kurdi

On the morning of 2 September 2015, the body of a 3-year-old Syrian boy called Aylan Kurdi – whose family had been fleeing the Syrian Civil War – washed up on a beach near the city of Bodrum, in southwestern Turkey. Kurdi, along with his mother and brother, had drowned when the boat that was carrying them from the Turkish coast to the Greek Island of Kos capsized. Shortly afterwards, local media cameramen took a series of still and moving images of the scene, which included one shot of a Turkish policeman carrying away Kurdi's lifeless body. When this picture was circulated through global media networks later that day, it drew an extraordinary response from audiences across Europe and around the world. It caused an immediate – and enormous – increase in donations to refugee and migration charities, and it also resulted in increased pressure being put on European leaders, in particular, to change their policy positions in relation to the burgeoning Syrian refugee crisis. It was as a direct result of this that, for example, Britain's then Prime Minister David Cameron later pledged to resettle up to 20,000 Syrian refugees in the UK, over a five-year period. Yet what was it about this particular picture that drew such a strong reaction from media audiences – especially in a context

Figure 2.17 *The Death of Aylan Kurdi*

in which media outlets had published other pictures of drowned refugees, including of Syrian refugees, in the months beforehand, none of which had generated anything like this scale of reaction? In the weeks and months following the photograph's publication, a large number of media commentators and scholars attempted to answer this question, often developing arguments around empathy and sentimentality as they did so. A good example of a scholarly treatment in this vein is an article by Nadine El-Enany, in which she shows how responses to the picture in the blogosphere and on Twitter were frequently characterized by media viewers imagining that Kurdi was their own son (El-Enany notes that in the hours following the photograph's publication, a trending hashtag on Twitter was #CouldBeMyChild). However, in my own original contribution on this subject, I would argue that the analysis of humanitarian imagery that I have developed in this chapter offers one further dimension for our understanding of precisely why this particular picture had such force. Specifically, I would argue that if much of the atrocity imagery that has been historically reproduced in global media outlets *does* reference four conventionalized scenes of biblical suffering, then this one picture of the Turkish policeman holding Kurdi's body reproduces key elements from three of these. Specifically, in picturing an adult cradling an infant, the picture reproduces elements of the 'Madonna and Child'; in showing someone holding a dead body, it reproduces the 'Pietà'; and in picturing a policeman, it reproduces the soldier-protector figure of 'The Fall'. However, the photograph also radically disrupts these conventionalized scenes in a number of ways. In particular, the fact that the photograph here is of a dead child disrupts both the biblical image of the Madonna and Child (in which the child represents hope for mankind) and the Pietà (in which the dead body is of the *adult* Jesus, who has died *after* having fulfilled his destiny to save mankind). In addition, the fact that the photograph shows a policeman who has clearly been unable to help this child also disrupts the image of 'The Fall' (in which the 'soldier' figure exists precisely to *protect* mankind). In these ways, then, it is my argument that at least part of the power of this image stemmed from the way in which it signalled to media audiences, by way of conventions with which many of them would already have been familiar, that the Syrian refugee crisis is again a disaster of 'biblical proportions', yet in a way that, by disrupting conventionalized narratives about how biblical stories should 'play out', was particularly unsettling.

Source: El-Enany (2016).

Conclusion

Between roughly the mid-1960s and the early 1990s, humanitarian atrocity images came to dominate the way in which all kinds of interventions into the developing world were represented through global media outlets. In trying to understand how this happened, we must recognize that the precise processes and relationships through which all news photographs are taken in the first place, are subsequently circulated through media networks, are broadcast on media outlets, and are ultimately viewed and made sense of by audiences, are all highly complex phenomena, in a constant state of change. Therefore, if we were to undertake a more 'fine-grained' analysis of the processes that we have been looking at here, it might be necessary for each photograph – or set of photographs – under discussion to look at: (1) the specific relationship that pertained between the photographer and the person or people pictured (i.e. between those who were party to the actual 'photographic encounter'); (2) the ways in which other individuals and agencies might have also shaped the situation in which the picture was taken (i.e. the context of the photographic encounter); (3) the role of photographic agents, or agencies, who may have purchased the image rights, and later circulated and sold the images to broadcasters around the world; and (4) the part played by the picture editors within those organizations who bought the images, as well as the news editors who chose which of the images purchased to then print or broadcast, and the typesetters and image mixers who actually inserted them within the news segment in which they finally appeared. And all of this before we have given any consideration to the hugely complex questions of audience reception. Moreover, the precise configuration of all of these relationships is in a constant state of flux – indeed, with each picture taken, let alone across entire emergencies (Gursel, 2016).

Nevertheless, even without going into such fine-grained analysis, and without opening up all of these complexities in greater detail, it is still possible to trace the contours of a general pattern as to why and how humanitarian imagery came to dominate in the way that it did. The general pattern here is that from the late eighteenth century onwards, but especially following the invention of photography in the nineteenth century, humanitarian organizations' general *modus operandi* became, in relation to crises in distant parts of the world, to either produce pictures of atrocity themselves or else to arrange for others to do so on their behalf. These pictures were then transmitted to audiences 'back home', in order to galvanize support for the issue at hand among donor publics in Europe, North America and Australia. From the mid-1960s onwards, these same basic practices became increasingly combined with then emergent global media networks, networks that had the capability to transmit many more images, to many more people, much more quickly, than could ever have been imagined beforehand. As a result, humanitarian organizations – and latterly also many other kinds of international development organizations as well – were able to use images of atrocity to galvanize support not just among small groups or 'committees of the concerned', which they had put together themselves, but from potentially limitless global media audiences.

For the humanitarian agencies involved, this hugely increased the impact of their images, over increasingly short periods of time.

This 'amplification effect' also resulted in the kinds of iconographic images that they had always relied upon – which themselves drew on an even older Christian 'Iconography of Suffering' – becoming amplified as well. Indeed, these soon became so ubiquitous that they even became 'fixed' within global media circuits, and possibly in the minds of global media audiences as well, as the primary way to visualize not only specific events and problems facing the developing world, but the *entire* developing world. One result is that even today, global media audiences are still sometimes surprised to see any picture in the news of an obese African child, or of a mother posing with her perfectly healthy baby (in a formal studio portrait, for example), or of a middle-class African suburb in which the large, well-built villas are spaced apart and surrounded by perfectly manicured lawns and well-tended streets. Another outcome, though, from the late 1980s onwards, was that humanitarian agencies and development organizations became increasingly concerned that the kinds of atrocity imagery upon which they had for so long relied, and which they had helped to circulate so widely, effective though this had been in generating short-term income, was in fact ultimately damaging their long-term efforts to educate global media audiences about the issues and problems facing the developing world, and about their own responses to those problems. These concerns, despite having generated a range of alternative media strategies, remain pertinent today.

Summary

- The era of 'modernization' witnessed a number of key trends in the way in which international development was represented in western media.
- In particular, it saw humanitarian imagery emerge as the primary genre through which all kinds of development interventions in the Global South were depicted.
- This dominance emerged from a long history of humanitarian practice, which had long used particular kinds of atrocity imagery to galvanize audiences to action.
- This imagery in turn drew on an even longer Christian 'Iconography of Suffering'.

- Over time, this approach came in for increasing criticism, for perhaps inducing compassion fatigue, but certainly for being patronizing towards the victims of famine and other disasters in the developing world.

Discussion questions

1. Close your eyes and think of one image of Africa, one of Latin America, and one of South Asia. What do you see, and to what extent are your mental images influenced by your own experiences and/or by images that you have seen on television and the internet?
2. Watch Amin and Buerk's 1984 report from Ethiopia (it is available on YouTube at www.youtube.com/watch?v= XYOj_6OYuJc). Does it retain its power to shock, even today?
3. How do images get from a crisis zone in the Global South to our television screens? What are all of the agents, organizations, and relationships involved here? How do aid agencies influence these actors and shape their connections, and how might they do so differently in an attempt to generate different media messages?
4. Critically assess the concept of 'compassion fatigue'.
5. Are 'post-humanitarian' media strategies a significant improvement on what went before?

Further reading

For the history of humanitarian photography, see: Sliwinski, S. (2011) *Human Rights in Camera*, Chicago, IL: University of Chicago Press; and Batchen, G., Gidley, M., Miller, N. and Prosser, J. (2012) *Picturing Atrocity: Photography in Crisis*, London: Reaktion Books.

For more on images of atrocity within media representations of development, see: Chouliaraki, L. (2006) *Spectatorship of Suffering*, London: Sage; and Franks, S. (2013) *Reporting Disasters: Famine, Aid, Politics and the Media*, London: Hurst.

Meanwhile, for more on post-humanitarian communication strategies, see: Chouliaraki, L. (2013) *The Ironic Spectator: Solidarity in the Age of Post-Humanitarianism*, Cambridge: Polity Press.

Readers who wish to take their studies of representations of development further, and beyond only the examination of news, and factual, media content, will also be interested in: Lewis, D., Rodgers, D. and Woolcock, M. (2014) *Popular Representations of Development: Insights from Novels, Films, Television and Social Media*, New York: Routledge.

Multimedia sources

Online guide: *Imaging Famine* Exhibition Catalogue (*The Guardian*, 2005) Available online at: www.david-campbell.org/wp-content/documents/Imaging_Famine_catalogue.pdf. See also David Campbell's main website: www.david-campbell.org

Documentary: *Jesus Christ Airlines* (dir. Lasse Jensen, 2001) [The Biafra Emergency, 1967–1970]

Documentary: *The Band Aid Story* (dir. Andy Baybutt, 2004)

Documentary: *The Salt of the Earth* (dir. Wim Wenders and Juliano Salgado, 2014) [Biographic of Sebastiao Salgado]

Documentary: *War Photographer* (dir. Christian Frei, 2001) [Biographic of war photographer James Nachtwey, which explores the ethics of humanitarian imagery]

Film: *Enjoy Poverty, Episode III* (dir. Renzo Martens, 2008)

Film: *Out of Africa* (dir. Sydney Pollack, 1985)

Film: *Xala* (dir. Ousmane Sembène, 1975)

Film: *Yaaba* (dir. Idrissa Ouedraogo, 1989)

Film: *Yeelen* (dir. Souleymane Cissé, 1987)

3 Media, empowerment, and agency

The promises of participatory communication

- Growing criticisms of modernization theory.
- Dependency theory and its implications for M4D.
- Feminist and environmentalist perspectives on media.
- 'Post-development' and the rise of 'participatory communication'.
- Indigenous media and its critics.

Introduction

Following Truman's famous speech in 1949, the field of international development soon became dominated by the paradigm of 'modernization', which posited that: (1) the societies of the Global South were both economically and socio-politically *lacking* compared with those of the rich world; (2) the *raison d'être* of international development was to try to address this lack, in order to allow the countries of the South to be entirely transformed, or 'modernized', in ways that would enable them to 'catch up' with those of the western world; and (3) the most effective way of doing this was through technical interventions, in which more 'advanced' technologies and knowledge of the west could be transferred into the developing world. All of this implied a relatively straightforward role for media, in which the spread of western-designed media devices and platforms into the developing world itself constituted one form of 'technology transfer', and in which those platforms would then become a key tool for communicating further knowledge transfers. Although at the time Truman made his speech much of this – both the model of development itself and its implied role for media – remained largely hypothetical (i.e. largely untested in practice), over the decades that followed, as practically all of the world's largest international development agencies became invested in the paradigm and used it to guide their development practice, a growing body of policy-oriented and academic literature appeared to provide ever greater justification of and for its logics. As a result, the key goals of modernization, and their implied role for M4D, became well established within the international development industry, and these have also, in one form or another, continued to influence the field ever since.

However, the fact that both modernization theory itself and a modernization approach to M4D *have* continued to be followed by at least some projects up until the present time does *not* mean that the paradigm itself or this approach to M4D have remained unchallenged ever since, or that no alternative approaches have ever been put forward. On the contrary, from around the mid-1960s onwards, a series of increasingly powerful critiques began to be levelled against modernization, all of which to a greater or lesser degree also reframed both the 'problems' for, and the goals of, international development, and the methods through which these goals might be achieved. Although these critiques were often informed by quite different political and theoretical points of view, and had quite different empirical emphases – some focused on different parts of the developing world, others on different kinds of places (such as urban or rural areas) – all of them began to gradually congeal around one relative simple central idea. This in turn implied an alternative orientation, or set of orientations, towards how international development should be carried out *in practice*. Moreover, this alternative orientation also suggested an entirely different role for media than that which had previously been forwarded by practitioners and theorists of the modernization approach to M4D.

Simply put, the various critiques from the mid-1960s onwards gradually congealed around the relatively simple idea that most, if not all, of the societies of the developing world were not inherently flawed, inferior, or 'backwards' compared with those of the west. Rather, their observed dearth of economic goods and political freedoms relative to the rich world stemmed more from the way in which developing world countries' *potential* for economic – or political – prosperity had been thwarted by the history of extractive – or coercive – interventions into those places, including interventions by Euro-American societies. This included not only colonial interventions, but also interventions that had been made in the name of international development itself. In this view, underdevelopment was not an intrinsic or an inevitable state for African, Asian, and Latin American societies, but was instead an outcome of the way in which those same places had been negatively impacted by actual external historical processes. By this logic, the aims of international development became recast as *less* an attempt to transform southern societies into 'carbon copies' of Euro-American polities – through the transfer of more 'advanced' technologies and knowledge – and *more* a process for understanding the qualities already possessed by societies in the developing world, and for assisting these qualities to flourish to their fullest potential. In this way, development practice also became reconceived as *less* a process of 'intervention', and *more* a process of 'facilitation' and 'empowerment': one which should be primarily characterized not by 'transfer' but by 'engagement' and 'dialogue' – one in which ordinary people living in the developing world 'participated' equally and exercised a degree of 'agency' of their own.

One result of this wider 'paradigm shift' was a recasting of the role for media within international development. For advocates of this new approach to development, the potential for media did *not* stem from the way in which radio, television, and other technologies might be used as a tool for the 'one-way' broadcasting of information and knowledge to the Global South by western development agencies and their broadcasting partners. Instead, its potential related to how those same devices might be used to facilitate 'two-way' communication (i.e. dialogue) between members of southern societies themselves, with a view to strengthening their common understandings, social bonds, and potential for problem solving. This in turn would have transformative effects upon their societies as a whole. In addition, media could also be used to facilitate dialogue between people in the developing world and the development agencies, with a view to improving both the nature and the quality of the interventions that the latter made into the Global South. Over time, this general approach – really set of approaches – became known as 'participatory communication'. The purpose of this chapter, then, is to trace all of these developments. It is beyond my scope here to examine *all* of the critiques of modernization theory that emerged from the mid-1960s onwards. However, it is necessary to briefly introduce the main arguments of at least three of these: (1) dependency theory; (2) feminist critiques; and (3) the environmental/sustainability critique. Each of these was a seminal critique of modernization in its own right. However, more importantly from our point of view, each also involved a specific set of criticisms of media and development, as a result of which each had a key bearing on what became 'participatory communication'.

Dependency theory

Somewhat curiously, what became known as dependency theory in fact dates to around the same time as Truman's speech, and therefore technically pre-dates the classic period of development as modernization. In late 1949, a German economist working in the then newly created Department of Economic Affairs at the United Nations in New York, Hans Singer, published what was to become one of the foundational texts for the theory, an article entitled 'Economic Progress in Under-developed Countries', in the journal *Social Research*. Just a few months later, an Argentine economist based at the Economic Commission for Latin America, Raoul Prebisch, published a second key text, a report called 'The Economic Development of Latin America and Its Principal Problems', which was published by Singer's department at the UN (1950). Taken together, these two texts – which became jointly known as the 'Singer-Prebisch hypothesis' (they are still known by that term today) – argued through technical economic analysis that within the global trading system, underdeveloped (i.e. poorer) countries were not only disadvantaged at the outset *vis-à-vis* wealthier ones, but were likely to become increasingly more disadvantaged over time. Put simply, this is because within the global system – given the way in which it had developed over time – underdeveloped countries were more likely to be reliant upon exports of primary commodities (i.e. raw materials). They exported these raw materials to more developed nations to feed the latter's relatively larger manufacturing bases. Meanwhile, developed nations were more likely to be reliant upon exports of manufactured goods, a significant portion of which they exported to poorer nations. This pattern placed underdeveloped countries at a comparative disadvantage that would only increase over time, given that the relative cost of raw materials tends to remain static, while the relative cost of manufactured goods usually rises more quickly (*ibid.*). As a result, with each passing year, underdeveloped countries needed to export more and more of their primary commodities to purchase the same volume of manufactured imports. In other words, given the nature of the global system, poor countries will become *increasingly* worse off, relative to richer countries, with each passing year.

Although the Singer-Prebisch hypothesis had some early impact among academic economists, it initially gained little traction within wider development circles (Leys, 1996: 110–118). This was partly because it was developed from a highly technical set of analyses, but more so because its logical conclusion was that the developing world needed to adopt more protectionist measures, and might even benefit from having *less* engagement with the western world. Yet this flew in the face of the fundamentally interventionist logics of modernization theory, and with the kinds of development practice that these informed. As a result, it was not until much later – into the late 1950s, and more so into the second half of the 1960s – that a group of Marxist scholars took up the key ideas of the hypothesis, and greatly expanded them into a more thorough-going theory – what became known as dependency theory (Cardoso, 1977). By that time, it had become increasingly obvious that for certain parts of the developing world, modernization theory simply *wasn't working*, even in the most basic of its own terms, in that it simply hadn't generated anything like the aimed for rise in national wealth for those developing nations – measured in terms of gross domestic product (GDP) – or significantly 'closed the gap' between the poorer nations and those of the richer North (Chambers, 1977). Whilst this was true across much of the developing world, for complex historical reasons modernization had come to be seen as a failure in Latin America in particular. As a result, much early dependency theory was developed by scholars who, like Prebsich, were from the continent or who worked in or on Latin American countries. Paul A. Baran, Professor of Economics at Stanford University, published the first extended exposition of dependency theory in 1957 in a book entitled *The Political Economy of Growth*. However, by far the most influential, and still the most well-known, contribution to the theory appeared nine years after that, when the polymath German-American scholar Andre Gunder Frank, who was at the time Professor of Sociology and Economics at the University of Chile in Santiago, published his seminal – and highly polemical – short book *The Development of Underdevelopment* (1966). This was followed a year later by his equally important *Capitalism and Underdevelopment in Latin America* (1967).

Dependency theory in general, and Frank's work in particular, extended Singer and Prebisch's insights by completely rejecting many of the central ideas that had animated modernization theory. It argued that underdevelopment was not internal to the societies of the developing world; it was not a reflection of their being 'backwards' or 'traditional', or of being in need of transformation through successive stages of 'modernization' to become more 'Euro-American'. Instead, the theory posited that underdevelopment was an outcome of the specific ways in which developing nations had been initially incorporated into the world economy, following the expansion of European markets, and later European capitalism and colonialism, from the sixteenth century onwards (Frank, 1966: 22). (Although all dependency theorists agreed that Southern underdevelopment *was* primarily an outcome of European economic and political expansion, they disagreed as to precisely when this expansion had begun.) The way in which this incorporation had occurred had created a set of unequal economic relations between nations, which had become persistently worse over time – as the Singer-Prebisch hypothesis had predicted they would. Thus, southern societies had, over several centuries, been systematically exploited, through an increasingly unfair extraction of their wealth and resources to the Global North, and this accelerated following the emergence of capitalism in north-western Europe, around the mid-eighteenth century. Moreover, the fact that southern societies' incorporation into the world economy had been more or less everywhere achieved through coercion had also created a set of prevailing political conditions in which most people living in the developing world remained powerless to challenge their relative economic disadvantage. This was especially true for societies brought into the world economy during the era of colonialism. However, Frank also described, for example, Brazil's integration into the world economy after the First World War as the outcome of an 'American economic invasion' (1966: 26). The only category of people living in the developing world who had done well from the process, and who therefore retained at least some influence, were narrow groups of elites who, from the outset, had supported foreign interests in pursuit of personal gain, rather than for the common good.

The conclusions to be drawn from all of this also turned the logic of modernization *practice* almost entirely upon its head (Leys, 1996). Because now, the solution to underdevelopment for the developing world lay not in any further interventions into these regions by, or transfers from, the rich world; or into the 'capitalist periphery' from the 'core countries' (to use dependency theorists' own terminology). After all, it was interventions from core countries that had caused their problems in the first place, and were making them worse over time. Instead, developing nations needed to wield whatever sovereignty they still retained in order to strategically protect certain sections of their own economies, in particular in order to strengthen their national manufacturing bases, and in so doing to pursue an 'autocentric' path to development – that is, one that first and foremost reflected their own national interests. However, within the various countries involved, this was *not* to be led by 'modern' educated elites – a category which by this time had become synonymous with those already in power – given that those elites were already dupes of foreign interests (or 'compradores' as dependency theorists called them: a Portuguese term which, from the sixteenth century onwards, was used to refer to the indigenous managers of European trading houses in East Asia; Evans, 1979) Instead, and reflecting the general Marxist leanings of most dependency theorists, the process should be led by a new political leadership, one that was in effect better connected to its population.

The main point here is that this general attack on modernization also implied a number of fundamental criticisms of the way in which media had been previously employed within development. In other words, it contained a nascent denunciation of the logics and practices of the entire field of M4D as it then existed, and in so doing it introduced the first – and even today, still the most powerful – challenge to the prevailing consensus that an expansion of mass media *always* had a generally positive effect upon development. These implied criticisms were to become increasingly explicit – and expanded – over the decades that followed. Firstly, dependency theory contained an implied criticism of the idea that any transfer of media technologies and infrastructures from the developed world to Africa, Asia, or Latin America was always a good thing. This stemmed not only from the fact that development theorists regarded all such transfers with general suspicion. It also stemmed from the growing realization that western countries, and the US in particular, may have deliberately exported mostly older – even obsolete – technologies to developing countries, thereby leaving the latter at a more or less permanent technological disadvantage (Nordenstreng and Varis, 1974).

Secondly, and more importantly, dependency theorists also rejected what had by that time become one of the key tenets of modernization and M4D: that the main problem faced by all societies in the Global South was a persistence of pre-existing forms of knowledge (i.e. cultural, or 'traditional', knowledge) that needed to be effectively displaced, or replaced, through an increased dissemination of 'modern' scientific and technical information, if those societies were to 'progress' – dissemination that could be most effectively achieved through mass communications. For dependency theorists, the problem of underdevelopment was *not* a reflection of traditional knowledge at all, and it therefore could *not* be remedied through the provision of more information (Hornik, 1988). Instead, underdevelopment was entirely an outcome of economic relations between nations, and of the political structures that had both generated those relations in the first place and that continued to sustain them in the present. The implication, then, was that the prevailing model for M4D was, at best, redundant.

A third criticism implied by dependency theory, and the one that was to become more widely expanded over the following decades, was the suggestion that the prevailing model for media may even have a detrimental effect upon the developing world, by helping to sustain underdevelopment and perhaps even make it worse (Boyd-Barrett, 1977). This criticism stemmed from the fact that a majority of the most important early theorists of modernization and M4D, beginning with Daniel Lerner, had posited that developmental change needed to begin with changing the attitudes and outlook of *individuals* living in the developing world. In other words, from Lerner onwards, theorists had assumed that the path to modernization for any nation lay in more and more individuals in those places becoming better educated and adopting modern values. Therefore, the main challenge for M4D was to identify the most effective means through which individuals' outlooks could be changed in and through their exposure to media. For example, it was this very logic that informed Rogers' attempts to identify different individuals' personality 'types' in relation to their adoption of new technologies, including media, and it was the same logic that drove all social marketing approaches to media. However, for dependency theorists, the problems of underdevelopment lay not at the individual level at all, but at the 'structural' level of the state and of relations between states – that is, at what would now be more commonly called the 'macro' level. In other words, what stopped people progressing was not their own worldview, or lack of knowledge, but instead the social and political environments in which they lived, and which, for the reasons described, resulted in their being unable ever to achieve equitable access to land/property, to credit markets, and to adequate healthcare (Fair, 1989). Again, this suggested that the prevailing focus of M4D was redundant.

Worse still, dependency theorists further argued that precisely because modernization and M4D *was* focused upon, and targeted at, individuals, there was a danger that it might even end up distracting people from the *real* causes of their relative disadvantage, which were structural. Worse still, it might even act to naturalize the very idea of 'individualism' itself, an idea that would have been largely alien to many of the societies of Africa, Asia, and Latin America prior to the expansion of the world economy (and in some senses is still alien in many of those places), yet which is of course a central ideology for capitalism itself – for the very process that for a long period drove the expansion of Euro-American power. Also, although it was development agencies that created the conditions for widening access to media in the developing world, and that advocated most strongly for its perceived benefits, it tended to be international commercial broadcasters that provided most of the actual content, initially at least. Yet most of these broadcasting companies were themselves large, and western, capitalist corporations, whose interests in the developing world stemmed from their own desires for commercial expansion into these regions – what McPhail (1981) refers to as a form of 'electronic colonialism'. Moreover, these broadcasters often had close ties with other, non-media, western corporations as well, and may therefore have had a stake in forwarding those other corporations' interests as well. There was a danger, then, that M4D might end up not only propagating a kind of 'false consciousness' (to use the Marxist language favoured by dependency theorists themselves), but also serving the interests of the very agents of unequal economic power that were the very cause of underdevelopment. From the 1970s onwards, all of the main academic theorists of modernization and M4D – including Lerner, Rogers, and Schramm – came in for sustained criticism for their failure to examine the relationship between media content and the institutional structures of the media organizations from which that content was generated (Melkote and Steeves, 2001: 218; see also Fjes, 1976).

One of the first dependency-oriented scholars to draw together these arguments about media in a sustained and explicit way was the Bolivian journalist-turned-scholar Luis Ramiro Beltran, especially in his seminal 'Alien Premises, Objects and Methods in Latin American Communication Research' (1976). However, by that time, the arguments had anyway begun to be bolstered by a number of other events and processes, and in particular by the emergence of the 'Media Imperialism Debate'. This debate stemmed from a complaint made by a number of developing world countries – but especially by the populous nations of Egypt, India, and Indonesia – that western nations wielded too much control over global media production, and that large Euro-American media outlets should have their access to all developing nations restricted. The complaint was taken very seriously by UNESCO, which in 1977 set up the International Commission for the Study of Communication Problems, chaired by the Irish politician Sean McBride – it is usually referred to as simply 'The McBride Commission' – and in 1980, the commission's final report found strongly in the complainants' favour. The report also defined the scope of a platform for addressing these parties' grievances called the New World Information and Communication Order (NWICO). The result was a minor diplomatic storm in which western nations strongly condemned the report – amongst other things, they argued that it would limit press freedoms – and both the UK and the US withdrew from UNESCO completely (they later rejoined in 1997 and 2003, respectively). Perhaps the most important, and long-lasting, effects of the Media Imperialism Debate – the phrase 'media imperialism' was not introduced by the protagonists themselves, but was coined by the scholar Boyd-Barrett in 1977 – were the effects that it had upon scholarship, in particular by influencing the ideas of the then also emergent 'Cultural Imperialism School' (Tomlinson, 1991).

The precise antecedents of cultural imperialism are in fact various, and dependency theory and media imperialism were only two of the multiple influences that shaped it (and it is beyond my scope here to provide a more exhaustive account of its intellectual heritage). Also, many cultural imperialists took issue with certain features of dependency theory, and in particular with the latter's primary emphasis upon economic domination, rather than claims to, and representations of, cultural superiority, as the key source of western power over the Global South – or 'hegemony' (to use cultural imperialists' own language; Dossa, 2007). The notion that claims to cultural superiority took precedence here was first proposed in a sustained way by the Palestinian-American scholar Edward Said in his seminal book *Orientalism* (1978). This work drew heavily on the ideas of the French theorist Michel Foucault, whose concept of 'governmentality' proposed that ways of knowing the world played a crucial role within, and were therefore in a sense 'imminent to', any attempts to control it (see Foucault, 1969). For cultural imperialists, the implication was that Euro-American representations of the Global South as 'backwards' or 'lacking', or as in some other way 'inadequate' – a discourse which could be traced to pre-colonial times, but was no less central to modernization theory – performed a crucial role in justifying, and therefore in facilitating, Euro-American domination of the developing world.

Despite these theoretical divergences from dependency, scholars of cultural imperialism nevertheless reached quite similar conclusions to dependency theorists as to the role that mass media had played, and continues to play, both in propagating a kind of false consciousness among audiences in the developing world, and in directly supporting capitalist structures and interests. Therefore, cultural imperialists also drew attention to the ways in which media content produced in the west, yet transmitted to the Global South, encouraged individualism – and also represented other traits of US culture as 'superior' to their non-western counterparts. One early, and seminal, example of this line of analysis was Dorfman and Mattelart's *How to Read Donald Duck* [in Latin America], which although first published in 1971, still reads well even today. More generally, they argued – and even today, they continue to argue – that western media corporations have frequently operated as kind of propaganda machines in support of expansionist capitalist interests. Today, this line of argument is most commonly associated with the American linguist Noam Chomsky, whose *Manufacturing Consent: The Political Economy of the Mass Media* (1988), co-authored with Edward Herman, remains the modern classic in the field.

Feminist critiques

A second major critique, really set of critiques, of modernization theory also traces to the late 1960s, although became most explicit – and therefore had its greatest impact – in the 1970s. This was the so-called 'feminist critique' of development, which, in broad terms, can be understood as an attempt by scholars to bring the ideas and insights of 'second wave feminism' to bear upon an understanding both of the causes of underdevelopment and of potential solutions for it. If the 'first wave' of the global feminist movement refers to the sustained attempts that were made by predominantly Euro-American women's groups to gain women's suffrage (i.e. the right to vote) during the late nineteenth and early twentieth centuries, the 'second wave' refers to those new kinds of groups, and activism, which emerged throughout the world, in response to ongoing inequalities that women continued to experience during the 1960s. These inequalities became manifest in multiple ways in different contexts, and included everything from persistent cultural perceptions that women's bodies, opinions, and/or practices were inferior to men's, to ongoing political and economic imbalances between women and men

– as may be characterized by, for example, women being underrepresented in a country's parliament, or their being unpaid *vis-à-vis* male workers.

Like dependency theory, the ideas and ideology of second wave feminist theory were strongly influenced by Marxist thought. As a result, already by the late 1960s – that is, even before a distinctly 'feminist critique of development' had been made explicit – it was becoming clear that both dependency theory and feminist theory shared certain key features, and in other ways mirrored each other. For example, just as dependency theory argued that underdevelopment was *not* an outcome of any inherently inferior qualities of societies in the developing world, so feminist theory argued that women's unequal position was not, in any given context, an outcome of any innate inferiority on their part; just as dependency theory argued that underdevelopment was instead an outcome of specific histories, and the structures of inequality that these histories had generated, so feminist theory argued that women's inequality was everywhere an outcome of historically specific, and structural, factors; just as dependency theory focused upon the role of elites for facilitating and perpetuating underdevelopment, so feminists argued that women's inequality invariably reflected elite interests – given that elites were almost always, and everywhere, predominantly male groups. However, over time, feminist ideas began also to expand dependency theory, in particular by showing how and why underdevelopment often had a disproportionately negative effect upon women living in the developing world. This, in turn, led to an even more thoroughgoing critique of the logics and practices of modernization.

In 1970, a Danish development professional-turned-scholar, Ester Boserup, published what was to become not only the seminal work for the feminist critique of development, but also one of the most devastating attacks on modernization ever presented: *Woman's Role in Economic Development*. It is not an overstatement to say that Boserup's book – which has remained in print since its publication, and was revised as recently as 2007 – uses feminist thought to comprehensively challenge not only all the assumptions upon which modernization was built but, more importantly, to also debunk the consequences of its implementation in practice. Based on a detailed empirical analysis of a range of societies across the developing world, but especially in Africa and Asia, over a long timeframe, and through a comparison of these with some European societies' histories,

Boserup found that the very model of development envisaged by modernization – in which 'traditional', agricultural societies are progressively transformed into 'modern' ones through increased education/literacy, which in turn leads to increased urbanization, industrialization and, ultimately, to economic growth (cf. Lerner, 1958, above) – systematically works to the detriment of women. In fact, wherever in the world these stages of 'progress' towards modernization had actually occurred, they had invariably left all of the women in those places in a relatively economically, politically, and socially weaker position than they had been before such progress had started. This is because in any predominantly agricultural context, increased educational provision is much more likely to be taken up by boys, rather than girls, given how integral girls are to the productive – and reproductive – fortunes of the household. As a result, when increased education leads to growing urbanization, it is much more likely to be young men, rather than young women, who migrate to towns. Yet this in turn removes men from the agricultural workforce, thereby leaving the women who have 'stayed back home' in the rural areas of origin with more work to do. In turn, this results in those same women then falling even further behind in terms of education and health outcomes. In short, for women, it is a 'downward spiral'. Moreover, this process and the problems that it generates become further exacerbated with growing industrialization. Therefore, even where these processes do generate economic 'lift-off' – as they did, for example, in Europe following the industrial revolution (*c.* 1750) – they still leave women in a more difficult position.

Over the course of the 1970s, arguments such as Boserup's gained increasing traction not only amongst scholars, but also among development organizations and practitioners. On the one hand, this resulted in a growing recognition that any focus upon *only* the processes for economic growth was fundamentally chauvinistic, and therefore flawed. Instead, new models for development were required that could better identify additional measures for developmental 'progress' as well, related directly to women's experiences (who, after all, constitute half of the population in the developing world). This notion of multiple measures was later codified as the Human Poverty Index (HPI), which was a system of metrics developed by the Pakistani economist Mahbub al Haq and the Indian economist Amartya Sen for the UNDP in the 1990s. In addition to measuring economic growth, the HPI also – for each developing country – related that growth to other measures of potential progress, including women's rights, but also economic and social inequality, democracy, health outcomes, and environmental quality. The HPI was in turn superseded by the Multi-dimensional Poverty Index (MPI), which was developed by an Oxford University project in 2010 and included an even wider range of measures still. On the other hand, the growing impact of the feminist critique led to practically all development agencies drawing up more policies, and creating more projects, that were focused specifically on women. Over time, these efforts – which were bolstered by the UN's declaration of the period of 1975–1985 as the 'Decade for the Advancement for Women' – drew in more and more feminist groups in the Global South, and eventually became collectively known as the 'Women in Development (WID)' approach (for the best overview of the WID approach, see Collier, 1988). Even though WID focused largely upon women, of course, it too was later criticized for sharing too many of the same individualistic assumptions as modernization, and for therefore not going far enough in addressing some of the more structural constraints that women in the developing world faced (see, for example, Parpart, 1995). Yet according to advocates for the slightly later Gender and Development (GAD) movement, it was precisely these structural factors – that is, the wider social relations and institutions through which gendered roles (both male and female) were assigned in the first place – that were the root cause of women's subordination (Reeves and Baden, 2000).

Once again, the feminist critique of modernization implied a number of significant criticisms of M4D, as it was then conceived. And once again, these also became more explicit over time. Firstly, like dependency theorists, feminist scholars were generally sceptical of the notion that a transfer of media technologies from the First World to the developing world, as part of more general processes of 'technology transfer', would indeed address underdevelopment. For feminists, the key problem here was that all such transfers predominantly involved men, in that the western media companies producing and distributing such technologies were still, and in many ways still are, predominantly controlled by men. In addition, and more significantly, as/when households in the developing world gained ownership of new media devices, these often remained under the control of men for an extended period of time. This, in turn, limited women's access to any of the content that was broadcast through those devices. In other words, media transfers often resulted in men having *increased* control over women's access to information. Over the course of the 1970s, an increasing number of empirical studies from throughout the developing world showed this to be the general pattern (Koczberski, 1998). Secondly, and again mirroring arguments made by dependency theorists, feminists argued that modernization projects' attempts to use media to educate people in 'modern values', tended to end up focusing upon the education of only men – and this was especially true of those projects that were informed by Rogers' models of 'opinion leaders', given that in many real-world contexts a majority of these opinion leaders were male. Conversely, the kinds of cultural or traditional knowledge that M4D sought to displace – with 'scientific' knowledge – was in many rural agricultural contexts disproportionally known by certain categories of people, including elders and *women* (Saunders, 2003).

Finally, and again echoing arguments made in relation to media content and cultural imperialism, feminist scholars also found that even when M4D *did* result in the developing world gaining increased access to media content, this content nevertheless tended to be heavily biased towards a male worldview. In consequence, it was in fact more likely to reinforce, rather than to challenge, any existing sense of inferiority that its female audience might already hold, and it certainly wouldn't inspire them to challenge the structural causes of their inequality. Over the course of the 1970s, these sorts of arguments gained increasing strength as a growing body of feminist scholarship on the media – based on media content produced and broadcast in Europe, America, and the developing world – produced detailed content analyses which showed that many forms of media content at that time were systematically biased towards a male perspective. For example, studies of television drama content often found that such dramas had more male characters than female ones, and that the female characters tended to conform to negative stereotypes of women (in that they were overly emotional or irrational; see Dow and Condit, 2005). Meanwhile, in 1975, a seminal article published by the British feminist film theorist Laura Mulvey, called 'Visual Pleasure and Narrative Cinema' – which amongst other things, is widely credited for having introduced psychoanalytic theory into film studies – argued that during the 'classic era' of Hollywood Cinema (1917–1960), all Hollywood films invited their audiences to see the world through a 'male gaze'. In other words, they all encouraged all of their viewers – be they male or female – to identify with films' male characters (and throughout this period, most films' characters were also predominantly male) as the active agents of its narrative, and the female characters as simply passive sites of pleasure. Given these findings, then, it was argued that it is simply impossible to imagine how increasing developing world access to mainstream radio, television, and/or film content could possibly further their empowerment.

Not all feminist scholars accepted the ideas of theorists such as Boserup, and their concerns began debates that extended feminist critiques still further. For example, in what became a seminal contribution in its own right, the Indian-born gender studies scholar Chandra Talpade Mohanty published an article called 'Under Western Eyes: Feminist Scholarship and Colonial Discourses' (1984), in which she challenged Boserup and others for regarding *all* women in the developing world as a single, monolithic category. For Mohanty, this inevitably obscured the fact that that experiences of development would be undoubtedly very different for different groups of women, such as for 'urban, middleclass, educated Egyptian housewives', as compared with 'their uneducated, poor maids' (to use Mohanty's own examples, 1984: 344). Not only would the 'structures of development' (as it were) be imposed very differently upon these two different groups of women, but the range of choices and strategies that were available to each as a means for 'navigating' those structures would also be highly variegated. As a result, for Mohanty, it is quite wrong to conclude, as Boserup does, that modernization necessarily results in *all* women in the developing world becoming victims. Instead, any such process of change is more likely to produce both 'winners' and 'losers'. More fundamentally, Mohanty also worried that the feminist critique's very focus upon the different experiences of 'men' vs. 'women', anyway defined everyone's experience of development in terms of *only* gendered identities. Yet, as she pointed out, experiences of, and responses to, development might be equally shaped by other kinds of identities besides, including one's sexuality, religion, ethnicity, or locality (*ibid.*, 336–337). Moreover, and although this point remains only implicit in Mohanty's article (*ibid.*, 337), these arguments also have a bearing upon our understanding of the relationship between media content and gender. Because they suggest that even if media content *is* biased towards a male worldview, such content may nevertheless have a different effect upon, and it will certain draw quite different responses from, different kinds of female viewers – depending on their class, occupation, age, sexuality, religion, ethnicity or locality. In other words, such content may draw very different interpretations or 'readings', even 'counter-readings', from different viewers. These ideas, which in some ways anticipated the arguments of 'third wave' feminism – which emerged from the 1990s onwards – were later explored in much greater depth in anthropologist Lila Abu-Lughod's ethnographic study *Dramas of Nationhood: The Politics of Television in Egypt* (2004).

Environmental critique

Finally, the early 1970s also saw the emergence of the environmental critique of modernization – and therefore the first currents of what we now know as the arguments for, and the models of, 'sustainable development'. Although the political and intellectual influences that shaped this critique were multiple and various – and included the anti-nuclear movement from the late 1950s onwards, the youth movements of the 1960s (especially the 'hippie movement'), the establishment of 'Earth Day' in 1970, the publication of James Lovelock's Theory of Gaia (1972), Arne Naess' philosophy of Deep Ecology (1973), and so on – they in fact came together into one quite simple, and fundamental, argument against modernization. This was the argument that modernization's central goal for societies of the Global South – that they should strive for economic progress, or growth, through increased urbanization and industrialization – was fundamentally flawed, because it did not take into account the negative impact that both increased urbanization and industrialization have on the environment. Further, such growth could not be sustained everywhere – and forever – anyway (i.e. not all societies could continue to become more and more 'modern' indefinitely), because this would require an endless input of natural resources as raw materials to sustain, and it would also – given the nature of both urbanization and industrialization – result in unlimited volumes of pollutants being put back into the atmosphere, and in an endless proliferation of other forms of waste besides. Yet as all of the movements and philosophies listed above directly argued (albeit each in its own quite different way): Earth's natural resources are *not* infinite, and a future based on endless waste is equally unsustainable – and we now know this for certain, of course, thanks to the burgeoning science of anthropogenic climate change (or 'global warming', as it is today more commonly known).

Although the environmental critique began as a diffuse set of arguments, it soon came to have a major impact upon international development practice. As early as 1972, the UN convened a major international conference on the subject, the Conference on the Human Environment (in Stockholm, Sweden), and this soon led to all of the major development agencies adopting a raft of new environmental policies, and implementing a wide range of new projects focused on the environment. In 1983, the Secretary General of the UN, General Javier Pérez de Cuéllar, partly in an attempt to keep the 'spirit' of the Stockholm Conference alive, set up the famous UN World Commission on Environment and Development (WCED), which, chaired by the former Norwegian Prime Minister Gro Harlem Brundtland, is today much better known as simply the 'Brundtland Commission'. Between 1983 and 1987, Brundtland spent over 900 days interviewing a large cross-section of the 'development elite' (i.e. senior development practitioners at USAID, the World Bank, UNDP, and other agencies) as a means both for understanding current development practice and for thinking about how this could be made more environmentally sustainable in the future. The results were published in the final report from the commission, the seminal *Our Common Future* (usually known as the 'Brundtland Report', 1987), which made a raft of recommendations as to how development might continue to be pursued, yet in ways that would not compromise the needs of future generations (i.e. in ways that wouldn't undermine 'inter-generational equality'). Of the report's many key insights was its first extended definition of the phrase 'sustainable development', which, today, has become probably one of the most important concepts in all of international development. In these ways, Brundtland remains a key document, even though it was later criticized along similar lines to the WID approach – that is, for ultimately accepting too many of the basic assumptions of modernization. In particular, and reflecting the fact that the report was based largely upon interviews with senior development officials, all of whom were at that time steeped in the theory and practice of modernization, it ultimately suggested that economic growth could be used to, in effect, 'offset' environmental degradation (in that, as developing countries got richer, they would have more money to spend on environmental protection measures). This notion that further growth might offset environmental challenges remains highly controversial, even today (for many environmentalists, the idea was at the time of Brundtland, and remains today, highly questionable). Nevertheless, despite these criticisms, the work of the Brundtland Commission remained highly influential, and it can be seen as in some ways the forerunner to later events such as the UN Earth

Summit (held in Rio de Janeiro, in 1992) and the UN World Summit on Sustainable Development (Johannesburg, 2002), both of which further extended our models for sustainable development.

Although few scholars or activists working within the environment critique of modernization ever engaged directly with the models and practices of M4D, the critique nevertheless had two important implications for the way in which we think about the role of media in international development. The first stemmed from its implied critique of the notion that ongoing transfers of physical media technologies (or any other kinds of technologies, for that matter), from the Global North to the South, were to be encouraged. This is because, irrespective of whether or not these transfers did, or did not, generate economic growth in Africa, Asia, and Latin America, they certainly did, always and everywhere, generate waste products – especially in urban areas – and these would only accumulate over time. In this way, and although the full implications of what was being suggested here were appreciated at the time, scholars contributing to the environmental critique were the first to anticipate the likely effects of (what we now call) 'e-waste' within the Global South. Today, this has become perhaps one of the most pressing issues in relation to media in the developing world, as we shall see in a later chapter. The second implication of the environmental critique was that modernization's goal of displacing, or replacing, traditional knowledge with modern scientific knowledge, through the latter's dissemination via mass media, was equally wrong-headed – albeit for a quite different set of reasons. For environmentalists, the entire premise of displacing traditional knowledge was misplaced because, if it were to be successful, it would lead to a significant loss of diverse cultural understandings, beliefs, and practices relevant for managing natural resources. This stemmed from the conviction that any cultural group that had inhabited a particular place for an extended period of time would likely have built up a significant depth of 'traditional environmental knowledge' (TEK) about how best to live within that environment in a sustainable way (today, TEK is more commonly referred to as 'indigenous knowledge', or IK). In different cultures, such knowledge could take many different forms, and might include elements of anything from cosmological stories to songs and dances to oral histories. However, the assumption was that in whatever form it took, such IK was not only always valuable, but was also something from which modern scientific knowledge might have a great deal to learn.

Post-colonial development

By the early 1980s, the three major critiques of dependency, feminism, and environmentalism had had such a profound impact that a number of scholars and other commentators were beginning to declare that the theories and practices of modernization were simply no longer 'fit for purpose'. Moreover, because since Truman's speech modernization had been synonymous with all forms of 'development', it followed that *development itself* was no longer fit for purpose either. A number of especially vocal critics – such as the Colombian-American anthropologist Arturo Escobar, the Mexican economist-turned-activist Gustavo Estevar, the Iranian Minister for Science (and later UN official) Majod Rahnema, and the German sociologist Wolfgang Sachs – even began to talk openly of development being 'dead' (Rahnema and Bawtree, 1997). The introduction to Sachs' famous edited collection on this subject, called *The Development Dictionary* (1992), is worth quoting at length. As part of a wider tract, which draws on many of the ideas of dependency, feminism, and environmentalism, as I have described them above, Sachs argues: 'The idea of development stands like a ruin in the intellectual landscape. Delusion and disappointment, failures and crimes have been the steady companions of development and they tell a common story: it did not work ... But above all, the hopes and desires which made the idea fly, are now exhausted: development has grown obsolete' (1992: 1).

Theorists such as Escobar, Estevar, Rahnema, and Sachs, like dependency theorists before them, emphasized that the issues and problems facing developing countries were *not* a result of any internal deficiencies, but were instead an outcome of the ways in which those places had become incorporated into European trading, and later political, empires, from the sixteenth century onwards. They also stressed that the idea of developing nations needing interventions from the Global North in order to 'progress' (i.e. Truman's definition of transitive development) was a fiction, an ideology that had been made up by the US and other wealthy countries, in order to justify their ongoing interventions into Africa, Asia, and Latin America in benevolent terms. Finally, they highlighted that this fiction bore a striking resemblance to the kinds of ideologies that European powers had used to justify their earlier colonial interventions into the Global South in similar terms – and in many parts of the developing world, the advent of the 'development age' also overlapped with the era of decolonization (Young, 2016). In other words, for these theorists, if development was first and foremost a discourse, it was a neo-colonial discourse at that (Rahnema and Bawtree, 1997). Reflecting these arguments, the ideas of theorists such as Escobar, Estevar, Rahnema, and Sachs are often referred to as 'post-colonial' development theory (for an excellent critical engagement on post-colonialism, see also Gupta, 1998). However, because their overall project primarily aimed at not only problematizing – or critiquing – modernization/development, but in fact at doing away with it altogether, I find it more useful to refer to this body of work as 'post-development' (Sachs, 1992).

For these theorists, the problems facing the societies of the developing world remained as pressing as ever, and they also did not deny that those same polities needed to undergo processes of change in order to address those problems. Rather, the theorists and activists of post-development argued that efforts to bring about those changes needed to give up on the earlier tenets of modernization – with its transitive approach, its overly economic focus, its emphasis upon individuals, its elitist (and in other ways 'top-down') orientation, and, above all, its 'one-size-fits all' methodology. Instead, efforts for purposive social change needed to begin from a much more 'participatory' approach – that is, one that: was cognizant of the actual problems that people living in the developing world faced (which are invariably a combination of economic, political, and social pressures); took into account the structural challenges that not just individuals, but entire categories of people, ran up against; that were sensitive to the needs not only of community leaders, but also of 'ordinary' people as well (i.e. that were more 'bottom-up' in orientation); and, above all, gave equal weight to people's own thoughts and ideas about these problems, and provided them with some opportunity to define their own potential solutions to them.

Participatory communication

The model for how this might work in practice derived from participatory action research (PAR). PAR did not, in fact, begin within international development *per se*, but was instead a slightly older, and more broad-based, intellectual movement in the Global South, which, inspired by the work of the Brazilian philosopher Paolo Freire – especially his seminal book *Pedagogy of the Oppressed* (1970) – sought to encourage people to define their collective problems on their own terms (using their own, evidence-based reasoning when doing so), and to come up with their own, community-based, responses to these. Moreover, the overall emphasis of PAR was to encourage groups to understand their problems less in narrowly economic terms, and more so as fundamentally political in nature (as a result of which, the overall goal for PAR was ultimately to facilitate communities to achieve their own forms of collective empowerment; Gegeo, 1998). In these ways, then, PAR clearly resonated with the aims for post-development, and it is therefore understandable why it should have quickly become so influential within the new forms of international development practice that emerged out of the three critiques outlined above – indeed, to such a degree that those same kinds of practices soon became collectively known as simply 'participatory development' (Rist, 2014).

Following the example of PAR, participatory development aimed to include community members in all aspects of project design, implementation, and evaluation, within all development interventions. However, from the outset, there was never one agreed way, or even set of ways, for how to do this. Instead, over the next decade or so, an extremely wide range of different kinds of tools and techniques for incorporating PAR into development work was developed both by academics and by development practitioners (Slocum, 2003). The kinds of PAR techniques that emerged, or were significantly elaborated upon, at this time included things like: *role reversal* – a method in which ordinary people in the Global South would be invited to imagine themselves as a development professional (for example, as an official from the World Bank), and to think about how they would design and implement development projects in this role; *transect walks* – a method in which a small group of people would be invited to guide a development practitioner on a route around their locality of residence, in order to identify different kinds of land use and crop distributions, and to discuss any issues or problems that they might be experiencing in relation to these (Kangalawe, 2017); *focus-group discussions* – in which a sample group from a given target population would be gathered together to collectively discuss the causes of a specific developmental problem or problems, and the possible solutions to those problems; *photo elicitation* – a technique in which groups of people would be invited to reflect on an issue or problem, and possible solutions to it, by being shown photographs of that issue or problem that could be passed around and collectively discussed (Collier and Collier, 1967); and *social mapping* – a technique in which ordinary people, and especially marginalized people, would be invited to make maps of what they themselves perceived to be the economic, political, and social resources available to them in their area of residence, and to think about how these various resources might relate to each other (Bell and Aggleton, 2016).

So diverse did the field become, that the first significant attempt to provide an overview of all of the methods of participatory development, Robert Chambers' *Rural Development: Putting the Last First* (1983), could do little more than to group them into four general categories of methods. These categories were constituted of: (1) *group dynamics techniques* – all of which focused upon improving empathy, and communication, between development subjects and development agencies (role reversal is one example of this kind of technique); (2) *sampling methods* – all of which involved recording 'typical' elements of a given social world in order to understand its totality (transect walks fit into this category); (3) *interview techniques* – all of which involved group interviewing methods of one kind or another (focus groups and photo elicitation are two examples); and (4) *visualization tools* – all of which, as the name suggests, attempted to get people to 'picture' their issues and problems in certain kinds of ways (social mapping is one example of this approach). Finally, I would also note here that during this period, the methods for participatory development were also sometimes referred to collectively as 'Participatory Rural Appraisal' (PRA) and as 'Rapid Rural Appraisal' (RRA; Chambers, 1983). Over the years, scholars of international development have tried to develop fine-grained distinctions between the definitions of participatory development in general, and of PRA and of RRA. However, because the very same sets of methods are referred by all of these terms, in practice it is probably easier to just think of them as in fact one and the same thing.

Diverse though all of the new methods for participatory development were, they also shared a number of key features in common. First, and most importantly, they all focused upon *not* individuals, but instead *group dynamics*, which reflects their underlying logic that developmental change is to be achieved not by changing individual outlooks or behaviours, but by altering social structures and contexts. Second, because of their emphasis upon gaining the input of ordinary people, and because literacy rates were sometimes quite low among populations in the developing world, they all relied primarily upon oral or visual communication, as opposed to reading and writing, as a means for data collection. Third, because they all aimed to secure the

Media, empowerment, and agency • 135

Figure 3.1 *Participatory methods in development*

Source: Image courtesy of Wikimedia

detailed, and the *extended*, input of local people, they were almost always 'non-linear' in nature. In other words, reflecting the fact that such detailed and extended input was unlikely to ever produce a neat, ideal 'pathway' from identification of problem → design of response → implementation of response → evaluation of response → 'lessons-learned' for future projects, participatory approaches almost always involved a much 'messier' process of back and forth, or multi-directional communication, between the participants and the agencies involved, at all stages of the ideal linear 'project cycle' described above. Fourth, and also because of this aim for the detailed and extended input of ordinary people, in practice these approaches usually ended up being quite small-scale in nature. In other words, not only did they in practice involve quite limited numbers of participants and in quite 'intimate' settings, such as in people's homes, they also ended up being employed more by smaller international development organizations – and especially by smaller non-governmental organizations (NGOs) – than by the larger development organizations such as USAID or the World Bank (Lewis and Kanji, 2009). Fifth, and again because of the emphasis upon having ordinary people's input, they all recast the role of development professionals – and by extension, development organizations as well – from that of 'provider' to that of 'facilitator'. In so doing, they attempted to alter the power dynamics within the 'development encounter', in an attempt to ensure that development interventions were not just 'handed down' by development agencies to people in the developing world, but were instead an outcome of some sort of 'dialogue' between the two (Gumucio-Dagron, 2001). In short, participatory methods aimed to ensure that ordinary people who were engaged in development projects did indeed have some agency over how those projects were carried out. Finally, they were all highly flexible in nature, in that, although they all involved some definitions of 'best practice', they were all also designed to be inherently adaptable to the specific contexts in which they were being used.

The key point here is that PAR implied an entirely different role for media within the development enterprise. Against the modernization approach to M4D – with its objectives of spreading media technologies as a form of technology transfer in its own right, and in then using those same technologies as a means for disseminating 'useful information' from the west to the developing world, or from urban centres in the developing world to their rural hinterlands – the emphasis now became upon working with the communications environments that people already had available to them, and with which they were already comfortable. Instead of thinking about media as a tool for the 'one-way' communication of information that development organizations had deemed in advance to be useful, it was now thought of instead as a tool for dialogical processes in which ideas could be shared between facilitating agencies and participants and, more importantly, within and between participant groups themselves. One of the key early advocates for, and theorists of, this shift was again Luis Beltran (see especially Beltran, 1976, 1980). By around the mid-1980s, this alternative approach was beginning to be seen as an entirely new 'paradigm' for M4D, called 'Participatory Communication for Social Change'. Rather confusingly, this is sometimes referred to as just 'participatory communication', at other times as only 'communication for social change'. It is sometimes also called 'communication for development', or 'C4D' for short. All of these phrases refer to more or less the same thing. For clarity here, I will use only the phrase 'participatory communication' throughout the remainder of this chapter.

However, whether or not participatory communication *was* ever an actual 'paradigm', in the strict meaning of that term (i.e. a clear and coherent framework for defining practice) is open to debate. On the one hand, a number of theorists, from the early 1990s onwards, *did* try to define a coherent underlying theoretical foundation for participatory communication, and to use this as a means for defining a definitive set of practices for the approach. For example, in 1991, the media studies scholar Jan Servaes argued that a basic human right to communicate, to speak, and to be heard was the underlying principle that held together what he called the 'multiplicity paradigm', which for him animated all forms of participatory communication (Servaes, 1991). The same year, another media theorist, Srivinas Melkote, argued that a co-equal process of knowledge sharing between sources and users of development information was the distinctive feature of what he called 'Another Development', which he thought drove participatory communication (Melkote, 1991). In 1992, John Friedmann saw an attempt to dissolve pre-existing hierarchies – between the genders, between the generations, and between other social categories – as the main dynamic of what he termed 'the empowerment framework', and within which he placed participatory communication (Friedmann, 1992). And in 1996, Raff Carmen argued that attempts to reclaim development subjects' own *agency* was the underlying principle that held together what he called 'autonomous development', the goals of which were forwarded by participatory communication (Carmen, 1996). On the other hand, however, and reflecting the overall diffuse nature of participatory development in general, and of the tools and techniques that were used in pursuit of it, it could be argued that participatory communication always meant different things to different people, and always involved a quite diffuse set of approaches. In this view, PAR is probably better thought of as not a distinct paradigm, so much as a set of generally similar – in some ways overlapping, in other ways distinct – strategies and approaches for using media within development research and for trying to achieve development goals (Waisbord, 2001; Lennie and Tacchi, 2013; Melkote and Steeves, 2015).

Nevertheless, whether or not one chooses to opt for a 'strong' or for a 'weak' definition of participatory communication, it is clear that the advent of the approach, and its various new methods, certainly did result in many of the old ideas concerning modernization and M4D becoming displaced, and in media becoming employed within development programmes and projects in entirely new kinds of ways.

For example, PAR's general emphasis upon concepts such as empathy and communal understanding, and its associated methods of role reversal, and other group dynamics techniques, led to the advent of what has come to be seen as perhaps the most influential of the many innovations associated with participatory communication: Theatre for Development (or TFD; it is sometimes also called Community-Based Theatre, or Popular Theatre). The concept of TFD traces, ultimately, to the 'Theatre in Education (TIE) Movement' that developed in the mid-1960s in the UK, as part of a then broader shift towards 'child-centric' pedagogical approaches – a shift that was particularly marked within the UK's public schooling sector (Epskamp, 2006). The basic premise of the TIE Movement was that children's learning could be improved by getting them to 'act out' situations in groups, in ways that required them to improvise and engage in role-play. This was thought not only to improve concentration, but also to increase argumentation, empathy, and collaboration (Nogueira, 2002; Kamlongera, 2005). In 1974, a Canadian-born educationalist, Ross Kidd, began an experiment to introduce these same approaches within an international development context in Botswana. The experiment, called 'Laedza Batanani', involved a theatre troupe touring villages to stage performances relating to issues and problems in the farming sector. These performances typically involved a combination of songs, dances, and puppetry, and were also highly interactive in nature, in that they required audience members not only to have input into the narrative of the drama, but also to come on stage and act out certain parts (Epskamp, 2006: 14–15). So popular did Laedza become in Botswana, that it became the focus for an annual nationwide 'Festival of Community Awakening'. Following this success, Kidd and his growing network of international collaborators introduced the concept to other parts of the developing world as well, such that by the time Kidd had finished his PhD thesis on the subject a few years later, TFD had become already established across Africa, in the Caribbean, and in parts of South Asia as well (Box 3.1). Its early development also benefitted from the input of some of Africa's greatest theatre directors of the period, such as that of Nigerian Steve Ogah Abah (Plastow, 2014). Later, the TFD movement gained some further impetus from the growing popularity of 'entertainment-education' with which it has at least some features in common (Epskamp, 2006).

Readers of this book may be wondering how our broader discussion of *media* for development has come to include a discussion of theatre

Box 3.1 Jana Sanskriti, India

Although Theatre for Development (TFD) was first developed in Africa, it quickly proved highly popular in other parts of the Global South as well, especially in areas that already had well-established dramaturgical traditions. Today, one of the best-known examples is the Jana Sanskriti Centre for the Theatre of the Oppressed, which was started by Indian theatre director Sanjoy Ganguly in a village outside Kolkata (Calcutta) in the state of West Bengal in 1985. As the full name of the organization suggests, Jana Sanskriti took its inspiration not only from the TIE Movement, and from Ross Kidd's experiments with this in a development setting, but also from the ideas of Brazilian theatre director Augusto Boal's 'Theatre of the Oppressed'. Boal's concept of Theatre of the Oppressed, which he outlined in a book of the same name in 1979, was that from classical Greece onwards, the western state had used theatre, and what Boal regarded as its later transformations such as radio and television soap operas, to extend its powers of oppression by propagating a kind of 'false consciousness' among its citizens. His vision, then, was for an alternative kind of theatre (i.e. a 'Theatre of the Oppressed') that moved in the other direction, by deliberately and explicitly challenging all forms of state control. Therefore, Theatre of the Oppressed, and the kinds of projects that took inspiration from it (such as Jana Sanskriti) were always much more politically motivated than other forms of TFD, and their performances were much more politically charged. Moreover, all of this resonated particularly strongly in West Bengal, where theatre had been historically controlled, first by powerful feudal landlords (almost all of whom were men) and later by the highly conservative Communist Party. Under both regimes, theatre had also remained very exclusive. Against this background, then, Jana Sanskriti's politically progressive and inclusive philosophy proved particularly attractive, especially to women. From the outset, this was put into practice by small teams of Jana Sanskriti members, who would travel out to villages and hold a series of participatory theatrical workshops in which local people were encouraged to 'act out' the ways in which they experienced oppression, and to perform their 'ideal' responses to this – no matter how angry, even violent, these might be. So popular did the format become, that by the late 2000s Jana Sanskriti had over 300 permanent members working in over 30 teams, who were travelling to villages not only throughout West Bengal, but all over India. Meanwhile, in its state of origin, Jana Sanskriti had developed into a full-blown social movement for the ending of traditional systems of patriarchy, and for the emancipation of women.

Sources: Mills (2009), Da Costa (2010), Ganguly (2010).

and dramaturgy, which is not really a type of 'media' at all – or, at least, not according to our most common definitions of that term. However, it must be remembered here that within participatory communication, the emphasis was not upon electronic media *per se*, but upon wider *communication contexts*, which included both electronic media and other kinds of 'communication channels' as well (Lennie and Tacchi, 2013). The idea was to understand the full range of ways through which people already communicated – be these through electronic means or through face-to-face communications – and to then engage these for development purposes. In this sense, the use of theatre as a primary means for getting people collectively to articulate and to explore the challenges they faced, presented itself as perhaps even the perfect medium (Box 3.2). This is because, on the one hand, TFD tended to make intuitive sense to people, wherever it was introduced (it still does), not least because practically all human societies – even if they do not have high degrees of literacy – have some sort of oral and dramaturgical traditions to which it can be related (Kamlongera, 2005). On the other hand, TFD also lent itself to the general features of PAR approaches as I have described them above, in that: it was particularly well suited for capturing extended engagements with development projects (as it allowed for the same plays to be reworked again and again, and changed each time); it lent itself to small-scale and intimate settings (and it is therefore no coincidence that TFD became particularly favoured by smaller NGOs); it is in practice highly effective at reworking the power dynamics within the development encounter, since within the 'play' of each TFD performance, development subjects can act out the roles of development professionals and/or invite – even require – the facilitators to act out their own positions (this is parodied to wonderful effect in Malian director Abderrahmane Sissako's 2006 film *Bamako*, in which local actors play the role of World Bank officials during a fictional trial in which the alleged 'crimes' of the Bretton-Woods Institution's failed development policies are prosecuted by an African 'village court'). It is also endlessly flexible and adaptable. Indeed, it is a truism to say that no two theatrical performances – anywhere in the world – are ever precisely the same, of course.

Box 3.2 Wan Smolbag, Vanuatu

Another part of the developing world in which TFD has made a significant impact is Oceania, which again has a long history of indigenous oral and dramaturgical traditions. In 1989, two British aid workers, Jo Dorras and Peter Walker, along with 15 local actors, set up a TFD troupe in Vanuatu – an island nation group in the Southern Pacific Ocean, roughly 1,000 miles east of northern Australia – and which, like other parts of Melanesia, has a long tradition of indigenous theatre. The troupe was called 'Wan Smolbag' (which is the local pidgin, Bislama, for 'one small bag'), the idea being that the group needed only one small bag to carry costumes, and a few props, in order to put on plays on any of Vanuatu's 65 inhabited islands. Wan Smolbag's approach to TFD was highly innovative, in that, rather than getting the audience to participate in the staged plays themselves (or the 'big plays' as the group called them), they would instead hold a series of small participatory theatre workshops and script-writing sessions beforehand, from which elements for the big play's dramaturgy and dialogue would develop. The members of Wan Smolbag would then perform the big play itself. From the outset, this format proved highly popular, given that the involvement of only professional actors in the big plays made these performances much more polished, while the involvement of local people in the initial development processes made them much more realistic and engaging of the actual issues and problems that ordinary people faced in their day-to-day lives. Indeed, so popular did Wan Smolbag's shows become, that one of its performances, *Zero Balans* (2011), was seen by more than 10% of the entire population of Vanuatu's capital, Port Vila. For six years, the troupe received core funding from Britain's Department for International Development, during which time it developed over 50 big plays – on subjects as wide-ranging as environmental management, good governance, maternal health, youth justice issues, and HIV/AIDS awareness – which it performed not only all over Vanuatu (including on some of the country's most remote islands), but increasingly across other parts of Oceania as well. From around the mid-1990s onwards, the group also increasingly branched out from live theatrical performances only, to embrace other media channels as well. Since then, Won Smolbag has also produced a large number of radio and video dramas, and spin-off leaflets and books from its many big plays.

Sources: Gumucio-Dagron (2001), Taylor and Gaskell (2007), and Woodward (2014).

Figure 3.2 *A TFD group, the Kigezi Rugo Actors*

Source: Author

Yet participatory communication also encompassed more than just TFD. It also involved radio, television, and latterly mobile phones and the internet being employed within development programmes in entirely new kinds of ways. For example, at around the same time that Kidd was beginning his experiment with T4D, development organizations working in Latin America were starting to explore ways in which radio phone-in shows, especially on local and community radio stations, could be used as a kind of focus group 'writ large'. In these experiments, potentially anyone with a stake in an issue under discussion could ring up the show to put their opinion forward, which would then be heard – and engaged with – by a *much* larger audience than could ever be achieved in a 'face-to-face' focus-group event. Such discussions could also be potentially sustained over a longer period of time, if and when a regular phone-in show returned to the same topic again and again (Huesca, 1995). This model proved highly effective and was later used extensively in participatory communications projects, especially in the literally thousands of projects that were begun in Africa, especially, in response to the HIV/AIDS epidemic. Radio phone-in shows, of the sort that were first trialled in Latin America, became one of the main tools through which medical NGOs working in Africa responded to that crisis (Adam and Harford, 1999). A similar approach has been also used in a variety of other contexts as well, including in contexts of post-war reconstruction. For example, in the early 2000s, Britain's Department for International Development set up an entire radio station in Northern Uganda, called Mega FM, in order to broadcast radio phone-in shows to a regional population that was still deeply traumatized by ongoing violence related to the insurgency of Joseph Kony's Lord's Resistance Army (Otim, 2009). It is testament to how effective Mega FM was in this mission that on a number of occasions, Joseph Kony himself phoned in to debate specific points that had been made by other callers (Vokes, 2007a). Participatory communication projects have also employed radio in other ways as well. For example, also in the early 2000s, I personally pioneered the use of 'radio elicitation' as a tool for conducting both one-on-one and focus group discussions. Like photo elicitation before it, this involves using radio programming about some or other development-related problem as the basis for interviews in which people are invited to reflect upon both the issue at hand and possible solutions to that problem (the techniques for doing this, and the potential advantages of it, are discussed in Vokes, 2007b). More recently, participatory communication projects have also used 'reality' television genres, mobile phones, and social media as means for exploring group dynamics, for sampling, and for gathering participants' testimonies and ideas, on ever-wider scales (Burger, 2015; Cupples, 2015; Artz, 2016). Following the mobile phone 'revolution' and the rise of the internet and social media, participatory geographic information systems (GIS) has been also a burgeoning field (see Chapter 5).

From the 1980s onwards, the impact of participatory communication was so great that it entered the 'mainstream' of M4D. It never completely replaced modernization approaches to M4D – which as we have seen, also continued to thrive throughout this period, and have in some areas remained influential, even up until the present time. Nevertheless, participatory communication gained growing recognition, even amongst the largest, and most important, international development organizations and forums. As a result, participatory techniques and methods became integrated into a greater range of development projects. One of the first major organizations to explicitly acknowledge participatory communication's utility was the UN's Food and Agriculture Organization (FAO), which, in 1984, even defined the entire field of M4D as 'a social process towards common understanding and concerted action of all involved in a development initiative' (Servaes, cited in Lennie and Tacchi, 2013: 5). In the late 1980s, the UN inaugurated a series of Inter-Agency Round Tables on Communication for Development, as a means for raising the profile of participatory communication, and for exploring ways in which it may be more effectively integrated across the entire international development industry. These round tables have continued to be held on a regular basis; the most recent and thirteenth was held in Rome in September 2014. In 1999, UNAIDS published what became its highly influential *Communications Framework for HIV/AIDS: A New Direction*, which in a sense formalized participatory communication's already dominant role within M4D responses to the epidemic (see above). And in 2006, the FAO and the World Bank co-organized the first World Congress on Communication for Development (WCCD), which also sought to raise the profile of participatory communication across the international development industry. Once again, the WCCD defined all forms of M4D as a 'social process based on dialogue', and as being 'about seeking change at different levels including listening, building trust, sharing knowledge and skills, building policies, debating and learning for sustained and meaningful change' (Lennie and Tacchi, 2013: 5).

Indigenous media

At around the same time that PAR and participatory communication were becoming established within international development, a broadly similar phenomenon was being elaborated upon by visual studies' scholars and ethnographic film-makers, which became known as 'indigenous media' (IM). Like participatory communication, IM also focused upon how electronic audio-visual media – in its case, video-cameras, VHS video-decks, and televisions – could be harnessed as tools for communicating collective understandings and issues, and for generating increased collective engagement with these. Like participatory education, IM was also animated by a broadly similar set of theoretical concerns, especially those that related to how electronic media might be used to further people's 'right to communicate', how these media could be used to challenge social identities and political hierarchies, and how media might empower people to reclaim their own sense of agency. However, unlike participatory communication, IM was concerned not with all populations throughout the developing world, but only – as its name suggests – with indigenous minorities, be they living in countries of the Global North or the South. Compared with participatory communication, IM's methods were if anything even more 'open ended' – indeed, they were in some ways entirely 'experimental' in nature. Finally, in a further divergence from participatory communication, IM also went on to have a more complicated political and institutional history, in that – a few notable exceptions aside – it was never broadly taken up by international development organizations, yet in some countries, at least, *did* go on to have a major impact within mainstream media industries.

In 1966, a Professor of Communication at the University of Pennsylvania, Sol Worth, and a Professor of Anthropology at San Francisco State University, John Adair, together with one of Worth's former students, Richard Chalfen, began the first ever IM project, with members of the indigenous Navajo Nation, in Pine Springs, Arizona, USA. The aim of the project was to examine whether this academic team could teach film-making techniques to members of a cultural group that was vastly different from their own, and if so, whether the resulting films would be in some ways (in what ways?) specifically 'Navajo' in character. In pursuit of these aims, the researchers identified Navajo participants who had had no – or very little – prior exposure to electronic media, and then provided these people with eight hours of film-making training per day over a two-month period. However, in what became the model for all IM projects worldwide, this training was carefully designed to focus upon only the technical aspects of film-making – such as how to operate a camera (the team used 16-mm film cameras), how to edit the resulting rushes, and how to project the finished film – and to avoid any discussion of *what* to film or *how* to film it. In other words, the instructions scrupulously avoided providing any guidance on such things as 'storyboarding', subject selection, image composition, scene design, filmic narrative, and character development – all of which would be routinely taught on any film production course in any US university – in order to avoid any biases being introduced into what kinds of filmic 'texts' that the participants might end up producing. In this way, like PAR, the methods of IM were ultimately designed to facilitate members of the community using media to tell stories in their own ways.

The project team ended up working particularly closely with three male and five female Navajo participants – Mike Anderson, Susie Benally, Al Clah, Alta Kahn, Johnny Nelson, Mary Jane Tsosie, and Maxine Tsosie – who between them produced seven silent films. These became known collectively as the 'Navajo Films Themselves', and later became famous both within international documentary film circles and also, more importantly, among the Navajo Nation itself. Certainly, all of the seven documentaries were technically highly accomplished. More significantly, though, and as Worth and Adair later argued in their book about the project, *Through Navajo Eyes* (1972), each of the films demonstrated structural patterns that made them distinctively 'Navajo'. In particular, the films' general lack of facial close-ups, their inclusion of extended sequences of people just walking, and their constant use of 'jump cuts', were all interpreted as reflections of Navajo oral traditions and social norms, and of the structures of the Navajo language. For example, Worth and Adair argued that the focus on walking reflected Navajo mythology (in which central characters are frequently depicted as walking between places and events); that the lack of facial close-ups reflected a Navajo taboo on 'looking people in the eye'; and that the jump cuts were an elaboration of the rules of Navajo grammar (although for alternatives to these interpretations, see especially Pack, 2012).

Although Worth, Adair, and Chalfen's project was primarily an academic experiment, its unique methodology demonstrated how film-making could be used as a tool for articulating distinct 'worldviews' – or, in other words, for communicating forms of cultural self-expression. Moreover, and as Faye Ginsburg later elaborated upon, this also made all of the Navajo films – and all other IM films, and other kinds of IM content, which followed them – inherently *political* in nature (see especially Ginsburg, 1989, 1991, 1996). This is because all forms of cultural self-expression are always implicated in processes of 'identity politics'. On the one hand, such films, or other media content, communicate to other members of the 'in-group' that which is distinctive about their own shared perspectives. In so doing, they inherently strengthen that group's social cohesion. In this sense, as Ginsburg puts it, such films are inherently 'conservative of identity' (1989: 19). On the other hand, such films simultaneously also communicate to people *outside* of the in-group where the 'boundaries' between the group and the wider world lie. In so doing, they subtly inform outsiders about the limits of the influence they have over the group, and of the incursions they may make within it. In this sense, such films are inherently '*assertive* ... of identity' as well (*ibid.*). In these ways, then, for Ginsburg, IM becomes a kind of 'discursive space' for indigenous peoples to assert both self-determination and resistance (and in this regard, her arguments for IM are in some ways similar to the arguments that were made in relation to theatre by advocates of TFD; Ginsburg, 1991). Because of all this, it is not surprising that in the years since Worth, Adair, and Chalfen's experiment, IM projects have tended to be most enthusiastically embraced by indigenous peoples who are experiencing particular external threats to their ways of life, to their political autonomy, and/or to their natural resource bases. For example, in one of the most widely cited cases, from the mid-1980s onwards, a series of IM projects – the best known of which was introduced by a Professor of Anthropology at Cornell University, Terence Turner – were widely taken up by the Kayapo people living in the Amazon Rainforest of Central Brazil. The outputs from these projects – which were made using portable VHS cameras, later to be played back on VCR decks – initially focused on Kayapo ceremonies, cultural performances, and public debates. However, within a short period of time, the films began to also document the Kayapo's many – and complex – confrontations with the Brazilian government, and with the World Bank, which, at the time, was funding a major hydro-electric dam that threatened to flood indigenous lands (Turner, 2002: 81–88). In another very well-known example, in the late 1990s, an IM project begun by an American documentary film-maker called Alexandra Halkin was enthusiastically adopted by the Maya people of

Chiapas State in Southern Mexico, and became an important social and political tool for them in the context of their long running insurgency against the Mexican government (Box 3.3).

Box 3.3 Chiapas Media Project, Mexico

The Chiapas Media Project is one of the best-known examples of an indigenous media movement to become engaged with participatory communication strategies and approaches. On 1 January 1994, the Zapatista National Liberation Army (EZLN), an indigenous Mayan organization based in Chiapas State, Southern Mexico, launched a war of independence against the country's central government. The uprising was a response to what the EZLN perceived as the government's neglect of indigenous people in general, and their signing of the North American Free Trade Agreement (NAFTA) – which had serious detrimental consequences for the agricultural livelihoods of most Mayan people – in particular. From the outset, the EZLN recognized that media were one of the most important tools in their 'arsenal' and, as a result, dedicated a great deal of time and energy into getting the message of their grievances 'out to the world', both through mainstream news channels and via the internet (one consequence of which is that the Zapatista uprising is sometimes referred to as having been 'the first internet war'). In 1998, an American documentary film-maker, Alexandra Halkin, visited the region with a humanitarian NGO, and recognized the need for additional video and

Figure 3.3 *The Chiapas Media Project*

Source: Francisco Vázquez, Chiapas Media Project/Promedios

Figure 3.4 A CMP cameraman at work

Source: Francisco Vázquez, Chiapas Media Project/Promedios

computer equipment and training to help not only the Zapatista leadership, but also ordinary EZLN sympathizers, to document and to broadcast their grievances more effectively. Halkin went on to play a leading role in the creation of the bi-national Chiapas Media Project (CMP)/Promedios NGO, which over the past 28 years has provided equipment and training at the 'village level', with a view to putting video cameras and editing equipment into the hands of ordinary people, including women. CMP also provides a global distribution network for the resulting outputs, which by 2008 had marketed more than 24 CMP films – although Halkin is keen to stress that the vast majority of the material produced through CMP has remained in Chiapas itself. In addition, over time, the CMP's village workshops became participatory in other ways as well, for example, in their increasing use of group 'brainstorming' sessions over the content and style of documentaries to be made. The CMP later became part of the larger Americas Media Initiative (AMI).

Sources: Halkin (2008), Wortham (2013), http://americasmediainitiative.org.

Therefore, if Ginsburg presented an optimistic view about the general political possibilities of IM, both the Kayapo and Chiapas examples demonstrated, to powerful effect, how these potentials might be even harnessed as a vehicle for 'media activism'.

Criticisms of participatory communication and indigenous media

Yet over the same period in which experiments in participatory communication were proliferating, and in which its methods were gaining a higher profile amongst international development policy-makers, so too criticisms of the approach were also growing. Although none of these criticisms ever developed into any kind of major and sustained critique on the scale of something like dependency theory, over time, they nevertheless became an increasing 'thorn in the side' for participatory communication practitioners and theorists. Perhaps the most pressing of these criticisms was that the effects of participatory communication were extremely difficult – for some commentators, almost impossible – to measure (Tufte and Mefalopulos, 2009). In other words, against a modernization approach to M4D, in which, for example, the scale of technology transfer could be easily quantified using somewhat objective measures (such as rates of media ownership or levels of media saturation), for participatory communication, goals such as heightened empathy or increased dialogue were always going to be much more elusive to evaluate. It was also argued that the very claim that participatory communication was, in fact, 'participatory' at all, was somewhat dubious. This stemmed from the fact that a vast majority of participatory projects were designed by, and implemented by, NGOs themselves. As a result, irrespective of how much empathy these projects generated, or dialogue they produced, among participants, they often remained under the direction and control of development professionals alone (Nelson and Wright, 1995). Given this, it is questionable how 'empowering' they ultimately were. It was also argued that precisely because participatory communication did include such a diffuse set of strategies and approaches, it lacked clarity and precision, which made it difficult to replicate in different locations and at different scales (Servaes, 2008).

Interestingly, a broadly similar set of criticisms was also levelled at IM. Therefore, some commentators similarly worried that the impacts of IM initiatives were difficult to measure (Curtis, 2011). Other critics raised concerns that despite IM's obvious political potential, and the existence of at least some projects that had clearly demonstrated how IM *could* become a vehicle for media activism in practice, in many other instances IM initiatives ultimately failed to overcome the kinds of uneven power relations that had historically affected indigenous people. One argument here focused on the fact that these projects invariably used *western* film technologies. It was argued that given that these technologies had for so long been used to represent indigenous peoples in stereotypical and derogatory ways, they could never be truly emancipatory for those same groups. In other words, the concern was the technologies' own 'embedded histories' (as it were) ultimately constrained IM's potential to empower indigenous users (Faris, 1992). Another argument was that against those cases in which IM projects had become vehicles for challenging state power, many other examples could be found of IM initiatives that had, conversely, become increasingly incorporated into state-run bureaucracies and reliant upon state-owned infrastructures.

This is what happened, for instance, from the mid-1970s onwards, with a series of IM projects that were organized by Inuit Tapirisat, an umbrella organization representing remote communities of indigenous Inuit in Northern Canada. These projects had been initially designed to increase the circulation of indigenous video content, and to expand Inuit-language newspapers and radio stations, precisely with a view to *limiting* the growing influence of Canadian national media into Inuit areas. However, quite quickly, their efforts became primarily focused upon making only television programmes, which were increasingly regulated by the government's Canadian Radio-Television and Telecommunications Commission (CRTC). In 1981, all of Inuit Tapirisat's initiatives were merged into an officially recognized company, the Inuit Broadcasting Corporation (IBC), which, with the CRTC's backing, was provided with programming slots on the recently launched and state-funded Anik B telecommunications satellite (IBC content was initially output on the Canadian Broadcasting Corporation's channels, and later on its own, dedicated channel). IBC was in many ways an enormous success. It was one of the first IM projects, anywhere in the world, to 'upscale' to the then new satellite television environments, as a result of which it also became the first media organization capable of broadcasting simultaneously across all of Northern Canada's remote communities. Influenced by the ideas both of M4D and of participatory communication, it output a range of content that focused upon, for example, women's health issues, drug and alcohol abuse, and domestic violence, and in a range of genres, from telenovelas to phone-in programmes (Rony, 1996; Roth, 2005). In addition, because a majority of its content was in the Inuit vernacular, Inuktitut, it also played a key role in minority language preservation – in a context in which Canada's national languages, English and

French, were increasingly displacing indigenous languages across Northern Canada (Brisebois, 1983). However, highly important though all of these successes were, it is still the case that the Inuit Tapirisat only achieved them by effectively giving up on its earlier projects' 'activist function' (as it were) by incorporating its IM projects within Canada's national broadcasting regulatory environment (as part of which IBC initially also received more than C$8 million in government subsidies), outputting its content on the national broadcaster, and by generally 'professionalizing' its operations. For example, to ensure the quality of IBC content, both the CRTC and CBC required IBC staff to undergo extensive, formal media training at a metropolitan institution. For some commentators, this meant that the IBC's content could no longer even be called 'IM', at least not according to the definition provided by Worth, Adair, and Chalfen (see the discussion in Roth, 2005). A similar political and institutional history for IM broadcasting also pertained in other countries as well, most notably in Australia (Ginsburg, 1993; Meadows and Molnar, 2002).

Advocates both for participatory communication and for IM have attempted to respond to each of these criticisms in turn. For example, scholars June Lennie and Jo Tacchi (2013) have recently attempted to develop a comprehensive model for evaluating the impacts of participatory communication projects, based upon the long-term and systematic ethnographic study of projects' design, implementation, and effects. Other advocates have responded to the criticism that participatory communication is too diffuse by developing more systematic kinds of theoretical models for the field. Indeed, it was partly in response to these kinds of criticisms that Melkote, Friedman, and Carmen developed their 'strong' paradigms for participatory communication (see above). A number of the major development agencies that have championed participatory communication in recent decades have also tried to address these criticisms. In particular, the UN devoted its entire 2001 Inter-Agency Round Table on Communication for Development to discussion of precisely the criticisms outlined above, and to finding suitable responses to these concerns (Deane, 2001). Meanwhile, advocates for IM have developed increasingly nuanced and sophisticated arguments concerning how and why, even where such projects *are* embedded within national regulatory regimes, and dependent upon state-run broadcasting infrastructures, they may nevertheless continue to play an important role in identity construction, language preservation, and indigenous rights (Wilson and Stewart, 2008). However, all of these responses have offered, at best, only partial rebuttals to the criticisms raised.

For some post-development theorists, the only genuine solution to the various issues raised here would be for participatory communication to shift its focus onto *only* those community, or 'grassroots', media projects that have been started by local people themselves, and have been continuously run as independent entities (a definition that would include some of the indigenous media projects described above, but not others). For some theorists, such a move might finally allow participatory communication to achieve its ultimate promise of only observing how people in Africa, Asia, and Latin America define their *own* development goals, and how they may go about trying to achieve these on their *own* terms (see the discussion in Gibson-Graham, 2010). However, in practice, it is very difficult to define precisely how and when a given community broadcaster can, and cannot, be defined as 'independent' – given that, in practice, a majority will have received at least *some* kind of external funding, training, and/or other support from, for example, a government body, an NGO or even just a wealthy benefactor (on this, and the many other definitional problems of community media, see especially Carpentier *et al.*, 2003). In addition, even this move does not fully address the various criticisms raised above, given that, even if participatory communication were to focus upon *only* community media that are 'independent', then this does not negate the fact that it is nevertheless still desirable to develop reliable ways to measure the effects that media projects have upon processes of social change, and to identify models for replicating 'best practice' across different contexts. It also does not overcome the issues relating to the 'embedded histories' of media technologies, described by Faris (1992). There may also still be power imbalances at play, for example, between those who had planned or set up the community broadcaster in the first place and those who ran it on a day-to-day basis (for a good discussion of the complex politics of community media projects, see Rennie, 2006).

Conclusion

From the end of the Second World War onwards, modernization theory defined a role for media within international development in terms of it being a tool, or tools, for accelerating technology transfers, and for communicating modern ideas and information from the western world to the Global South (or within the South itself, from urban areas to rural ones). Given this context, it followed that growing criticisms of modernization – in particular, those associated with dependency theory, but also those forwarded by feminist and environmentalist scholars – and the subsequent emergence of post-development theory, would require this role to be rethought. What eventually emerged was participatory communication. This was a new set of strategies and approaches for M4D, in which the importance of all kinds of media stemmed not from their potential to disseminate messages, but from their ability to facilitate new kinds of dialogue and interactions, both amongst groups of local people themselves and between local people and development professionals. The possibilities for these new approaches to participatory communication were first demonstrated, to powerful effect, in T4D, although they subsequently went on to involve radio, television, and more recently the internet and social media as well. These possibilities were also explored in other areas of media theory and practice, most notably in IM. Both participatory communication and IM remain highly influential, and widely practised, even today, although certain criticisms of the approaches have never been fully resolved.

Summary

- From the mid-1960s onwards, a growing number of critiques were levelled against modernization theory.
- Amongst these were dependency theory, feminist critiques, and the environmental critique – each of which attacked previous approaches to media and development in a number of ways.
- Out of these critiques emerged a new paradigm for international development – participatory development.
- This in turn gave rise to an entirely new set of theories and methods regarding media and development, which together were referred to as participatory communication.
- Some key examples of participatory communication in action include the Theatre for Development movement and the increasing use of radio phone-in shows in development projects. The latter were widely taken up in HIV/AIDS programmes.

Discussion questions

1. Does dependency theory have continuing relevance for understanding the contemporary world order? Can you think of one argument in favour of this, and one against?
2. What were the differences between 'first wave', 'second wave', and 'third wave' feminism, and what implications do these have for international development?
3. Can you list the ways in which detrimental environmental impacts may be exacerbated both by media technologies and media content?
4. Design a short dramatic production that would be suitable for use in an HIV/AIDS education programme in rural Pakistan.
5. What issues would be involved in trying to evaluate the impacts of a participatory communication project over one-month, one-year, and ten-year timeframes?

Further reading

Once again, there are enormous literatures relating to all of the topics discussed in this chapter. The best general introductions to dependency theory and cultural imperialism remain: Cardoso, F. and Enzo, F. (1979) *Dependency and Development in Latin America*, Berkeley, CA: University of California Press; and Wolf, E. (2013) *Europe and the People Without History*, 2nd Edition, Berkeley, CA: University of California Press.

However, for a recent application of the theory to the current world order, see also: Muthee, P. (2013) *Dependency Theory: The Reality of the International System*, Nairobi: CreateSpace Independent Publishing.

For more on feminist perspectives on development, see: Visvanathan, N., Duggan, L., Wiegersma, N. and Nisonoff, L. (2011) *The Women, Gender and Development Reader*, 2nd Edition. Kaapstad: New Africa Books.

For more on environmentalist critiques, see: Adams, B. (2008) *Green Development: Environment and Sustainability in a Developing World*, 3rd Edition, New York, Routledge.

For a practical guide to participatory methods in general, see: Slocum, N. (2003) *Participatory Methods Toolkit: A Practitioner's Guide*, Maastricht: United Nations University.

The best introductions to the theory and practice of participatory communication, specifically, are: Gumucio-Dagron, A. (2001) *Making Waves: Stories of Participatory Communication for Social Change*, New York: Rockefeller Foundation; Mefalopulos, P. (2008) *Development Communication Sourcebook: Broadening the Boundaries of Communication*, Washington, DC: World Bank; Tufte, T. and Mefalopulos, P. (2009) *Participatory Communication: A Practical Guide*, Washington, DC: World Bank; and McPhail, T. (2009) *Development Communication: Reframing the Role of the Media*, Malden, MA: Wiley.

For more on the complexities of evaluating participatory communication, readers are also encouraged to look at: Lennie, J. and Tacchi, J. (2013) *Evaluating Communication for Development: A Framework for Social Change*, New York: Routledge.

The best introduction to indigenous media is: Wilson, P. and Stewart, M. (2008) *Global Indigenous Media: Cultures, Poetics and Politics*, Durham, NC: Duke University Press.

For much more on media activism in general, see: Downing, J. (2011) *Encyclopedia of Social Movement Media*, London: Sage.

Multimedia sources

Online guide: Participatory Methods Portal (Institute of Development Studies). Available online at: www.participatorymethods.org

Online guide: The Chiapas Media Project. Available online at: www.chiapasmediaproject.org

Online guide: The Navajo Film Themselves Project. Available online at: www.penn.museum/sites/navajofilmthemselves/

Documentary: *Dreams of Change* (dir. Ditte Haarlov-Johnsen, 2006) [The story of Hopangalatana, a TFD group in Mozambique]. Available online at: www.youtube.com/watch?v=1gHQrL6oO7A&index=6&list=PL_a5kP08zUgKoZZOUx7Jfge6qiAyLHffi

Documentary: *Starting Fire with Gunpowder* (dir. William Hansen and David Poisey, 1991) [History of the Inuit Broadcasting Corporation]

Film: *Atanarjuat the Fast Runner* (dir. Zacharias Kunuk, 2002) [Made by a Canadian IM production house, Isuma Igloolik Productions, the film is an epic retelling of an Inuit legend]

Film: *Bamako* (dir. Abderrahmane Sissako, 2006)

4 Structural-adjustment and media globalization

- The rise of the Washington Consensus.
- Media globalization.
- Press freedoms in the developing world.
- The expansion of community media.
- The mobile phone revolution in the developing world.

Introduction

From around the mid-1960s onwards, a series of interrelated and increasingly strong critiques were levelled against the ideas and practices of 'modernization', including those of dependency theory, feminism, environmentalism, and post-colonialism. However, powerful though all of these critiques were, even collectively they were not sufficiently strong to dislodge all elements of the dominant paradigm. In particular, one of modernization's central ideas – that 'progress' and social and economic development are best led by a developing world country's own *government* (i.e. by its own '*state*') – remained largely intact. What finally dislodged this idea then was the global economic crisis, and the subsequent downturn, of the 1970s. The global economic tumult that began in this period left many of the states in the developing world in dire circumstances, and resulted in western donor countries and the major multi-lateral development agencies effectively giving up on what had become the modernization paradigm's central premise: that a poor country's development is best led by its own government. This became replaced by an alternative series of policies that instead emphasized reducing the state's involvement in its own country's economic and social affairs, in favour of market-led mechanisms for growth. Although these policies were introduced in different places at different times, by the early 1990s they had become 'the new orthodoxy' within international development. Even today, although some of the specific policies and approaches of what came to be known as 'the Washington Consensus' have been greatly modified, many of the underlying logics and ideas of this newer paradigm remain highly influential within international development (Serra and Stiglitz, 2008; Khan and Christiansen, 2011).

The aim of this chapter is to explore what effects this new orthodoxy for international development had upon media landscapes in the poorest parts of the world. It will argue that the new policies and approaches either directly caused, or else created the general conditions for, a vast expansion not only in media ownership but also in media infrastructures – including broadcasting, ICT, and telecommunications infrastructures – across the developing world. Equally importantly, they also greatly accelerated the globalization of media content, and led to a significant expansion both of press freedoms and of community media initiatives throughout Africa, Asia, and Latin America. Various elements of these changes also played a key role in what was to soon become the most profound shift in the media landscape to date in the developing world: the mobile phone 'revolution', and the concomitant rise of the internet and social media. This study provides the background for the next chapter, which goes on to look at the implications that these changes had for the evolving fields of M4D and participatory communication (although as a result of the shifts described here, both of these fields became increasingly subsumed under the umbrella term 'Information-Communication Technologies for Development', or ICT4D. This reflects the fact that both fields now included not only radio, television, and print media, but also increasingly computers, mobile phones, the internet and social media as well. For clarity, then, I will use only 'ICT4D' throughout this chapter, and in the remainder of the book).

The economic crises of the 1970s and the 'neo-liberal turn'

By the early 1970s, a majority of countries in Africa, Asia, and Latin America, with the support of western donors, had been following policies of government-led 'modernization' for at least 25 years. Although the precise policies varied from country to country, and also changed over time, in broad terms the driving logic was that of 'state-led industrialization' (Cardenas et al., 2000). In all cases, this involved governments investing heavily in the building of new towns and factories, and in their associated technologies and infrastructures – especially in energy and transportation infrastructures – as the main engines for economic growth. These investments were funded by a combination of government taxes, Official Development Assistance (ODA, or 'aid' as it is more commonly called), and government borrowing, especially from European or American-based banks. From the 1960s onwards, as the ideas of dependency theory became more popular, an increasing number of developing world governments had begun also to routinely intervene in their economies in other ways besides. In particular, they had begun to intervene in ways that would, they hoped, make their *own* industries' products more competitive within their own internal (i.e. national) markets, *vis-à-vis* manufactured imports from richer nations. The aim was to try to break the 'uneven' balance of global trade that dependency theorists had identified, as described above.

Developing world governments tried to make their own manufacturers more competitive within internal markers in a number of ways, including by: providing subsidies to selected national industries – which made their products cheaper than equivalent imported goods; applying quotas for and tariffs on imported goods – which limited the availability of imports, and made them more expensive anyway; and manipulating exchange rates – especially with a view to making imports that had to be paid for in foreign currencies impossibly expensive to buy. Collectively, all of these policies became known as 'protectionist measures'. Between 1945 and the early 1970s, practically every country in the developing world adopted some sort of protectionist measures at one time or another. However, during this period, Latin American governments became especially perceived as protectionist in orientation. This is mainly because Latin American governments tended to employ groups of protectionist measures in 'clustered' and strategic ways, with a view to protecting not just national industry in general, but instead specific national industries, or industrial sectors, as might face particularly fierce competition from international competitors (Ocampo and Ros, 2011). The use of such focused clusters of protectionist policies became known as Import Substitution Industrialization (ISI).

However, by the early 1970s, this general pursuit of state-led industrial strategies was beginning to falter. In particular, it was becoming increasingly obvious that developing governments' borrowing to fund state-led industrialization programmes was growing faster than the presumed 'returns' on those investments, in the form of economic growth – measured in terms of gross domestic product (GDP). In this context, there was an increased risk that a large number of developing world countries might be heading for national debt crises. Meanwhile, it was also becoming increasingly obvious that protectionist measures were of only limited utility – given that both transnational companies (TNCs) could find ways around them via legal loopholes, and ordinary consumers could circumvent them via black markets (Grindle, 1996). This combination of risk factors represented a growing time bomb for the developing world, and the event that eventually 'lit the fuse' was the oil crisis of 1973.

The oil crisis began in late October 1973, when the main oil-producing countries of the Middle East worked collectively to restrict oil exports to western industrialized countries – especially to America, but also to some European countries. The group's main reasons for generating the embargo were political, and related, in particular, to anger over the United States' support for Israel in the Arab–Israeli War that took place between 6 and 25 October 1973 (the conflict is also known as the Yom Kippur War and the October War). However, the group's actions also had major economic effects, in particular by driving up oil prices – which, within a short time, rose from US$3 per barrel to US$12 per barrel, and which then continued to rise continuously for another seven years. The effects of this 'first oil shock', as it became known, were various and profound. For example, it was a major cause of the global stock market crashes of late 1973 and 1974 – although there were other causal factors for these as well – as a result of which it was also a key driver of the major recessions that many western countries, including the US and the UK, experienced from the mid-1970s onwards. More significant for our purposes here was the effect that it had upon nations in the developing world, in exposing modernization not only as flawed, but as even a potentially *disastrous* approach to development.

The first oil shock hit many countries in the developing world particularly hard: unable to afford adequate volumes of oil at the new, higher prices, urbanization slowed and industrial output declined. This in turn made it more difficult for those countries to keep up the repayments on the loans they had taken out to pay for all of their new towns, factories, and associated infrastructure in the first place. This created all sorts of financial difficulties for the governments involved, including a reduced tax base, devaluation of their currencies, and rising inflation (for an extended discussion about, and literature review of, the negative impacts of the 1970s oil crisis on developing world economies, see African Development Bank and African Union, 2009). In response, many developing world countries tried to 'spend their way out of trouble' – by borrowing still more money to fund yet more investment in industry and infrastructure (*ibid.*). In a cruel irony, many of the Middle Eastern oil-producing countries that had profited from the oil price spike had begun to 'park' their newfound profits in western commercial banks. As a result, these banks were themselves experiencing 'excess liquidity' (i.e. they were cash-rich) and they were thus willing to lend ever-increasing sums to developing world countries (Danso, 1990). However, given those countries' declining industrial output, and the ongoing existence of protectionist measures – which produced all sorts of inefficiencies throughout their national economies – this new borrowing did little to arrest their general 'spiral of decline'. Instead, it simply left developing world countries with higher volumes of external debt (Ocampo and Ros, 2011). Finally, as interest rates in America and some European countries themselves began to climb – as a result of the 'monetarist' economic policies that those nations adopted in response to their own recessions of the 1970s – so this new external debt became increasingly expensive for developing world governments to service (Lipson, 2009). In other words, levels of external debt became increasingly unsustainable – and for many developing world countries, they were to remain so until the 1990s, if not beyond.

Across the developing world, different nations began to experience the worst effects of these rising debt burdens at different times and in different ways. However, by the early 1980s, a general pattern had started to emerge, in which developing countries' foreign debt commitments had typically begun to exceed their earning power to repay those same commitments (Ferraro and Rosser, 1994). In other words, *they were bankrupt*. Initially, the problem became particularly associated with Latin America, with the emergence of what became known as the Latin America Debt Crisis. Following the pattern described above, after the first oil crisis, almost all Latin American countries – and especially the five biggest economies of Argentina, Brazil, Chile, Colombia, and Mexico – had massively increased their external debt burdens. Across the continent, between 1975 and 1983, external debts – many of which were owed to commercial banks – had risen by more than 400%, to a total of US$315 billion, or 50% of the continent's entire GDP (World Bank, 1989). And by the early 1980s, it had become increasingly clear that none of these countries – including the 'big five' listed above – could afford to meet even the interest payments owed on these debts. The first country to openly declare that this was the case was Mexico, in 1982, after which other countries followed suit. Moreover, although the problem became initially apparent in Latin America, it was quickly realized that the same situation pertained, to a greater or lesser degree, across other parts of the developing world. In particular, by 1988, the same set of factors had resulted in African countries owing a collective external debt of US$230 billion, which was driving a major African debt crisis as well (Danso, 1990).

The response of donor countries, and multi-lateral agencies such as the World Bank and the International Monetary Fund (IMF), was to give up on some of the key ideas that had previously animated international development policy. In particular, the notion that development could be most effectively achieved by developing world governments themselves, who would 'manage' their nations' progress through a series of carefully designed stages towards industrialization, was jettisoned in favour of a new set of policies that significantly reduced governmental influence. Instead, western donor governments – led by the newly elected Reagan and Thatcher governments in the US and UK, respectively – and multi-lateral development organizations now began to champion an alternative approach to international development. In this alternative approach, it was not developing world governments, but instead market forces, that would become the main driver of growth across the developing world. Not surprisingly, given that it was the continent on which the effects of unsustainable debt first emerged, it was in Latin America that these policies were first implemented. However, they soon became a prescription for practically all other developing nations as well. Indeed, by the late 1980s and early 1990s, they were being more or less forced upon developing nations, and especially upon the nations of Africa, as part of World Bank and IMF-led 'structural-adjustment programmes' (SAPs).

Donor governments' and development agencies' newfound belief that unfettered market forces could be an alternative, and perhaps more effective, driver for economic growth for the developing world was based upon a body of economic theory that traces, ultimately, to the work of Enlightenment economists such as Adam Smith (1723–1790). Smith believed that all human beings are 'rational' economic actors, in that they will always seek to maximize their own personal gains. However, because all individuals' needs are also always finite, even the most selfish of economic behaviours will still produce a surplus, which the individual involved will then likely 'reinvest'. This reinvestment in turn benefits others as well. In consequence, and as Smith first elaborated in his *The Theory of Moral Sentiments* (1759), even the initially most selfish of economic actions is likely to still generate wider economic benefits. This he called the 'invisible hand' of economics (*ibid.*). Later, Smith extended this model, especially in *An Inquiry into the Nature and Causes of the Wealth of Nations* (1776), to argue for the overwhelmingly positive effects of markets and of capitalism. From around the mid-1950s onwards, but with increasing vigour following the first oil shock, a group of economists based at the University of Chicago, who became known as the 'Chicago School', returned to the 'classic' economic theories of people like Smith, and began to see them as a model for macro-economic policy – including for international development policy – for the late twentieth century as well. Led by the Nobel Prize-winning economist Milton Friedman – today, the Chicago economics department has produced no less than 12 Nobel laureates, more than any other academic department in the world – members of the Chicago School argued that if states' involvement in their economies could be generally reduced, to facilitate individuals, private companies and ultimately, therefore, *markets*, to operate in a more or less unrestricted way, then this would result in mechanisms such as the 'invisible hand' both generating further growth, and redistributing this in a way that benefitted the common good (Mirowski, 2013). This general way of thinking is today commonly referred to as *laissez-faire* economics, or simply as 'neo-liberalism' (although one must be careful, because the ideas of the Chicago School are in some ways quite different to an earlier body of 'neo-liberal' theory that emerged in Germany in the 1930s; in other words, 'neo-liberalism' can refer to different ideas, in different places and times).

In the context of international development, following the perceived failure of modernization, and of its model of an elite-led/state-led approach to growth, these ideas of the Chicago School appeared to provide an attractive alternative. As a result, by the late 1980s, a group of the larger, Washington, DC-based agencies – including USAID, the World Bank, and the IMF – were using them to inform a wide range of policies. For this reason, the policies later became known, collectively, as the 'Washington Consensus', a term that was coined by the British economist John Williamson in 1989 (although he later distanced himself from the phrase; Williamson, 1990). Although the precise elements of these policies varied from country to country, as did the combinations in which they were introduced – depending on a host of country-specific factors – in all instances, the overall policy package required developing world governments to undertake economic and legal reforms aimed at reducing their own interventions in their economies, and to in other ways create more 'market-friendly' conditions in their nations. Examples included requiring developing world governments to: (1) stop providing subsidies to national industry; (2) privatize state enterprises; (3) improve their fiscal discipline, in order to reduce the size of their deficits; (4) undertake tax reform to increase their tax income, again with a view to reducing deficits; (5) set interest rate targets that reflected actual, or 'real', market activity – as opposed to a government's aspirations on trade targets; (6) allow exchange rates for currencies to be similarly market-determined; (7) remove tariffs on imports, thereby allowing free movement of goods into the country; (8) remove legal barriers on Foreign-Direct Investment (FDI), thereby allowing free movement of capital into the country; (9) recognize international property rights, in order to build confidence among international companies and investors who may wish to 'do business' in that country; and (10) generally 'deregulate', i.e. generally remove any other regulations, across all sectors, which might unreasonably deter international companies or investors from entering those markets, or which might restrict their competitiveness once they had entered them. In this context, the only regulation that was allowed to remain in place was that relating to workers' health and safety, environmental protection, and consumer rights (Williamson, 1990).

What effects did this major shift in the approach to international development have upon both the volume and the types of media that were available to people living in the developing world, and upon the amount and kinds of media content that ordinary people living in the developing world could access and use? The remainder of this chapter will examine these questions in detail, and will look at how the policies and practices associated with the Washington Consensus produced a wide range of both intended and unintended consequences.

Globalization of the media

It is tempting to see the advent of the Washington Consensus as heralding the beginning of 'the globalization of media'. However, we must exercise a degree of caution here, not least because other periods could be also seen as marking the start of this 'global spread'. For

example, the nineteenth century witnessed the dissemination of various forms of new media throughout the world. Following the confirmed invention of the first reliable form of photography, the *daguerreotype*, in France in 1839, the objects and techniques of this media were quickly conveyed around the world, via steamships. Already by the end of 1839 – that is, just a few months after the invention had been announced – photography had reached Africa: it was introduced by the French painter Horace Vernet, who was resident in Egypt at the time (Haney, 2010). By the end of the following year, it had reached large parts of Latin America. Conventional wisdom has it that the French ship *L'Orientale* introduced photography to Argentina, Brazil, Chile, Peru, and Uruguay during its stops in those countries (Lanctot, 2015: 2). And by 1841, it had even reached Oceania, on board another French ship, *Justine* (Wood, 1994: 4). Similar was the invention of the moving film camera, the cinematograph, also in France, in the early 1890s (the *cinematograph* had the capacity not only to record moving images but also to project them back afterwards onto a screen – as such, its invention marks the birth both of moving imagery and of 'cinema'). Again, within just a few years of its invention, this technology had become established across the world, not least following a 'world tour' of the device by its confirmed inventors, the brothers Auguste and Louis Lumiere,
in 1896. In addition to taking in Canada, the UK, and the US, the Lumieres' tour also included stops in Argentina and India (Barnouw, 1993). Finally, following the invention of wireless telegraphy – the first form of radio – by the Italian Guglielmo Marconi in 1895, the infrastructures required to convey that medium were quickly established throughout the world. By the turn of the twentieth century, they had already been established not only in Europe and North America, but also in Africa, Latin America, and elsewhere (Fahie, 1971). The late 1890s and early 1900s also saw the first newspapers, and other forms of print media, becoming established throughout the developing world (Peterson *et al.*, 2016).

If the nineteenth century was an important period in the globalization of media, so too was the period from roughly the mid-1950s onwards. In particular, following the invention of the transistor radio set, by the United States' Bell Labs in the late 1940 – which compared to the earlier vacuum tube radio was much smaller, lighter, and most importantly of all *cheaper* – personal radio ownership rose dramatically throughout the world, including in the developing world.

For example, a former researcher for the BBC World Service, Graham Mytton, has estimated that between the late 1950s and the early 1970s, in one African country alone, Tanzania, the number of personal radios rose from less than 72,000 to 1.7 million (Mytton, 2000). In some African countries, rates of ownership grew even faster than that, as governments subsidized their import and/or manufacture. In addition, with the development of increasingly small and affordable television sets – which followed the production of the first commercially viable cathode ray tube (CRT) sets – by Germany's Telefunken, this medium also became increasingly globalized. CRTs remained the basis for most television systems, worldwide, until the advent of digital television in the 1990s. Already by 1970, sub-Saharan Africa – to stay with that example – had 299 million television sets, and by the mid-1980s, this number had grown to almost 750 million, according to UNESCO estimates (Mano, 2008). This growth in television ownership is particularly remarkable, given that throughout sub-Saharan Africa, and indeed throughout the developing world, television ownership was then, and it remains today, primarily associated with people living in urban areas and/or with elites.

It was not only the spread of the physical technologies themselves and their associated infrastructures that contributed to the 'globalization' of media during these periods. The *content* that was produced in and through these material forms also became a medium for the transnational movement of forms, styles, and ideas, and for the development of new kinds of hybridities and global imaginaries. For example, recent research has shown how the spread of photographic technologies between Africa and the Americas in the nineteenth century helped to cement an emergent Atlantic 'visualscape' through which aesthetic forms and styles from West Africa became incorporated into the visual cultures of Caribbean societies, and vice versa (e.g. Thompson, 2006; Schneider, 2010). New studies have shown how interactions between film-makers across the world during the early years of cinema resulted in South Asian dramatic styles becoming incorporated into a wide range of American and European films (Jhala, 2011). Meanwhile, both scholars and activists have long argued that the expansion of television throughout the world in the period after the Second World War resulted in Euro-American programming becoming the primary content for *all* television viewers, throughout the world. This argument first rose to prominence in the context of the Media Imperialism Debate in the 1970s (see above).

It was with the advent of global 'media events' that the sheer power of media content as a force for globalization first became clear. A 'media event', sometimes called a 'pseudo-event', as defined by the Chicago-based historian Daniel Boorstin – who first coined the term, in his book *The Image, or, What Happened to the American Dream?* (1961) – is an event, or other happening, that occurs solely for the purpose of generating as much media coverage of itself as possible (without revealing that to the audience, i.e. in an 'immediate' way). In so doing, the event generates a collective experience for everyone who is viewing it – even if all of those people are, in fact, watching in isolation – and as such, it becomes part of collective memory. In addition, and in order to generate as much publicity for itself as possible – in order that it can increase the degree of collective engagement, and so become more effectively embedded within collective memory – media events tend also to appeal directly to *emotion*. In other words, they are specifically designed to make their audience feel proud, or angry, or shocked (Rowe, 2000). From Boorstin onwards, scholars have taken the quintessential examples of media events to be things like political speeches, news conferences, and 'photo shoots' (Rowe, 2000). But the point is that following the global spread of media such as radio and television in the period after 1945, and especially following the launch of the first television satellites in the mid-1960s, such media events could now be staged, and be affective, on a global scale. The first truly global media event was the Our World television programme, which was broadcast for two and a half hours on 25 June 1967, to 14 countries, each of which produced one section for it – although only two of the countries involved were in the developing world: Mexico and Tunisia. The programme was explicitly non-political, in that no politicians were allowed to take part in it, as a result of which most of the national sections were constituted of a mixture of documentary-style content and creative materials. For example, the UK's section included a live performance by the Beatles. Throughout, the programme displayed a high degree of self-consciousness of its global reach, in that all of the sections made frequent reference to the notion of a 'shared planet' – which was still a relatively novel concept in the late 1960s – and all talked directly to audiences living in other parts of the world (for a segment from the programme, see www.youtube.com/watch?v=wbWMBiz2z7k). In addition, Canada's section included an interview with the philosopher Marshall McLuhan, who was one of the earliest scholars to explore ideas of the globalization of media, and whose concept of the 'global village' remains part of our common parlance today (McLuhan, 1962).

Later, the Live Aid concerts of 1985 constituted another major global media event, as we have already seen.

However, the key point here is that even against this background of a long history of different forms of media globalization, what happened after the policies of the Washington Consensus were adopted by/imposed upon countries throughout the developing world was still qualitatively new, and different, compared with anything that had gone before it. In particular, the new policies' emphasis upon the free movement of goods and capital across borders – by requiring nations to remove any barriers that might prevent this from happening – not only resulted in a massive increase in the volume of media technologies that could be imported into those countries, but also enabled private, transnational media corporations to expand markedly the size of their investments into developing countries, a large part of which, initially at least, went into establishing new broadcasting infrastructures. To continue with the examples already cited, if by 1970 sub-Saharan Africa had 33 million radio sets and 299 million televisions, by the late 1990s, as a direct result of the policies introduced by the SAPs from the late 1980s onwards, these numbers had risen to 158 million and 1,396 million, respectively (Mano, 2008). By that time, the region had also seen a huge growth in private investment in broadcasting infrastructures. Perhaps the most significant of these was the South African company Nasper's creation of a continent-wide infrastructure capable of delivering its pay-TV service, DStv (Digital Satellite Television). The success of this investment is demonstrated by the fact that, today, Nasper's systems have more than 8.5 million subscribers across the continent, and the head of the company, Koos Becker, is one of the richest men in Africa, with a net worth of US$2.3 billion.

The Washington Consensus policies' additional emphasis upon the dissolution of all state-owned monopolies, including those held by national broadcasting companies, and upon the more general deregulation of all sectors, including the media sector, were to have even more profound effects. It is important to emphasize here that prior to structural-adjustment, a majority of states in sub-Saharan Africa had one single large, state-owned broadcaster, whose monopoly over the country's entire broadcasting landscape was protected by national law. In practically all cases, this one broadcaster operated a single nationwide radio station and one television channel (Myers, 2008: 12). Yet as part of their adoption of the new policies, all sub-Saharan African states were required to dissolve said monopolies, and to allow new broadcasters to enter the marketplace, through the passing of new legislation to establish more liberal media environments. Initially, the effects of this were most profoundly felt in relation to radio. Prior to the Washington Consensus, the entire sub-Saharan African region, in the context of state monopolies, had just ten private (i.e. non-state) radio stations (*ibid.*, 12). Within just a few years of structural-adjustment, the region had literally thousands of new radio stations broadcasting over various spatial scales (some of them started by civil society groups, others operating on a more commercial basis). Certainly, at least some of these new stations were still controlled by, or had links with, governing regimes (Myers, 2008: 13). Nevertheless – and although precise numbers are difficult to come by – the sheer growth and diversity of stations were impressive. For example, by 2008, it was estimated that the Democratic Republic of Congo (DRC) alone had 250 radio stations, Ghana had 130, and Mali had no less than 300 (these estimates are based on a variety of sources, that are cited in Myers, *ibid.*, 11). Over the same period, the number of print media titles also increased dramatically. For example, in one country alone, Uganda, the period since structural-adjustment has seen the establishment of several hundred newspapers and news-magazine titles (although the majority of these have not lasted very long – in some cases, just a few months or even weeks; BBC, 2012: 5). Since the early 1990s, the situation with television has been more complicated, with some countries allowing new broadcasters to enter the market – for example, by 2006, Uganda had 13 television stations operating in the country – whilst others, despite passing new laws to establish liberalization, have *de facto* allowed their state-own monopolies to remain intact (Gicheru, 2014: 8–9). Nevertheless, the overall picture is still one of a major transformation in all media environments.

This enormous growth in media providers also radically altered both the range and the nature of the material that African audiences were able to access. Prior to liberalization, the output of state-owned monopolies tended to be characterized by: a primary focus upon the activities of the government, and in particular upon those of the head of state; the policies and ideas of the administration, often broadcast in a more or less uncritical fashion; and generally low production and editorial values and standards. As anyone who has ever listened to, or watched, the content of state-owned media monopolies, where these still exist, will testify, none of this adds up to the most gripping of viewing experiences. For example, I vividly recall watching

Channel 1 of the Zimbabwe Broadcasting Corporation (ZBC) one evening in the mid-1990s, when the main evening section, from roughly 6.00 to 7.30 pm, consisted entirely of a single long-shot (i.e. one single, unedited sequence) of a speech made by the country's president, Robert Mugabe (ZBC still controls most radio and television channels in Zimbabwe. However, the country does have a number of independent newspapers, and access to other media is also available in the country through satellite television services such as DStv). Compare this, then, to the current situation in many other sub-Saharan African countries, in which most users are likely to have the potential to access several dozen radio stations, a handful of newspapers and magazines, and a number of television stations. In other words, like media users everywhere in the world, these audiences now have exposure, in theory at least, to a potentially limitless range of media content, of all genres and styles, including news content, other forms of factual programmes, fictional drama, music, and commercial advertising.

The profound effects of the Washington Consensus in transforming media environments were felt not only in sub-Saharan Africa but across the developing world. Thus, although the scale and combination of effects varied from place to place – depending on a wide range of historical, political, and cultural factors – in general terms, the period following structural-adjustment, as a direct result of the kinds of policies outlined above, saw similar spikes across the developing world in media technologies ownership, in investment in media infrastructures, in numbers of media providers, and in the sheer scale and variety of media content to which users had access.

Media development

Structural-adjustment programmes' emphasis upon policies that required states to dissolve their former media monopolies, and to allow for all manner of additional broadcasters to enter their national media markets, also galvanized a renewed interest in wider notions of media development. In particular, they led to a significant renewal of interest in ways for improving freedoms of the press throughout the developing world. Once again, there was nothing new about the concept of 'press freedom' itself. On the contrary, the idea can be traced back to the Enlightenment philosopher John Milton, and his polemical tract *Areopagitica* (1644). *Areopagitica* was published at the height of the English Civil War (1642–1651), and in direct response to the Parliamentarians' passing of a censorship component within its Licencing Order of 1643. The component sought to stifle the publication of dissenting views, not only from Royalists, with whom Parliamentarians were at war, but also from factions within the Parliamentarian camp with whom legislators disagreed. Although Milton broadly sympathized with the Parliamentarian cause, he was vehemently against this kind of censorship. According to him, not only would the news laws be unworkable, but more importantly, they violated a fundamental individual right to seek truth – which, for Milton, was a process whereby all possible ideas and opinions had first to be carefully considered, with a view to rejecting as many of them as possible. Whatever remained at the end of this deductive process (i.e. whatever had not been 'ruled out') could be considered 'the truth'. In forwarding these arguments, Milton began what was to become an important tradition within western thought, which is sometimes referred to as 'libertarianism' (although Milton himself was not, strictly speaking, a libertarian). The root of libertarianism is the idea that it is a basic *right* for individuals to be able to access a free press, and to enjoy their own freedoms of thought and expression in relation to this (Russomanno, 2008). In evidence of how important these ideas became, it is noteworthy that England's Bill of Rights (1689), the United States' Bill of Rights (1789), and France's Declaration of the Rights of Man and of the Citizen (also 1789), although they all defined the very notion of 'rights' in slightly different ways, all included explicit provisions for freedoms of the press and free speech.

Yet libertarian arguments about freedoms of the press and free speech, perfectly reasonable though they appear at first blush, are in fact not quite as straightforward as they might seem. This is because they focus primarily upon what lawyers refer to as 'freedoms *to*' – that is, freedoms to access a wide range of ideas and opinions, and freedoms to reach, and to express, one's own thoughts and ideas. However, as other Enlightenment philosophers already realized, especially Rousseau (1762), responsible states also have a duty to provide their citizens with 'freedoms *from*' – that is, freedoms from being exposed to ideas, opinions or other media content that are derogatory, or in other ways damaging, and freedoms from defamation by printed materials or spoken words. For these reasons, in all real-world contexts, freedoms of the press and freedoms of expression must always be *balanced* with the protection of citizens from exposure to inflammatory, or in other ways dangerous, materials, and from attacks in media content and in speech. Yet where the precise balance between these two things should lie is not always clear, and it anyway varies across places and times (Beger, 2010). For these reasons, no definitive, 'hard and fast' rules can be ever reached, which is one reason why debates over the limits of media censorship and defamation laws – libel and slander – and, more recently, over the boundaries of privacy, remain as keen today as they always have been. Nevertheless, these public policy and legal complexities aside, it remains the case that the right to a free press and to free speech remains deeply embedded within the 'cultural imaginary' (as it were).

Moreover, if the dangers of an *unfree* press were already obvious to Milton (at which time the primary medium for mass communications was still the printing press), they became even more obvious in the twentieth century (by which time mass communications had come to encompass a much wider range of media technologies besides). In particular, the first half of the twentieth century demonstrated the acute dangers that followed monopolistic media regimes becoming tools for state-led propaganda. Again, the concept of propaganda was not new at that time. The concept can be traced back to classical Greece and it was widely used, for example, in the seventeenth century by the Catholic Church, and in the eighteenth century during the French Revolution (Wilke, 1998). However, in the period between the two World Wars, the way in which state-controlled broadcasters – especially those in the fascist states of Germany and Italy, and in Japan – used modern mass communications to expose their citizens to radical and racist ideas and ideologies, and to generate deep emotional engagements with the same, was qualitatively different from anything that had gone before (Welch, 1983). As a result, following the end of the Second World War, the governments of the US and its allies not only wanted to distance themselves from the use of the term 'propaganda' altogether – usually by simply renaming it as 'public relations' (Cutlip, 1994) – but also by forcibly restating the by now 'age old' libertarian principles of the right to a free press and free speech. Indeed, it was as a direct result of this very impulse that in 1948, Article 19 of the UN's Universal Declaration of Human Rights enshrined the right to 'seek, receive and impart information and ideas through any media' within international law (UNGA, 1948). Therefore, if into the era of modernization a majority of international development organizations generally perceived that 'there was no such thing as too much media', so too they also held the view that there 'was no such thing as too much media pluralism'. One consequence of this was that arguments regarding 'press freedoms' were used by western governments to support a wide range of political agendas, especially during the Cold War – as we have already see in relation to their response to the McBride Report (1980).

Yet it was also the case that throughout the era of modernization, although western donor governments liked the *idea* of media pluralism, they generally lacked the means to bring this about in many countries in the developing world. Certainly, there were a number of initiatives that attempted to forward the agenda, particularly UNESCO's International Bureau for the Development of Communication, which was set up in 1980, and the US NGO Freedom House's *Freedom of the Press* reports, the first of which was published that same year (Box 4.1). However, other than monitoring the situation in developing world countries, and/or lobbying for greater press freedoms in those states, there wasn't really much that these initiatives could really do. Therefore, it was only following the introduction of the SAPs – with their requirement for governments in Africa, Asia, and Latin America to dissolve their state-led media monopolies, and to establish new, market-focused, regulatory environments – that press freedoms could begin to be developed across the developing world in anything like a systematic and sustained way (Vokes, 2007a).

At the same time this was happening, there was a growing recognition that media pluralism and press freedom were not the *only* elements necessary for the establishment of 'healthy and vibrant' media environments. Therefore, the phrase 'media development' was increasingly expanded beyond its original – and primary – reference to freedom of the press *per se*, to also include a wide range of other things as well, including: (1) the professionalization of journalism – through the development of programmes aimed at improving the extent and quality of training programmes for journalists and other media professionals (Mottaz, 2010); (2) the extent and reach of the media sector – by way of initiatives aimed at strengthening connections between the media industries and other institutions, and people of influence, in order to make these more 'embedded' within wider society (Scott, 2014a); (3) the sustainability of media – especially through attempts to support media 'start-ups', and to help them survive in the new marketplace (Prahalad and Hammond, 2002); (4) the quality of media law – through reviews of existing legislation, and lobbying for additional laws (Tettey, 2001); and (5) rates of

Box 4.1 Freedom of the Press Report

In October 1941, a group of highly placed US political figures – including the First Lady Eleanor Roosevelt, Mayor of New York Fiorello La Guardia, and presidential candidate Wendell Wilkie – set up a research-based NGO/'think-tank' called Freedom House, in New York (it later moved to Washington, DC). The initial aim of the organization was to gather evidence, and to generate publicity, in support of America becoming involved in the Second World War (this was still two months before Pearl Harbor, when various constituencies in the US were still advocating for America to 'appease' the Axis powers of Germany, Italy, and Japan). However, following the conclusion of that conflict, the organization's purview expanded much further, and it went on to become a powerful advocate of – amongst other things – international development (from 1949 onwards), the US Civil Rights Movement (in the 1950s and 1960s), and South Africa's anti-apartheid struggles (especially in the 1980s and early 1990s). Since 1972, one of the main ways in which Freedom House has advocated for these causes is through its annual Freedom in the World Reports, which famously categorize all countries in the world – based on a wide range of measures relating to political and civil rights – as 'free', 'partly free', or 'not free'. From the late 1970s onwards, the organization also became particularly engaged with issues of global press freedom – as part of its wider concern for human rights – and from 1980 onwards, has also published an annual Freedom of the Press Report. Modelled on the NGO's main publication, this similarly categorizes the news media in most countries around the world – based on factors such as the national political environment in which the press operates, the strength of the legal and regulatory environments in which they practise, and the economic health of the national media sector, as again 'free', 'partly free', or 'not free'. Yet, although these annual Freedom of the Press Reports provide an important 'snap-shot' of variations in press freedom around the world, and highlight additional areas in which further interventions in media development could be targeted, they have not been without criticism. In addition to using crude metrics (which because they are applied as a country-level comparison, may mask important regional variations, and may miss, for example, improvements that have been made within one country over time), the reports have also been criticized for effectively making western media environments the 'benchmark' against which all developing world countries are measured. In addition to smacking of modernization thinking, this may be trying to hold up developing world countries to standards of media development that are simply impossible for them to obtain, given the significantly lower resource bases they have available to them.

Sources: Martin et al. (2016), https://freedomhouse.org/report/freedom-press/freedom-press-2015#.VwSOwGNUNO4.

'media literacy' – via programmes to improve not media production, but the ability of media users to develop more sophisticated interpretations of the media content that they are exposed to (Moeller, 2009; Berger, 2010). Indeed, so wide did the field of media development become, and so numerous were the elements that became included under its umbrella, that as one media studies scholar has recently put it, attempts to definitely define the boundaries of the field – that is, to specify precisely what it does and does not include – have become akin to 'nailing jelly to a wall'! (Scott, 2014a). Nevertheless, diffuse though the field certainly became, its general concern with removing constraints upon media environments, and upon improving the capabilities of media production and consumption, had transformative effects throughout the developing world. We will return to some of these in the next chapter.

Community media

Of the many thousands of new radio and television stations that were established throughout the developing world following structural-adjustment, a large proportion could be characterized as community, or 'grassroots', in nature. In other words, in hindsight, the Washington Consensus also created the conditions necessary for a vast expansion of specifically indigenous and other kinds of community broadcasting – of a kind that advocates for participatory communication had been long arguing for (see above). In fact, neoliberal policies, and their effects, facilitated the growth of community media in a number of different ways. First, and most obviously, the liberalization of national media environments meant that groups could launch their own community media initiatives – with or without external support – without fear of arrest and prosecution and/or without having to worry about how to incorporate their stations into regulatory, and other national legal, regimes. Of course, the history of community media is replete with examples of broadcasters who, for one reason or another, were never concerned about breaking the law in the first place, or about how to bring their operations within regulatory regimes. Certainly, this was very much the case with what is taken to be one of the first ever examples of community media in the developing world, Bolivian tin miners' radio stations, which began operating in the 1940s (Box 4.2). It was also the case with all forms of 'guerrilla media' that is, media operations that were set up as part of armed opposition groups. Examples of guerrilla media include Radio Venceremos (*lit.* 'Radio We Shall Overcome'), a station that was set up by the insurgent Farabundo Marti National Liberation Front (FMLN) to output anti-government propaganda during El Salvador's Civil War (1979–1992; see Vigil, 1994), and the later Chiapas Media Project (see above).

Figure 4.1 *Image of Radio Venceremos*

Source: Cortesía MUPI

Box 4.2 Miners' radio in Bolivia

One of the best-known examples of a communication movement that was used by its participants to resist state power was a series of community radio stations that were set up across the tin mining regions of Bolivia, in Latin America, by local branches of the Bolivian Tin Workers' Union (FSTMB). Some of these stations date back to 1947 – making them one of the oldest examples of community radio in the world – and from the time of Bolivia's nationalist revolution in 1952, have been seen has a key 'space' in which miners – who have always had various means for putting their opinions out over the airwaves – can express their political views, can mobilize around grassroots causes, and can engage in a 'cultural sphere' that is outside of the control of the state. For all of these reasons, Bolivian miners' radio has long been seen as the very paradigm of 'community and participatory media' and as a model of the political possibilities of decentralized communication regimes. However, it was following the military coup in Bolivia in 1980, and the subsequent crackdown on mining communities by the new junta – given that tin miners were the most militant and well-organized social group in the country at that time, they were regarded as an enemy by the new military government – that the miners' radio stations really came into their own. As soldiers moved from village to village, arresting FSTMB organizers, and closing down radio stations as they went, remaining stations formed what became known as a 'chain of democracy'. In this way, the stations 'closest to the action' (as it were) would broadcast what they knew about what was happening.

Other stations further away would then 'rebroadcast' this content (in some cases simply by tuning in to the first station on a transistor radio set, and holding this up to the microphone in their own studios). By these means, in a context of military oppression, the network of stations was able to maintain a continual flow of information about what was happening across the entire tin mining regions – and on to the outside world. Many international broadcasters relied on what they could pick up from these miners' radio signals for the content of their own reports on the situation. Eventually, the military authorities did manage to shut this network down, although it took them a full three weeks to do so. However, the stations have since been re-established, and today are still widely recognized for the key role they play in keeping alive the strongly collectivist values of the mining communities, and the rich oral traditions that are associated with them.

Sources: Huesca (1995), O'Connor (2004).

However, prior to structural-adjustment, a more general trajectory for community media initiatives was more akin to that of the Inuit Tapirisat's projects described in the last chapter. In other words, stations would begin as effectively illegal broadcasters, or 'pirate

Figure 4.2 *Community radio in Kinshasa, the Democratic Republic of Congo*

Source: Photo courtesy of Katrien Pype

stations', and would then – if they survived the 'complex and contradictory' ways in which regulatory regimes were everywhere enforced (Howley, 2005: 47) – gradually be incorporated into regulatory regimes: yet with all of the problems of subsidization, professionalization, and loss of control that that might entail (see above). Against this pattern, then, following structural-adjustment's general liberalization of media markets, it became much easier for community media operations to secure licences, and to maintain at least some degree of independence over time.

Secondly, the liberalization of national media environments, precisely because this facilitated a potentially limitless range of media content to be broadcast across the developing world, revived earlier concerns over cultural imperialism (above). In other words, the fact that the Washington Consensus removed many of the barriers that had previously prevented media organizations from broadcasting their content across international borders, once again raised concerns that American and European media organizations, in particular, might now 'swamp' the developing world with their own content. Thus, although by this time the New World Information and Communication Order (NWICO) had largely 'run out of steam', the UN's Economic, Social and Cultural Organization (UNESCO), in particular, began to revisit some of NWICO's key debates – albeit now in different forums. For example, in 1998, UNESCO published its first *World Culture Report* – a second was published in 2000 – which re-examined some of the NWICO debates, and observed that the advent of neo-liberal models of development, and the commercialization of media environments and globalization of media content that had resulted from this, certainly had expanded western media and cultural influence over the developing world (Thussu, 2007: 10). Nevertheless, the report went on to conclude that this was likely to be only a short-term phenomenon and that, in the longer run, commercialization and globalization would likely also increase the potential for other, non-western, models of 'different cultural, institutional and historical backgrounds ... to multiply', and to eventually produce 'greater diversity than uniformity' (UNESCO, 1998: 23). In reaching this conclusion, the UNESCO report in a sense captured the general mood amongst the international development community at that time, which may be summarized as a perception that although the liberalization of the airwaves was likely to result in an initial spike in global content, over time this would be tempered by increases in the production and broadcasting of more local material.

However, it was believed that the key to this movement would be a proliferation of community media broadcasters. Or, to put it more simply, the negative effects of more globalized media content could be offset by the production of more community content. As a result, from the early 1990s onwards, media development initiatives began also to focus upon advocating for national policy environments that were conducive to a proliferation of community media projects as one further aspect of their wider drive towards the creation of healthy and vibrant media environments (Coyer, 2011). Once again, this made it much easier for community media operations to become established – and to survive.

Finally, neo-liberalism's general shift away from elite-led/state-led approaches to development resulted in the onus for managing all kinds of social change being anyway effectively 'passed on' to local communities. In keeping with the wider ethos of the Washington Consensus, this was again cast in largely optimistic terms. For example, the general expansion of global capital flows was framed as conferring great opportunity, by providing access to new markets in which different 'localities' (to use the parlance of the day) could sell their own unique products, skills or experiences (Rennie, 2006: 152–153). And the general dissolution of state-run bureaucracies and institutions around everything from domestic welfare to agricultural extension was represented as a great opportunity for local communities both to develop more robust mechanisms for coping with major social change and, from that, to design their own, bespoke solutions for everything from welfare to farming (*ibid.*; see also Howley, 2005). Interestingly, advocates for neo-liberalism often couched these ideas in a language that was effectively identical to that of participatory development. Thus, their key jargon made frequent use of phrases such as 'community empowerment', 'community resilience', 'people-focused approaches', and 'stakeholder-led initiatives'. However, as Wendy James has demonstrated, within neo-liberal policy environments, such phrases were effectively drained of their former sense of humanistic holism (above), and instead tended to refer to only *economic* dispositions and practices. In other words, when advocates for structural-adjustment spoke about 'empowerment', they were often referring to only *economic* empowerment, and when they discussed 'resilience', they were invariably referring to only *economic* resilience (see James, 1999). The key point, though, is that if these perceived new opportunities for localities to market themselves, to develop more robust mechanisms for coping with change, and to forge their own approaches to welfare, then it was recognized that these could only be realized if those same localities had effective forums in which to communicate and debate these: and this again gave impetus to the drive towards a vastly expanded community media sector. It was as a combined result of all of these factors, then, that throughout the 1990s and into the 2000s, the number of community media broadcasters grew exponentially, across the developing world. For example, Kaplan estimates that 'across Africa, community radio [alone] grew, on average, by 1386 per cent between 2000 and 2006' (cited in Scott, 2014a: 132).

The mobile phone revolution

Structural-adjustment programmes' emphasis upon the free movement of goods and capital across borders – by requiring nations to remove any barriers that might prevent this from happening – also created the conditions for what was to become the most profound shift in the media landscape ever to have occurred in the developing world: the mobile phone 'revolution'. Just as the removal of barriers on the free movement of goods and capital had created the conditions for a huge growth in the numbers of radios and televisions, and for major new investments in media infrastructures, they also facilitated the arrival of masses of mobile phone handsets, and the entry of the finance required to develop digital telecommunications networks. Just as the dissolution of state-owned enterprises had created the conditions that ended – or at least significantly undermined – national media monopolies, thereby allowing new commercial providers to enter the market, so too it also ended public telecommunications monopolies, with a similar result. And just as all of this had brought about a major transformation of African, Asian, and Latin American people's experience of radio, print media, and television, so too it had a similar effect upon their experience of telephone communications.

A note of caution, however, must be sounded in thinking that the Washington Consensus was the *only* cause of the mobile revolution. On the contrary, simply creating the conditions in which some or other sea-change in technology *might* occur does not necessarily guarantee that that will then happen. For one thing, and as we have already seen, a host of factors shape the speed at which different categories of people in a society take up any new technology. And interestingly, in 2003, Everett Rogers released an updated fifth edition

Figure 4.3 *Shop selling mobile phone services, south-western Uganda*

Source: Author

of his famous book, which examined how his model for the *Diffusion of Innovations* might be applied to the mobile phone revolution, and other recent technological developments. More generally, recent research in anthropology has emphasized the fact that, across all cultural groups: 'People [always] understand each new medium, each of which possesses its own historicity, largely in terms of how it alters previously established possibilities for storage, and for communicating across time, distance, and with different numbers of people' (Hinkson, cited in Gershon and Bell, 2013: 260). One implication of this is that even if people across Africa, Asia, and Latin America – indeed, across the whole world for that matter – are all taking up a similar communication technology, they may nevertheless be doing so for very different reasons (depending on how that technology relates to the ways in which they used to communicate beforehand).

Nevertheless, whatever the precise causal factors were for the mobile revolution, the effects of the process were undisputable, in that it entirely transformed communications infrastructures and environments in both profound and irreversible ways. The revolution really began in the mid-1990s, when a relatively small group of multinational operators – led by companies such as South Africa's MTN Group (formerly M-Cell) in Africa, Mexico's America Movil Telefonica and Brazil's Vivo Participacoes (VP) in Latin America (VP is jointly owned by Portugal Telecom and Spain's Telefonica), and India's Bharti Airtel in South Asia – began to establish significant regional platforms across their respective areas of operation. These growing infrastructures, combined with the increasing availability of cheap handsets – the vast majority of which were in fact made by just two companies, the US company Motorola and Finland's Nokia, yet which by the mid-1990s were being traded all over the world by a myriad of companies – created the context for the 'boom' in mobile phone ownership and usage that was shortly to follow. Between 2000 and 2013, the number of 'unique mobile subscribers' in Africa grew from less than 10 million to more than 311 million – the fastest rate of growth in the world – as a result of which, at least one-third of all Africans now have a mobile phone subscription (GSMA Intelligence, 2014a). By 2020, the number of unique subscribers in Africa is projected to rise to 504 million, or roughly half the continent's population (note that the number of 'unique mobile subscribers' refers to the total number of individuals who own a handset, and at least one SIM card). However, there are two other possible measures of mobile phone penetration as well, 'mobile connections' and 'mobile users'. The first of these refers to the total number of SIM cards in circulation, the second to the total number of people who have some sort of access to a phone. Typically, the number of unique subscribers will be much lower than either of the latter numbers, given the common practices in Africa – as throughout the developing world – for individuals to use multiple SIM cards and handsets at the same time, and to share their phone with sometimes quite sizeable networks of family and friends. During this same period, the number of subscribers grew at a staggering rate across all other parts of the developing world as well. For example, by 2013, the number of unique mobile subscribers in Latin America had reached 320 million, which represents just over half of the continent's total population (GSMA Intelligence, 2014b: 7). By 2014, the number of unique subscribers in India had reached 453 million, or 36% of the population (GSMA Intelligence, 2015: 4).

Following the later introduction of 3G and 4G networks, and a concomitant rise in access to 'smartphone' handsets, the mobile revolution has also delivered internet access to many parts of Africa for the first time – and in so doing, at least partly addressed some of the issues and problems associated with the 'global digital divide' (Box 4.3).

In 2004, the Mauritius-based telecom company Emtel launched the first ever 3G network in Africa. But it was from 2008 onwards that these technologies really 'got going' with the start of an estimated US$45 billion investment in network upgrades across Africa, which massively improved bandwidth and network coverage. throughout the continent (again, these were led by the MTN group; GSMA Intelligence, 2014a: 3). The timing of these investments also broadly coincided with the arrival on the market of a new generation of much cheaper smartphones, which in recent years have retailed throughout Africa for less than US$50 (Gicheru, 2014: 7). Prior to these developments, internet access – via personal computers and modems – had been heavily concentrated in just three African countries: Nigeria, South Africa, and Sudan, which by the mid-2000s, accounted for more than three-quarters of all internet users across the continent (Mano, 2008). Since the arrival of 3G networks and smartphones – and the new kinds of 'media convergence' that these technologies have facilitated (Grant and Wilkinson, 2009) – such access has become available to potentially the vast majority of Africans. Thus, although a 2013 survey by the long-term research project

Box 4.3 The 'digital divide'

Between 1991 and 1996, the number of personal computers in the United States exploded, from less than 300,000 to more than 10 million. However, in 1995, a report by the US National Telecommunications and Information Administration (NTIA) used subscription rates to the country's new high-speed fibre optic network (i.e. 'the internet') to deduce that computer ownership was not evenly distributed across the country. Instead, it was concentrated in wealthier, and more socially privileged, urban and rural areas, and thus appeared to have created a new 'digital divide'. Although the NTIA report referred to only the situation in the US, its findings particularly resonated with international development agencies such as UNESCO, which, from the mid-1950s onwards, had been trying to map inequalities in access to media technologies and infrastructures between the developed and developing worlds, and across different parts of the Global South, and to address the economic and social inequalities which shaped these. As a result, development agencies widely adopted the concept of the 'digital divide', and the phrase soon came to refer primarily to an international development context. It was sometimes also referred to as the 'global digital divide'. However, effective though the term was in highlighting inequalities in digital media ownership and use between the wealthier and poorer parts of the world, and in tempering some of the more utopian predictions that accompanied the early growth of the internet, it soon proved to be highly problematic in a number of ways. On the one hand, as a metaphor, it suggested that there were two clearly defined groups, with a 'gap' between them that was 'fixed' or at least very difficult to bridge. Yet in reality, patterns of media ownership and use worldwide have been always highly varied and complex. In addition, and as the mobile phone revolution was shortly to show, media 'gaps' can be very

Figure 4.4 *Worldwide Internet access*

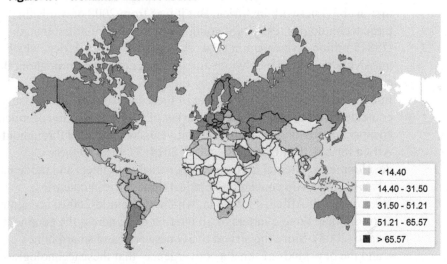

Source: Based on World Bank data

rapidly bridged if the right conditions prevail. More fundamentally, and as Faye Ginsburg has pointed out, any notion of the developing world being on the wrong end of a 'gap' risked repeating modernization theory's patronizing assumptions about Africa, Asia, and Latin America needing to 'catch up' with the Euro-American world. On the other hand, it also proved quite difficult in practice to make any precise measurements of the 'digital divide'. Early attempts to do so tended to focus primarily upon rates of ownership (of physical digital media technologies) and of subscriptions (to digital media services). Yet a raft of empirical studies soon showed that both measures could easily result in either underestimates or overestimates of inequalities of access. For example, following the mobile revolution, a range of studies showed how women might own mobile phones, yet have their access to them circumscribed by men (such as their husbands). Conversely, multiple individuals might share access to a single mobile phone subscription, as a result of which, all mobile research now routinely distinguishes between various categories of subscribers and of users. In response, some researchers have suggested using other measures instead, such as volumes of digital traffic, or rates of 'digital literacy'. However, these alternative measures may be just as problematic in their own ways. Nevertheless, the concept of the digital divide continues to resonate within international development, and is still a key driver for a number of contemporary initiatives aimed at bringing internet access to everyone in the world.

Sources: Gunkel (2003), van Dijk (2005), Ginsburg (2008), Rapaport (2009).

Afrobarometer found that only 18% of mobile subscribers in Africa used their phones to access the internet, since then mobile internet access has grown rapidly (Afrobarometer, 2013). By 2020, more than half of all phone connections on the continent will be internet-enabled (GSMA Intelligence, 2014a; Box 4.4).

In recent years, Africa's mobile phone landscape has also been further transformed by the introduction of mobile phone-based money transfer systems, often known as 'm-pesa' systems, after *pesa*, the Swahili word for money. These systems enable all mobile users, irrespective of whether they are using a 'standard' handset or a smartphone, to use their phone accounts to deposit and withdraw funds, and to transfer funds to other users. In effect, m-pesa has turned people's phone subscriptions into bank accounts – and in so doing has transformed mobile phone companies into banks – and has turned their handsets into mobile ATMs. It is also important to note that Africa has always had the lowest number of actual ATMs of any continent. In 2004, the first mobile money system in the world was tested in Mozambique, and in 2007, the system was rolled out in Kenya and Tanzania as well (Hughes and Lonie, 2010). It is today available across more than 80% of African countries, and has become an integral part of many mobile phone users' lives (GSMA Intelligence, 2014c: 15). And once again,

Box 4.4 Global internet access

There are currently around 7.2 billion people in the world, of whom an estimated 2.9 billion have access to the internet, which leaves roughly 4.3 billion who are not yet online – the majority of whom live in the developing world (including in remote rural areas). Thus, although the mobile phone revolution has done much to improve equality of access to media worldwide, there is clearly still a very long way to go to get the remaining 60% of humanity into cyberspace. At present, a number of major initiatives are underway to do just that. Although these programmes have the strong support of traditional development agencies such as UNESCO, it says much about our current 'neo-liberal age' that the two largest, and most important, of these initiatives are in fact being driven by Facebook and Google – whose projects are called 'Internet.org' and 'Project Loon', respectively. As is always required for any major media advancement, to achieve their goals these initiatives must both create the necessary infrastructure to bring internet access to even the remotest parts of the planet and work out ways to then deliver meaningful content (i.e. that people will actually want to engage with) via that infrastructure. In regard to infrastructure, Facebook's initiative is concentrating on developing a system of huge solar-powered drones, each of which will fly for months at a time at an altitude of around 60,000–90,000 feet (i.e. around double the typical cruising altitude of a Boeing 747), providing constant internet access in a 50-km radius as it does so. Meanwhile, Google's project is designed around sending hundreds of high-pressured helium balloons into the stratosphere (i.e. at an altitude of between 18 and 25 km), which will act like satellites in relaying internet signals across a huge area. However, it is in terms of content delivery that Internet.org currently has the lead. In 2013, Facebook signed a deal with six major telecom and internet companies (Ericsson, Opera Software, MediaTek, Nokia, Samsung, and Qualcomm) to develop an app – now called 'Free Basics' – which would deliver free internet content across the developing world. In a typical piece of social marketing, the approach was to first carry out market research to find out which 'bits' of internet content would be of most interest to consumers in country x, y, or z, and then to bundle only those parts into Free Basics. To date, the app has been rolled out across more than 17 countries across the Global South – beginning with Zambia (in July 2014) and including India (in February 2015), Guatemala (March 2015), Pakistan (May 2015), and Iraq (December 2015). The plan is for Free Basics to be available eventually to the whole of humanity, using Facebook's new drones. Yet until these come on-stream, the app is being delivered using existing 3G and 4G mobile infrastructures instead. However, whilst few commentators have challenged Internet.org or Project Loon's plans for new infrastructure, Free Basics has been widely criticized. In particular, both ICT4D practitioners and scholars have taken issue with the fact that it allows users to access only small parts of the internet. On the one hand, this can be seen as a form of censorship – in that, in all of the countries in which it operates, the designers have been careful not to include any content that might offend the government involved – as a result of which it violates principles of press freedom and of internet neutrality. On the other hand, by locking users into an app that Facebook ultimately controls, it provides the company with what some commentators have called a 'walled garden' in which they may be able to decide, for example, precisely which kinds of advertising users are exposed to.

Sources: Levy (2013), Grossman (2014).

over the same period, these general patterns in Africa have been repeated in most other parts of the developing world. Thus, following the introduction of 3G and 4G networks in Latin America – the first of which was introduced by Chile's Entel in 2006 – and the growth of smartphones, internet access had grown exponentially on that continent as well. By 2020, around 80% of the phone connections in Latin America will be internet-enabled (GSMA Intelligence, 2014b: 7). Similarly, by that date, around 42% of the connections in India will have similar capabilities (GSMA Intelligence, 2015: 4). Finally, in recent years, mobile money – following its invention in Africa – has also grown exponentially across both Latin America and South Asia. As of 2014, m-pesa systems have become available in 85 of the 136 countries across the developing world, and have become a ubiquitous part of social life across many of those places (GSMA Intelligence, 2014c: 14).

Conclusion

The economic crisis of the 1970s set in motion a series of broad shifts in international development policy that eventually became fully institutionalized in the World Bank and IMF-led structural-adjustment programmes of the late 1980s and early 1990s. By design or otherwise, these completely revolutionized media environments across the developing world. On the one hand, they led to a huge growth in media ownership across Africa, Asia, and Latin America, and to a simultaneous expansion of broadcasting infrastructures. On the other hand, they also generated a concomitant and huge acceleration in the globalization of media, which, amongst other things, vastly expanded the range of media content to which ordinary people living in the developing world could access (Box 4.5). In addition, they created the conditions for the mobile phone revolution that shortly was to follow, which provided many parts of the developing world with their first ever access to adequate telecommunications, and later to the internet and social media as well.

In trying to understand just how profound the effects of all of this must have been for ordinary people living in the developing world, it is worth pausing to consider how those individuals' everyday engagements with media would have changed between the period before and after the emergence of these new media environments. Beforehand, most people's only access to a media device such as a

Box 4.5 Global Bollywood

The liberalization of national media environments across the developing world enabled American and European media organizations to broadcast more of their material across larger parts of the globe. Yet it also allowed African, Asian, and Latin American producers to increase the global reach of their own content. In other words, it also increased 'reverse flows'. A particularly good example of this is the post-1980s deepening globalization of Hindi-language cinema produced in and around the Indian city of Bombay, commonly known as *Bollywood* cinema. Again, it is important to recognize that the 1980s did not mark the start of Hindi film's global distribution. On the contrary, from the early twentieth century, Bombay producers' then silent films were already being widely distributed, especially amongst South Asian diasporas in Eastern and Southern Africa, the Middle East, and Europe. Nevertheless, even against this historical background, the period after 1991 – the year in which India began its major structural-adjustment reforms – still witnessed an unprecedented expansion in the global reach of Bollywood cinema. These years saw Hindi-language films reaching vast new audiences throughout the world, including audiences other than the South Asian Diaspora. They witnessed a major increase in the number of films being made, and a concomitant rise in revenues. By 2012, Bollywood was making 745 films per year – compared with Hollywood's 476 – while by 2014, the Indian film industry as a whole was worth approximately US$2.28 billion, making it a major national industry. Equally importantly, these years also saw Hindi-language cinema actors becoming elevated to global celebrity status, and the signs and symbols of Bollywood become embedded within the 'global ecumene'. For example, actors such as Salman Khan and Aishwarya Rai are today famous all over the world, while the tropes of Bollywood are today referenced in everything from Oprah Winfrey to collections presented at London Fashion Week. In my favourite example, a Hindi-film dance closed an episode of *The Simpsons* in which the family travelled to India (see www.youtube.com/watch?v=wJkw24zxizw). The period since 1991 has also seen a number of global intellectual movements develop 'counter-readings' of Bollywood films, as a means for destabilizing more taken-for-granted narratives about global history (narratives which, as we have seen, may be hegemonic in their effects). For example, subaltern historians have developed interpretations of Bollywood films that challenge narratives about the generally positive effects of British colonialism; poststructuralist thinkers have interpreted them in ways that destabilize our notions of spectatorship and fame; and queer theorists have read them as sites for the articulation of LGBTI desires. Moreover, Bollywood is not the only example of a regional – and non-European language – cinema that has had similar, global effects. In recent decades, other regional film industries that have had at least some of these same effects include those originating from Gujarat in Western India ('Gollywood'), Tamil Nadu in Southern Indian ('Kollywood'), Lahore in Pakistan ('Lollywood'), Malaysia ('Mollywood'), Nigeria ('Nollywood'), Taiwan ('Tollywood'), and Zimbabwe ('Zollywood').

Sources: Kavoori and Punathambekar (2008), McCarthy (2014).

radio or television would have been likely through a member of their household, or possibly a local political leader in their locality. As a result, they would likely have had very little control over where, when, and for how long they engaged with these media devices. In addition, the main source of content on those radios and televisions would have been a single government broadcaster, whose programming directly served the interests of the state. Furthermore, most people would have had no access whatsoever to telephony. Compare this, then, to the situation afterwards, whereby the vast majority of people now owned their own radio sets, and sometimes televisions as well, which they could use, where, when, and for however long they liked, to access a large number of stations, and a wide range of content from around the world. Furthermore, most people now had some way of accessing a mobile phone. In short, people's engagements with media had been utterly transformed. Certainly, these changes occurred at different times, in different places. For example, in relation to my own field site in Uganda, the period between roughly the late 1990s and the mid-2000s was crucial. However, in other parts of the developing world, the main effects of these transformations were felt during other periods besides. Yet everywhere, these were rapid and profound transformations.

Yet what possibilities and challenges did these changes, and the new engagements with media that they generated, present for international development more broadly? In other words, what new possibilities and constraints did they engender for how media might be used, or might in other ways contribute to wider goals in relation to poverty reduction, good-governance agendas, and health programming? Which is also to say, what opportunities and challenges did these transformations present for an evolving field of ICT4D? It is to this question that we turn in the next chapter.

Summary

- The era of 'state-led development' came to an end following the oil crisis of 1973, and the subsequent economic downturn.
- Following this, both western donor governments and multi-lateral agencies began to impose market-led approaches to development upon countries in Africa, Asia, and Latin America.

- Among their many effects, these policies led to a huge rise in media ownership, and a massive expansion of media infrastructures, across the developing world.
- They also vastly improved press freedoms in the Global South, and generated a huge growth in community media.
- They also created the conditions for the mobile phone revolution, and for the spread of the internet and social media, throughout the developing world.

Discussion questions

1. International development is *not* just all about the money. Discuss.
2. How were the effects of the global economic crisis of the 1970s similar to, or different from, those of the Global Financial Crisis of 2007–2008 for developing world countries?
3. Can you think of a global media event you have engaged with? To what extent have terrorist attacks become the quintessential global media events of our times?
4. To what extent have debates concerning 'freedoms *to*' vs. 'freedoms *from*' in relation to media development become even more complicated since the advent of the internet and social media?
5. In what ways were the effects of Africa's mobile phone revolution different from those of the European and North American mobile phone revolutions, which occurred shortly beforehand?

Further reading

For more on the Washington Consensus, and its effects in different parts of the Global South, see: Dixon, C. and Drakakis-Smith, D. (1993) *Economic and Social Development in Pacific Asia*, London: Routledge; Naim, M. (1994) *Latin America's Journey to the Market: From Macroeconomic Shocks to Institutional Therapy*, San Francisco, CA: ICS Press; and Sahn, D., Dorosh, P. and Younger, S. (1999) *Structural Adjustment Reconsidered: Economic Policy and Poverty in Africa*, Cambridge: Cambridge University Press.

For a particularly critical view of the 'neo-liberal turn' in general, see: Bello, W., Cunningham, S. and Rau. B. (1993) *Dark Victory: The United States and Global Poverty*, Oakland, CA: Food First Books.

For more on the ongoing influence of the Washington Consensus on the developing world, see: Serra, N. and Stiglitz, J. (2008) *The Washington Consensus Reconsidered: Towards a New Global Governance*, Oxford: Initiative for Policy Dialogue; and Khan, S. and Christiansen, J. (2011) *Towards New Developmentalism: Market as Means Rather than Master*, New York: Routledge.

For more on globalization of the media, see: Lule, J. (2015) *Globalization and Media: Global Village of Babel*, London: Rowman & Littlefield. For media development, see: Coyne, C. and Leeson, P. (2009) *Media, Development and Institutional Change*, Northampton: Edward Elgar Publishing.

For community media, see: Howley, K. (2005) *Community Media: People, Places, and Communication Technologies*, Cambridge: Cambridge University Press; and Rennie, E. (2006) *Community Media: A Global Introduction*, New York: Rowman & Littlefield.

And for the mobile phone revolution, see: de Bruijn, M., Nyamnjoh, F. and Brinkman, I. (2009) *Mobile Phones: The New Talking Drums of Africa*, Leiden: African Studies Centre.

Multimedia sources

Online resource: *Community Media: A Good Practice Handbook* (UNESCO, 2011). Available online at: unesdoc.unesco.org/images/0021/002150/215097e.pdf

Documentary: *Frame by Frame* (dir. Alexandria Bombach and Mo Scarpelli, 2015) [Photojournalism and media development in Afghanistan]

Documentary: *Hello Africa* (ICT4D.at, 2011) [Mobile phone revolution in Africa]. Available online at: www.youtube.com/watch?v=mIGEg2PDbMA

Documentary: *Nollywood Babylon* (dir. Ben Addelman and Samir Mallal, 2008) [Nigeria's film industry]. Can be compared with …

Documentary: *Welcome to Nollywood* (dir. Jamie Meltzer, 2007) [Nigeria's film industry]

Film: *Something in the Air*. Original Portugese title: *Uma Onda No Ar* (dir. Helvecio Ratton, 2002) [Community radio in Brazil]

5 ICT4D in new media worlds

- The effects of the neo-liberal turn upon ICT4D.
- The potential economic and political benefits of new media environments in the developing world.
- The telecentre movement, responses to the mobile phone revolution, and mobile money.
- The potential drawbacks of new media environments in the developing world.
- E-waste and toxic media content.

Introduction

The emergence of the 'new orthodoxy' for international development, one that centred on market-driven rather than state-led approaches to global growth, had profound effects in transforming media landscapes across the developing world, in deepening the globalization of media more generally, and in advancing media development and community media. It also created the conditions for the mobile phone, and the internet and social media, 'revolutions' that were to shortly follow. The purpose of this chapter, then, is to explore what effects these media shifts had upon socio-economic development more broadly in the developing world. In other words, it will look at the wider ramifications of these media transformations for the economic, political, and social lives of people living in the developing world. It approaches these issues through an examination of how international development organizations conceived of the possibilities for these media shifts to generate entirely new kinds of economic, political, and social action. It then evaluates these possibilities in relation to the *actual effects* that the new media environments went on to have in Africa, Asia, and Latin America over the past 25 years or so. Finally, it goes on to look at how these new media environments also posed a range of largely unforeseen challenges as well.

Development agencies' initial excitement about the possibilities afforded by these new environments is quite understandable, not least in terms of the new opportunities that they appeared to confer for ICT4D interventions (a label that by now had come to subsume all manner of M4D and participatory communication approaches). In other words, if nothing else, these media transformations certainly did result in *everyone* in the developing world – even its poorest and most marginalized people – having far greater access to a much wider range both of media technologies and media content than they would ever have done beforehand. In this context, and as outlined at the very start of this book, western donors, multi-lateral agencies, non-government organizations (NGOs), and developing world governments began to foresee myriad ways in which ICT might be used to advance their goals in relation to all manner of development-related issues and problems, including poverty reduction, health programming, good-governance agendas, disaster reduction, and conflict transformation. As outlined in the Introduction to this book, this in turn led to a raft of new policies and initiatives oriented towards an 'ICT4D of the future', or 'ICT4D 2.0' as the field has become to be known from around the late 2000s onwards.

Over time, however, those same donors, organizations, and governments have also increasingly come to recognize that these new media environments also present a range of challenges for achieving these development goals. In particular, the sheer volume of media technologies and media content now in circulation in the developing world has meant that development agencies have effectively lost control over the ways in which their target audiences (i.e. ordinary people living in the developing world) engage with media, and over the kinds of media content these people are exposed to. As a result, ICT4D interventions became more reliant than ever before upon simply waiting to see what patterns of media usage emerged in the developing world, and then finding ways – indeed, increasingly inventive ways – of 'intervening' to forward development goals (be these educational, health or governance related). A corollary to this is that ICT4D programmes were also now operating in increasingly 'crowded' media environments, in which they found themselves competing with greater numbers of commercial, political, local, and community broadcasters, who were using an ever-wider range of genres across more and more media platforms – themselves undergoing increasing 'media convergence' (Cupples, 2015) – to gain media users' attention. ICT4D practitioners had been aware of the complexities of genre and reception at least since the publication of Hall's Theory (1973), of course, and they had been aware of the importance of selecting the right balance of different media channels – or the most effective 'cross-platform' approach, as we would now call it – from the advent of social marketing onwards. However, the sheer scale of new providers, genres, and media channels, and the speed of convergence, that emerged within these new media environments nevertheless provided challenges on a scale hitherto never seen. As a result of these factors, ICT4D projects now found themselves at best losing 'market share', and at worst having to 'run to catch up' with media-driven political and social changes in which they had played no part – and which, in some cases, they frankly did not understand.

It is extremely important to recognize that the emergence of these new media environments also generated a range of outcomes that are in fact detrimental to the goals of international development; in other words, they had a *negative* impact upon economic, social, and political outcomes in the developing world. In particular, the massive increase in production of personal computers, mobile phones, and other new digital devices, which these new media environments engendered, created huge new demand for certain kinds of mineral ores, and especially for columbite-tantalite (usually known by its acronym, 'coltan'). At the time, coltan was predominantly mined in developing world countries. This spike in demand for these minerals generated a rush to secure their supply, which inevitably resulted in some unscrupulous practices. In a number of African countries, in particular, this either caused armed conflict or, more commonly, significantly exacerbated wars that were already underway. In addition, the massive increase in the numbers of computers, phones, and other digital devices in circulation soon began also to generate major new problems of e-waste across large parts of the developing world. For example, in places such as the now famous – or infamous – suburb of Agbogbloshie in Accra, Ghana, it generated mountainous new e-waste rubbish dumps. Although these dumps did generate new economic opportunities of sorts, the sheer volumes of poisonous elements contained in the millions of obsolete machines deposited in them has had cataclysmic environmental and health impacts in those localities, and has produced a range of other social problems besides. It is not for nothing that Agbogbloshie is known locally as 'Sodom and Gomorrah' (Hugo, 2011). Moreover, the problems of e-waste – including the general problems they generate, and the specific issues relating to its 'dump sites' – have continued to worsen with each passing year.

Finally, these new media environments, by exposing practically everyone in the developing world to exponentially more media content than they could ever have imagined beforehand, did of course have significant positive effects as well. Yet, they have inevitably also provided those same people with much wider access to all sorts of unsavoury content as well, including all sorts of 'mis-information' – such as 'conspiracy theories' or 'fake news' – as well as political propaganda, racist material, radical content, pornography, fraudulent content, and simply junk. All of this content has presented challenges for development goals. In some instances, it has specifically generated, or contributed to, episodes that such media has the potential to produce, or exacerbate, in all times and places, including rioting and other forms of civil unrest, outbreaks of racist violence, increased radicalization, and media-driven 'moral panics' (none of which are mutually exclusive, of course). In this context, then, for the field of ICT4D as a whole, new media environments have certainly presented great opportunities, but they have also generated a range of new challenges as well.

New media environments – the opportunities for ICT4D

Responses to the globalization of radio, television, and print media

It is not surprising, given their commitment to the Washington Consensus, that from the early 1990s onwards, almost all international development organizations hailed the growth of radio, print, and television infrastructures, and the spread of media technologies, across the developing world as an unmitigated success. From that time onwards, donor governments, multi-lateral agencies, and NGOs have generally done everything in their power to speed up these processes still further. For example, in one of the slightly more unusual development initiatives of recent years, in 2007 the British government of then Prime Minister Gordon Brown tried to help a British company, Gateway TV (GTV), set up an additional satellite-TV infrastructure across Africa – as an alternative to DStv – by intervening to secure GTV the rights to broadcast live English Premier League (EPL) football. The logic was that GTV's system was far more likely to become established if it carried live EPL games, which have always been incredibly popular throughout the African continent – and this intervention was initially successful.

Thus, following the British government's engagement, GTV was successful in wresting 80% of the EPL broadcasting rights for Africa from DStv (previously, DStv had held a near-monopoly on EPL content), and the company did then use this as a vehicle to achieve dramatic growth. Indeed, within barely a year of launching their services in Africa, GTV had over 100,000 subscribers, across more than 20 countries (Vokes, 2010: 12).

Certainly, donors, multi-lateral agencies, and NGOs did have some initial concerns that the liberalization of media environments might result in American and European media organizations 'overwhelming' developing world countries with their own media content. However, as we have seen, the consensus was that, over time, the worst effects of this would be mitigated by a vastly expanding community media sector. More broadly, though, the general sentiment was that even if the increasing globalization of media content might have at least some drawbacks, then these were more than offset by the enormous benefits that it would likely also deliver. First, advocates of ICT4D saw in such increased exposure to radio, print, and television content, a number of potential economic benefits – and in taking this view, they were in a sense simply re-applying some of the older thinking of the modernization approach to the new media age. In particular, it was argued that exposure to ever more content, including more global content, would provide ordinary people in the developing world with more and better quality information about such things as price fluctuations, market conditions, and market analysts' projections, on both national and international scales. This would in turn enable those same people to both maximize their profits on goods being sold and to make more effective, and timely, investment decisions (see www.mdif.org). For example, through exposure to real-time information about national and international coffee prices and markets, or even to news of global weather patterns, coffee farmers would be able to make better informed choices about to when to sell their crops or when to plant new trees, and in so doing would reduce their chances of being 'ripped off', of losing their crops to bad weather, or of selling during a period of depressed prices. Throughout the development literature, any information that could potentially produce a beneficial economic outcome of this kind is commonly known as 'useful information'. For advocates of ICT4D, the thinking was that, over time, as more and more individuals made better economic decisions of their own, it would increase the pressure on economic policy-makers to 'coordinate' (i.e. to align) national policies with actors' best interests, thereby also improving the overall economic outlook (see Coyne and Leeson, 2004: 22). Finally, it was also felt that increased exposure to media advertising would further stimulate consumer demand for national and global brands, which would in turn provide a further boost to economic activity – given that consumers would have to try to earn more money in order to purchase those branded products (*ibid.*, 32–34).

However, it was in relation to its potential *political* benefits that advocates for ICT4D perceived the greatest advantages to this increased exposure to media content. The arguments here proceeded in stages. First, based on a growing body of academic research in media studies, it was recognized that in most countries throughout both the developed and developing worlds, the vast majority of citizens receive a majority of their information about political leaders and political parties specifically, and about politics in general, from media sources (Panos, 2007). As a result, most citizens' political general knowledge and – more importantly – many of their political opinions are shaped by their exposure to media. As we have seen, the relationship of media content to political opinions is not a straightforward one, given the complexities of reception. Nevertheless, by the early 1990s, a general consensus had emerged that such content at least 'sets the agenda' – that is, it shapes the context within which people form their political opinions and debate these with other people in their everyday lives (for more on what media scholars call 'agenda-setting effects', see McCombs, 2004). It followed that the earlier contexts of state broadcasting monopolies must have had markedly detrimental political effects, not only in stifling the ability of opposition groups to 'get their message across' to ordinary citizens, but – more insidiously – by limiting the range of political opinions that those people held and communicated with others. Given this, it followed that western governments' and development agencies' renewed emphasis upon political pluralism (i.e. multi-partyism) and democracy in the Global South – both of which followed the Washington Consensus, and were in a sense part of its same 'neo-liberal settlement' – would be more likely to succeed in a context of wider and more diverse media content. At the very least, this increased content would break governments' former 'monopoly of ideas', and would expose ordinary citizens to the perspectives of opposition political parties specifically, and to a much wider range of political ideas and opinions more generally – including perspectives that originated in other countries. At best, it might even engender new forums for 'civic engagement', in which political ideas could be debated, and possibly even a new kind of 'civic structure' of its own, one capable of acting as a counter-balance to state knowledge and authority (Minderhoud, 2009). One early focus here was on the political 'phone-in shows' that proliferated on the new radio stations, across the developing world, following liberalization (Myers, 2008: 20; Brisset-Foucault, 2016). Throughout this period, all of these arguments were also bolstered by the renewed interest in, and the new initiatives regarding, 'media development' throughout the developing world (see above).

Responses to the mobile phone revolution, and the rise of the internet and social media

Development agencies' initial response to the growth of radio, print media, and television across the developing world was overwhelmingly positive. However, against this, their response to the later advent of the mobile phone revolution was markedly more 'lukewarm' in tone. Indeed, it is fair to say that still by the early 2000s, at least some agencies remained sceptical about mobile phones. This is something that I have already illustrated with my anecdote from 2010, of a senior development official publically stating his organization's view that Uganda '[wasn't] ready for mobile phones yet' (Vokes, 2010). The reasons for this scepticism were partly to do with the ongoing influence of modernization thinking – which, although the theory had by then more or less explicitly been rejected for many years, continued to cast a kind of 'shadow' over development policy and practice – with its emphasis upon development occurring through a series of structured stages. By this logic, countries in Africa, Asia, and Latin America couldn't just 'jump to' mobile phones and latterly mobile internet, without having first developed efficient fixed-line telephone infrastructures – which were then still woefully inadequate in many developing world countries – and adequate computer-based internet facilities. However, in addition to this frankly derogatory perception, development agencies' scepticism was also fuelled by another more compelling concern. This was the concern that the personal mobile phone economy effectively encouraged the world's poorest people to outlay relatively *enormous* sums of money on mobile handsets, sim cards, and airtime, and this money was simply much better spent on other things, not least on such pressing things as more nutritious food, healthcare, and education. Moreover, if this argument was first made in the 1990s, it has, if anything, become even more compelling in the period since then. This much was highlighted by the 2016 *World Development Report* – which is one of the World Bank's flagship annual publications – which points out, pertinently, that today, more people in Africa own a mobile phone than have sustained food security, clean drinking water or electricity. This pattern is repeated elsewhere as well. Indeed, across the entire developing world, more than 80% of people now have a mobile phone, considerably more than are fully nourished, complete high school or have adequate healthcare. If the World Bank's figures are accurate here, then it would suggest that Castells' vision of 'the network society' (2000) – a vision in which people's increasing access to digital technologies will provide them with more effective means for meeting their productive needs, and for securing all kinds of other resources besides – hasn't yet come to pass.

For these reasons, throughout the late 1990s and into the early 2000s, the ICT4D community remained largely focused upon computers, not mobile phones (Kenny, 2006). However, given agencies' desire not to pass on the costs of these to individuals, neither development policy nor practice ever developed any sustained focus upon achieving significant densities of personal computer ownership in Africa, Asia, and Latin America – or at least, not in any of their poorest areas, such as rural areas and urban slums. Instead, and drawing their inspiration from the United States' 'Community Technology Centre' movement (which had been driven from the early 1990s by a Washington, DC-based NGO called CTCnet) and from Europe's 'Electronic Village Halls' (which were the brainchild of Danish media scholar Lars Qvortrup), development agencies initially focused their efforts upon establishing networks of 'telecentres' across these areas (Herman, 2008: 904–906). The concept of the telecentre basically refers to a free 'internet cafe' – although, in practice, they are not all entirely free, but fall onto a spectrum ranging from those that charge nothing to those that are entirely commercial – in which members of local communities can gain access to the internet in order to view informational or educational material. Again, there is a spectrum here, from those that police users' activities to make sure that they are viewing only 'useful information', to those that allow their users to freely 'surf the web'. From the outset, the concept also had a strongly feminist dimension, which in practice meant that they were particularly targeted towards female users (*ibid.*, 906–908). Initially, the growth of telecentres for development was driven by a partnership involving three large development organizations: UNESCO, the International Telecommunications Union (ITU), and Canada's International Development Research Centre (IDRC). From the mid-1990s onwards, these agencies funded a series of sizeable telecentres, beginning in four African countries: Mali, Mozambique, South Africa, and Uganda. In an attempt to encourage the users of these facilities to focus upon 'useful information', these were mostly sited in places like schools, hospitals, and public libraries (Benjamin, 2000). However, over time, the telecentre movement within ICT4D became increasingly dominated by smaller NGOs, who might typically set up just one or two telecentres, focused around their specific areas of operation. Sometimes, these NGOs used only their own funds, whereas others entered into commercial funding partnerships (Box 5.1). For example, I once worked with an Italian medical NGO, which, as part of its efforts to improve healthcare services in south-western Uganda, had set up one telecentre in Mbarara Hospital – the main town in that region – with the specific aim of allowing doctors there to use the internet to access the latest medical research literature. By the early 2000s, there were several thousand NGO-founded telecentres operating across Africa, albeit with different densities in different countries. For example, by that time Senegal already had more than 9,000 in operation – partly because the telecentre movement there was also supported by one of the country's largest telecommunications companies, Sonatel – while some countries, such as Madagascar, still had none.

Once the mobile phone revolution did get going, however, most donors, multi-lateral organizations, and NGOs realized that there was really nothing they could do to influence the situation, and that they therefore had little choice but to engage with the phenomenon, and to examine how it might be harnessed towards their wider development goals. The key period here, in which the general thinking changed, was roughly the years 2003–2005. This much can be evidenced by comparing the content of the two UN-sponsored World Summits on the Information Society (WSIS), which were held in Switzerland and Tunisia in 2003 and 2005, respectively. In short, the first of these WSIS summits was still dominated by discussions of telecentres, whilst the latter firmly embraced the possibilities for ICT4D of mobile phones and mobile internet. Indeed, by 2005, some development agencies had even begun to extol the virtues of the

Box 5.1 The Telecentre *Cookbook*

In 2001, two researchers at UNESCO, Mike Jensen and Anriette Esterhuysen, produced what became the quintessential developmental manual for ICT4D. Entitled *The Community Telecentre Cookbook for Africa: Recipes for Self-Sustainability (How to Establish a Multi-purpose Community Telecentre in Africa)*, the book quickly became a key resource for NGOs that were attempting to expand the internet across Africa and elsewhere in the developing world. What was so engaging about the *Cookbook* (and it remains compelling, even today) was the clear and concise way in which it took the reader through each step in the process of setting up, running, and achieving sustainability for a telecentre, including creating a 'steering group' to oversee the project, holding a public meeting to inform community members about the centre, selecting the right hardware and software to use in the facility, training staff to operate it, handling the day-to-day management issues, and so on. In addition, it explored each of these elements in the finest of detail. For example, the sections on developing a telecentre's infrastructure discussed the precise kind of lighting to use, and the best kind of generator and batteries to power these. Elsewhere, it warned the reader that: 'The Telecentre operator is expected to know how to operate all the equipment in the Telecentre. For example, how to replace a toner, a cartridge, carbon paper for the management system, paper for the printer, etc. Telecentre operators must also be able to find faults even before they occur and if possible, be able to fix them.' Meanwhile, in the section on day-to-day management issues, it included a section on handling complaints. Here, the reader was advised that: 'A customer who is not satisfied with the service of the Telecentre may complain to you ... Always try to stay in a calm and friendly mood when dealing with complaints; never become angry. The customer is the most important person in the Telecentre!' In these ways, the *Cookbook* set a new standard as a textbook for project design, and presented this in a way that was highly accessible (and, one suspects, at least partly tongue-in-cheek as well). It was for these reasons that the manual became so popular among development practitioners. It is also because of them that readers of this book would also find the *Cookbook* a particularly good place to start when thinking about the fundamentals of project design and management – whether these projects are in ICT4D or in any other branch of international development.

Source: Jensen and Esterhuysen (2001).

mobile revolution precisely in terms of the fact that it could help developing world countries to 'leapfrog' the stages of development (Archambault, 2011: 445), whilst a number of ICT4D practitioners had gone as far as to label the revolution as Africa's 'saviour' (e.g. Butler, 2005). As part of this sea-change in thinking, development agencies now simply transposed the arguments that they had previously made about the development potential for radio, print media, and television, onto mobile phones and mobile internet. In order words, just as they had previously argued for the virtues of increasing access to those other media in terms of their potential economic benefits – given their capacity to disseminate 'useful information' – so too agencies now made the same arguments about mobile phones. From 2005 onwards, these positions were greatly bolstered by the publication of a highly influential report by the multinational telecommunications company Vodafone, called *Africa: The Impact of Mobile Phones*, which argued very strongly, based on a range of empirical data, that increased densities of mobile phone ownership *did* result in individual productivity becoming more efficient, and that this in turn led to higher growth rates. The report also found that these effects were especially pronounced in low-income countries and amongst people engaged in mobile productive activities, such as fishing. Around the same time, a raft of other research studies, from around the developing world, were drawing similar conclusions (for an excellent overview of the vast literature on ICT4D and mobile phones from this period, see Donner, 2008: 140–159).

Development agencies also found that growing mobile phone markets were also generating a wide range of entirely *new* economic opportunities for people to engage in in their own right, such as: mobile phone companies employed increasing numbers of local people to run their in-country operations; traders opened shops to sell and to repair handsets and their associated paraphernalia; and entrepreneurs set up a myriad of phone-related services, ranging from money transfer schemes to food delivery businesses to dating services. Throughout Africa, Asia, and Latin America, people were also increasingly using mobile phones to remain in contact with their friends and relatives living overseas, and this in turn increased the volumes of remittances that the latter sent back (for an extended discussion of mobile phones and economic activities, see Aker and Mbiti, 2010). A growing number of developing countries, the most significant being China and India, were also using the new global demand for mobile phones and other digital ICT as catalysts for growing their own IT industries (i.e. industries that could manufacture digital technologies, develop software for the same, and provide a range of IT-related services). By the mid-2000s, it was becoming increasingly clear that these strategies could also have a major effect in boosting at least some developing countries' GDP growth. By 2013, the mobile phone industry, and its associated 'ecosystem' of economic activities, employed at least 2.4 million people and was worth about US$75 billion, or 5.4% of GDP, across sub-Saharan Africa (GSMA Intelligence, 2014a). By the same year, it employed at least one million people and was worth about US$242 billion, or 4.1% of GDP, across Latin America (GSMA Intelligence, 2014b). And by 2014, it employed 2.2 million and was worth more than US$100 billion, around 6.1% of GDP, in India alone (GSMA Intelligence, 2015). Moreover, across all of these places, all of these figures are still rapidly rising. According to current projections, by 2020 the mobile economy will account for a staggering 6.2%, 4.5%, and 8.2% of GDP across sub-Saharan Africa, Latin America, and India, respectively.

Mobile money

By 2005, international development agencies had put aside their former misgivings about the mobile phone revolution, and had begun instead to explore ways in which they might try to 'steer' – or to 'harness' – it towards broader development goals such as poverty reduction, improved health outcomes, and increasing access to education. And it was in their attempts to do precisely this that they were to generate what became the most socially significant innovation in relation to mobile phone markets in the developing world: mobile money. As we have seen, following the emergence of the Washington Consensus, donors and multi-lateral development agencies were heavily invested in the idea of expanding all kinds of markets across the developing world. However, this expansion would always be limited unless ordinary people in the developing world could fully participate in these, as consumers, in the same way that people living in western countries all do. To put it the other way around, markets would only become truly transformative once they became accessible to even the poorest people. This idea would become later elaborated by the neo-liberal Harvard economist Coimbatore Prahalad as the 'Bottom of the Pyramid' (BoP) approach to development, especially in his highly influential book, *The Fortune at the Bottom of the Pyramid: Eradicating Poverty Through Profits* (2004). However, a major barrier existed for very many Africans, Asians, and Latin Americans to becoming consumers, in the form of a lack of access to formal banking, credit, and other financial services. This was an outcome both of the lack of banking infrastructure in many developing countries, especially in their rural areas, and of the fact that the poorest members of those societies sometimes often did not hold land titles, or any other legally recognizable property, as might be used as collateral on loans or other forms of credit. It is against their property, of course, that consumers in the west secure a majority of their personal credit.

In this context, the challenge that was taken up by a number of the larger development agencies, in particular, was to find ways in which to deliver rudimentary banking services, including financial flows and basic credit services, to even the poorest people in the developing world – yet without these involving formal banking infrastructures, or requiring formal securities. In an attempt to meet this challenge, throughout the early 2000s a range of experiments were tried, and a good deal of research was carried out, on how this might work in practice. Perhaps the most well known of the experiments was one that was set up by the UK's Department for International Development (DfID), which equipped a fleet of 4-wheel drive vehicles to operate as mobile banks in several remote parts of rural Kenya. These vehicles would drive from village to village, according to a fixed timetable of visits, and during each stop would allow people to make deposits and withdrawals, and would also provide them with some at least rudimentary credit facilities. The vehicles' visits might also include some educational workshops, which were designed to 'up-skill' people in how to most effectively use credit, once they had secured it (Ngugi *et al.*, 2010: 4). However, it was ultimately the associated research that development agencies funded into the issue that was to produce the most lasting effects. Interestingly, from the outset, much of this research was heavily informed both by models such as Rogers' *Diffusion of Innovations*, and by the more general ideas of an anthropology of technology (described above). As a result, it was generally assumed that people living in the developing world would be much more likely to take up new banking services if those services conformed to their pre-existing practices of exchanging and storing value. Yet this would be impossible, of course, without first understanding the nature of those pre-existing practices. It was in this context, then, that much of the initial research effort went into trying to understand the kinds of exchange practices in which people were already engaging. And it was in 2002, during one of these studies – one that was also funded by DfID – that a group of researchers working on a comparative study of Botswana, Ghana, and Uganda, noticed how people in all three of those countries were by then regularly engaging in frequent, and at times highly elaborate, exchanges of mobile phone airtime vouchers, as a means both for making and receiving payments, and for circulating credit to each other (see McKemey *et al.*, 2003). It was directly from this study that m-pesa was born. The systems involved in delivering these new mobile banking services – which from the outset allowed mobile phone users to deposit, withdraw, and to exchange not only airtime, but also money as well – were therefore initially championed by DfID, in partnership with a range of the major commercial mobile phone companies. However, as the 2000s wore on, it was taken up by a range of other major international development agencies as well, including the World Bank, the Consultative Group to Assist the Poor (CGAP), and the Bill and Melinda Gates Foundation (BMGF). In 2009, these organizations led a consortium to launch a 'Mobile Money for the Unbanked' grant scheme, which had the aim of using mobile phones to provide banking to at least 20 million formerly 'unbanked' people in the developing world by 2012 (Maurer, 2012: 589). As we have already seen, they very quickly vastly surpassed this target, as mobile money became quickly incorporated within all of the different kinds of economic activities described above, including the transfer of remittances from people living in the diasporas, back to their friends and relatives in Africa, Asia, and Latin America.

Finally, by around 2005, a growing number of development agencies had begun to realize some of the problems involved in using telecentres as the primary means for expanding internet access across the developing world. By this time, it had become increasingly clear that, in addition to their high setup costs, telecentres had serious problems of sustainability. These stemmed both from the need to frequently upgrade both their equipment and software – given the speed at which both of these things become obsolete – and the need to train sufficient numbers of local staff to continue operating them after the organization that had set them up had withdrawn. In this context, and following the advent of 3G networks, donors, multi-lateral agencies, and even NGOs – who had been the driving force behind the telecentre movement – realized that the mobile revolution, given the speed at which it was occurring 'under its own steam' as it were, represented a much cheaper, quicker, and more efficient means for increasing internet access across the developing world, and for thereby at least partly closing the global 'digital divide'.

Media activism

Just as donors, multi-lateral agencies, and NGOs had also extolled the virtues of increasing access to radio, print media, and television in terms of their potential political advantages, especially in relation to their potential to engender new civic arenas, and spaces for activism, so too similar arguments were now made in regard to mobile phones and social media (World Bank, 2012; Brisset-Foucault, 2016). By the mid-2000s, these arguments had gained particular force following a series of influential publications that had interpreted the downfall of President Joseph Estrada of the Philippines, in January 2001, as *primarily* an outcome of popular street protests that had been organized at very short notice, and almost entirely via mobile phones and SMS text messaging. Following the failure of a specially convened court to impeach Estrada for corruption, these protests had emerged throughout the capital, Manila. Confronted with the speed and scale of the gatherings, the army decided to withdraw its support for the president, which forced him to resign. Following these events, the highly influential cultural studies theorist cum 'tech guru' Howard Rheingold, famously labelled these apparently popular gatherings as 'smart mobs' – a term that immediately gained common currency (Rheingold, 2002). However, an even more dramatic demonstration of mobile phones' political potential began in December 2010, with the emergence of the so-called 'Arab Spring' (Box 5.2). The Arab Spring was a series of political protests that began in Tunisia, but soon spread across international borders. It eventually led to the downfall of authoritarian governments in Egypt, Libya, Tunisia, and Yemen, and to sustained political pressure being brought to bear against illiberal regimes in at least 12 other countries across the Middle East and North Africa as well, including Bahrain, Iraq, Jordan, Kuwait, and Syria. From the start of the Arab Spring, mobile phones played a key role in the creation of protests, in the later coordination of the protestors' activities, and in the evolving political discussions and debates that took place among the various groups involved. Crucially, mobile phones also played a vital role in the protest spreading from Tunisia to other North African and Middle Eastern countries as well. Indeed, before mobile phones, protests of this kind could simply not have happened in the way that they did – not least given the fact that prior to the Arab Spring, many of the countries involved continued to have relatively 'closed' broadcasting environments. Therefore, mobile phones and their associated technologies provided an alternative forum for 'civic debate', and even a communications space in which popular discontent could be mobilized to overthrow entire regimes – potentially in many different countries at the same time. As a result, some commentators even hailed mobile phones as having therefore inaugurated a new era for global democracy (see, for example, Howard *et al.*, 2011).

Box 5.2 Media and the 'Arab Spring'

The so-called 'Arab Spring' – also called 'The Arab Awakening' – was a wave of non-violent and violent protests directed at authoritarian governments across North Africa and the Middle East, which led to the overthrow of the regimes in Egypt, Libya, Tunisia, and Yemen – although also resulted in a wave of counter-revolutionary violence, and in several civil wars (at least three of which – in Libya, Syria, and Yemen – continue to rage). The Arab Spring began on 17 December 2010, when a street vendor named Mohamed Bouazizi in the Tunisian capital, Tunis, set himself on fire in protest at being harassed by public officials. Such was the level of public anger, and empathy, at Bouazizi's plight, that it sparked a wave of huge demonstrations across the country, which eventually forced the country's autocratic president, Zine el Abidine Ben Ali, to step down after 23 years in power. Within just a few weeks, media broadcasts of what was happening in Tunisia had resulted in similar popular protests emerging in Egypt, Morocco, Syria, Oman, and Yemen, and by the end of 2011, these had spread to 13 other countries and territories across the region as well. From the outset, outside commentators argued that these protests would simply not have been possible before the mobile phone revolution. Noting that the national media environments of many of the countries involved were still characterized by state-owned monopolies, it was argued that the Tunisian protests had only grown so quickly, and spread to other countries so rapidly, because of the ways in which they were coordinated through social media. Indeed, for this reason, the protests were seen to demonstrate the potential for new, transnational 'smart mobs' to be created in and through social media platforms. However, later scholarly research on the events of 2010–2011 sounded a more cautious note over the role that social media had played here. Specifically, a raft of studies published from late 2011 onwards found that the early protests in Tunisia had been initially driven by word of mouth, and that people in the other countries involved had discovered what was happening in Tunisia mostly through what they had learned on 'traditional' media platforms (i.e. radio and the television), rather than through social media. At certain times during the Arab Spring, both mobile phones and the internet had played a key role. However, the most significant form of mobile phone use involved SMS text messaging rather than social media platforms, and the main use of the internet was for email and blogs also. Indeed, the main role that social media – such as Facebook, Instagram, and Twitter – had played in the events was in spreading awareness of them in countries outside of North Africa and the Middle East. Therefore, the overall picture to emerge here is of complex media environments, in which word of mouth interacted with various media platforms – in different ways, at different times – to produce the outcomes observed. Whilst this reality is more in keeping with what many ICT4D theorists' – from Rogers onwards – have recognized as the 'socially embedded' nature of media, it did also temper some of the more 'utopian' claims that had been made for the democratic possibilities for social media during the early months of this major transnational political event.

Sources: Howard et al. (2011), Khondker (2011).

In the years since the Arab Spring, mobile phones – and increasingly social media as well – have played an ever more important role within all sorts of political activism, in countries across the developing world. For example, in Africa, the period since 2010 has witnessed an increasing use of mobiles and social media platforms to mobilize and to coordinate various kinds of opposition activities. In 2010–2011, Nigeria's presidential and parliamentary election campaigns witnessed the extensive use of mobile phones and social media by opposition groups for just about everything, including organizing rallies, political advertising, gaining feedback on their own policies, fact-checking government campaign promises, and collecting unofficial polling data (Fadoju, 2015). On the polling days themselves, SMS messages sent from polling stations around the country were monitored at opposition party headquarters to check for any patterns of vote-rigging or other kinds of electoral fraud. This was an early example of mobile technologies being used to engage in a 'popular', real-time form of what is technically known as 'Parallel Vote Tabulation' (PVT). PVT refers to any method of election-monitoring in which any non-governmental actor gathers its own, independent voting tallies, in order for these to then be cross-checked against official results (Garber and Cowan, 1993).

In March 2015, South Africa saw mobile phones and social media being used to mobilize and coordinate the 'Rhodes Must Fall' campaign, which began at the University of Cape Town (UCT) and subsequently spread to other universities. Rhodes Must Fall was a student-led protest that began with an effort to pressure UCT to take down its statue of Cecil John Rhodes – who was Prime Minister of the colonial Cape Colony from 1890 to 1896, a key architect of British imperial expansion in Southern Africa, and well known for his deeply racist views of black Africans. From the beginning of the campaign, students used Facebook and especially Twitter (#RhodesMustFall) to coordinate a series of spontaneous direct action protests focused upon the statue that were eventually successful: UCT eventually took down the statue on 9 April 2015.

As importantly, though, Facebook and Twitter were also key venues for participants in the campaign to debate the wider issues that the Rhodes statue symbolized, especially the ongoing legacies of South Africa's colonial past in general, and the perceived institutional racism of its tertiary education sector in particular. These same social media have since been used to coordinate other student protests in South Africa as well, such as the later #FeesMustFall campaign (see Africa is a Country's video on the campaign, which is available online at http://africasacountry.com/2015/10/watch-our-11-minute-film-capturing-the-energies-of-feesmustfall-in-south-africa/). Finally, in 2016, Zimbabwe witnessed social media being used to generate a major 'viral' opposition protest called #ThisFlag. 'This Flag' began when Pastor Evan Mawarire posted on Facebook a passionate critique of President Robert Mugabe and his government, which is framed in terms of how the regime's recent actions have sullied the symbolism of the Zimbabwean national flag: a powerful symbol of nationalist pride in the country. In the video, Mawarire is draped in the flag, and encourages other Zimbabweans to record their own criticisms of the government, and to post these online, also whilst wearing the flag (Mawarire's video can be viewed online at www.youtube.com/watch?v=Ut9F5d3vxUY). Several thousand people took up the call, thereby effectively beginning an organic digital protest movement – which later evolved into a declared 25 days of digital activism. In May, two opposition MPs were even evicted from Zimbabwe's parliament for wearing the flag to a sitting (Allison, 2016).

Over the past decade or so, mobile phones and social media have also played an increasingly important role in galvanizing political activism *across* international borders – or, in other words, within 'transnational fields' (Ginsburg *et al.*, 2002). Of particular relevance for international development have been those cases in which these new media have been used for political mobilization among *diasporas* – to create diasporic activist movements which may then go on to shape political environments 'back home' (i.e. back in those diasporic groups' countries of origin; Sheffer, 2006; Lyons and Mandaville, 2012). In recent years, these kinds of diasporic constituencies have come to be seen as especially effective in shaping post-war or other 'transitional' political contexts, and/or in checking the powers of authoritarian national regimes (Jones, 2016). For example, the period since 2000 has seen social media playing an increasingly important role in the mobilization of support both for existing political parties and for new political movements among the Kurdish diaspora in Germany. These new constituencies have been highly influential in the predominantly ethnically Kurdish regions of both Turkey and Iraq (Ostergaard-Nielsen, 2003). Over the past decade or so, the internet has been crucial in the formation of a coherent Zimbabwean opposition-in-exile, which has become in effect the main force for political opposition within Zimbabwe itself (McGregor and Primorac, 2010). Meanwhile, in recent years, social media have also played a key role in the mobilization of the Sri Lankan Tamil diaspora – which is located throughout the world – around post-war reconstruction efforts, following the end of the country's long-running civil war, which lasted from 1983 to 2009 (Orjuela, 2008). (The above three examples are all cited in Jones, 2016, who develops the further case study of diasporic politics and Rwanda.) Moreover, it is also interesting to note that many of these diasporic movements have been mobilized not just through the internet and social media in general, but through *community* webpages and social media sites in particular. For example, my own research has shown how during the run-up to the Ugandan elections of 2016, an increasing number of parliamentary candidates used social media platforms such as WhatsApp to mobilize support – including financial support – for their bids among diasporic populations. In one case that I documented, a candidate created a dedicated WhatsApp group that eventually included several hundred people, all of whom were from his home 'community' – in that they had all been born in the same village as him (and in most cases were members of just a handful of families from that village) – yet who now live all over the world (see Vokes, 2016b).

Participatory GIS

Finally, just as donors, multi-lateral agencies, NGOs, and community groups had previously explored how radio and television might be used to significantly extend, and to deepen, the reach of participatory communication projects, they also began to explore how mobile phones might do likewise. In other words, all of these groups began to explore how mobile phones – through their capacities both to make calls and to send and receive SMS messages – might be used to make participatory communication both more direct, and more personally engaging, than ever before. They also looked at how these technologies could increase the scale of participatory projects – to now potentially garner the input of, and to thereby deepen social empathy amongst, *all* mobile phone and internet users within a given region, or even country. These possibilities were expanded further still following the advent of 4G mobile phone networks, which also brought social media software such as Facebook and WhatsApp. Following this, there was an explosion in the number of participatory communication projects and initiatives using mobile phones, initially in the area of health programming (Pettit *et al.*, 2009; Chou *et al.*, 2013). Over time, development agencies and community groups also explored ways in which participatory communication projects might make use of, or in other ways engage with, the new kinds of civic activism that mobile phones and social media were already generating (see above). This, of course, had the potential to give participatory communication an even greater role within purposive social change in general (Goggin and Clark, 2009).

Over the past decade or so, an emerging field of participatory 'geographic information systems (GIS)' has further explored ways in which the techniques of participatory communication may be combined with geo-spatial management data – such as 2D maps, satellite imagery, and 3D spatial models – in order to gain people's input into, and their own perspectives on, emerging situations, and to plot these onto 'dynamic' maps (i.e. maps which update in 'real time'). In most cases, this involves gathering people's input and perspectives (i.e. 'crowdsourcing' their views) via email, Twitter or, more commonly, SMS, and then inputting these into relevant GIS software (excellent general introductions to participatory GIS are provided by Abbot *et al.*, 1998; McCall and Minang, 2005; Elwood, 2006a, 2006b). The resulting dynamic maps may then be used by the relevant authorities, or development agencies, to guide their interventions, and/or they can be output to the public at large, via websites, as a means for helping people to make sense of their own experiences in relation to the wider contexts in which they are located. In other words, they can be used as a means for 'mediating' people's own experiences of a given event or place. In this sense, participatory GIS is also part of the emergent 'Web 2.0', which refers to the phenomenon whereby around the world people increasingly use the internet, and cloud-based services, for collaborative projects aimed at the co-production of information (see Zook *et al.*, 2010). The techniques of participatory GIS have proved especially effective for rapidly mapping people's experiences of, and for designing relevant responses to, various kinds of fast-changing – and large-scale – events, such as large-scale political violence, wars, and natural disasters (Gao *et al.*, 2011). For example, one of the earliest cases to demonstrate the potential power of participatory GIS to great effect was a project set up by a group of Kenyans in response to the large-scale political violence that engulfed their country from late 2007 onwards, following the contested general elections on 27 December of that year (Okolloh, 2009). The project tried to create a dynamic map of the scale and nature of the unrest throughout the country, by gathering eyewitness accounts of individual acts of violence, which were mostly submitted via SMS. The project then used its own specially designed piece of software, called Ushahidi in Swahili (*lit.* 'witness'), to map these onto Google Maps, which could then be viewed in real-time on any web browser (see www.ushahidi.com). So successful was the project – with a later academic analysis showing that it mapped the Kenyan crisis far more accurately than did any 'traditional' data gathering techniques, or conventional media outlets – that the Ushahidi software itself, or later versions of it, have been subsequently taken up in a range of other major crisis contexts. For example, the software has since been used to create dynamic maps of, and to help the design of dynamic responses to, the Haiti Earthquake disaster of 2010 (Box 5.3), the Libyan Civil War from 2011 onwards (Stottlemyre and Stottlemyre, 2012), and the LRA emergency, also from 2011 (Box 5.4).

Box 5.3 GIS and the Haiti earthquake disaster, 2010

At 4.53 pm on 12 January 2012, an earthquake of magnitude 7.0 struck 25 km west of Haiti's capital, Port-au-Prince. The seismic event, and its subsequent aftershocks, caused massive damage to the city's built environment, killed at least 100,000 people (and probably many more), and left up to 3 million people without adequate shelter, food or sanitation. Over the days and weeks that followed, a major international relief operation was launched in response to the crisis, which was led by the US military, but involved dozens of other international humanitarian organizations as well. However, one of the major problems that all these agencies experienced from the outset was a general lack of sufficient maps for the disaster zone (given that Port-au-Prince was, at the time, not adequately covered by standard web mapping services such as Bing Maps and Google Maps). In response, in the first 24 hours after the initial earthquake struck, a number of commercial satellite imaging companies – including DigitalGlobe, GeoEye, and Google – worked collaboratively to generate high-quality and real-time imagery of the zone, and to make this available to all of the agencies involved. However, what the humanitarian agencies really needed were detailed geographical information databases that could be merged onto these satellite images, which would enable them to navigate the urban landscape (for example, by telling them where important infrastructure such as hospitals, water mains, and electricity junctions were sited), and to save lives by helping them to pinpoint where injured survivors might be located. Yet such detailed GIS databases typically take years to develop. What happened, then, was the emergence of an online volunteer community of web designers and software engineers, based all over the world, who worked collaboratively to generate the necessary GIS data. They did this by gathering as much geographical information as they could from online sources, and recoding this into unified and usable formats. They also developed simple web-based tools through which the people of Port-au-Prince could upload critical information onto the resulting GIS platforms, in real-time, via SMS and emails. A number of networks and structures to support this collaborative technical effort were already in place.

In particular, in 2009, a group of government agencies, NGOs, private companies, and interested citizens had formed a worldwide network called CrisisCommons, with a view to just such a situation. Following the 12 January earthquake, this group organized a series of 'CrisisCamps' (Haiti), which physically brought together web designers and software engineers to work on the technical solutions required. The first of these camps was held in the US, with others subsequently taking place in more than 20 other countries around the world. Similar collaborative efforts also emerged from communities associated with GeoCommons, OpenStreetMap, and Ushahidi. As a result of all of these efforts, within just a few days, an entire infrastructure for participatory GIS had been set up, and this was used to guide the relief efforts, in real-time, over the following weeks and months. Indeed, so effective was the work of this global online community of web designers and software engineers, that their efforts might be even described as the world's first ever 'virtual relief operation'.

Source: Zook et al. (2010).

Box 5.4 KONY 2012

The KONY 2012 campaign is a good example of how development and humanitarian work has been afforded new opportunities while also facing new problems since the advent of the internet and social media. The campaign was the work of a US-based advocacy group called Invisible Children, which was set up in 2004 by three former film students from California, in response to ongoing violence by the Uganda-originating insurgent group The Lord's Resistance Army (LRA), which is led by Joseph Kony. Prior to KONY 2012, Invisible Children was best known for its work in creating – along with its partner organization the Resolve LRA Crisis Initiative – a participatory GIS system for mapping incidents of LRA-related violence across the Democratic Republic of Congo–Central African Republic borderlands, the region in which the LRA has been most active since 2008. The system used crowdsourced data plotted on Ushahidi from radios that Invisible Children had distributed throughout the troubled areas, to map the location and nature of LRA attacks in 'real time'. This later became the 'LRA Crisis Tracker' website, which in addition to mapping attacks, also includes personal testimonies from LRA victims (including in photographic and video diary formats), and aggregates media reports on the insurgent group. The Tracker is also now available as a mobile app. However, with KONY 2012, Invisible Children used the internet in another way also: to mobilize support for their own lobbying efforts aimed at stopping LRA violence among global media audiences. This was done primarily through a 30-minute campaign film that was initially uploaded to the video sharing websites Vimeo and YouTube. The film quickly 'went viral', especially over Facebook, and within one week had been viewed more than 21 million times (as of the time of writing, the YouTube video alone has now been viewed over 100 million times). Within barely a few days of the video's launch, a great many theories had already been put forward – both in traditional media outlets and in the 'blogosphere' – as to precisely why the film was so rapidly and so widely circulated. At least part of the answer here may lie in the film's general reliance upon an appeal to emotion, in particular in relation to its representation of the general 'fear' that LRA-affected populations may experience, rather than upon a balanced assessment of the facts and in this regard, the film can be said to draw on the techniques of 'post-humanitarian communication' (see above). Yet whatever the reasons for its appeal, there is no doubt that the video vastly increased public awareness of the LRA insurgency and its effects. However, also within a few days of its release, both Invisible Children and the KONY 2012 film began to come in for a range of criticisms as well. These ranged from attacks on the video's style of 'celebrity humanitarianism' (the opening sections of the film, in particular, are terribly self-indulgent on the part of Invisible Children founder Jason Russell), to its central thesis that the best way to deal with the LRA is through military intervention. However, one of the most widespread criticisms was that having won the attention of such a large global media audience – at least some of whom must have watched the film for its full 29 minutes and 59 seconds – requested them to do very little at all, other than to recirculate the video (i.e. to click their mouse), to buy an 'action kit' for the campaign, and to put up the posters from this kit in their home towns on 20 April 2012 (although only a minute fraction of the people who watched the video appear to have actually done this). In these ways, the campaign was criticized for encouraging a form of what Ozard and Clark have called 'slactivism'. This largely explains why, despite its massive global media reach, the KONY 2012 campaign arguably had very little impact at all upon anti-LRA policy or operations.

Sources: Gregory (2012), Vokes (http://bit.ly/H6giiY), https://lracrisistracker.com.

Yet Participatory GIS is used not only in major crisis contexts; it has been employed in other development contexts as well, including the Map Kibera project (Box 5.5).

Box 5.5 Map Kibera, Kenya

One of the best-known examples of a participatory communication project that has made innovative use of new media technologies, including social media and the internet, as a means for 'upscaling' community participation in its work, is the Map Kibera Project (MKP). Launched in 2009 by Erica Hagen and Mikel Maron – who went on to form the GroundTruth Initiative – in collaboration with a number of Kenyan partner organizations, the project focuses on Kibera, one of the largest informal settlement, or 'slum', areas in the Kenyan capital of Nairobi (the area has an estimated population of around 250,000 people). Although Kibera has been a site of intense activity by a wide range of international development agencies, government bodies, and NGOs over many decades, prior to the advent of the MKP very little of vast amounts of map data and other information that these organizations had produced had ever been made available to the area's residents themselves. In an attempt to facilitate ordinary citizens to access and to produce data of their own – with the ultimate aim of enabling them to have greater control over their own lives – Hagen and Maron began by holding a series of workshops in which local people were taught how to use GPS technologies. At first, these were used to simply map out the slum in an accurate way, and in a format that could be made available to everyone (via the OpenStreetMap platform). However, within a short space of time, the technologies were also employed to generate a kind of broad-scale *social map* as well, in which residents also plotted sites that were of particular economic, political, and social interest to them (such as shops, NGO offices, toilets, water points, and electric lights). Over time, the project developed into a major community information resource, one that increasingly included many other forms of multimedia content as well. Today, the whole thing has evolved into the Voice of Kibera community website, to which any resident of the slum can now post news and information of their own choosing via SMS or webform, which is automatically geo-located on the Open map, and which is posted in more-or-less real-time. A team of young people connected to the Map Kibera Trust can then follow up on certain items that are posted, by producing short videos on those topics (which are then posted to YouTube) and/or by organizing community workshops around the issues. Following the MKP, the GroundTruth Initiative have gone on to develop similar projects in other informal urban settlement areas as well, including Tandale in Dar es Salaam (Tanzania) and al Walajeh, a Palestinian settlement in Jerusalem, Israel.

Sources: Hagen (2011), Donovan (2012), http://voiceofkibera.org.

New media environments: the challenges for ICT4D

Over this very same period – that is, from the early 1990s onwards – donor governments, multi-lateral agencies, and NGOs began to recognize how the spread of media technologies across the developing world was also starting to generate a series of significant challenges as well. First, the general growth of media ownership, regardless of the potential economic and political advantages it might confer (see above), certainly did also generate a series of material and financial *burdens* for ordinary people living in the developing world. These related to the time and money it took to get these media machines and their associated paraphernalia running in the first place, to keep them working over time – something which always required either a fixed electricity supply or replaceable batteries – and/or to fix them when they broke down. In many developing world contexts, and especially for households in rural areas and in urban slums, any of these factors could represent a significant challenge. Although these kinds of material and financial burdens have always been an issue in relation to all media technologies – for example, even today, although a majority of households in my main field site in rural Uganda own a radio set, less than half can afford the batteries required to keep them running on a regular basis – they have become particularly acute in relation to mobile phones. This is because anyone wishing to make a mobile phone call must first assemble not only the mobile phone handset itself, but also, as a minimum list, a charged battery – which usually requires a phone charger as well – a sim card, and a 'loaded' airtime card (Vokes, 2016a). Yet each of these separate items may require significant investments of time and money to acquire – and again, this is particularly true for people living in rural areas and urban slums. Furthermore, a raft of recent studies have shown how, precisely because each of these items does require significant investments of time and money, they may result in people entering into exchange relations in which they are open to manipulation. For example, Burrell (2010: 238) has shown how women in rural Uganda can only get mobile handsets if they are purchased by their husbands, yet they are then vulnerable to their husbands using the phones to control their movements by 'checking up' on their whereabouts. Archambault (2013: 95–96) has shown how young women in Mozambique may typically secure airtime from their extra-martial lovers, yet again be forced into obligations as a result (for example, to ring their lovers at certain times). And Pype (2016) has shown how, in the Democratic Republic of Congo (DRC), elderly people are entirely reliant for mobile phones upon their children and other young relatives, yet may become beholden to them as a result. In these ways, then, all media technologies, but especially mobile phones, far from empowering women or the elderly, may in fact generate new avenues for them to become *dis*empowered, and new ways for them to be controlled by others as well.

Secondly, the general expansion of media infrastructures and media providers, all of which were more deeply integrated into global markets, also made consumers in the developing world more vulnerable to the vagaries of market forces – such that, for example, they may be more exposed to the kinds of economic 'shocks' that may follow from sudden market slowdowns. This kind of risk was demonstrated to dramatic effect in relation to the British government-backed expansion of GTV in Africa from mid-2007 onwards. As described above, GTV's securing of English Premier League (EPL) football rights acted as a vehicle for the company to massively expand both its broadcasting infrastructure and its subscription base across Africa within a relatively short period of time. By mid-2008, barely a year after its arrival on the continent, GTV had already secured over 100,000 subscribers, across more than 20 African countries (Vokes, 2010). However, disaster was shortly to follow, when in 2008 the 'Global Financial Crisis' (GFC) and the concomitant 'credit-crunch' struck. It transpired that GTV's initial US$200 million investment into Africa, which had been used to develop its broadcasting infrastructure and to subsidize the sale of TV equipment to its subscribers (and which was, incidentally, the largest ever single investment in media ever made in Africa), had been funded almost entirely through loans, and that following the GFC, these were no longer sustainable. As a result, in January 2009, GTV went into liquidation, its broadcasting signal was switched off, and its entire infrastructure and all of the equipment it had subsidized for its subscribers was rendered useless. Moreover, for many of the subscribers themselves, the negative effects of this event went way beyond a mere economic inconvenience. For example, in one case study I carried out, I documented the situation of one young man in rural Uganda who had used a subscription to GTV – and the EPL games this accessed – to build up a small business centred around a 'cinema hall'. Following the GTV turn-off, not only did this business collapse but the young man was left to manage a series of debts and other obligations that had been secured against the cinema hall. Unable to manage these himself, at one stage it looked as though he might even end up in jail (although thankfully, this was eventually avoided; see Vokes, 2010). However, the key point remains: if an expansion of media infrastructures and media providers across the Global South *has* accelerated globalization, then so too has it further exposed people in the developing world to the potentially toxic effects of global crises as well.

Finally, the general increase in media ownership, and expansion of media infrastructures, also resulted in an unprecedented growth in demand for the raw materials required to make radios, televisions, computers, and mobile phones, and this in turn generated a rush to secure their supply – a rush that, in some cases, inevitably resulted in unscrupulous practices. As the raw materials involved here were themselves mined in developing world countries, there was also an increased risk that this rush – and its associated practices – might produce a range of damaging effects in its own right, including everything from exacerbating corruption to stoking armed conflict. In relation to the latter, from the late 1990s onwards, a number of NGOs – including Amnesty International and Global Witness – and subsequently the UN as well, drew particular attention to the way in which attempts to control the supply chains of columbite-tantalite (or 'coltan') from the Democratic Republic of Congo (DRC) had played a significant role in exacerbating ongoing armed conflict in that country (Montague, 2002). Because of this, coltan – an element that is vital for the production of tantalum capacitors, which are found in practically every kind of electronic device – has become regarded, in the popular imagination, as a 'conflict mineral' par excellence. As a result, it has also engaged everyone from development organizations to the world's largest technology companies – including Apple, Intel, and Nokia – in major efforts to improve the mineral's 'supply-chain transparency' (Bleischwitz et al., 2012).

The general increase in media ownership also exponentially increased volumes of e-waste worldwide. The concept of e-waste refers to 'all items of electrical and electronic equipment (EEE) and its parts that have been discarded by its owner as waste without the intent of reuse' (Step Initiative, cited in Baldé et al., 2015). However, some electrical and electronic items, and their parts, may of course represent more of a health and environmental hazard than others (and thus, may be more or less difficult to reuse, to recycle, or to dispose of). For example, cathode ray tube (CRT) televisions – which accounted for the vast majority of television sets worldwide before the major uptake of liquid crystal display (LCD) televisions in the developed world from around 2012 onwards – are especially hazardous, given that the CRTs themselves invariably contain high levels of lead and other highly toxic elements. So too, the central processing units (CPUs) found in all computers – and now smartphones as well – usually also contain lead, together with cadmium and beryllium (albeit in smaller quantities than are found in CRTs). In addition, mobile phones handsets may contain up to 40 toxic elements, although many phone manufacturers are increasingly trying to reduce these toxins, in order to make their handsets as 'green' as possible. However, the significant challenge of e-waste stems not just from the nature of specific devices and the toxins they contain, but also the sheer volume of discarded EEE that is now in circulation throughout the world, and/or has been put into rubbish dumps.

In recent decades, this volume has been significantly increased by each of a series of media 'revolutions', including: the advent of mass ownership of personal computers (which in Europe and North America really 'got going' from around the late 1980s onwards); the arrival of mobile phones (and in the western world, the mobile 'revolution' dates from slightly earlier than in the developing world) and the subsequent advent of smartphones; the change from VHS video to DVD technologies during the late 1990s; and the more recent broad switch from CRT to LCD televisions. Each of these revolutions generated mass waves of new e-waste, as consumers replaced their existing technologies with the newer, incoming products. (To complete the picture on volumes of e-waste, it would also be necessary to consider key developments in relation to other consumer devices as well, such as fridges, dishwashers, and other domestic appliances. However, consideration of such a wide range of devices is beyond our scope here.) Moreover, with each of these revolutions, the likelihood that consumers would replace their existing products, rather than persist with their older models, and/or fix their existing technologies, was increased through the actions of the technology companies themselves. Specifically, in recent decades, big tech companies have increasingly adopted 'planned obsolescence' – a design concept invented by General Electric's light bulb division in the 1920s, in which a new product is deliberately manufactured either to break, or to run out, or to in some other way become obsolete, within a finite period of time. The result is that consumers have no choice but to replace the technology in question. And big tech companies have increasingly engaged in even more aggressive marketing of their incremental – and usually extremely minor – upgrades to existing product lines (think: the difference between the iPhone 5S and its predecessor, the iPhone 5), again with a view to encouraging consumers to replace their existing products with newer ones (Guiltinan, 2009). As a result of these various forces, then, the sheer scale of EEE as a 'waste stream' – as it is technically known – in today's world is nothing short of mind-boggling. For example, a recent publication by the United Nations University's Institute for the Advanced Study of Sustainability, called 'The Global E-Waste Monitor 2014' (Baldé et al., 2015), a report which developed the most accurate framework yet for measuring volumes of e-waste, estimated that in the 5 years between 2010 and 2014 alone, a staggering 189 million tonnes of new e-waste was generated worldwide. And by 2018, global volumes of e-waste are projected to reach almost 50 million tonnes per annum (*ibid.*, 24).

Moreover – and this is really the key point here – the burden of e-waste has in some respects always fallen disproportionately upon the societies of the developing world. This is because from around the late 1980s onwards (i.e. from the period following the advent of mass personal computer ownership in Europe and North America), western countries have increasingly 'dumped' toxic EEE into developing world countries. This was partly a result of improved legislation over the disposal of e-waste in the western countries themselves

– legislation which, ironically, *increased* the incentive to transport these materials to the generally less robust legislative environments found in many African, Asian, and Latin American countries. The result was the emergence of a series of 'mega-dumps' for e-waste across the developing world. Perhaps the best known of these dumps are Agbogbloshie in Accra, Ghana and Guiyu near Shantou, China (both of which have been extensively researched, and the subject of various films and even art projects; for examples of films and art projects focused on the Accra and Guiyu dumps, see Hugo, 2011 and Chung and Getty, 2016, respectively). However, in truth, sites like these now exist all over the developing world, albeit not always on the scale of Agbogbloshie or Guiyu (Box 5.6).

Box 5.6 Guiyu, China

Guiyu is a group of four interconnected villages – with a combined population of about 150,000 people – situated close to the large port city of Shantou, in Guangdong Province, China. From the 1990s onwards, it became established as the largest e-waste dump on earth (although some sources claim that this dubious honour is now held by Agbogbloshie in Ghana). From the 1980s onwards, Guiyu became a key location for waste companies based across Guangdong, and in the major cities along China's south-east coast (including Quanzhou and Xiamen, as well as Macau and Hong Kong) to ship their e-waste to. Guiyu's proximity to the Port of Shantou, as well as other major transport routes (Guiyu also sits on the River Lianjiang), made it relatively cheap and easy to offload to. Later, Guiyu also became a major site for western waste management companies, including several from the US, to also offload their e-waste. Ironically, it was as regulations relating to the safe disposal of e-waste became stricter in the US – which made it more expensive for waste management companies to dispose of such materials in their home country – that places like Guiyu became more attractive, and cost-effective, as sites for dumping. As the volumes of e-waste coming into the place increased, so too did the number of small businesses – the majority of them family-owned enterprises – that were involved in 'recycling' these items. In most cases, this process involves two sets of businesses. The first set break the machines down into their component parts, and then sell the different parts off to various 'specialists'. This second set of businesses then employ various methods for extracting valuable metallic elements from the different parts, including gold, copper, and lead. By 2012, it was estimated that by these means, Guiyu was processing more than 700 million tonnes of e-waste per year, through more than 5,500 of these small enterprises. However, from 2001 onwards, a number of international environmental groups, including the Basel Action Network and Greenpeace, have drawn attention to the massive detrimental health and environmental impacts of Guiyu's industries. In particular, the 'second stage' processes of extracting metallic elements often involve crude methods of burning the e-waste – which is made up mostly of plastics, rubber, and paint – in open smelters to give up the metals contained therein. Not only are large volumes of toxic gases released

Figure 5.1 *Agbogbloshie e-waste dump in Ghana*

Source: Photo courtesy of Andrew McConnell

into the air, but the waste products from these smelters are often simply poured out onto the ground afterwards. And a series of major health population health studies of Guiyu residents has highlighted just how dangerous all of this is to human health. For example, one major study done by Shantou University's Medical School found that over 82% of children in Guiyu had dangerous levels of lead in their bloodstream. In recent years, a number of NGOs have been working with Guiyu companies, in an attempt to get them to employ safer methods for stripping the e-waste. However, the responsibility for addressing the kinds of problems associated with places like Guiyu may ultimately reside with the major international tech companies themselves – and their consumers. If tech companies made their machines from more environmentally safe materials in the first place, which they will be especially encouraged to do if their customers demand it, then the hazards for Guiyu might be 'addressed at their source', as it were.

Source: Chung and Getty (2016).

At all of these sites, large numbers of urban dwellers, who are often extremely poor, are willing to run the massive health risks that come with exposure to the kinds of toxic chemicals that are contained in e-waste, so as to try to derive a basic living from salvaging items of value. Yet in so doing, they are storing up major public health crises for the future for the governments of Ghana and China. More recently, and especially following the mobile phone revolution in the Global South, the burden of e-waste has disproportionately fallen upon the developing world in another way as well, in that the Global South is now producing a growing amount of e-waste of its own (which, again because of weak legal regimes, is more likely to end up being disposed of in an unsafe manner). For example, the Global E-Waste Monitor 2014 found that India and China already produce a combined 7.7 million tonnes of e-waste per annum (about 18% of the global total), and this figure is set to grow significantly in the coming years (Baldé et al., 2015: 42). In response, a raft of initiatives have been started in recent years, with a view to tackling the problems associated with e-waste in the developing world. In particular, in 2007, the UN, together with the tech giant Hewlett-Packard and various other partner organizations, launched the 'Solving The E-Waste Problem' (STEP) initiative, which today conducts a wide range of research and intervention projects aimed at tackling the issue. However, as of 2017, it appears highly likely that the problems associated with e-waste in the developing world will likely become significantly worse – probably over several decades or more – before they start to get better.

'Toxic' media content

From the early 1990s onwards, donor governments, multi-lateral agencies, and NGOs also began to realize that it was not only physical media technologies that contain toxic elements – media content can as well. Thus, agencies' initial optimism that following liberalization the early 'spike' in global content would eventually be replaced by more and more locally produced content (see above), was tempered by the realization that there was really nothing to stop this new wave of locally produced content from outputting inflammatory, racist or in other ways derogatory content. In this respect, the age-old libertarian arguments that an increasingly free press will *always* produce positive social outcomes – because it will inevitably result in toxic content being 'drowned out' by other kinds of more moderate media content – were exposed as at best overly optimistic, and at worst dangerously naïve. The problem with these kinds of libertarian arguments – which by the early 1990s had been significantly revived under the umbrella of 'media development' (see above) – was that they failed to account for the existing political and social structures that might pertain in a particular country at the point at which increased press freedoms were first introduced. Yet these existing structures might have the potential to subvert the very process of 'opening up' the airwaves, to control the emerging marketplace, and potentially at least to use this control to do damage before more moderate content has had a chance to 'catch up'.

As it turned out, the international development community did not have to wait long before these potential dangers were demonstrated in reality – and indeed, in a devastating way – by a radio station, Radio-Television Libre des Milles Collines (RTLM) in the small Central African country of Rwanda. Prior to 1994, there appeared to be little that was remarkable about the history of radio in Rwanda, compared with other countries in sub-Saharan Africa. Thus, prior to the First World War, radio ownership in the country had been relatively low, given the prohibitive costs of sets. But from around the mid-1950s onwards, following the invention of the cheap transistor radio, ownership had risen dramatically and by the late 1980s – partly as a result of a government policy to subsidize radios – private ownership was amongst the highest in Africa. At that time, the government-owned broadcaster, Radio Rwanda, enjoyed a broadcasting monopoly throughout the country. However, following the debt crises of the mid-1970s onwards, and also the sharp fall in coffee prices during the late 1980s (Rwanda's main export commodity), in 1990 the IMF and World Bank imposed the first of a series of SAPs on the country – and as part of these, the country's media environment was liberalized, and the airwaves were opened up to new broadcasters (Uvin, 1998). Unfortunately, this occurred at a time when Rwanda was experiencing a civil war in the north of the country, and when (we now know) a network of highly influential Hutu extremists called the *akazu* (*lit.* 'little house') were beginning to plot – and to secretly position themselves – to take over the country, in the event that the war should take a 'turn for the worse' or that some other political 'shock' should occur in the country (for the best account of the rise of Hutu-extremism in the context of Rwanda's political landscape during this period, see Prunier, 1995; Des Forges and Liebhafsky, 1999).

Following the liberalization of the airwaves in Rwanda, the first new station to open was RTLM, which began broadcasting on 8 July 1993 (the following section is based on my extended analysis of RTLM, published in Vokes, 2007a). Being the first privately owned radio station in the country, RTLM was probably guaranteed a broad listenership from the start. However, to begin with, at least, its popularity was also bolstered by the station's extensive collection of 'hot' Congolese and Caribbean music, which was very attractive to younger listeners in particular. However, in October 1993, the tone and content of RTLM's output changed dramatically, and its schedule became increasingly dominated not by music, but by a series of talk shows hosted by a number of charismatic 'shock jocks' (as we would now call them), including Valerie Bemeriki, Gaspard Gihigi, Kantano Habimana, Noel Kitimana ('Noheli'), and later Georges Ruggiu (an Italian national). Each show was typically hosted by one of these presenters and, following a Q&A format, some of which involved phone-ins, would focus on a specific political issue or event. Although punctuated with good humour, the shows were usually serious in content and intense in tone, and often engendered heated debate. At the time, observers from the international community were generally impressed with the station's broadcasts, and felt that its debates did indeed represent the kind of hoped-for emergent 'civic structure' – except that, as it turned out, RTLM was in fact owned by several members of the *akazu*, including Ferdinand Nahimana and Jean-Bosco Barayagwiza, and all of its presenters were therefore in fact mouthpieces for the Hutu extremist network. As a result, during late 1993 and early 1994, RTLM's output (the majority of which was in Rwanda's national language, *Kinyarwanda*), became increasingly racist towards the country's other major ethnic group, the Tutsi.

On 6 April 1994, a plane carrying President Juvenal Habyarimana was shot down over the capital, Kigali, which provided the political shock necessary for the *akazu* to seize control of the country, and to put into action a genocide plan that they had been working on for some months (even today, debate still rages over precisely who shot down Habyarimana's plane). The *akazu*'s aim was nothing short of the killing of all Tutsi in Rwanda, a goal which, through their control of the security services, local village 'defence units', and a body of armed militia called the *Inteerahamwe* (*lit.* 'those who strike together'), they came very close to achieving. Between 6 April and late July 1994, the Rwandan genocide resulted in the deaths of an estimated 800,000 Tutsi, together with moderate Hutu, the fastest rate of killing ever recorded. But the point is that throughout this period of the genocide itself, RTLM appears also to have played a significant role in stoking the general climate of ethnic hatred and fear in which the mass killings took place (not least by constantly referring to Tutsi people as 'cockroaches', and in other de-humanizing ways); in praising the actions of the army, defence units, and *Inteerahamwe*

Figure 5.2 *A scene from the play 'Hate Radio' (a South African play that reconstructed hate radio in the Rwandan genocide of 1994)*

Source: Photo courtesy of Daniel Seiffert

(albeit through only oblique references to their actual acts of mass murder); and in encouraging the general public to participate in the killings. At least one scholar, Scott Straus, has found – through a detailed analysis of a wide range of the available empirical evidence – that these messages alone 'could not account for either the onset of most Rwandan genocidal violence or the participation of most perpetrators' (2011: 85). Nevertheless, they clearly had an important 'conditional effect' upon the genocide (i.e. they formed part of the overall context) – along with a range of other factors – in which the conditions were created for the mass killings to occur (Vokes, 2007a). For this reason, a number of people connected with the station, including its owners Nahimana and Barayagwiza, were indicted by the UN's International Criminal Tribunal for Rwanda (ICTR) – which was set up in late 1994 to prosecute the senior figures responsible for the Rwandan Genocide – and were later tried by the court which sat in Arusha, Tanzania. In 2003, Nahimana and Barayagwiza were both found guilty of genocide, of crimes against humanity, and of incitement to genocide, and sentenced to 30 years and 32 years in prison, respectively (Nahimana is today still in prison in Mali, whilst Barayagwiza died in prison in Benin, in 2010). At the same trial, Nahimana and Barayagwiza's co-defendant, Hassan Ngeze – who was the owner of a Hutu extremist newspaper, *Kanugura*, in 1993–1994 – was found guilty of the same crimes, and sentenced to 35 years' imprisonment (which he is also still serving, in Mali).

Although RTLM is the most notorious example of a 'hate radio' station that was established in the wake of liberalization, it is far from being the only example of a toxic broadcaster to emerge from that time onwards. For example, similar kinds of ethnically divisive radio stations emerged in the context of the Second Congo War (1998–2003), the Second Liberian Civil War (1999–2003), and in the Kenyan emergency, which followed that country's disputed general election in 2007 (to name just a few more examples from Africa). In response, the creation of alternative, 'peace radio' stations to act as a counter-influence to hate broadcasters, has become a key tool for conflict transformation for a range of development agencies in recent years. For example, since 2002, the UN's current Stabilization Mission in the Democratic Republic of Congo (MONUSCO) has operated Radio Okapi, which broadcasts across the DRC in a range of languages, including French, Lingala, Kituba, Swahili, and Tshiluba; whilst since 1995, the conflict transformation NGO Search for Common Ground has run the Radio for Peacebuilding (R4P) network across Africa. The network began with Studio Ijambo in Burundi, but has subsequently expanded to include stations in more than 18 other African countries as well. Interestingly, R4P is heavily informed by the histories of both M4D and participatory communication, and thus included a wide range of entertainment-education content, much of which included participatory elements. However, despite these initiatives, the threat posed by 'hate broadcasters' has not gone away. As recently as mid-2014, the UN published a report attacking the output of a South Sudanese radio station, Radio Bentiu FM, for inciting ethnic-based violence in the context of that country's ongoing civil conflict. Meanwhile, at the present time, throughout the Middle East and North Africa, a growing number of satellite television broadcasters – many of which only emerged, ironically, following the Arab Spring and in the context of the more liberal media environments that stemmed from it – continue to broadcast material that is intended to inflame Sunni–Shia sectarian divisions. A majority of these stations are physically based in Egypt, but may receive funding from other countries across the Middle East as well. Their output is then broadcast across the region, through satellite TV stations and the internet (Losifidis and Wheeler, 2016). A recent investigation by the BBC's Arabic Service found that such broadcasts could be linked directly to a number of murders and more general outbreaks of violence that have occurred in Egypt, Iraq, and elsewhere in recent years (Farmar, 2014). The broadcasts by these stations also form part of the same media context into which groups such as ISIS output their extreme, and highly graphic, content.

It was not only in contexts of war and political upheaval – or, indeed, through the actions of such extreme broadcasters – that toxic media effects could be produced. So too the establishment of media markets, and the kind of intense competition for 'market share' that this frequently caused, sometimes resulted in what might otherwise be moderate media producers trying to sensationalize their content – and in a number of instances, this resulted in their producing, or amplifying, what Marshall McLuhan called 'moral panics' among their readerships or viewerships (McLuhan, 1964). For example, in the two decades or so following the liberalization of Uganda's media environment in the early 1990s, the country's media landscape has become increasingly crowded. During this period, literally hundreds of new print media – both newspaper and magazine titles – have been started, the majority of which have lasted for only a month or two before folding. In such circumstances, new media start-ups have tended to become as sensationalist as possible, with a view to increasing the impact of their publication – thereby, hopefully, increasing the chances that it will be one of the titles to survive. However, such intense competition, and the increasing sensationalism that it engenders, has at times produced toxic effects. For example, in October 2010, one media start-up, a newspaper called *Rolling Stone*, tried to establish itself by harnessing the wave of homophobia that was then sweeping the country – in relation to debate surrounding a draft of what became the Anti-homosexuality Act, 2014 – in the most sensational way possible. The newspaper published the photographs, names, and addresses of 100 allegedly gay individuals – among them those of a prominent gay rights activist called David Kato, and an Anglican Bishop – alongside a banner headline which read: 'Hang Them'. The publication stoked an already simmering moral panic over homosexuality in Uganda, and resulted in several of the people named in the newspaper being attacked – including David Kato, who was murdered in his home on 26 January 2011 (Strand, 2011; Sadgrove et al., 2012). All of the elements here, the *Rolling Stone* publication, the wider wave of homophobia upon which it was playing, and the violence it incites, were all widely condemned by the international community. However, for me the most damning aspect of the whole story was that for *Rolling Stone* itself, the publication of the names and faces served no purpose at all, in that, despite being so sensationalist, it failed to get the newspaper established and the enterprise folded a short time later.

Conclusion

The emergence of new media environments in the developing world had both widespread and profound ramifications for the economic, political, and social lives of people throughout the developing world. At first, donor governments, multi-lateral agencies, and NGOs regarded these effects as generally positive in nature, emphasizing, for example, the economic possibilities of greater access to 'useful information' and the political possibilities of media to engender new kinds of 'civic spaces', and political activism, including transnational activism. However, this initial optimism soon became tempered in light of the way in which these same new media environments appeared also to be generating a growing number of new challenges as well, including those related to conflict minerals, the environmental, health, and other social consequences of the exponential rise in volumes of e-waste, as well as repeated instances of 'hate broadcasting' and other toxic content. In addition, there was a growing recognition that these media revolutions, whatever else they had done (good or ill), had certainly resulted in all ICT4D projects – irrespective of whether these were run by development agencies or community groups – now operating in vastly more crowded, and more complex, media environments than ever before (and these environments have become even more complicated over time, in the context of accelerating media convergence).

In light of all of this, the outlook of many development agencies concerning the role of media in international development in general became somewhat 'schizophrenic'. On the one hand, the fact that these new media environments had developed so fast, and had such profound effects across the developing world, acted as a 'wake-up call' across the development industry, that ICT4D was not just a niche sub-field, or methodology, within international development, but had to be made, in one way or another, central to the whole enterprise – hence the raft of new initiatives with which I opened this book. Yet on the other hand, the fact that these new environments were so complicated, the fact that they had generated such a 'crowded marketplace' in terms of platforms, providers, and genres of media content, and that they were capable of generating such largely unforeseen negative effects (Box 5.7), meant that those same agencies were less willing to commit to one or other central paradigm for how ICT4D should be carried out. As a result, ICT4D now became increasingly constituted of a wide range of mixed models and mixed methods. In addition, some of the fundamental questions that I posed at the outset of this book in many ways became more contested than ever before; questions such as: which are the best types of media, or combinations of types, to use for different sorts of development interventions? Are some genres of media content better suited to poverty reduction programmes and others to health projects? Can media really be used to 'empower' people in the Global South? The next chapter will examine another effect of our now much more complex global media environments.

Box 5.7 Internet scams

Email-based extortion is another example of a kind of media content that may have a detrimental impact upon socio-economic development. One of the most notorious forms of this fraud is the so-called 'Spanish Prisoner Scam', or 'Advanced-Fee Scam', in which an unsolicited message is sent to a recipient from a purported dignitary, or his/her emissary, requesting that the recipient send their bank details in order that a large amount of the dignitary's wealth can be transferred into it – for which the recipient will be handsomely rewarded. Sometimes, the message will also ask for the recipient to pay an up-front 'transaction fee' to facilitate the larger transfer. Although this kind of extortion in fact traces back to the Spanish-American War of 1898 – from which it takes its name – and is today carried out mostly by fraudsters based in the US (for example, one recent report by the FBI's Internet Crime Complaint Center estimated that 61% of all email frauds worldwide originate from within America), over the last 30 years the fraud has become synonymous with scammers from Nigeria (and, to a lesser extent, with criminals from other West African countries as well, including Côte d'Ivoire, Ghana, and Togo). Indeed, today, this form of extortion is more commonly referred to as a '419 Scam', after Article 419 of the Nigerian Criminal Code (which is in the Chapter there dealing with extortion). The association of this kind of fraud with Nigerians, specifically, is a result of two things. On the one hand, it reflects that fact that from the 1980s onwards, Nigerian criminals began to send out larger numbers of advanced-fee letters, in hard (paper) copies, to businesses and individuals throughout Europe and the US. Following the spread of telecentres throughout West Africa from the mid-1990s onwards, and the (roughly) contemporaneous development of powerful emailing harvesting software, these same fraudsters also made increasing use of the internet to send out '419 emails' as well. On the other hand, the association of this kind of fraud with Nigeria, specifically, also reflects the particularly elaborate language, and overblown narratives, that Nigerian 419 scammers tended to use (both in their paper letters and in their later emails). Specifically, these missives often invoked not only striking images of the opulence of African royalty and other leaderships, but also – in their descriptions of the putative problems that these fictional dignitaries were now facing – equally powerful representations of the effects of poverty, political violence, and African 'victimhood'. There is no doubt that all Advanced-Fee Scams can produce hugely negative consequences. For example, in 2003, the Nigerian government set up the Economic and Financial Crimes Commission, and within the first four years it had seized criminal assets worth over $750 million, which had been defrauded by Nigerians from victims throughout West Africa and elsewhere in the world. However, the particular way in which Nigerian criminals have appropriated the scam can also be read as a form of media-based 'empowerment' of a sort (albeit of a rather perverse sort), in that it has, after all, involved a creative mobilization of media resources for wealth generation, one that has also 'played' upon dominant media representations of Africa as poor, wartorn, and a place of 'victims', as a means for forwarding its subversive ends.

Sources: Rosenberg (2007), Burrell (2008).

Summary

- Following the Washington Consensus, most international development agencies hailed the spread of media across the Global South as a wholly positive thing.
- Their response to the mobile phone revolution was initially more qualified, although their concerns were soon overcome.
- The possibilities for mobile phones to both meet and exceed development goals were amply demonstrated with the advent of mobile money.
- However, the challenges presented by these new media environments cannot be overlooked.
- In addition to the issues of conflict minerals and e-waste, the growth of media in the Global South has also seen a growth in toxic media content contributing to political violence.

Discussion questions

1. In hindsight, was the development community's initial optimism over new media environments in the Global South a little naïve?

2. What are the pros and cons of telecentres? Do they still have a role, even in the era of smartphones?
3. Can you think of five ways in which mobile money might alter everyday life for someone living in a rural area in the developing world?
4. How much e-waste have you produced over your lifetime? What steps could you take to reduce the amount of e-waste you generate in the future, and would you be willing to take those steps?
5. Watch the BBC Arabic Service's documentary 'Freedom to Broadcast Hate', 2014 (available on YouTube at www.youtube.com/watch?v=qjNBsvwcAoQ). What more should regional governments and the international community be doing to curb the volume of inflammatory media content in the Middle East and to limit its effects?

Further reading

For more on new media environments and their potentials for international development, see: Unwin, T. (2009) *Information and Communication Technologies for Poverty Alleviation*, Cambridge: Cambridge University Press.

For more on conflict minerals in the DRC, see: Eichstaedt, P. (2011) *Consuming the Congo: War and Conflict Minerals in the World's Deadliest Place*, Chicago, IL: Chicago Review Press.

The best introductions to the multiple, and complex, issues relating to E-waste are: Grossman, E. (2006) *High-Tech Trash: Digital Devices, Hidden Toxins and Human Health*, Washington, DC: Island Press; Baichwal, J. (2007) *Manufactured Planet*, New York: Zeitgeist Films; and Alexander, C. and Reno, J., eds. (2012) *Economies of Recycling: Global Transformation of Material Values and Social Relations*. London: Zed Books.

The main source on RTLM and the Rwandan Genocide is: Article 19 (1996) *Broadcasting Genocide: Censorship, Propaganda and State-sponsored Violence in Rwanda, 1990–94*, London: Article 19.

For the most comprehensive account of the genocide as a whole, including the role of RTLM within it, see: Des Forges, A. and Liebhafsky, A. (1999) *Leave None to Tell the Story: Genocide in Rwanda*, New York: Human Rights Watch.

Multimedia resources

Documentary: *Call Me Kuchu* (dir. Katherine Fairfax Wright and Malika Zouhali-Worrall, 2012) [Anti-homosexuality and media-fuelled 'moral panics' in Uganda]

Documentary: *Freedom to Broadcast Hate* (dir. Sam Farmar, 2014) [Sectarian 'Hate Broadcasting' in the Middle East]. Available online at: www.youtube.com/watch?v=qjNBsvwcAoQ

Documentary: *Manufactured Landscapes* (dir. Jennifer Baichwal, 2007) [E-waste]

Documentary: *The Square* (dir. Jehane Noujaim, 2013) [The Arab Spring]

Transmedia documentary: *Girl Rising* (dir. Richard Robbins, 2013) [Social media and activism for girls' education]. Available online at: http://girlrising.com

Transmedia documentary: *Love Radio* (dir. Anoek Steketee and Eefie Blankevoort, 2014) [Peace radio and entertainment-education in post-genocide Rwanda]. Available online at: www.loveradio-rwanda.org/episode/1/onair/intro

6 Development and celebrity

- The post-Washington Consensus and 'the third way'.
- The rise of development targets, and new aid conditionalities.
- The development–celebrity nexus.
- Spectatorship and celebrity.
- Product RED.

Introduction

The final shift in development policy and practice with which we are concerned here began in 1997, and has continued to dominate the field ever since – and so brings us right up to the present time. Once again, the key shift here was precipitated by an international financial crisis and the general economic downturn thus generated. However, in this case, the crisis involved didn't result in western donors governments, multi-lateral agencies, and developing world governments simply rejecting – or replacing – their existing approaches to international development, as they had done following the 1970s financial crisis, with the wholesale turn away from state-led industrialization. The financial crisis of 1997 onwards didn't lead to any kind of 'paradigm shift' away from market-led approaches. Instead, it resulted in development agencies in effect refining their existing thinking, and adopting a series of measures aimed at tempering some of the potentially weaker aspects, and negative effects, of a purely 'neo-liberal' approach. These measures, which together have been variously described as 'the post-Washington Consensus' (Birdsall and Fukuyama, 2011) and international development's 'third way', continue to dominate development thinking and practice today.

The precise combinations of policies and practices that are included in the post-Washington Consensus have again varied from place to place and over time. However, in general, they have involved a series of measures aimed not at *limiting* market activities, but instead *guiding them* in ways that might produce more beneficial outcomes for the nations and peoples of the developing world. Such measures typically have involved policies aimed at, for example: allowing developing world governments to regain at least some control over economic planning and industrial policy, although not in ways that allow them to provide subsidies to, or make any other kind of direct interventions into, their favoured sectors; encouraging those same governments to build up their bureaucracies again, especially in the key areas of economic planning, health, and education – although, increasingly, these bureaucracies have been set up not as publically owned enterprises, but instead as 'public–private partnerships' (PPPs); and reintroducing at least some controls on flows of capital both into and out of developing world countries (Carroll, 2010).

Yet by far the most significant element of the post-Washington Consensus, and really central to everything, was its policies aimed at providing a series of 'safety nets' for the poorest people in society – that is, for those most impoverished within any developing country (Serra and Stiglitz, 2008). This stemmed from the recognized failure of earlier neo-liberal models for development to generate any significant 'trickle down' of wealth and prosperity to the people at the 'bottom of the pyramid' in the counties of the developing world (Prahalad, 2004). When the Washington Consensus first emerged it had been widely argued by advocates of market-led approaches to development that, by generating national-level economic growth, neo-liberalism would effectively benefit everyone living in the developing world. The thinking was that even if only a few people and companies were driving that growth (i.e. making more money), they would nevertheless have to spend it – and invest it – in their countries, which in turn would eventually generate more broad-based prosperity. This imagined process was referred to as 'trickle down' (*ibid.*). However, already by the late 1990s, it was beginning to be appreciated that expanded markets in the developing world – or any markets anywhere in the world for that matter – generally *don't* produce these effects. Instead, capitalist markets, even when they do generate significant growth, tend to produce vastly more benefits for the people and companies at the top, and in so doing tend towards greater inequality within societies (Collier, 2007). In other words, everywhere that markets are allowed to operate in a more or less unregulated way, they make the rich richer and the poor relatively poorer. Today, a growing body of detailed economic scholarship has established the precise mechanisms why this happens (see especially Piketty, 2013).

By the late 1990s, it was becoming clear that if the policies of the Washington Consensus weren't benefitting the poorest people in countries in the developing world, then donors, multi-lateral agencies, and developing world governments would need to find new ways to provide those same people with a minimal level of services and welfare support at least (i.e. a 'safety net') in order to meet their basic needs. Yet this in turn raised three key questions: (1) For any given country in Africa, Asia, or Latin America, how precisely is one to establish who are 'the poorest people' in that society? (2) How does one define those people's 'basic needs'? And (3) how does one know when those needs have been met? Of course, the fundamental issues underlying these questions – of poverty, social welfare, and aid effectiveness, respectively – are themselves nothing new to international development. Rather, the emergence of the post-Washington Consensus simply gave new impetus, even urgency, to the need for *specifying* these issues more accurately, for developing means for *measuring* them in value-neutral (i.e. 'objective') ways, and for *evaluating* when these had been met. What happened, then, was a whole raft of new definitions, new metrics, and new targets – or 'goals', to use development agencies' own parlance – focused upon the people of lowest socio-economic status in the developing world or, in other words, people living in the greatest poverty (see below).

The post-Washington Consensus also promoted the use of 'private aid', or public–private partnerships, as a means for funding development interventions. As opposed to public aid, which ultimately comes from western taxpayers, private aid comes from charitable foundations who are funded by a combination of corporations' profits, the interest on their own financial investments, and donations they receive from individuals (Sumner and Mallett, 2012). From the advent of the modern era of development onwards, most donor governments had strongly favoured public over private aid, mostly because public aid allowed them to set the theoretical agendas for international development and to control the money that was distributed in pursuit of those agendas. However, following the advent of the post-Washington Consensus, the development industry became less driven by theoretical models and more so by pragmatic concerns. In other words, rather than being informed by grand theories of society, by models for progressive social and political transformation, as had been the case since the advent of the era of modernization, it was now increasingly organized around only the production of, and the meeting of, specified goals (Booth and Mosley, 2003). This context created the conditions in which donor governments were no longer so concerned as to whether the money for funding all of this came from public or private funding streams, or from a combination of the two (this shift in thinking has sometimes also been referred to as the 'California Consensus'; Desai and Kharas, 2008).

The emergence of the post-Washington Consensus cemented a number of the trends in ICT4D that we have looked at in previous chapters. For example, the new consensus' general focus upon metrics and targets led to a renewal of interest in the gathering of data on, and the setting of targets regarding, media ownership and access rates in the developing world. Being focused more upon rates among those of lowest socio-economic status, rather than among the entire populations of developing world countries, the approach was in a sense no different to that which had first been explored by UNESCO in the early 1960s – a focus that was captured by the new concept of 'information poverty' (UNICTTF, 2005; see also Gebremichael and Jackson, 2006). Similarly, the new focus on metrics and goals also led to a renewed interest in the methods of participatory communication, it having long been established that any attempts to define measures and targets without local actors' input were inevitably doomed to failure, and that media had a key role to play in harnessing that input. For example, participatory communication methods were used in what became the central metrics and goals for international development: the Millennium Development Goals (UNDESA, 2008). In addition, the increasing presence of large private aid foundations within international development, including several foundations that had been created by big tech companies, also advanced the overall agenda of ICT4D. For example, the Microsoft-derived Bill and Melinda Gates Foundation has always championed the increased integration of ICTs across all sectors of international development, one instance of which was their participation in the 'Mobile Money for the Unbanked' consortium (see above).

However, the main focus of this chapter is to understand how and why the post-Washington Consensus also created the conditions for a significantly expanded role for media celebrities within international development. As we have seen, the relationship between celebrity and development is itself nothing new, and dates back to at least Band Aid/Live Aid in 1984–1985. Nevertheless, in the context of the post-Washington Consensus, a context which continues to prevail, this relationship became much wider still – to the point, in fact, that today a huge number of celebrities are attached to some or other project or programme in the developing world, whilst development agencies now begin to design their campaigns with 'the first question: which celebrity is going to front it' (as the former head of a major UK-based development organization recently put it to me). Indeed, so deep has this relationship become, that it may today be useful to think in terms of what, following David Hulme, I will call a 'celebrity–development nexus' (Hulme, 2015).

The Asian financial crisis and beyond

In July 1997, the value of Thailand's currency, the *baht*, suddenly collapsed, precipitating a major financial crisis that soon spread to practically every other country in the Southeast Asian region. Even before its currency fell, Thailand, like other developing countries in the region – especially members of the Association of Southeast Asian Nations, or ASEAN (Indonesia, Malaysia, the Philippines, Singapore, and Thailand) – had been already struggling to service their massive – and growing – foreign debts. With first the baht and then other regional currencies collapsing, these nations were all left effectively bankrupt. The 'contagion' effect of these nations' bad debts then very rapidly spread to other Southeast Asian countries as well, including to a number of its 'newly industrialized countries' or NICs (i.e. countries which had once been classified as 'developing', but which, as a result of huge economic growth from the 1970s onwards, had come to be classified as higher-income countries instead). Indeed, two of the worst hit countries in the region were the NICs of Hong Kong (which at the time was still a British overseas territory, and therefore independent of China) and South Korea. As the political economists Kanishka Jayasuriya and Andrew Rosser have described it: the crisis that erupted 'so suddenly and violently during 1997 irrevocably altered the political and economic landscape of the region. Major Asian companies went bankrupt, anxious domestic and foreign investors relocated vast amounts of capital abroad, interest rates skyrocketed, and inflation and unemployment soared' (2001: 381). The crisis even affected the region's then strongest economy, Japan, and was one of the causes of that country's recession, which began in 1998 (and from which, in some respects, the country has never fully recovered).

Economists and other scholars today still debate the causes of the Asian Financial Crisis, although it is beyond my scope to rehearse those arguments here. What is of greater relevance for this book is how the major development organizations, and especially the IMF and the World Bank, *responded* to it. Because to begin with, these agencies responded using the same formula they had deployed following earlier financial crises from the 1970s onwards, in Latin America, Africa, the Middle East, and elsewhere – that is, they sought to impose policies that generally conformed to the Washington Consensus, and would require the countries affected by the crisis to 'open up' their economies through the privatization of state-owned enterprises, fiscal discipline, and foreign investment deregulation (*ibid.*, 382). However, it very quickly became obvious that a *lack* of free markets was not the problem. Instead, the problem seemed to be that national governments were unable to control the development of the industrial sector's transnational capital flows in ways that might protect it from international financial storms. In other words, the more open these economies were, the more vulnerable they were as well. In addition, as the IMF and World Bank looked more closely at the crisis states, they also realized that one of the biggest problems these countries had, from a development point of view, was the presence of well-established cultures of 'crony capitalism'. In other words, they were all characterized by societies in which government officials enjoyed close ties with leading business people and companies, and would patronize and support them through the gifting of government grants, special tax arrangements, legal permits, and so on, all of which served to keep wealth 'at the top of society'.

For both of these reasons, then, the international development consensus began to shift towards a new overall policy framework, one that was animated by the dual intentions of: (1) allowing governments more autonomy over their development planning (especially with a view to allowing them to better protect themselves against international financial shocks), yet at the same time (2) making sure that they also adopt policies which ensure greater protections – both financial and in relation to health, education, and so on – for the lowest socio-economic strata of their societies. In these ways, donors and multi-lateral agencies hoped to facilitate policy environments in developing world countries that would be *both* 'pro-growth' *and* 'pro-poor' *at the same time* – and hence why the post-Washington Consensus is sometimes also linked to a 'third way' (Porter and Craig, 2004). I should also note here that some scholars and development practitioners often describe pro-growth and pro-poor policy agendas as antithetical to each other. Certainly, individual policies, in specific countries, can be at times more pro-growth, or more pro-poor, in orientation. However, it is crucial to recognize that the very foundation of the post-Washington Consensus was the assumption that development policy environments could be created that would be *both* pro-growth *and* pro-poor *at the same time* (Serra and Stiglitz, 2008). And it was the second part of this equation that led to the inexorable promotion of new definitions, metrics, and targets by donor governments and multi-lateral agencies (Hulme, 2009). Although these new policy environments were developed in Southeast Asia, they soon came to be seen as desirable for many others parts of the developing world as well.

The reason why the post-Washington Consensus came to dominate development policy across the developing world was in one sense only a matter of timing. Because at around the same time that the IMF and World Bank were starting to lead the international response to the Asian Financial Crisis, from which the post-Washington Consensus emerged, they were also beginning what became the Highly-Indebted Poor Countries Initiative (HIPC; Allen and Weinhold, 2000). By the late 1990s, it was becoming increasingly clear that the policies of the Washington Consensus were simply not succeeding in significantly easing the enormous debt overhangs that many developing world countries had been burdened with from the 1970s onwards. In other words, the poorest countries in the world – most of which were in Africa and Latin America, although some in other parts of the developing world – remained crippled by interest payments on external debts and, in some cases, they even remained effectively bankrupt. In this context, the IMF and the World Bank had begun to look at ways of paying off some of the debts of the world's poorest nations, and restructuring others in ways that would provide countries with relief on the interest they owed on the loans (for a good introduction to this subject, see Easterly, 2001). As a simple analogy for this, imagine how a consumer might do a balance transfer on their credit card debt, in order to move it from a card with a higher rate of interest to one with a lower rate. The first round of HIPC was introduced in 1996, and the programme has since grown to include 39 countries that are eligible for some level of debt relief, although some of these states have not yet received any money from the initiative. The 39 countries are made up of 33 in Africa, together with Afghanistan, Bolivia, Guyana, Haiti, Honduras, and Nicaragua and, as of 2014, the IMF, World Bank, and western donor governments had spent more than US$76 billion on the programme. However, as part of the planning for HIPC, it was realized that there was no point 'freeing up' this new money for the HIPC governments, if they weren't then able to have some control over how that money was spent, and were not able to better protect themselves against future financial shocks. In addition, it also recognized that free-market approaches had failed to generate significant 'trickle down' of wealth and services in many of these countries as well (Kakwani and Pernia, 2000). For these reasons, the very same policy prescriptions that the IMF and World Bank were then developing in response to the Asian Financial Crisis were considered appropriate for these HIPC nations as well. As a consequence, before they received any money from the initiative, any country that qualified for HIPC had first to demonstrate how they were going to re-organize their national economic policies, and how they were going to implement a pro-poor agenda, through the production both of a development plan and a country-specific Poverty Reduction Strategy Paper (PRSP).

It was the pro-poor element of these equations that resulted in much greater emphasis being placed upon poverty-related metrics, and targets, than ever before. Of course, western donors, development agencies, and developing world governments had always collected demographic data related to the their populations' wealth and income, health status, and levels of education, and they had always tried to design interventions on the basis of these data (see Chapter 3). However, prior to 1990, there had never been any attempt to define a set of global 'minimum standards' for income, health (measured in terms of, for example, infant mortality or levels of nutrition) or education (measured on the basis of, for example, number of years spent in school or standards of literacy), or to integrate these different sorts of data and measures into a single, integrated framework for understanding levels of 'poverty'. In short, there had never been any attempt to work out precisely who – in different places and times – really are 'the poorest of the poor'. However, in 1990, two different metrics were developed in an attempt to do exactly these things. The first was the World Bank's development of a 'global poverty line', which tried to define the absolutely minimum amount of money that any human being would need to meet his or her very most basic needs in terms of food, health requirements (safe drinking water, minimum sanitation, basic shelter) and education (access to some sort of information). This figure was initially set at US$1 per day, adjusted up or down for different countries, depending on how relatively cheap or expensive they were compared with other countries (this method of adjustment is known as 'purchasing power parity', or PPP). The figure – which is still widely used today, as a threshold for defining 'absolute poverty' – was later revised upwards, most recently in October 2015, when it was put up to US$1.90 per day PPP. Also in 1990, UNDP published the first of its Human Development Reports. Intended to provide an annual 'snapshot' of economic and social development around the world, in preparation for the first report, a team of UNDP researchers, led by the economist Mahbub ul Haq, began to develop a single framework for integrating different sorts of data on income, health, education, and so on. This became the Human Development Index (HDI), which, in 2010, was expanded to become the Multi-dimensional Poverty Index (MPI). The MPI remains the main framework through which all development agencies measure and understand poverty indicators throughout the world (Alkire and Santos, 2013).

It followed that having developed these much more global, and much more integrated, methods for measuring poverty indicators, that donor governments and development agencies would then become focused on setting targets based upon them. This led to the formation of the now famous Millennium Development Goals (MDGs) that were agreed at the UN's Millennium Summit in New York, in September 2000 unanimously, by all of the UN's then 189 member states.

The MDGs, which were constituted of 21 specific targets for improving the lives of 'the poorest of the poor' within 15 years (i.e. by the end of 2015), set goals based on a combination of the World Bank's 'global poverty line' (for example, MDG Target 1A aimed to halve the number of people living below the line between 1990 and 2015) and the MPI (for example, Target 2A aimed that all children throughout the world would have access to a full course of primary school education by 2015, while Target 4A aimed to reduce mortality rates of children under five years of age by two-thirds between 1990 and 2015). They also drew on other indexes in order to set goals in relation to various other areas as well, including ICT4D (for example, Target 8F set targets for media density rates for telephone subscriptions, personal computers, and internet users worldwide). In these ways, then, the MDGs sharply defined and quantified the overall aspirations for international development for a 15-year period. And in elevating specific goals in this way, they also

Figure 6.1 *Poster of Millennium Development Goals*

Source: © United Nations

inaugurated a new culture within the development industry for metrics and targets. Thus, although the MDGs are (by far) the best known of the sets of goals associated with development since 2000, in practice this period has seen the emergence of target setting and evaluation at all levels of the development enterprise (in one example, throughout this period, the goals for most country-level PRSPs were similarly defined in terms of goals based on absolute poverty, MPI indicators, and other factors besides).

Finally, and as I have already indicated, the period since 2000 has also seen a steady rise in the prominence of private aid, and of public–private partnerships, within international development (Desai and Kharas, 2008). Indeed, greater use of both of these was already embedded within the MDGs themselves – especially in Goal 8 ('Develop a global partnership for development'), which included explicit reference to a greater role for private capital within development. Following the MDGs' adoption, donor governments and development agencies also promoted public–private partnerships as their favoured vehicles for reaching these. For example, in 2002, donor governments, multi-lateral agencies, and developing world governments entered into a major PPP consortium with a large number of private aid foundations and private education providers that was focused specifically around Goal 2 ('To achieve universal primary education'). The consortium, the Global Partnership for Education (GPE), is today headed by former Australian Prime

Minister Julia Gillard, and has now become the pre-eminent organization for education and development in the world. The increasing importance of private aid is also demonstrated in the major development initiatives that have emerged since the end of the MDG period. In 2010, in preparation for the coming expiry of the MDG timeline, the UN held a High Level Plenary Meeting to review what progress had been made towards reaching the MDG targets, and to plan for a new global development agenda beyond the end of 2015. This led to the creation of the UN System Task Team (made up of the World Bank and no less than 60 UN agencies) and a High Level Panel of Eminent Persons (constituted mostly of present and former world leaders) to provide guidance and oversight of this. What is interesting is that the Task Team quickly published a series of reports arguing for an expansion of PPP contracts both within international development and in developing countries themselves. The World Bank, in particular, has championed these, and in 2012 spent US$2.9 billion in support of them across the Global South. Meanwhile, the High Level Panel also included, in addition to its present and former world leaders, a number of prominent businesspeople, such as the CEO of Unilever, Paul Polman, and the CEO of the Kenyan Manufacturers Association, Betty Maina.

In 2013, the Task Team launched what effectively became the world's largest ever exercise in participatory communication, when it set up a collaborative website called the 'World We Want 2015' (available online at www.beyond2015.org/world-we-want-2015), which allowed potentially anyone in the developing world to have a say in how future global development policy around, for example, inequality might be developed. This was accompanied by a range of workshops around the developing world (they were eventually held in more than 100 countries), as well as a range of SMS and Interactive Voice Response (IVR) surveys on related issues – most of which were implemented in local languages. In the end, it was estimated that the whole cross-platform approach was engaged with by at least a million people across the Global South, and probably very many more. In these ways, the Task Team effectively harnessed the potential of mobile phones and mobile internet to effectively 'crowdsource' the next generation of 'development goals' from a broad cross-section of the people who are, ultimately, most affected by the outcomes of international development policy – that is, ordinary people living in the developing world themselves. The project was later continued as the ongoing 'World We Want 2030' (available online at www.worldwewant2030.org).

The celebrity–development nexus

The emergence of the post-Washington Consensus created a much deeper relationship between celebrity and international development, to the point at which the two phenomena are today intrinsically inter-connected and even constitute what, following Hulme, I am calling a 'celebrity–development nexus' (2015). There are a number of reasons for this. The first and most well-known reason is that the new consensus' particular focus upon an *anti-poverty* agenda moved international development more directly into an area in which a number of then well-known celebrities were already highly active. Following Band Aid/Live Aid, a number of the high-profile celebrities who had taken part in that campaign/media event – people like Bob Geldof, Bono, and Sting – had continued to campaign on development-related issues and to support development-focused NGOs and lobby groups. From around the mid-1990s onwards, these individuals became particularly attached to a number of groups who were pushing for increased debt relief for developing world countries (Cooper, 2008). Most notably, they became especially connected to a UK-based lobby group called Jubilee 2000. Jubilee 2000 was in fact started in 1990 by an academic political scientist at Keele University, Martin Dent, and a former British High Commissioner to Malawi, William Peters, as a primarily faith-based organization. Motivated by their own Christian faiths, the two men believed that the levy of such massive debts on the world's poorest nations was essentially immoral. The name 'Jubilee 2000' is in fact a reference to the Old Testament's Book of Leviticus, which, in Chapter 25, says that God will cancel all of the debts of the faithful in a 'Jubilee year' to come. As a result, it initially grew mostly through church networks – especially within the Church of England – where it appealed in particular to youth groups. However, from the mid-1990s onwards, the organization became elevated to global prominence, when one of its campaigners, Jamie Drummond, along with journalist Mike Christie, launched a media campaign to raise wider awareness of the issue (Pettifor, 2006). The campaign, called 'Drop the Debt', was joined by the celebrities listed above – as well as Quincy Jones, Muhammad Ali, and Youssou N'dour – who quickly gave it a global media profile.

In addition to drawing on their existing media profiles, these celebrities also developed strategies for giving Drop the Debt maximum political impact (*ibid.*). In particular, they linked the campaign and its associated media events to Group of Eight (G8)

Figure 6.2 *Drop the Debt campaign, 'Haven't we taken enough?'*

Source: Courtesy of Jubilee Debt

Summits – events which bring together the leaders of Canada, the European Union, France, Germany, Italy, Japan, the UK, and the US for an annual meeting (the summits used to include the president of Russia as well, until that country was suspended in 2014).

In the run-up to the 2001 G8 Summit in Genoa, Italy, Bob Geldof launched a now famous, or infamous, media campaign on behalf of Drop the Debt, called 'Haven't we taken enough?' In a reversal of the iconic humanitarian image of the mother and starving child (which was discussed at length in Chapter 2), the image for this campaign showed an emaciated African mother breastfeeding a very *well-nourished* Caucasian baby. The implication was that Africa's poverty is the result of it being 'sucked dry' by Euro-American countries, in the form of their debt repayments to western governments and financial institutions. The image caused a huge media storm at the time of its release – although this, ironically, only increased the media profile of the campaign itself. However, it was in relation to the 2005 G8 Summit in Gleneagles, Scotland (UK), that Geldof, Bono, and the others had their greatest impact. In the lead up to the summit, the celebrities organized a series of media events, which included documentaries, studio debates, and a special edition of a then very popular UK sitcom called *The Vicar of Dibley*, all of them focused on the Drop the Debt campaign. By early 2005, this had grown to become the Make Poverty History campaign, which was itself a part of the larger Global Call to Action Against Poverty (the best overview of the Make Poverty History campaign, and the way in which this was mediated, is Harrison, 2010). This coalition had itself come into existence in pursuit of MDG Goal 8: 'To develop global partnership for development'.

This season of media events culminated on 2 July 2005 – 11 days before the 20th anniversary of the Live Aid concerts – in the 'Live 8' concerts, which involved simultaneous music events in all of the G8 countries, as well as South Africa (Sireau, 2008). The concerts involved performances from more than 1,000 musicians, including many of the world's biggest superstars, including Coldplay, Elton John, Madonna, Pink Floyd (Live 8 was the first time that the 'classic' Pink Floyd line-up had played together in 24 years), Snoop Dogg, and Stevie Wonder. It was broadcast on no less than 182 television networks and 2,000 radio stations, and achieved a worldwide audience of millions (it reached a peak viewing of 9.6 million people in the UK alone). The concerts did also have a significant effect upon the world leaders who were gathered at Gleneagles. Specifically, those leaders agreed at the meeting to double their Official Development Assistance (ODA) commitments, from a combined US$25 billion per year in 2004 to US$50 billion per annum by 2010 – half of it to go to Africa. In addition, a major portion of this money would be given directly to the IMF and World Bank for use in their HIPC programme – with the aim of cancelling between US$40 billion and US$55 billion of the money owed by the HIPC nations. In practice, a majority of these pledges never came to pass. In the years after 2005, the G8 countries simply didn't expand their ODA spending in the way they had promised (Kharas, 2007). Nevertheless, the fact that so much of the money pledged at Gleneagles was earmarked for debt relief specifically, demonstrates the scale of the impact that this group of committed celebrities, and the concerts/media events they organized, had on shaping development policy – and on forging one key plank of the emergent post-Washington Consensus – at this time. Thus, although these celebrities didn't invent the drop the debt agenda – as the IMF and World Bank have been at pains to point out ever since – they certainly did play a major role in raising public consciousness about the potentials of this policy shift, and in so doing created the conditions in which it became a central concern for not just the multi-lateral financial institutions, but for the entire international development enterprise.

It is also important to emphasize that if, alongside public aid, the post-Washington Consensus included a *much* greater role for private aid, as well as an increasing number of PPPs, within international development, then this also created the conditions for a much deeper relationship between celebrity and development (Ponte and Richey, 2014). In general terms, this is because media celebrities have always been the individuals who quintessentially, and perhaps uniquely, bridge the public and private domains. In other words, these individuals are essentially at the same time both public figures and key representatives of private interests. They are public because, by definition, lots of people know who they are, and therefore feel a sense of engagement, even identification, with them. It is this engagement that made them famous in the first place, and it also explains why media audiences have an endless fascination with even the smallest of details of their lives (for example, what shoes they are wearing, the name of their cat, and the person they went out on a date with last night). Some celebrities may be even perceived as a 'public good', such that they 'belong to the nation'. This is particularly the case with sports stars, such as the one-time England football team captain David Beckham (Andrews and Jackson, 2001). Yet celebrities are also – again, by definition – inextricably linked with private interests, including not only the record labels for whom they record, the film studies they make films for, the sports clubs that they play for, but also the sometimes extensive networks of other private companies who provide them with sponsorship to endorse their brands in the hope that this will increase their sales. In these ways, then, the phenomenon of celebrity provides an almost unique kind of bridge between the public and the private, and it is therefore not surprising that in the context of a move towards PPPs that this should have come to the fore (Wilkins and Enghel, 2013).

In addition, and as Professor of Geography at the University of Manchester Dan Brockington has demonstrated through detailed empirical research, the increasing involvement of corporate money in development has also produced even more direct drivers for the celebrity–development nexus (2014b). As Brockington shows, corporations have always recognized the economic benefits of having their brands associated with particular celebrities which is why they invest so much in 'celebrity endorsements'. However, in purely commercial contexts, such endorsements are often very costly – and the more famous the celebrity, the more costly they are. Yet in the context of international development, they become, in effect: *free*.

Simply put, were a corporation such as Microsoft to employ a high-profile celebrity to appear in a television advert, it would cost them a lot of money. Yet if the Microsoft Foundation funds a development programme, and then convinces a celebrity to front *that* instead, then it costs them nothing at all – yet arguably delivers broadly similar economic benefit in terms of their brand recognition through association with the celebrity (and possibly even more, given that the latter scenario also promotes the corporation through its association with a 'good cause', rather than through purely commercial advertising). Yet as Brockington's research also shows (*ibid.*), corporate executives often also derive significant *personal* gains from these kinds of celebrity engagements. Specifically, executives may be simply 'star struck', and therefore enjoy 'rubbing shoulders' with particular celebrities, especially when the latter are physically attractive and/or lead glamorous lifestyles. It is also noteworthy that unlike with celebrity endorsements in corporate advertising, corporate-celebrity-development engagements often provide contexts in which executives can interact with the celebrities over an extended period of time (such as over the course of a fundraising dinner, or even over a day-long field trip, see below). In addition, Brockington found that at least some executives also benefitted from the access to senior political figures that some celebrities could facilitate (*ibid.*). However, in furthering corporate interests in all of these ways, these kinds of relations opened up the celebrities themselves to the criticism that they were forwarding the interests of global capitalism, which itself produces the very structures of inequality that – from dependency theory onwards – has been recognized as the primary cause of poverty in the developing world (Kapoor, 2012).

One outcome of these increasingly complex relations between corporate interests, celebrity engagements, and development has been the emergence of campaigns that are fronted by celebrities, and which attempt to achieve development outcomes (which are framed in terms of the public good) by buying certain products (which are sold by private corporations). In some senses, the prototype for this was the Product RED brand (Richey and Ponte, 2011).

In 2006, Bono, together with development campaigner Bobby Shriver, launched the RED brand as a vehicle for raising awareness and funds for the HIV/AIDS pandemic in Africa. The concept for RED was that major private companies – including Apple, Armani, Coca-Cola, Gap, Hallmark, Nike, and Starbucks – would include RED branded items within their existing product lines, such that, for

Figure 6.3 *Product Red poster (GAP)*

example, Apple sold a RED iPod and Armani sold a variety of RED clothes. The profits from these sales were then divided 50/50 between Product RED itself – which was a private company, which aimed to make a profit – and the Global Fund to Fight AIDS, Tuberculosis, and Malaria. The Global Fund to Fight AIDS is a PPP coalition of organizations set up in 2002 to address MDG Goal 6: 'To combat HIV/AIDS, malaria, and other diseases'. For the companies actually selling the products (i.e. Apple, Armani, Coca-Cola), there was also the added advantage that selling RED products, which were themselves 'ethical products', also bolstered the companies' claims to be addressing 'corporate social responsibility' (CSR; see Moon, 2015). In addition, selling RED products also boosted their overall sales, not least because having bought a RED item many consumers went on to buy further products from those same companies as well. In these ways, then, Bono's Product RED achieved an almost complete suturing of social goals, such as addressing the HIV/AIDS pandemic, with private interests, especially that of making a profit (Richey and Ponte, 2011). In so doing, it showed what the future of international development campaigns might increasingly look like – or at least, what it will look like as long as the post-Washington Consensus continues to hold sway. In 2012, the One Campaign, an organization founded in 2004 by Bono and Jubilee 2000's Jamie Drummond, and which itself involves a coalition of 11 private-aid foundations, including the Bill and Melinda Gates Foundation, bought out Product RED.

Celebrity–humanitarian spectatorship

In recent years, the emergence of ever more complex global media landscapes has been another key driver of the deepening celebrity–development nexus. As we have already explored at length, these new landscapes have resulted in all development agencies operating in increasingly 'crowded' media contexts, in which they are competing with more and more commercial, political, local, and community broadcasters, across an ever wider range of media platforms – which are themselves undergoing increasing 'media convergence' – for users' attention. It is thus not surprising that these agencies should have increasingly turned to celebrities to draw, and to hold, users' attention – given that all celebrities, by definition, already have media users' attention. It is also unsurprising, perhaps, that it has also led to a resurgence of media portrayals of humanitarianism, specifically. As we have seen, since at least the eighteenth century, humanitarian organizations, and latterly international development ones as well, have disseminated images of war, famine, and/or other disasters through global media circuits, as a means for galvanizing global media audiences' support for their causes. However, since around the early 2000s, in the context of the emerging celebrity–development nexus, a key shift occurred, in which these same agencies began to circulate an increasing number of images and other media content, not of the *victims* of famine, war, and disaster, but instead of the celebrities who were engaged in the agencies' own responses to those crises (Chouliaraki, 2012). Ironically, some organizations, including Oxfam, did this at precisely the same time that they were promoting an increased use of 'post-humanitarian' communication strategies within their other campaigns (see above).

From the early 2000s onwards, humanitarian and development agencies engaged in some or other war, famine, or other disaster in the developing world tended to no longer put as much energy into facilitating journalists to visit their field operations as they might previously have done (in line with the 'Biafra model'; see Chapter 2). Instead, these agencies now shifted their attention and resources to a new *modus operandi*, in which they instead facilitated some

Figure 6.4 *Julien Clerc, UNHCR Goodwill Ambassador for Francophone Countries in Chad*

Source: Getty Images

celebrity-advocate to undertake a field trip to that place. This field trip, which typically lasted between four and ten days, would then draw journalists' attention to the celebrity and, through them, to the situation/place they were visiting. In this way, celebrities became key 'mediators' of humanitarian emergencies throughout Africa, Asia, and Latin America (Scott, 2014b).

Returning to Brockington's research, what made these field trips so newsworthy was not only the fact that a celebrity was involved; in addition, their fascination – for at least some media users – lay in the way in which they put that celebrity into a usually uncomfortable situation, and moreover one in which the celebrity was often, and very genuinely, emotionally moved (2014b). In both of these ways, these field trips played to media constructions of 'authenticity' in the age of reality television (Hill, 2005). In other words, they served to cast the celebrity's own experience as authentic, which, by extension, established the crisis situation as a genuine emergency as well (see also Chouliaraki, 2013). However, as a growing body of scholarly criticism has highlighted, this new approach also raises a number of potentially quite serious issues and problems as well.

First, the entry of a celebrity into the 'humanitarian frame' as it were, encourages the audience – who are more familiar with looking at the celebrity than with anyone else in the picture – to focus upon the celebrity themselves. In other words, with the celebrity's presence, the audience's gaze, and spectatorship, is immediately drawn *away* from the *local* people's lived experiences (i.e. their issues and problems). As a simple demonstration of this, consider a series of press images that were taken of David Beckham during a visit he made to Sierra Leone in 2008, as part of his duties as a UNICEF Goodwill Ambassador. In each picture, the viewer's gaze is almost certainly, and subconsciously, drawn towards the figure of Beckham – and therefore away from the Sierra Leoneans who are also present in the scene.

Across many examples of this sort, one might even argue that the very iconography of humanitarianism has now shifted away from its previous focus upon the suffering African – or Asian, or Latin American – body, towards the celebrity's perfect form. In extreme cases, the celebrity's figure may even come to 'stand in for' the very cause that he or she is advocating for.

Figure 6.5 *David Beckham working as a UNICEF Goodwill Ambassador in Sierra Leone*

Source: Getty Images

Figure 6.6 *Bono and Africa*

Source: Photo by David Shankbone

Yet there may be something peculiarly unsettling about this, given that celebrities are, by definition, persons that audiences usually gaze upon primarily for reasons of *pleasure*, and as objects of fantasy (see especially Kapoor, 2012). Second, and because the viewer's gaze *is* drawn towards the celebrity, the viewer is also encouraged to identify emotionally not with the people who are suffering, but instead with the celebrity. In other words, whereas earlier humanitarian imagery – no matter how flawed it was in many respects – invited its viewers to empathize with the mother cradling her dying child, or with the relative carrying the body of his loved one, and to imagine how they might respond in similar circumstances, the new humanitarian imagery instead invites its viewers to empathize only with the celebrity's discomfort, as stems from their being placed in such a challenging environment. Yet the celebrity is, by definition, only ever a visitor – and an essentially voyeuristic one at that – to that crisis. Therefore, the viewer is also encouraged to adopt what Chouliaraki (2012) calls a 'narcissistic disposition of voyeuristic altruism' towards the war, famine, or disaster at hand. Third, the placement of a celebrity at the centre of the frame may encourage audiences to have an erroneous confidence in that celebrity's ability – and by extension the ability also of the humanitarian or development organization they represent – to successfully intervene. This confidence may be particularly elevated when the audience has previously seen the celebrity involved play a heroic figure in a movie, as might be the case with celebrity–development activists such as Ben Affleck or Matt Damon (Richey, 2015).

Finally, and perhaps most significantly, there is also an inherent risk that by drawing the media focus onto the celebrity-advocate

Figure 6.7 *Matt Damon with Zimbabwean refugees in South Africa*

Source: AAP Images

themselves, such coverage might also invite the audience to perceive that celebrity to be an expert on the crisis at hand. Yet oftentimes, the celebrity involved may know little or nothing about the context they have just jetted into. Indeed, given their lack of specialist knowledge, there is even a danger that they might end up repeating ill-informed stereotypes about African, Asian, or Latin American contexts. For example, Rinna Yrjola shows how Bob Geldof and Bono's descriptions of African poverty – even after both men have spent several decades acting as spokespeople for humanitarian and development projects, across the continent – still bears a striking resemblance to colonial discourses of 'the white man's burden'. In this way, both men continue to describe humanitarian and development engagement with Africa as a 'specifically Western project and calling', and even as a 'moral duty' for western states (Yrjola, 2009; see also Harrison, 2010). Yet in so doing, they both continue to reproduce the very ideology that, as we have seen, was used to justify Euro-American historical expansion into Africa in the first place, which ultimately created the structural conditions for the continent's economic subordination (Rodney, 1972). A given celebrity's lack of expert knowledge may also produce more specific risks. A recent case that highlighted this directly was George Clooney's engagement in South Sudan. When the newly independent country descended into civil conflict in 2013, Clooney – a long-standing celebrity-advocate for the region – was accused by journalists and other commentators of having been a 'dupe' of the new government in Juba, and in particular of its President Salva Kiir. The argument ran that Clooney, precisely because of his lack of specialist knowledge of the region, had played a key role in helping South Sudan to achieve its independence in the first place, by championing Kiir's narrative that the new country would be a united, and therefore peaceful, place. In so doing, he had become partly responsible for the new conflict – which was primarily an outcome of the fact that South Sudan had become independent too quickly, *before* it could be properly united as a new nation (see, for example, Howden, 2013). As the expert on South Sudan Douglas Johnson has demonstrated, the argument being made against Clooney here was entirely unfair: the celebrity played only a very minor role in processes that led to independence, and the argument that the conflict that began in 2013 was primarily caused by the country having moved too quickly to independence is a gross distortion of history (one that fails to take any account of the 'twenty-two years of civil war, and six years of political contestation' that led up to the self-determination referendum; Johnson, 2014). Nevertheless, the incident demonstrates the dangers of how celebrities may unwittingly become politically embroiled in the very contexts they are hoping to transform.

Conclusion

The emergence of the post-Washington Consensus led to a new emphasis – by donors, multi-lateral agencies, and developing world governments – upon poverty reduction agendas, and also opened up a vastly expanded role for private aid within international development. Both of these factors in turn created the conditions for the emergence of a new celebrity–development nexus that would shortly follow. On the one hand, the renewed focus upon poverty brought 'mainstream' development thinking into an area in which a small, but highly committed group of celebrity-activists had been working consistently for many years. On the other hand, the expanded role for private aid led to an increasing overlap between corporate interests and international development, which for a number of reasons conferred an elevated role upon celebrities. The fact that all of this was happening in a context of increasingly complex global media environments further fuelled the rise of celebrity humanitarianism.

The result of all of these factors has been a deepening relationship between international development and media celebrity. Indeed, over the past 15 years or so, development agencies' use of celebrities as 'front people' for their projects increased dramatically, and also became increasingly institutionalized with international development in general. The latter point is perhaps best illustrated in UNICEF's appointment of an increasing number of 'Goodwill Ambassadors' from 2000 onwards. Goodwill Ambassadors are celebrities who are engaged by the UN to travel around the developing world, visiting sites of particular humanitarian and/or development activity, and – simply by dint of who they are – garnering media coverage for those sites as they go. Although the institution of the Goodwill Ambassadors has existed since 1954, after the turn of the millennium the number of these appointments grew significantly, and the they included increasingly high-profile celebrities. For example, current Goodwill Ambassadors include David Beckham, Orlando Bloom, Lionel Messi, Katy Perry, and Serena Williams. In addition, it is interesting to note that one of the first Goodwill Ambassadors to be appointed after 2000 was Sebastiao Salgado, the photojournalist who had previously produced some of the most iconic images of the Sahelian famines of the 1980s (see Chapter 2). Since 2000, other UN agencies have also instituted programmes for celebrity ambassadors, as have many NGOs. In addition in recent years, it has become also a commonplace for larger NGOs, at least, to maintain full-time, dedicated celebrity liaison officers. According to Brockington, by 2014 three-quarters of the 30 largest charities in the UK had such positions (Brockington, 2014b). In recent years, a number of celebrities have also founded their own development-focused NGOs. The best known of these is undoubtedly Madonna's 'Raising Malawi', which was co-founded by the singer with Michael Berg in 2006, to provide assistance for Malawi's one million orphans (see www.raisingmalawi.org).

What have been the effects of this? The primary outcome has been that representations of development in international global media outlets have become once again dominated by images of *humanitarian* emergencies – that is, images of war, famine, and disaster – although now with a focus upon the celebrity-advocates who visit those crises, rather than upon the people who have actually experienced them. This, in turn, has significantly altered the dynamics of humanitarian/development spectatorship, and in so doing has changed the ways in which international media audiences may interpret, and respond to, complex emergencies in the developing world. Yet so too, precisely because the celebrity–development nexus has emerged from and into such a complex global media environment, it has also highlighted a range of other possibilities, some of which may in fact point to the future directions for the relationship between media and development in general. For example, it has pointed to how ICT4D projects might in the future engage more extensively with local and national celebrities – for example, Bollywood or Nollywood celebrities – as a means for forwarding their development goals. It has shown how participatory projects might be expanded still further through the involvement of global celebrities – who, by definition, are likely to be already well known among audiences in the developing world. It has also pointed to how, in the future, those who have experienced war, famine, or disaster may themselves achieve global celebrity status, and thereby become celebrity-advocates in their own right. Perhaps the first truly global humanitarian celebrity to emerge in our current media age has been Malala Yousafzai, the Pakistani blogger and activist who, at the age of 15, survived being shot by the Taliban. Yousafzai went on to become a globally recognized advocate for women's education, eventually winning the Nobel Peace Prize for her efforts. It is likely that as the celebrity–development nexus deepens still further, and as the media environments within which it exists becomes increasingly complex, examples like Yousafzai's will become more and more common in the future – with the potential to radically alter both representations of development and international media audiences' interpretations of these as they do so.

Summary

- Following the Asian Financial Crisis in 1997, international development agencies began to temper neo-liberal approaches to development.
- These efforts congealed around the 'post-Washington Consensus', which still focused on market-driven growth, but gave developing world governments more control over how they managed this, and also required them to provide economic and social 'safety nets' for their most vulnerable citizens.
- The emergence of these 'pro-poor' agendas led to greater emphasis upon the 'poverty agenda', and to the setting of goals for improving these.
- The post-Washington Consensus has had various implications for media and development, the most significant of which has been the emergence of a new 'celebrity–development nexus'.
- This nexus has produced important outcomes, including a renewed focus on developing world debt. However, it also raises difficult questions about the role of spectatorship, and potential conflicts of interest between public and private goals.

Discussion questions

1. In what ways was the 'post-Washington Consensus' simply a continuation of what went beforehand, and in what ways was it entirely different?
2. To what extent was the Asian Financial Crisis of 1997 a portent of the Global Financial Crisis to come (from 2008 onwards)?
3. Do some internet research on Poverty Reduction Strategy Papers (PRSPs) for a developing world country of your choice. How 'participatory' are these papers, really?

4. In what ways has Bono's personal career as a 'development-celebrity' produced complicated outcomes?
5. Design a fictional public–private partnership to address anthropogenic climate change in a developing world country of your choosing. In doing so, try to incorporate as wide a range of public and private interests as you can. To what extent can these different interests be made to support each other, and in what ways do they inevitably conflict?

Further reading

For more on the Asian Financial Crisis, and the IMF and World Bank's responses to it, see: Blustein, P. (2003) *The Chastening: Inside the Crisis that Rocked the Global Financial System and Humbled the IMF*, New York: Public Affairs.

The best critical introductions to the post-Washington Consensus in general (and its implications for future development policy) are: Fine, B. and Lapavitsas, C. (2003) *Development Policy in the Twenty-First Century: Beyond the Post-Washington Consensus*, New York: Routledge; and Carroll, T. (2010) *Delusions of Development: The World Bank and the Post-Washington Consensus in Southeast Asia*, London: Palgrave Macmillan.

There is now a growing academic literature on celebrity and development. The best starting points are: Brockington, D. (2014a) *Celebrity Advocacy and International Development*, New York: Routledge; and Richey, L. (2015) *Celebrity Humanitarianism and North–South Relations: Politics, Place and Power*, New York: Routledge.

Finally, for a detailed case study of one particular development-celebrity, Bono, see the (albeit provocative): Browne, H. (2013) *The Frontman: Bono (In the Name of Power)*, London: Counterblasts.

Multimedia sources

Online resource: Huffington Post's Web Portal on 'Celebrity Activism'. Available online at: www.huffingtonpost.com/news/celebrity-activism/

Online resource: The Radiator Awards/Radi-Aid [A spoof website set up to satirize media representations of development, and the celebrity–development nexus. Includes the spoof charity single: 'Africa for Norway' (www.youtube.com/watch?v=oJLqyuxm96k) and a spoof gameshow: 'Who Wants to be a Volunteer' (www.youtube.com/watch?v=ymcflrj_rRc)]. Available online at: www.rustyradiator.com

Documentary: *He Named Me Malala* (dir. Davis Guggenheim, 2015)

Documentary: *I Am Because We Are* (dir. Nathan Rissman, 2008) [Madonna's charitable organization 'Raising Malawi']

Documentary series: *Why Poverty?* (Democracy Pictures/Steps International, 2012) [An eight-part series on global poverty. See especially episode 2, 'Give Us the Money', which focuses on the celebrity–development nexus]. Available online at: http://documentaryheaven.com/why-poverty/

Bibliography

Abbot, J., Chambers, R., Dunn, C., Harris, T., Merode, E., Porter, G., Townsend, J. and Weiner, D. (1998) Participatory GIS: Opportunity or Oxymoron. *PLA Notes*, 33, 27–33.

Abu-Lughod, L. (2004) *Dramas of Nationhood: The Politics of Television in Egypt*, Chicago, IL: University of Chicago Press.

Adam, G. and Harford, N. (1999) *Radio and HIV/AIDS: Making a Difference – A Guide for Radio Practitioners, Health Workers and Donors*, Geneva: UNAIDS.

Adams, W. (2008) *Green Development: Environment and Sustainability in a Developing World*, 3rd Edition, New York: Routledge.

African Development Bank and African Union (2009) *Oil and Gas in Africa*, Oxford: Oxford University Press.

Afrobarometer (2013) *Policy Paper 3: The Partnership of Free Speech and Good Governance in Africa*. Available online at: http://afrobarometer.org/publications/pp3-partnership-free-speech-and-good-governance-africa [Accessed 29.9.16].

Aker, J. and Mbiti, I. (2010) *Mobile Phones and Economic Development in Africa*, Working Paper #211. Washington, DC: Center for Global Development.

Alexander, C. and Reno, J., eds. (2012) *Economies of Recycling: Global Transformation of Material Values and Social Relations*, London: Zed Books.

Alkire, S. and Santos, M. (2013) *Measuring Acute Poverty in the Developing World: Robustness and Scope of the Multidimensional Poverty Index*, Working Paper #59. Oxford: Oxford Poverty and Human Development Initiative.

Allen, T. (2006) AIDS and Evidence: Interrogating Some Ugandan Myths. *Journal of Biosocial Science*, 38(1), 7–28.

Allen, T. and Weinhold, D. (2000) Dropping the Debt for the New Millennium: Is it Such a Good Idea? *Journal of International Development*, 12(6), 857–875.

Allison, S. (2016) The Man Behind #ThisFlag, Zimbabwe's Accidental Movement for Change. *The Guardian*. Available online at: www.theguardian.com/world/2016/may/26/this-flag-zimbabwe-evan-mawarire-accidental-movement-for-change [Accessed 29.9.16].

Anderson, B. (1983) *Imagined Communities: Reflections on the Origin and Spread of Nationalism*, London: Verso.

Andreasen, A. (1994) Social Marketing: Its Definition and Domain. *Journal of Publication Policy & Marketing*, 13(1), 108–114.

Andrews, D. and Jackson, S., eds. (2001) *Sport Stars: The Cultural Politics of Sporting Celebrity*, New York: Routledge.

Archambault, J. (2011) Breaking Up 'Because of the Phone' and The Transformative Potential of Information in Southern Mozambique. *New Media and Society*, 13(3), 444–456.

Archambault, J. (2013) Cruising Through Uncertainty: Cell Phones and the Politics of Display and Disguise in Inhambane, Mozambique. *American Ethnologist*, 40(1), 88–101.

Article 19 (1996) *Broadcasting Genocide: Censorship, Propaganda and State-sponsored Violence in Rwanda, 1990–94*, London: Article 19.

Artz, L. (2016) Politics, Power and the Political Economy of Media: Nicaragua and Bolivia. *Perspectives on Global Development and Technology*, 15(1/2), 166–193.

Atkin, C. and Wallack, L., eds. (1990) *Mass Communication and Public Health: Complexities and Conflicts*, New York: Sage.

Baichwal, J. (2007) *Manufactured Planet*, New York: Zeitgeist Films.

Bajorek, J. (2012) 'Ca Bousculait!': Democratization and Photography in Senegal. In Vokes, R., ed., *Photography in Africa: Ethnographic Perspectives*, Oxford: James Currey.

Baldé, C., Wang, F., Kuehr, R. and Huisman, J. (2015) *The Global E-Waste Monitor 2014*, Bonn: UN University, ISA – SCYCLE.

Bandura, A. (1977) *Social Learning Theory*, Englewood Cliffs, NJ: Prentice-Hall.

Baran, P. (1957) *The Political Economy of Growth*, New York: Monthly Review Press.

Barendregt, B. (2006) Mobile Modernities in Contemporary Indonesia: Stories from the Other Side of the Digital Divide. In Schulte Nordholt, H. and Hoogenboom, I., eds., *Indonesian Transitions*, Yogyakarta: Pustaka Peljaar.

Barnett, S. (2013) Leveson Past, Present and Future: The Politics of Press Regulation. *The Political Quarterly*, 84(3), 353–361.

Barnouw, E. (1993) *Documentary: A History of Non-Fiction Film*, New York: Oxford University Press.

Batchen, G., Gidley, M., Miller, N. and Prosser, J., eds. (2012) *Picturing Atrocity: Photography in Crisis*, London: Reaktion Books.

BBC (2012) *Country Case Study Uganda: Support to Media Where Media Freedoms and Rights are Constrained*, London: BBC Media Action.

Bell, S. and Aggleton, P., eds. (2016) *Monitoring and Evaluation in Health and Social Development: Interpretive and Ethnographic Perspectives*, London: Routledge.

Bello, W., Cunningham, S. and Rau. B. (1993) *Dark Victory: The United States and Global Poverty*, Oakland, CA: Food First Books.

Beltran, L. (1976) Alien Premises, Objects and Methods in Latin American Communication Research. *Communication Research*, 3(2), 107–134.

Beltran, L. (1980) *Farewell to Aristotle: 'Horizontal' Communication*, Paris: UNESCO.

Benjamin, P. (2000) African Experience with Telecenters. *On the Internet*. Available online at: www.isoc.org/oti/printversions/1000benjamin.html [Accessed 29.9.16].

Berger, C. (2005) Interpersonal Communication: Theoretical Perspectives, Future Prospects. *Journal of Communication*, 55(3), 415–447.

Berger, G. (2010) Problematizing 'Media Development' as a Bandwagon Gets Rolling. *International Communication Gazette*, 72(7), 547–565.

Berlin, I., ed. (1984) *The Age of Enlightenment: The 18th Century Philosophers*, London: Plume.

Birdsall, N. and Fukuyama, F. (2011) The Post-Washington Consensus: Development After the Crisis. *Foreign Affairs*, 90(2), 45–53.

Bleischwitz, R., Dittrich, M. and Pierdicca, C. (2012) *Coltan from Central Africa, International Trade and Implications for Any Certification*, Bruges: Department for European Economic Studies.

Blustein, P. (2003) *The Chastening: Inside the Crisis that Rocked the Global Financial System and Humbled the IMF*, New York: Public Affairs.

Boal, A. (1979) *Theatre of the Oppressed*, London: Pluto Press.

Boorstin, D. (1961) *The Image, or, What Happened to the American Dream?* London: Weidenfeld & Nicolson.

Booth, A. and Mosley, P., eds. (2003) *The New Poverty Strategies*, London: Springer.

Boserup, E. (1970) *Woman's Role in Economic Development*, New York: St. Martin's Press.

Boyd-Barrett, O. (1977) Media Imperialism: Towards an International Framework for the Analysis of Media Systems. In Curran, J., Gurevitch, M. and Woollacott, J., eds., *Mass Communication and Society*, London: Edward Arnold.

Boyd-Barrett, O. and Braham, P., eds. (1987) *Media, Knowledge, and Power*, London: Croom Helm.

Brisebois, D. (1983) The Inuit Broadcasting Corporation. *Anthropologica*, 25(1), 107–115.

Brisset-Foucault, F. (2016) Serial Callers: Communication Technologies and Political Personhood in Contemporary Uganda. *Ethnos*, 83, 1–18.

Brockington, D. (2014a) *Celebrity Advocacy and International Development*, New York: Routledge.

Brockington, D. (2014b) The Production and Construction of Celebrity Advocacy in International Development. *Third World Quarterly*, 35(1), 88–108.

Browne, H. (2013) *The Frontman: Bono (In the Name of Power)*, London: Counterblasts.

Brundtland, G. (1987) *Our Common Future*, New York: United Nations.

Buettner, A. (2011) *Holocaust Images and Picturing Catastrophe: The Cultural Politics of Seeing*, Burlington, VT: Ashgate.

Burger, M. (2015) Public Self-expression, Identity and the Participatory Turn: The Power to Re-imagine the Self. *Communication*, 41(3), 264–286.

Burrell, J. (2008) Problematic Empowerment: West African Internet Scams as Strategic Misrepresentation. *Information Technologies and International Development*, 4(4), 15–30.

Burrell, J. (2010) Evaluating Shared Access: Social Equality and the Circulation of Mobile Phones in Rural Uganda. *Journal of Computer-Mediated Communication*, 15(2), 230–250.

Butler, R. (2005) *Cell Phones May Help 'Save' Africa*. Available online at: https://news.mongabay.com/2005/07/cell-phones-may-help-save-africa/ [Accessed 29.9.16].

Campbell, D. (2002) Salgado and the Sahel: Documentary Photography and the Imaging of Famines. In Debrix, F. and Weber, C., eds., *Rituals of Mediation: International Politics and Social Meaning*, Minneapolis, MN: University of Minnesota Press.

Campbell, D. (2012) *The Myth of Compassion Fatigue*. Available online at: www.david-campbell.org [Accessed 29.9.16].

Cardenas, E., Ocampo, J. and Thorp, R., eds. (2000) *Industrialization and the State in Latin America: The Postwar Years*, New York: Palgrave Press.

Cardoso, F. (1977) The Consumption of Dependency Theory in the United States. *Latin American Research Review*, 12(3), 7–24.

Cardoso, F. and Enzo, F. (1979) *Dependency and Development in Latin America*, Berkeley, CA: University of California Press.

Carmen, R. (1996) *Autonomous Development: Humanising the Landscape – An Excursion into Radical Thinking and Practice*, London: Zed Books.

Carpentier, N., Lie, R. and Servaes, J. (2003) Community Media: Muting the Democratic Media Discourse? *Continuum: Journal of Media and Cultural Studies*, 17(1), 51–68.

Carroll, T. (2010) *Delusions of Development: The World Bank and the Post-Washington Consensus in Southeast Asia*, London: Palgrave Macmillan.

Castells, M. (2000) *The Rise of the Networked Society: The Information Age – Economy, Society and Culture*, Volume 1, New York: Wiley.

Chambers, R. (1977) *Botswana's Accelerated Rural Development Programme 1973–1976: Experiences and Lessons*, Gaborone: Government Printer.

Chambers, R. (1983) *Rural Development: Putting the Last First*, London: Longman.

Chou, W.-Y., Prestin, A., Lyons, C. and Wen, K.-Y. (2013) Web 2.0 for Health Promotion: Reviewing the Current Evidence. *American Journal of Public Health*, 103(1), 9–18.

Chouliaraki, L. (2006) *Spectatorship of Suffering*, London: Sage.

Chouliaraki, L. (2010) Post-humanitarianism: Humanitarian Communication Beyond a Politics of Pity. *International Journal of Cultural Studies*, 13(2), 107–126.

Chouliaraki, L. (2012) The Theatricality of Humanitarianism: A Critique of Celebrity Advocacy. *Communication and Critical/Cultural Studies*, 9(1), 1–21.

Chouliaraki, L. (2013) *The Ironic Spectator: Solidarity in the Age of Post-Humanitarianism*, Cambridge: Polity Press.

Chung, C.-M. and Getty (2016) China's Electronic Waste Village. *Time Magazine*. Available online at: http://content.time.com/time/photogallery/0,29307,1870162,00.html [Accessed 29.9.16].

Clark, D. (2004) The Production of a Contemporary Famine Image: The Image Economy, Indigenous Photographers and the Case of Mekanic Philipos. *Journal of International Development*, 16(5), 693–704.

Collier, J. and Collier, M. (1986 [1967]) *Visual Anthropology: Photography as a Research Method*, Albuquerque, NM: University of New Mexico Press.

Collier, P. (1988) *Women in Development: Defining the Issues*, Policy, Planning and Research Working Paper #129. Washington, DC: World Bank.

Collier, P. (2007) *The Bottom Billion: Why the Poorest Countries are Failing and What Can be Done About it*, Oxford: Oxford University Press.

Cooper, A. (2008) *Celebrity Diplomacy*, Boulder, CO: Paradigm.

Coyer, K. (2011) Community Media in a Globalized World: The Relevance and Resilience of Local Radio. In Mansell, R. and Raboy, M., eds., *The Handbook of Global Communication Policy*, London: Wiley.

Coyne, C. and Leeson, P. (2004) Read All About It! Understanding the Role of Media in Economic Development. *Kyklos*, 57(1), 21–44.

Coyne, C. and Leeson, P. (2009) *Media, Development and Institutional Change*, Northampton: Edward Elgar Publishing.

Cupples, J. (2015) Development Communication, Popular Pressure and Media Convergence. In Mains, S., Cupples, J. and Lukinbeal, C., eds., *Mediated Geographies and Geographies of Media*, Dordrecht: Springer.

Curtis, D. (2011) Broadcasting Peace: An Analysis of Local Media Post-Conflict Peacekeeping Projects in Rwanda and Bosnia. *Canadian Journal of Development Studies*, 21(1), 141–166.

Cutlip, S. (1994) *The Unseen Power: Public Relations – A History*, Hillsdale, NJ: Lawrence Erlbaum.

Da Costa, D. (2010) *Development Dramas: Reimagining Rural Political Action in Eastern India*, New York: Routledge.

Danso, A. (1990) The Debt Crisis and Africa's Maldevelopment. *Southeastern Political Review*, 18(2), 61–84.

Davies, K. (2009) *Flat Earth News*, London: Random House.

Deane, J. (2006 [2001]) Communication for Social Change: Why Does it Matter? In Gumucio-Dagron, A. and Tufte, T., eds., *Communication for Social Change Anthology: Historical and Contemporary Readings*, South Orange, NJ: CSCC.

de Bruijn, M., Nyamnjoh, F. and Brinkman, I., eds. (2009) *Mobile Phones: The New Talking Drums of Africa*, Leiden: African Studies Centre.

De Mul, S. (2011) The Holocaust as a Paradigm for the Congo Atrocities: Adam Hochschild's *King Leopold's Ghost*. *Criticism*, 53(4), 587–606.

Desai, R. and Kharas, H. (2008) The California Consensus: Can Private Aid End Global Poverty? *Survival: Global Politics and Strategy*, 50(4), 155–168.

Des Forges, A. and Liebhafsky, A. (1999) *Leave None to Tell the Story: Genocide in Rwanda*, New York: Human Rights Watch.

de Waal, A. (1997) *Famine Crimes: Politics and the Disaster Relief Industry in Africa*, Oxford: James Currey.

de Waal, A. (2008) The Humanitarian Carnival: A Celebrity Vogue. *World Affairs*, 171(2), 43–55.

Dixon, C. and Drakakis-Smith, D., eds. (1993) *Economic and Social Development in Pacific Asia*, London: Routledge.

Dogra, N. (2014) *Representations of Global Poverty: Aid, Development and International NGOs*, London: I.B. Tauris.

Donner, J. (2008) Research Approaches to Mobile Use in the Developing World: A Review of the Literature. *The Information Society*, 24(3), 140–159.

Donovan, K. (2012) Seeing Like a Slum: Towards Open, Deliberative Development. *Georgetown Journal of International Affairs*, 13(1), 97–104.

Dorfman, A. and Mattelart, A. (1971) *How to Read Donald Duck: Imperialist Ideology in the Disney Comic*, New York: International General.

Dossa, S. (2007) Slicing Up 'Development': Colonialism, Political Theory, Ethics. *Third World Quarterly*, 28(5), 887–899.

Dow, B. and Condit, C. (2005) The State of the Art in Feminist Scholarship in Communication. *Journal of Communication*, 55(3), 448–478.

Downing, J., ed. (2011) *Encyclopedia of Social Movement Media*, London: Sage.

Drahos, P. (2014) *Intellectual Property, Indigenous People and their Knowledge*, Cambridge: Cambridge University Press.

Easterly, W. (2001) Debt Relief. *Foreign Policy*, 127, 20–26.

Eichstaedt, P. (2011) *Consuming the Congo: War and Conflict Minerals in the World's Deadliest Place*, Chicago, IL: Chicago Review Press.

El-Enany, N. (2016) Aylan Kurdi: The Human Refugee. *Law Critique*, 27(1), 13–15.

Elwood, S. (2006a) Critical Issues in Participatory GIS: Deconstructions, Reconstructions, and New Research Directions. *Transactions in GIS*, 10(5), 693–708.

Elwood, S. (2006b) Negotiating Knowledge Production: The Everyday Inclusions, Exclusions, and Contradictions of Participatory GIS Research. *The Professional Geographer*, 58(2), 197–208.

Entertainment-Education Network Africa (2001) *Case Study 5: India – Tinka Tinka Sukh*. Available online at: www.comminit.com/edutain-africa/content/institutional-review-educational-radio-dramas-case-study-5-india-tinka-tinka-sukh [Accessed 29.9.16].

Epskamp, C. (2006) *Theatre for Development: An Introduction to Context, Applications and Training*, London: Zed Books.

Evans, P. (1979) *Dependent Development: The Alliance of Multinational, State and Local Capital in Brazil*, Princeton, NJ: Princeton University Press.

Fadoju, L. (2015) 8 Ways Technology is Influencing Nigeria's 2015 Elections. *TechCabal*. Available online at: http://techcabal.com/2015/03/26/8-ways-technology-is-influencing-nigerias-2015-elections/ [Accessed 29.9.16].

Fahie, J. (1971) *A History of Wireless Telegraphy*, New York: Arno Press.

Fair, J. (1989) 29 Years of Theory and Research on Media and Development: The Dominant Paradigm Impact. *Gazette*, 44(2), 129–150.

Faris, J. (1992) Anthropological Transparency: Film, Representation, and Politics. In Crawford, P. and Turton, D., eds., *Film as Ethnography*, Manchester: Manchester University Press.

Fehrenbach, H. and Rodongo, D., eds. (2015) *Humanitarian Photography: A History*, Cambridge: Cambridge University Press.

Ferraro, V. and Rosser, J. (1994) Global Debt and Third World Development. In Klare, M. and Thomas, D., eds., *World Security: Challenges for a New Century*, New York: St. Martin's Press.

Fidler, R. (1997) *Mediamorphosis: Understanding New Media*, New York: Sage.

Fine, B. and Lapavitsas, C., eds. (2003) *Development Policy in the Twenty-First Century: Beyond the Post-Washington Consensus*, New York: Routledge.

Fjes, F. (1976) *Communications and Development*. Unpublished paper, College of Communications, University of Illinois, Urbana-Champaign, IL.

Foucault, M. (1969) *L'Archéologie du Savoir*, Paris: Gallimard.

Fox, K. and Kotler, P. (1980) The Marketing of Social Causes: The First 10 Years. *Journal of Marketing*, 44(4), 24–33.

Frank, A. (1966) *The Development of Underdevelopment*, Boston, MA: New England Free Press.

Frank, A. (1967) *Capitalism and Underdevelopment in Latin America: Historical Studies of Chile and Brazil*, New York: Monthly Review Press.

Franks, S. (2013) *Reporting Disasters: Famine, Aid, Politics and the Media*, London: Hurst.

Freire, P. (1970) *Pedagogy of the Oppressed*, New York: Herder & Herder.

French, J., Blair-Stevens, C., McVey, D. and Merritt, R. (2009) *Social Marketing and Public Health: Theory and Practice*, Oxford: Oxford University Press.

Friedmann, J. (1992) *Empowerment: The Politics of Alternative Development*, Oxford: Blackwell.

Friedrich, E. (1924) *Krieg dem Kriege! Guerre a la Guerre! War against War! Oorlog aan den Oorlog!* Berlin: Freie Jugend.

Ganguly, S. (2010) *Jana Sanskriti, Forum Theatre and Democracy in India*, New York: Routledge.

Gao, H., Barbier, G. and Goolsby, R. (2011) Harnessing the Crowdsourcing Power of Social Media for Disaster Relief. *IEEE Intelligent Systems*, 26(3), 10–14.

Garber, L. and Cowan, G. (1993) The Virtues of Parallel Vote Tabulations. *Journal of Democracy*, 4(2), 95–107.

Geach, H. (1973) The Baby Food Tragedy. *New Internationalist*, 6 (August).

Gebremichael, M. and Jackson, J. (2006) Bridging the Gap in Sub-Saharan Africa: A Holistic Look at Information Poverty and the Region's Digital Divide. *Government Information Quarterly*, 23(2), 267–280.

Gegeo, D. (1998) Indigenous Knowledge and Empowerment: Rural Development Examined from Within. *The Contemporary Pacific*, 10(2), 289–315.

Gershon, I. and Bell, J. (2013) Introduction: The Newness of New Media. *Culture, Theory and Critique*, 54(3), 259–264.

Gibson-Graham, J. (2010) Post-Development Possibilities for Local and Regional Development. In Pike, A., Rodriguez-Pose, A. and Tomaney, J., eds., *Handbook of Local and Regional Development*, London: Routledge.

Gicheru, C. (2014) *The Challenges Facing Independent Newspapers in Sub-Saharan Africa*, Oxford: Reuters Institute for the Study of Journalism.

Ginsburg, F. (1989) *Contested Lives: The Abortion Debate in an American Community*, Berkeley, CA: University of California Press.

Ginsburg, F. (1991) Indigenous Media: Faustian Contract or Global Village? *Cultural Anthropology*, 6(1), 92–112.

Ginsburg, F. (1993) Screening Politics in A World of Nations: Aboriginal Media and the Australian Imaginary. *Public Culture*, 5(3), 557–578.

Ginsburg, F. (1996) 'From Little Things, Big Things Grow': Indigenous Media and Cultural Activism. In Fox, R. and Starn, O., eds., *Between Resistance and Revolution: Cultural Politics and Social Protest*, New Brunswick, NJ: Rutgers University Press.

Ginsburg, F. (2008) Rethinking the Digital Age. In Hesmondhalgh, D. and Toynbee, J., eds., *The Media and Social Theory*, New York: Routledge.

Ginsburg, F., Abu-Lughod, L. and Larkin, B., eds. (2002) *Media Worlds: Anthropology on New Terrain*, Berkeley, CA: University of California Press.

Goetz, N. (2001) *Humanitarian Issues in the Biafra Conflict*, New York: United Nations High Commissioner for Refugees, Evaluation and Policy Analysis Unit.

Goggin, G. and Clark, J. (2009) Mobile Phones and Community Development: A Contact Zone Between Media and Citizenship. *Development in Practice*, 19(4/5), 585–597.

Golding, P. (1974) Media Role in National Development: Critique of a Theoretical Orthodoxy. *Journal of Communication*, 24(3), 39–53.

Gourevitch, P. (2010) Alms Dealers. *The New Yorker*, 11 October.

Graham, A. (2014) One Hundred Years of Suffering? 'Humanitarian Crisis Photography' and Self-Representation in the Democratic Republic of Congo. *Social Dynamics*, 40(1), 140–163.

Grant, A. and Wilkinson, J., eds. (2009) *Understanding Media Convergence: The State of the Field*, Oxford: Oxford University Press.

Gregory, S. (2012) KONY 2012 through a Prism of Video Advocacy Practices and Trends. *Journal of Human Rights Practice*, 4(3), 463–468.

Grindle, M. (1996) *Challenging the State: Crisis and Innovation in Latin America and Africa*, Cambridge: Cambridge University Press.

Grossman, E. (2006) *High-Tech Trash: Digital Devices, Hidden Toxins and Human Health*, Washington, DC: Island Press.

Grossman, L. (2014) Inside Facebook's Plan to Wire the World. *Time Magazine*. Available online at: http://time.com/facebook-world-plan/ [Accessed 29.9.16].

GSMA Intelligence (2014a) *The Mobile Economy: Sub-Saharan Africa 2014*, London: GSMA Intelligence.

GSMA Intelligence (2014b) *The Mobile Economy: Latin America 2014*, London: GSMA Intelligence.

GSMA Intelligence (2014c) *State of the Industry: Mobile Financial Services for the Unbanked*, London: GSMA Intelligence.

GSMA Intelligence (2015) *The Mobile Economy: India 2015*, London: GSMA Intelligence.

Guiltinan, J. (2009) Creative Destruction and Destructive Creations: Environmental Ethics and Planned Obsolescence. *Journal of Business Ethics*, 89(1), 19–28.

Gumucio-Dagron, A. (2001) *Making Waves: Stories of Participatory Communication for Social Change*, New York: Rockefeller Foundation.

Gumucio-Dagron, A. and Tufte, T., eds. (2006) *Communication for Social Change Anthology: Historical and Contemporary Readings*, South Orange, NJ: CSCC.

Gunkel, D. (2003) Second Thoughts: Toward a Critique of the Digital Divide. *New Media and Society*, 5(4), 499–522.

Gupta, A. (1998) *Postcolonial Developments: Agriculture in the Making of Modern India*, Durham, NC: Duke University Press.

Gursel, Z. (2016) *Image Brokers: Visualizing World News in the Age of Digital Circulation*, Berkeley, CA: University of California Press.

Hagen, E. (2011) Mapping Change: Community Information Empowerment in Kibera. *Innovations*, 6(1), 69–95.

Halkin, A. (2008) Outside the Indigenous Lens: Zapatistas and Autonomous Videomaking. In Wilson, P. and Stewart, M., eds., *Global Indigenous Media: Cultures, Poetics and Politics*, Durham, NC: Duke University Press.

Hall, S. (1973) *Encoding and Decoding in the Television Discourse*, Birmingham: Centre for Cultural Studies.

Haney, E. (2010) *Photography and Africa*, London: Reaktion Books.

Harrison, G. (2010) The Africanization of Poverty: A Retrospective on 'Make Poverty History'. *African Affairs*, 109(436), 391–408.

Hattori, M. (2003) The Moral Politics of International Aid. *Review of International Studies*, 29(2), 231–249.

Heeks, R. (2008) ICT4D 2.0: The Next Phase of Applying ICT for International Development. *Computer*, 41(6), 26–33.

Heffelfinger, E. and Wright, L. (2005) *Visual Difference: Postcolonial Studies and Intercultural Cinema*, New York: Peter Lang.

Herman, C. (2008) Crossing the Digital Divide in a Women's Community ICT Centre. In Van Slyke, C., ed., *Information Communication Technologies: Concepts, Methodologies, Tools, and Applications*, Hershey, PA: IGI Global.

Herman, E. and Chomsky, N. (1988) *Manufacturing Consent: The Political Economy of the Mass Media*, New York: Pantheon Books.

Hill, A. (2005) *Reality TV: Audiences and Popular Factual Television*, New York: Routledge.

Hjarvard, S. (2008) The Mediatization of Religion: A Theory of the Media as Agents of Religious Change. *Northern Lights, Film and Media Studies Yearbook*, 6(1), 9–26.

Hobbs, R. (1998) The Seven Great Debates in the Media Literacy Movement. *Journal of Communication*, 48(1), 9–29.

Hornik, R. (1988) *Development Communication: Information, Agriculture and Nutrition in the Third World*, New York: Longman.

Hornik, R., ed. (2002) *Public Health Communication: Evidence for Behaviour Change*, Hillsdale, NJ: Lawrence Erlbaum.

Howard, P., Agarwal, S. and Hussain, M. (2011) *The Dictators' Digital Dilemma: When Do States Disconnect Their Digital Networks?*, Issues in Technology Innovation #13. Washington, DC: Brookings Institution.

Howden, D. (2013) How Hollywood Cloaked South Sudan in Celebrity and Fell For the 'Big Lie'. *The Guardian*. Available online at: www.theguardian.com/world/2013/dec/28/reality-of-south-sudan-and-hollywood-stars [Accessed 29.9.16].

Howley, K. (2005) *Community Media: People, Places, and Communication Technologies*, Cambridge: Cambridge University Press.

Huesca, R. (1995) A Procedural View of Participatory Communication: Lessons from Bolivian Tin Miners' Radio. *Media, Culture and Society*, 17(1), 101–119.

Hughes, N. and Lonie, S. (2010) M-PESA: Mobile Money for the 'Unbanked' – Turning Cellphones into 24-Hour Tellers in Kenya. *Innovations*, Winter/Spring, 63–81.

Hugo, P. (2011) *Permanent Error*, New York: Prestel Art.

Hulme, D. (2009) *The Millennium Development Goals: A Short History of the World's Biggest Promise*, BWPI Working Paper #100. Manchester: Brooks World Poverty Institute.

Hulme, D. (2015) *Global Poverty: Global Governance and Poor People in the Post-2015 Era*, New York: Routledge.

Ingold, T. (1986) *Evolution and Social Life*, New York: Routledge.

Jacobs, S. (2016) Journal Work: Africa is a Country. *Small Axe*, 20(2), 52–57.

James, W. (1999) Empowering Ambiguities. In Cheater, A., ed., *The Anthropology of Power: Empowerment and Disempowerment in Changing Structures*, London: Routledge.

Jayasuriya, K. and Rosser, A. (2001) Economic Orthodoxy and the East Asian Crisis. *Third World Quarterly*, 22(3), 381–396.

Jensen, K. (2010) *Media Convergence: The Three Degrees of Network, Mass and Interpersonal Communication*, London: Routledge.

Jensen, M. and Esterhuysen, A. (2001) *The Community Telecentre Cookbook for Africa: Recipes for Self-Sustainability (How to Establish a Multi-purpose Community Telecentre in Africa)*, Paris: UNESCO.

Jhala, A. (2011) *Royal Patronage, Power and Aesthetics in Princely India*, London: Pickering & Chatto.

Johnson, D. (2014) Briefing: The Crisis in South Sudan. *African Affairs*, 113(451), 300–309.

Jones, W. (2016) Victoire in Kigali, or: Why Rwandan Elections are Not Won Transnationally. *Journal of Eastern African Studies*, 10(2), 343–365.

Kakwani, N. and Pernia, E. (2000) What is Pro-Poor Growth? *Asian Development Review*, 16(1), 1–22.

Kamlongera, C. (2005) *Theatre for Development in Africa*, Buenos Aires: CLASCO.

Kangalawe, R. (2017) Climate Change Impacts on Water Resource Management and Community Livelihoods in the Southern Highlands of Tanzania. *Climate and Development*, 9(3), 191–201.

Kapoor, I. (2012) *Celebrity Humanitarianism: The Ideology of Global Charity*, New York: Routledge.

Karlyn, A. (2001) The Impact of a Targeted Radio Campaign to Prevent STIs and HIV/AIDS in Mozambique. *AIDS Education and Prevention*, 13(5), 438–451.

Kavoori, A. and Punathambekar, A., eds. (2008) *Global Hollywood*, New York: New York University Press.

Kendall, C., Foote, D. and Martorell, R. (1983) Anthropology, Communications and Health: The Mass Media and Health Practices Program in Honduras. *Human Organization*, 42(4), 353–360.

Kenny, C. (2006) *Overselling the Web? Development and the Internet*, Boulder, CO: Lynne Rienner.

Khan, S. and Christiansen, J., eds. (2011) *Towards New Developmentalism: Market as Means Rather than Master*, New York: Routledge.

Kharas, H. (2007) *The New Reality of Aid*, Washington, DC: Brookings Institution.

Khondker, H. (2011) Role of the New Media in the Arab Spring. *Globalizations*, 8(5), 675–679.

Koczberski, G. (1998) Women in Development: A Critical Analysis. *Third World Quarterly*, 19(3), 395–410.

Kotler, P. (1979) Strategies for Introducing Marketing into Non-profit Organizations. *Journal of Marketing*, 43(1), 37–44.

Kovarik, B. (2011) *Revolutions in Communication: Media History from Gutenberg to the Digital Age*, London: Bloomsbury.

Kuper, A. (1988) *The Invention of Primitive Society: Transformations of an Illusion*, New York: Routledge.

Lanctot, B. (2015) The Tiger and the Daguerreotype: Early Photography and Sovereignty in Post-Revolutionary Latin America. *Journal of Latin American Cultural Studies*, 24(1), 1–17.

La Pastina, A., Rego, C. and Straubhaar, J. (2003) The Centrality of Telenovelas in Latin America's Everyday Life: Past Tendencies, Current Knowledge, and Future Research. *Global Media Journal*, 2(2), 1–15.

Lee, N. and Kotler, P. (2015) *Social Marketing: Changing Behaviours for Good*, 5th Edition, New York: Sage.

Lennie, J. and Tacchi, J. (2013) *Evaluating Communication for Development: A Framework for Social Change*, New York: Routledge.

Lerner, D. (1958) *The Passing of Traditional Society: Modernizing the Middle East*, Glencoe, IL: Free Press.

Leveson, B. (2012) *Report into the Culture, Practices and Ethics of the Press*, London: The Stationery Office.

Levy, S. (2013) How Google Will Use High-Flying Balloons to Deliver Internet to the Hinterlands. *Wired Magazine*. Available online at: www.wired.com/2013/06/google_internet_balloons/all/google.com/loon [Accessed 29.9.16].

Lewis, D. and Kanji, N. (2009) *Non-Governmental Organizations and Development*, London: Routledge.

Lewis, D., Rodgers, D. and Woolcock, M., eds. (2014) *Popular Representations of Development: Insights from Novels, Films, Television and Social Media*, New York: Routledge.

Leys, C. (1996) *The Rise and Fall of Development Theory*, Bloomington, IN: Indiana University Press.

Lipson, C. (2009) The International Organization of Third World Debt. *International Organization*, 35(4), 603–631.

Lissner, J. (1981) Merchants of Misery. *New Internationalist*, 1 June. Available online at: https://newint.org/features/1981/06/01/merchants-of-misery/ [Accessed 29.9.16].

Lizarzaburu, J. (2006) *How Telenovelas Conquered the World*, London: BBC News.

Lorber, H. and Cornelius, M. (1982) Bottle Babies: Grave Markers. *Jump Cut, A Review of Contemporary Media*, 27, 33–34.

Losifidis, P. and Wheeler, M. (2016) *Public Spheres and Mediated Social Networks in the Western Context and Beyond*, London: Springer.

Lousley, C. (2014) Band Aid Reconsidered: Sentimental Cultures and Populist Humanitarianism. In Lewis, D., Rodgers, D. and Woolcock, M., eds., *Popular Representations of Development: Insights from Novels, Films, Television and Social Media*, New York: Routledge.

Lovelock, J. (1972) Gaia as Seen Through the Atmosphere. *Atmospheric Environment*, 6, 579–580.

Lule, J. (2015) *Globalization and Media: Global Village of Babel*, London: Rowman & Littlefield.

Lynch, M., Freelon, D. and Aday, S. (2014) *Syria's Socially Mediated Civil War* (Blogs and Bullets Part III), Washington, DC: US Institute of Peace.

Lyons, T. and Mandaville, P., eds. (2012) *Politics from Afar: Transnational Diasporas and Networks*, London: Hurst.

Mano, W. (2008) Emerging Communities, Emerging Media: The Case of a Zimbabwean Nurse in the British Big Brother Show. *Critical Arts*, 22(1), 101–128.

Martin, J., Abbas, D. and Martins, R. (2016) The Validity of Global Press Ratings. *Journalism Practice*, 10(1), 93–108.

Maurer, B. (2012) Mobile Money: Communication, Consumption and Change in the Payments Space. *Journal of Development Studies*, 48(5), 589–604.

McBride, S. (1980) *Many Voices, One World*, Paris: UNESCO.

McCall, M. and Minang, P. (2005) Assessing Participatory GIS for Community-Based Natural Resource Management: Claiming Community Forests in Cameroon. *The Geographical Journal*, 171(4), 340–356.

McCarthy, N. (2014) Bollywood: India's Film Industry by the Numbers. *Forbes Magazine*. Available online at: www.forbes.com/forbes/welcome/?toURL=http://www.forbes.com/sites/niallmccarthy/2014/09/03/bollywood-indias-film-industry-by-the-numbers-infographic/&refURL=https://www.google.com.au/&referrer=https://www.google.com.au/ [Accessed 29.9.16].

McCombs, M. (2004) *Setting the Agenda: The Mass Media and Public Opinion*, Cambridge: Polity.

McGregor, J. and Primorac, R., eds. (2010) *Zimbabwe's New Diaspora: Displacement and the Cultural Politics of Survival*, Oxford: Berghahn Books.

McKee, N. (1999) *Social Mobilization and Social Marketing in Developing Communities: Lessons for Communicators*, Penang: Southbound.

McKemey, K., Scott, N., Souter, D., Afullo, T., Kibombo, R. and Sakyi-Dawson, O. (2003) *Innovative Demand Models for Telecommunications Services: Final Technical Report*, Reading: Gamos.

McLuhan, M. (1962) *The Gutenberg Galaxy: The Making of Typographic Man*, Toronto: University of Toronto Press.

McLuhan, M. (1964) *Understanding Media: The Extensions of Man*, New York: McGraw-Hill.

McPhail, T. (1981) *Electronic Colonialism: The Future of International Broadcasting and Communication*, London: Sage.

McPhail, T., ed. (2009) *Development Communication: Reframing the Role of the Media*, Malden, MA: Wiley.

McQuail, D. (1994) *Mass Communications Theory: An Introduction*, London: Sage.

Meadows, M. and Molnar, H. (2002) Bridging the Gaps: Towards a History of Indigenous Media in Australia. *Media History*, 8(1), 9–20.

Mefalopulos, P. (2008) *Development Communication Sourcebook: Broadening the Boundaries of Communication*, Washington, DC: World Bank.

Melkote, S. (1991) *Communication for Development in the Third World*, New Delhi: Sage.

Melkote, S. and Steeves, H. (2001) *Communication for Development: Theory and Practice for Empowerment and Social Justice*, 1st Edition, New York: Sage.

Melkote, S. and Steeves, H. (2015) *Communication for Development: Theory and Practice for Empowerment and Social Justice*, 3rd Edition, New York: Sage.

Mills, S. (2009) Theatre for Transformation and Empowerment: A Case Study of Jana Sanskriti Theatre of the Oppressed. *Development in Practice*, 19(4/5), 550–559.

Milton, J. (1644) *Areopagitica: A Speech by Mr. John Milton for the Liberty of Unlicenced Printing, to the Parliament of London*, London.

Minderhoud, A.-M. (2009) *Africa's Private Radio Stations: The Next Big Thing for African Democracy?* Unpublished thesis. Available online at: https://anniemieminderhoud.wordpress.com/africa's-private-radio-stations-the-next-best-thing-for-african-democracy/ [Accessed 29.9.16].

Mirowski, P. (2013) *Never Let a Serious Crisis go to Waste: How Neoliberalism Survived the Financial Meltdown*, New York: Verso.

Moeller, S. (1999) *Compassion Fatigue: How the Media Sell Disease, Famine, War, and Death*, New York: Routledge.

Moeller, S. (2009) *Media Literacy: Citizen Journalists*, Washington, DC: Center for International Media Assistance.

Mohanty, C. (1984) Under Western Eyes: Feminist Scholarship and Colonial Discourses. *Boundary 2*, 12(3)/13(1), 333–358.

Montague, D. (2002) Stolen Goods: Coltan and Conflict in the Democratic Republic of Congo. *SAIS Review*, 22(1), 103–118.

Moon, J. (2015) *Corporate Social Responsibility: A Very Short Introduction*, Oxford: Oxford University Press.

Mottaz, L. (2010) *US Government Funding for Media Development*, Washington, DC: Center for International Media Assistance.

Muller, M. (1974) *The Baby Killer*, London: War on Want.

Mulvey, L. (1975) Visual Pleasure and Narrative Cinema. *Screen*, 16(3), 6–18.

Muthee, P. (2013) *Dependency Theory: The Reality of the International System*, Nairobi: CreateSpace Independent Publishing.

Myers, M. (2002) *From Awareness to Action: Tackling HIV/AIDS Through Radio and Television Drama*, Unpublished manuscript, London: Benfield Greig Hazard Research Centre.

Myers, M. (2008) *Radio and Development in Africa: A Concept Paper*, Ottawa: IDRC.

Mytton, G. (2000) From Saucepan to Dish: Radio and TV in Africa. In Fardon, R. and Furniss, G., eds., *African Broadcast Cultures: Radio in Transition*, Oxford: James Currey.

Naess, A. (1973) The Shallow and the Deep, Long-range Ecology Movement: A Summary. *Inquiry*, 16(1–4), 95–100.

Naim, M. (1994) *Latin America's Journey to the Market: From Macroeconomic Shocks to Institutional Therapy*, International Center for Economic Growth Occasional Paper #62, San Francisco, CA: ICS Press.

Nelson, N. and Wright, S., eds. (1995) *Power and Participatory Development: Theory and Practice*, London: ITDG.

Ngugi, B., Pelowski, M. and Ogembo, J. (2010) M-Pesa: A Case Study of the Critical Early Adopters' Role in the Rapid Adoption of Mobile Money Banking in Kenya. *Electronic Journal of Information Systems in Developing Countries*, 43(3), 1–16.

Nielinger, O. (2004) *Assessing a Decade of Liberal Sector Reforms in African Telecommunications*, Hamburg: Institute of African Affairs.

Nielsen, N. (2009) Enjoy Poverty. *Foreign Policy Blog*. Available online at: http://foreignpolicyblogs.com/2009/05/11/enjoy-poverty/ [Accessed 29.9.16].

Nissinen, S. (2012) *In Search of Visibility: The Ethical Tensions in the Production of Humanitarian Photography*. Unpublished PhD thesis, The Open University.

Nogueira, M. (2002) Theatre for Development: An Overview. *Research in Drama Education*, 7(1), 104–108.

Nordenstreng, K. and Varis, T. (1974) *Television Traffic: A One Way Street? A Survey and Analysis of the International Flow of Television Programme Material*, Paris: UNESCO.

Ocampo, J. and Ros, J., eds. (2011) *The Oxford Handbook of Latin American Economics*, Oxford: Oxford University Press.

O'Connor, A., ed. (2004) *Community Radio in Bolivia: The Miners' Radio Stations*, New York: Edwin Mellen Press.

Okolloh, O. (2009) Ushahidi, or 'Testimony': Web 2.0 Tools for Crowdsourcing Crisis Information. In Ashley, H., ed., *Change at Hand: Web 2.0 for Development*, London: International Institute for Environment and Development.

Orjuela, C. (2008) Distant Warriors, Distant Peace Workers? Multiple Diaspora Roles in Sri Lanka's Violent Conflict. *Global Networks*, 8(4), 436–452.

Ostergaard-Nielsen, E. (2003) *Transnational Politics: The Case of Turks and Kurds in Germany*, New York: Routledge.

Otim, P. (2009) *An Interactive Media: Reflections on Mega FM and its Peacebuilding Role in Uganda*. Available online at: www.beyondintractability.org/casestudy/otim-interactive [Accessed 29.9.16].

Ott, B. and Mack, R. (2014) *Critical Media Studies: An Introduction*, 2nd Edition, Malden, MA: Wiley-Blackwell.

Oxfam (2011) *Growing a Better Future: Food Justice in a Resource-Constrained World*, Oxford: Oxfam.

Pack, S. (2012) 'Uniquely Navajo?': The Navajo Film Project Reconsidered. *Visual Ethnography*, 1(2), 1–20.

Palecanda, M. (2015) *Imagery Strategies and the UNHCR: UNHCR Appeals Images, and their Contribution to a Negative Portrayal of Aid Recipients from the Global South*. Unpublished thesis. Available online at: http://dca.ue.ucsc.edu [Accessed 29.9.16].

Pande, S., Keyzer, M., Aminou, A. and Sonneveld, B. (2008) Addressing Diarrhea Prevalence in the West African Middle Belt: Social and

Geographic Dimensions in a Case Study for Benin, *International Journal of Health Geographies*, 7(17).

Panos (2007) *At the Heart of Change: The Role of Communication in Sustainable Development*, London: Panos Institute.

Parpart, J. (1995) *Gender, Patriarchy and Development in Africa: The Zimbabwean Case*, East Lansing, MI: Michigan State University.

Parvez, N. (2011) Visual Representations of Poverty. *City: Analysis of Urban Trends, Culture, Theory, Policy, Action*, 15(6), 686–695.

Paul, E. (1996) Japan in Southeast Asia: A Geopolitical Perspective. *Journal of the Asia Pacific Economy*, 1(3), 391–410.

Peet, R. and Hartwick, E. (2015) *Theories of Development: Contentions, Arguments, Alternatives*, 3rd Edition, New York: Guilford Press.

Peterson, D., Hunter, E. and Newell, S., eds. (2016) *African Print Cultures: Newspapers and Their Publics in the Twentieth Century*. Ann Arbor: University of Michigan Press.

Pettifor, A. (2006) The Jubilee 2000 Campaign: A Brief Overview. In Jochnick, C. and Preston, F., eds., *Sovereign Debt at the Crossroads: Challenges and Proposals for Resolving the Third World Debt Crisis*, Oxford: Oxford University Press.

Pettit, J., Salazar, J. and Gumucio-Dagron, A. (2009) Citizens' Media and Communication. *Development in Practice*, 19(4/5), 443–452.

Pfau, M., Haigh, M., Logsdon, L., Perrine, C., Baldwin, J., Breitenfeldt, R., Cesar, J., Dearden, D., Kuntz, G., Montalvo, E., Roberts, D. and Romero, R. (2005) Embedded Reporting During the Invasion of Iraq: How the Embedding of Journalists Affects Television News Reports. *Journal of Broadcasting and Electronic Media*, 49(4), 468–487.

Philo, G. (1993) From Buerk to Band Aid: The Media and the 1984 Ethiopian Famine. In Eldridge, J., ed., *Getting the Message*, London: Routledge.

Piketty, T. (2013) *Capital in the Twenty-First Century*, Cambridge, MA: Harvard University Press.

Plastow, J. (2014) Domestication or Transformation? The Ideology of Theatre for Development in Africa. *Applied Theatre Research*, 2(2), 107–118.

Ponte, S. and Richey, L. (2014) Buying into Development? Brand Aid Forms of Cause-Related Marketing. *Third World Quarterly*, 35(1), 65–87.

Porter, D. and Craig, D. (2004) The Third Way and the Third World: Poverty Reduction and Social Inclusion in the Rise of 'Inclusive' Liberalism. *Review of International Political Economy*, 11(2), 387–423.

Pottier, J., Bicker, A. and Sillitoe, P., eds. (2003) *Negotiating Local Knowledge: Power and Identity in Development*, London: Pluto Press.

Potts, M. (1996) The Crisis in International Family Planning. *Health Transition Review*, 6(1), 114–119.

Prahalad, C. (2004) *The Fortune at the Bottom of the Pyramid: Eradicating Poverty Through Profits*, Harlow: Prentice-Hall.

Prahalad, C. and Hammond, A. (2002) *Serving the World's Poor, Profitably*, Cambridge, MA: Harvard University Press.

Prebisch, R. (1950) *The Economic Development of Latin America and its Principal Problems*, Lake Success, NY: United Nations Department of Economic Affairs.

Bibliography

Prunier, G. (1995) *The Rwanda Crisis: History of a Genocide*, New York: Columbia University Press.

Pype, K. (2016) Dead Media Objects and the Experience of the (Once) Modern: Ethnographic Perspectives from the Living Rooms of Kinshasa's Old Aged. *Ethnos* [doi: 10.1080/00141844.2015.1119177].

Rahnema, M. and Bawtree, V., eds. (1997) *The Post-Development Reader*, London: Zed Books.

Rapaport, R. (2009) A Short History of the Digital Divide. *Edutopia.* Available online at: www.edutopia.org/digital-generation-divide-connectivity [Accessed 29.9.16].

Reeves, H. and Baden, S. (2000) *Gender and Development: Concepts and Definitions*, Brighton: Institute of Development Studies.

Rennie, E. (2006) *Community Media: A Global Introduction*, New York: Rowman & Littlefield.

Rheingold, H. (2002) *Smart Mobs: The Next Social Revolution*, Cambridge: Perseus.

Rice, R. and Paisley, W., eds. (1981) *Public Communication Campaigns*, Beverly Hills, CA: Sage.

Rice, T. (2010) Colonial Film Unity. *Colonial Film: Moving Images of the British Empire.* Available online at: www.colonialfilm.org.uk/production-company/colonial-film-unit [Accessed 29.9.16].

Richey, L., ed. (2015) *Celebrity Humanitarianism and North–South Relations: Politics, Place and Power*, New York: Routledge.

Richey, L. and Ponte, S. (2011) *Brand Aid: Shopping Well to Save the World*, Minneapolis, MN: University of Minnesota Press.

Rist, G. (2002) *The History of Development: From Western Origins to Global Faith*, 2nd Edition, London: Zed Books.

Rist, G. (2014) *The History of Development: From Western Origins to Global Faith*, 4th Edition, London: Zed Books.

Roberto, E. (1975) *Strategic Decision-Making in a Social Program: The Case of Family-Planning Diffusion*, Lexington, MA: Lexington Books.

Rodenbeck, M. (2014) Iraq: The Outlaw State. *New York Review of Books.* Available online at: www.nybooks.com/articles/2014/09/25/iraq-outlaw-state/ [Accessed 29.9.16].

Rodney, W. (1972) *How Europe Underdeveloped Africa*, London: Bogle-L'Ouverture Publications.

Rogers, E. (1962) *Diffusion of Innovations*, 1st Edition, New York: Free Press of Glencoe.

Rogers, E. (2003) *Diffusion of Innovations*, 5th Edition, New York: Free Press of Glencoe.

Rogers, E. and Antola, L. (1985) Telenovelas: A Latin American Success Story. *Journal of Communication*, 35(4), 24–35.

Rogers, E. and Svenning, L. (1969) *Modernization Among Peasants: The Impact of Communication*, New York: Holt, Rinehart & Winston.

Rony, F. (1996) *The Third Eye: Race, Cinema and Ethnographic Spectacle*, Durham, NC: Duke University Press.

Rosenberg, E. (2007) US Internet Fraud at All-Time High: 'Nigerian' Scam and Other Crimes Cost $198.4 Million. *SF Gate.* Available online at: www.sfgate.com/crime/article/U-S-Internet-fraud-at-all-time-high-Nigerian-2576989.php [Accessed 29.9.16].

Roth, L. (2005) *Something New in the Air: The Story of First Peoples Television Broadcasting in Canada*, Montreal: McGill-Queens University Press.
Rousseau, J.J. (1762) *The Social Contract*, trans. 1782 G. D. H. Cole, Public domain.
Rowe, D. (2000) Global Media Events and the Positioning of Presence. *Media International Australia*, 97, 11–21.
Ruggiero, T. (2000) Uses and Gratification Theory in the 21st Century. *Mass Communication and Society*, 3(1), 3–37.
Russomanno, J. (2008) Concept of Freedom of the Press. In Donsbach, W., ed., *The International Encyclopedia of Communication*, Oxford: Wiley-Blackwell.
Sachs, W., ed. (1992) *The Development Dictionary: A Guide to Knowledge as Power*, London: Zed Books.
Sadgrove, J., Vanderbeck, R., Andersson, J., Valentine, G. and Ward, K. (2012) Morality Plays and Money Matters: Towards a Situated Understanding of the Politics of Homosexuality in Uganda. *The Journal of Modern African Studies*, 50(1), 103–129.
Sahn, D., Dorosh, P. and Younger, S. (1999) *Structural Adjustment Reconsidered: Economic Policy and Poverty in Africa*, Cambridge: Cambridge University Press.
Sai, F. (1986) Family Planning and Maternal Healthcare: A Common Goal. *World Health Forum*, 7, 316–339.
Said, E. (1978) *Orientalism*, New York: Pantheon Books.
Salgado, S. (2004) *Sahel: The End of the Road*, Berkeley, CA: University of California Press.
Saunders, K., ed. (2003) *Feminist Post-Development Thought: Rethinking Modernity, Post-colonialism, and Representation*, London: Zed Books.
Schelling, T. (1968) The Life You Save May be Your Own. In Chase, S., ed., *Problems in Public Expenditure Analysis*. Washington, DC: Brookings Institution.
Schneider, J. (2010) The Topography of the Early History of African Photography. *History of Photography*, 34(2), 134–146.
Schramm, W., ed. (1954) *The Process and Effects of Mass Communications*, Urbana, IL: University of Illinois Press.
Schramm, W. (1964) *Mass Media and National Development: The Role of Information in the Developing Countries*, Stanford, CA: Stanford University Press.
Scott, M. (2014a) *Media and Development*, London: Zed Books.
Scott, M. (2014b) The Role of Celebrities in Mediating Distant Suffering. *International Journal of Cultural Studies*, 18(4), 1–18.
Serra, N. and Stiglitz, J., eds. (2008) *The Washington Consensus Reconsidered: Towards a New Global Governance*, Oxford: Initiative for Policy Dialogue.
Servaes, J. (1991) Toward a New Perspective for Communication and Development. In Camir, F., ed., *Communication in Development*, Norwood, NJ: Ablex Publishing.
Servaes, J., ed. (2008) *Communication for Development and Social Change*, Thousand Oaks, CA: Sage.
Shawcross, W. and Hodgson, F. (1987). Sebastiao Salgado, Man in Distress. *Aperture*, 108, 2–31.

Sheffer, G. (2006) *Diaspora Politics: At Home Abroad*, Cambridge: Cambridge University Press.

Sillitoe, P. (2009) *Local Science vs. Global Science: Approaches to Indigenous Knowledge in International Development*, Oxford: Berghahn.

Singer, H. (1949) Economic Progress in Underdeveloped Countries. *Social Research*, 16(1), 1–11.

Singhal, A. and Rogers, E. (1999) *Entertainment-Education: A Communication Strategy for Social Change*, Mahwah, NJ: Lawrence Erlbaum.

Singhal, A., Cody, M., Rogers, E. and Sabido, M., eds. (2003) *Entertainment-Education and Social Change: History, Research and Practice*, New York: Routledge.

Sireau, N. (2008) *Make Poverty History: Political Communication in Action*, London: Palgrave Macmillan.

Skuse, A. (2011) Radio Sound and Social Realism: In the Terrain of Drama for Development Production. *International Communication Gazette*, 73(7), 595–609.

Sliwinski, S. (2011) *Human Rights in Camera*, Chicago, IL: University of Chicago Press.

Slocum, N. (2003) *Participatory Methods Toolkit: A Practitioner's Guide*, Maastricht: United Nations University.

Smith, A. (1759) *The Theory of Moral Sentiments*, London: Millar in the Strand.

Smith, A. (1776) *An Inquiry into the Nature and Causes of the Wealth of Nations*, London: Strahan & Cadell.

Smith, W. (2009) Social Marketing in Developing Countries. In French, F., Blair-Stevens, C., McVey, D. and Merritt, R., eds., *Social Marketing and Public Health: Theory and Practice*, Oxford: Oxford Scholarship Online.

Sontag, S. (1977) *On Photography*, New York: Farrar, Straus & Giroux.

Sontag, S. (2003) *Regarding the Pain of Others*, New York: Farrar, Straus & Giroux.

Stottlemyre, S. and Stottlemyre, S. (2012) Crisis Mapping Intelligence Information During the Libyan Civil War: An Exploratory Case Study. *Policy & Internet*, 4(3/4), 24–39.

Stowe, H. (1852) *Uncle Tom's Cabin, or, Life Among the Lowly*, Boston, MA: John P. Jewett.

Strand, C. (2011) Kill Bill! Ugandan Human Rights Organizations' Attempts to Influence the Media's Coverage of the Anti-Homosexuality Bill. *Culture, Health and Sexuality*, 13(8), 917–931.

Straus, S. (2011) What is the Relationship Between Hate Radio and Violence? Rethinking Rwanda's 'Radio Machete'. In Ligaga, D., Moyo, D. and Gunner, L., eds., *Radio in Africa: Publics, Cultures, Communities*, Johannesburg: Witwatersrand University Press.

Struk, J. (2004) *Photographing the Holocaust: Interpretations of the Evidence*, London: I.B. Tauris.

Sumner, A. and Mallett, R. (2012) *The Future of Foreign Aid: Development Cooperation and the New Geography of Global Poverty*, London: Palgrave.

Taylor, R. and Gaskell, I. (2007) Turning Up the Volume: A Study of the Wan Smolbag Theatre Company. *Journal of Language Teaching, Linguistics and Literature*, 13, 9–28.

Tettey, W. (2001) The Media and Democratization in Africa: Contributions, Constraints and Concerns of the Private Press. *Media, Culture and Society*, 23(1), 5–31.

Thompson, K. (2006) *An Eye for the Tropics: Tourism, Photography and Framing the Caribbean Picturesque*, Durham, NC: Duke University Press.

Thussu, D., ed. (2007) *Media on the Move: Global Flow and Contra-Flow*, New York: Routledge.

Tomlinson, J. (1991) *Cultural Imperialism: A Critical Introduction*, London: Pinter Publications.

Tufte, T. (2001) *Entertainment-Education and Participation: Assessing the Communication Strategy of Soul City*, New York: IAMCR.

Tufte, T. and Mefalopulos, P. (2009) *Participatory Communication: A Practical Guide*, Washington, DC: World Bank.

Turner, T. (2002) Representation, Politics, and Cultural Imagination in Indigenous Video. In Ginsburg, F., Abu-Lughod, L. and Larkin, B., eds., *Media Worlds: Anthropology on New Terrain*, Berkeley, CA: University of California Press.

Twomey, C. (2012a) Framing Atrocity: Photography and Humanitarianism. *History of Photography*, 36(3), 255–264.

Twomey, C. (2012b) Severed Hands: Authenticating Atrocity in the Congo, 1904–13. In Batchen, G., Gidley, M., Miller, N. and Prosser, J., eds., *Picturing Atrocity: Photography in Crisis*, London: Reaktion Books.

UNAIDS (1999) *Communications Framework for HIV/AIDS: A New Direction*, Geneva: UNAIDS.

UNDESA (2008) *Participatory Governance and the Millennium Development Goals*, New York: UNDESA.

UNESCO (1998) *World Culture Report 1998: Culture, Creativity and Markets*, Paris: UNESCO.

UNESCO (2000) *World Culture Report 2000: Cultural Diversity, Conflict and Pluralism*, Paris: UNESCO.

UNGA (1948) *The Universal Declaration of Human Rights*, Paris: United Nations.

UNICTTF (2005) *Measuring ICT: The Global Status of ICT Indicators*, New York: UNICTTF.

Unwin, T., ed. (2008) *ICT4D: Information and Communication Technology for Development*, Cambridge: Cambridge University Press.

Unwin, T. (2009) *Information and Communication Technologies for Poverty Alleviation*, Cambridge: Cambridge University Press.

Uvin, P. (1998) *Aiding Violence: The Development Enterprise in Rwanda*, West Hartford, CT: Kumarian Press.

van der Gaag, N. and Nash, C. (1987) *Images of Africa: The UK Report*, Oxford: Oxfam.

Vandevoordt, R. (2016) Humanitarian Media Events: On the Symbolic Conditions of Moral Integration. In Fox, A., ed., *Global Perspectives on Media Events in Contemporary Society*, Hershey, PA: IGI Global.

van Dijk, J. (2005) *The Deepening Divide: Inequality in the Information Society*, Thousand Oaks, CA: Sage.

Vaughan, P. and Rogers, E. (2000) Entertainment-Education and HIV/AIDS Prevention: A Field Experiment in Tanzania. *Journal of Health Communication*, 5(2), 203–227.

Vestergaard, A. (2013) Humanitarian Appeal and the Paradox of Power. *Critical Discourse Studies*, 10(4), 444–467.

Vigil, J. (1994) *Rebel Radio: The Story of El Salvador's Radio Venceremos*, Evanston, IL: Curbstone Press.

Visvanathan, N., Duggan, L., Wiegersma, N. and Nisonoff, L., eds. (2011) *The Women, Gender and Development Reader*, 2nd Edition, Kaapstad: New Africa Books.

Vodafone (2005) *Africa: The Impact of Mobile Phones*, London: Vodafone Group.

Vokes, R. (2007a) Charisma, Creativity and Cosmopolitanism: A Perspective on the Power of the New Radio Broadcasting in Uganda and Rwanda. *Journal of the Royal Anthropological Institute*, 13(4), 805–824.

Vokes, R. (2007b) (Re)constructing the Field Through Sound: Actor-networks, Ethnographic Representation and 'Radio Elicitation' in South-western Uganda. In Hallam, E. and Ingold, T., eds., *Creativity and Cultural Improvisation*, Oxford: Berg.

Vokes, R. (2010) Arsenal in Bugamba: The Rise of English Premier League Football. *Anthropology Today*, 26(3), 10–15.

Vokes, R. (2012) Introduction. In Vokes, R., ed., *Photography in Africa: Ethnographic Perspectives*, Oxford: James Currey.

Vokes, R. (2016a) Before the Call: Mobile Phones, Exchange Relations, and Social Change in South-western Uganda. *Ethnos* [doi: 10.1080/00141844.2015.1133689].

Vokes, R. (2016b) Primaries, Patronage and Political Personalities in South-western Uganda. *Journal of Eastern African Studies*, 10(4), 660–676.

Vokes, R. (unpublished) Signs of Development: Exhibitions, Photographs and the Politics of Affect in Late-Colonial Uganda. Unpublished manuscript.

Waisbord, S. (2001) *Family Tree of Theories, Methodologies and Strategies in Development Communication*, New York: Rockefeller Foundation.

Wakefield, A. (2015) One in Ten South Africans Living with HIV. On *News24*. Available online at: http://www.news24.com/SouthAfrica/News/One-in-10-South-Africans-living-with-HIV-Stats-SA-20150723 [Accessed 29.9.16].

Walsh, D., Rudd, R., Moeykens, B. and Moloney, T. (1993) Social Marketing for Public Health. *Health Affairs*, 12(2), 104–119.

Wasserman, H., ed. (2011) *Popular Media, Democracy and Development in Africa*, New York: Routledge.

Wasserman, H. (2013) *Press Freedom in Africa: Comparative Perspectives*, New York: Routledge.

Welch, D., ed. (1983) *Nazi Propaganda*, London: Croom Helm.

Wilke, J., ed. (1998) *Propaganda in the 20th Century: Contributions to History*, Cresskill, NJ: Hampton Press.

Wilkins, K. and Enghel, F. (2013) The Privatization of Development Through Global Communication Industries: Living Proof? *Media, Culture and Society*, 35(2), 165–181.

Williamson, J., ed. (1990) *Latin American Adjustment: How Much Has Happened?* Washington, DC: Institute for International Economics.

Wilson, P. and Stewart, M., eds. (2008) *Global Indigenous Media: Cultures, Poetics and Politics*, Durham, NC: Duke University Press.

Wolf, E. (2013) *Europe and the People Without History*, 2nd Edition, Berkeley, CA: University of California Press.

Wood, D. (1994) *The Arrival of the Daguerreotype in New York*, New York: American Photographic Historical Society.

Woodward, H. (2014) A Patchwork of Participation: Wan Smolbag Theatre's 'Big Plays' in Vanuatu. *Australasian Drama Studies*, 64, 223–242.

World Bank (1989) *World Development Report 1989*, New York: Oxford University Press.

World Bank (2012) *Maximizing Mobile: Information and Communication for Development*, Washington, DC: World Bank.

Worth, S. and Adair, J. (1972) *Through Navajo Eyes: An Exploration in Film Communication and Anthropology*, Bloomington, IN: Indiana University Press.

Wortham, E. (2013) *Indigenous Media in Mexico: Culture, Community and State*, Durham, NC: Duke University Press.

Young, R. (2016) *Postcolonialism: An Historical Introduction*, Oxford: Wiley-Blackwell.

Yrjola, R. (2009) The Invisible Violence of Celebrity Humanitarianism: Soft Images and Hard Words in the Making and Unmaking of Africa. *World Political Science Review*, 5(1), 279–292.

Zook, M., Graham, M., Shelton, T. and Gorman, S. (2010) Volunteered Geographic Information and Crowdsourcing Disaster Relief: A Case Study of the Haitian Earthquake. *World Medical and Health Policy*, 2(2), 7–33.

Index

Abah, Steve Ogah 138
Abbot, J., Chambers, R., Dunn, C., Harris, T., Merode, E., *et al.* 211
Abu-Lughod, Lila 11, 128
Academy for Educational Development 43
Adair, John 144, 145, 151
Adam, G. and Halford, N. 142
Affleck, Ben 254
Africa: The Impact of Mobile Phones (Vodafone) 202
'Africa is a country' (blog) 100
African Arts 99
African Development Bank 161
African Union (AU) 161
africasacountry.com 208–9
Afrobarometer 185
Aker, J. and Mbiti, I. 202
Ali, Muhammed 244
'Alien Premises, Objects and Methods in Latin American Communication Research' (Beltran, L.R.) 120–21
Alkire, S. and Santos, M. 241
Allen, T. 58
Allen, T. and Weinhold, D. 239
Allison, S. 209
Americas Media Initiative (AMI) 147–8
Amin, Mohamed 25, 75–6, 86, 96
Anderson, B. 2
Anderson, Mike 145
Andrews, D. and Jackson, S. 247
Anti-homosexuality Act (2014) 227
Applegate, Bill 25
Arab Spring, media and 206–7
Archambault, J. 201, 216
Areopagitica (Milton, J.) 170–71

Artz, L. 143
Asian financial crisis (1997), effects of 237–43
Association of Southeast Asian Nations (ASEAN) 237
atrocity imagery: power of 95; variations in effects of 95–6
autocratic development 117–18
automated teller machines (ATMs) 185

baby milk, investigation on use of 49–51, 52
Bajorek, J. 2
Baldé, C., Wang, F., Kuehr, R. and Huisman, J. 218, 219, 222
Band Aid 76–7, 236, 244
Bandura, Albert 53
Baran, Paul A. 116
Barayagwiza, Jean-Bosco 224, 225–6
Barendregt, Bart 20
Barnett, S. 23
Barnouw, E. 165
BBC (British Broadcasting Corporation): Arabic Service 227; TV News 25, 75; World Service 165–6
Becker, Koos 168
Beckham, David 247, 252, 256
Beecher Stowe, Harriet 78
Bell, S. and Aggleton, P. 134
Bello, W., Cunningham, S. and Rau. B. 18
Beltran, Luis 17, 136
Bemeriki, Valerie 224
Ben Ali, Zine el Abidine 207
Benally, Susie 145
Benjamin, P. 200

Berg, Michael 257
Berger, G. 22, 174
Berlin, I. 12
Bernstein, Sidney 80
Biafra emergency 94
biblical crises 87–94; 'Crossing the Red Sea' image 91, 93; 'Deposition from the Cross' image 90–91; disaster settings, humanity in 88, 90, 91–3; 'Fall of Adam and Eve' image 91, 92; 'Iconography of Suffering' 93–4; 'identifiable victim effect' 88; 'Madonna and Child' image 88–9; 'sentimentality' 88; soldier-protector image 88, 90, 91; suffering, Christian iconography of 87–8, 89–93, 93–4; 'visual memory' 93
Bill and Melinda Gates Foundation (BMGF) 205, 236, 250
Birdsall, N. and Fukuyama, F. 233
Bleischwitz, R., Dittrich, M. and Pierdicca, C. 218
Bloom, Orlando 256
Boal, Augusto 139
Bolivian Tin Workers' Union (FSTMB) 176
Bollywood 58, 188, 257
Bono 244, 245, 248–9, 249–50, 253
Boorstin, Daniel 167
Booth, A. and Mosley, P. 236
Boserup, Ester 123–4, 127
Bottom of the Pyramid (BoP) approach 203–4
Bouazizi, Mohamed 207
Boyd-Barrett, O. 119, 121
Bretton-Woods Institution 140
Brisebois, D. 151
Brisset-Foucault, F. 198, 206
British Colonial Film Unit (BCFU) 9–10, 52
Brockington, Dan 247–8, 251, 257
Brown, Gordon 195
Brundtland, Gro Harlem 129
Buerk, Michael 25, 75–6, 86, 94, 96
Buettner, A. 80
Burger, M. 143

Burrell, J. 216, 229–30
Butler, R. 201

Cameron, David 105–6
Campbell, David 93, 94–6
Canadian Broadcasting Corporation (CBC) 150–51
Canadian Radio-Television and Telecommunications Commission (CRTC) 150–51
Capitalism and Underdevelopment in Latin America (Frank, A.G.) 116
capitalist markets, inequalities and 234–5
Cardenas, E., Ocampo, J. and Thorp, R. 158
Cardoso, F. 116
Carmen, Raff 137, 151
Carpentier, N., Lie, R. and Servaes, J. 152
Carroll, T. 234
Castells, M. 199
cathode ray tubes (CRTs) 166, 218–19
'C4D' (communication for development) 136, 138, 143, 151
celebrity, development and 30, 233–60; Asian financial crisis (1997) and beyond 237–43; Association of Southeast Asian Nations (ASEAN) 237; capitalist markets, inequalities and 234–5; celebrity-development nexus 244–50, 256; celebrity-humanitarian spectatorship 250–56; discussion questions 258–9; further reading, suggestions for 259; Global Partnership for Education (GPE) 242–3; Goodwill Ambassadors (UNICEF) 252, 256–7; Group of Eight (G8) 244–5, 246; Highly-Indebted Poor Countries (HIPC) Initiative 239–40, 246; Human Development Index (HDI) 241; 'information poverty,' concept of 236; Interactive Voice Response (IVR) surveys 243; International Monetary Fund (IMF) 238, 239–40, 246; market activities, guiding beneficial outcomes from 234; Millennium Development Goals (UNDESA, 2008) 236, 241–3,

246, 249; multimedia sources 259–60; newly industrialized countries (NICs) 237; non-governmental organizations (NGOs) 244, 257; 'post-Washington Consensus,' development of 233–4; 'post-Washington Consensus,' emergence of 235, 236, 244, 256; 'post-Washington Consensus,' encouragement of private aid and PPPs 235–6; 'post-Washington Consensus,' media celebrities and 236–7; 'post-Washington Consensus,' metrics and targets focus of 236; public-private partnerships (PPPs) 234, 247; purchasing power parity (PPP) 241, 242, 243; 'safety nets,' provision of 234; SMS surveys 243; summary 258; 'third way' in development 233; 'trickle-down' process 234; UN Children's Fund (UNICEF) 252; UN Economic, Social and Cultural Organization (UNESCO) 236; UN High Commission for Refugees (UNHCR) 251; UN High Level Plenary Meeting (2010) 243; UN Information and Communication Technologies Task Force (UNICTTF) 236; UN Millennium Summit (New York, 2000) 241; UN System Task Team 243; UNDP Human Development Reports 241; Washington Consensus, poorest people and policies of 235; World Bank 238, 239–40, 243, 246; World Bank global poverty line, development of 240, 241; worldwewant2030.org 243
central processing units (CPUs) 218
Chalfen, Richard 144, 145, 151
Chambers, Robert 16, 116, 134
Chiapas Media Project (CMP) in Mexico 147–8
Chicago School 163
Chomsky, Noam 122
Chou, W.-Y., Prestin, A., Lyons, C. and Wen, K.-Y. 210
Chouliaraki, L. 27, 28, 66, 102–3; celebrity, development and 250, 251, 254

Christie, Mike 244
Chung, C.-M. and Getty Images 220–21
Cissé, Souleymane 99
Clah, Al 145
Clark, D. 24, 97
Clerc, Julien 251
Clooney, George 255
Coldplay 246
Collier, J. and Collier, M. 133
Collier, P. 234
colonialfilm.org.uk 9
Communications Framework for HIV/AIDS (UNAIDS, 1999) 143
community media 175–80; Bolivian tin miners' radio stations 175, 176; broadcasters, need for proliferation of 179; Chiapas Media Project (CMP) in Mexico 175; community radio in Kinshasa (DRC) 177; liberalization of national media environments 175, 178; neo-liberalism and 179; Radio Venceremos 175; social change, community management of 179–80; stakeholder-led initiatives 179
compassion fatigue 94–8; atrocity imagery, power of 95; atrocity imagery, variations in effects of 95–6; Biafra emergency 94; Enjoy Poverty Project (Renzo Martens) 97–8; Ethiopian famine 94, 96; flaws in idea of 95; Haiti earthquake (2010) 95; humanitarian imagery, overexposure to 94–5; Kroo Bay 'slum' area in Freetown, Sierra Leone 96; negative imagery, ethical implications of 97; 'numbing effect' upon audiences 94; Second Congo War (1997-2003) 96; World Lutheran Foundation 94–5
Compassion Fatigue (Moeller, S.) 95
Congo: Reform Association (CRA) 67, 69, 70; Second Congo War (1997-2003) 96; *see also* Democratic Republic of Congo (DRC)
Consultative Group to Assist the Poor (CGAP) 205

Cornell University 146
Coyer, K. 179
Coyne, C. and Leeson, P. 19, 197
'Crossing the Red Sea' image 91, 93
'crowded' media environments 193–4
Cruickshank, Isaac 68
CTCnet 199
cultural imperialism: antecedents of 121; dependency theory and 122
Cultural Imperialism School 121
Cupples, J. 143
Curtis, D. 149
Cutlip, S. 172

Da Costa, D. 139
Damon, Matt 254
Danso, A. 19, 161, 162
Davies, Howard 86
Davis, Nick 100
De Mul, S. 98
De Waal, A. 72, 75, 76–7
Deane, J. 151
Deep Ecology 128
Democratic Republic of Congo (DRC) 169, 216, 217–18; UN Stabilization Mission in Democratic Republic (MONUSCO) 226
Dent, Martin 244
dependency theory 115–22; 'Alien Premises, Objects and Methods in Latin American Communication Research' (Beltran, L.R.) 120–21; autocratic development 117–18; *Capitalism and Underdevelopment in Latin America* (Frank, A.G.) 116; cultural imperialism, antecedents of 121; *The Development of Underdevelopment* (Frank, A.G.) 116; media and detriment to developing world 119; Media Imperialism Debate 120, 121; 'modern' scientific and technical information, dissemination of 118–19; modernization theory, interventionist logics of 115–16, 117; modernization theory, undermining logic of 117–18, 119–20;

Singer-Prebisch hypothesis 115–16, 117; *Social Research* 115; systematic exploitation of southern societies 117; technological disadvantage 118; underdevelopment and 116–17
'Deposition from the Cross' image 90–91
Des Forges, A. and Liebhafsky, A. 223
Desai, R. and Kharas, H. 236, 242
development, representations of 29–30, 64–111; Africa is a country 100; Band Aid 76–7, 236, 244; biblical crises 87–94; compassion fatigue 94–8; *Compassion Fatigue* (Moeller, S.) 95; Congo Reform Association (CRA) 67, 69, 70; 'development as modernization,' era of 64; disaster, iconographies of 77–87; discussion questions 110; further reading, suggestions for 110–11; global media audiences, development of 65–6; humanitarianism, histories of 66–77; humanitarianism and international development, elision in media imagery of 64–5; iconographic imagery 65; international development agencies, increase in numbers of 66; Joint Church Aid (JCA) 72, 73, 95; Kurdi, Aylan, tragic death of 105–7; Live Aid 25, 76–7, 168, 236, 244, 246; Médecins sans Frontières (MSF) 72; multimedia sources 111; Overseas Development Institute (ODI) 105; Oxfam, suffering mother and child poster 81; Oxfam's GROW campaign 103–4; post-humanitarian communication 99–107; Society for Effecting the Abolition of the Slave Trade (SAST) 67–8, 93; summary 109–10; UN Food and Agriculture Organization (FAO) 76; World Food Programme (WFP) 102
The Development Dictionary (Sachs, W.) 131
Development Media International (DMI) 60
The Development of Underdevelopment (Frank, A.G.) 116

Diffusion of Innovations (Rogers, E.) 38–9, 182, 204
digital divide 184–5
disaster: iconographies of 77–87; settings of, humanity in 88, 90, 91–3
discussion questions: celebrity, development and 258–9; development, representations of 110; globalization of media, structural-adjustment and 190; ICT4D in new media worlds 230–31; media and development, relationship between 32; media empowerment 154; 'Media for Development' ('M4D') 61
Dixon, C. and Drakakis-Smith, D. 18
DKT International 43
Doheny, Father Kevin 72, 86
Donner, J. 202
Donovan, K. 214–15
Doordarshan, India 54
Dorfman, A. and Mattelart, A. 122
Dorras, Jo 140–41
Dossa, S. 121
Dow, B. and Condit, C. 126
Dowler, Millie 23
Drahos, P. 16
Dramas of Nationhood (Abu-Lughod, L.) 128
Drummond, Jamie 244, 249–50
DStv (Digital Satellite television) 168, 170, 196

Easterly, W. 239
electrical and electronic equipment (EEE) 218–19
Elton John 246
Elwood, S. 211
El-Enany, Nadine 107
England: Bill of Rights (1689) 171; English Premier League (EPL) football 195–6, 216–17
Enjoy Poverty Project (Renzo Martens) 97–8
entertainment-education, media and 52–9
Entertainment-Education Network Africa 58
Epskamp, C. 138
Escobar, Arturo 131–2
Esterhuysen, Anriette 201
Estevar, Gustavo 131–2
Estrada, Joseph 206
Ethiopian famine (1983-5) 25, 74–5, 76, 77, 78, 80, 86–7, 94, 96, 101
European Recovery Programme (ERP) 33
Evans, P. 15, 118
e-waste 218–19; generation of 194

Fadoju, L. 208
Fahie, J. 165
Fair, J. 119
'Fall of Adam and Eve' image 91, 92
Farabundo Marti National Liberation Front (FMLN) 175
Faris, J. 150, 152
FBI Internet Crime Complaint Center 229
Fehrenbach, H. and Rodongo, D. 26, 96
feminist critiques of modernization theory 122–8; Gender and Development (GAD) 125; Human Poverty Index (HPI) 124–5; industrialization, growth of 124; inequalities, economic imbalances and 122–3; media bias 126–7; Multi-dimensional Poverty Index (MPI) 125; second wave feminist theory, ideas and ideology of 123; UN 'Decade for the Advancement for Women' 125; 'Under Western Eyes: Feminist Scholarship and Colonial Discourses' (Mohanty, C.T.) 127–8; urbanization, growth of 124; *Woman's Role in Economic Development* (Boserup, E.) 123–4; Women in Development (WID) 125, 129
Ferraro, V. and Rosser, J. 161
Fidler, Roger 7
Fjes, F. 120
foreign direct investment (FDI) 18, 164
Forsyth, Frederick 73
Foucault, Michel 121
4G networks 183, 186, 187, 210

Fox, K. and Kotler, P. 48
France, Declaration of the Rights of Man and of the Citizen (1789) 171
Frank, Andre Gunder 15, 116–17
Franks, S. 75
Freedom House *Freedom of the Press Reports* 22, 173–4
Freire, Paolo 132–3
Friedman, Milton 163
Friedmann, John 137, 151
Friedrich, Ernest 11
further reading, suggestions for: celebrity, development and 259; development, representations of 110–11; globalization of media, structural-adjustment and 190–91; ICT4D in new media worlds 231; media and development, relationship between 32; media empowerment 154–5; 'Media for Development' ('M4D') 62
Futures Group 43

Gaia Theory 128
Ganguly, Sanjoy 139
Gao, H., Barbier, G. and Goolsby R. 17, 211
Garber, L. and Cowan, G. 208
Gateway TV (GTV) 195–6, 216–17
Geach, H, 49
Gebremichael, M. and Jackson, J. 236
Gegeo, D. 133
Geldof, Bob 76, 244, 245, 255
Gender and Development (GAD) 125
Gentileschi, Orazio 89, 91
geographic information systems (GIS) 17, 29, 143, 211–12; Haiti earthquake disaster (2010) and 212–13; KONY 2012 campaign and 213–14; Map Kibera Project (MKP) and 214–15
Gershon, I. and Bell, J. 4, 7, 182
Gibson-Graham, J. 152
Gicheru, C. 169, 183
Gihigi, Gaspard 224
Gill, Peter 75
Gillard, Julia 242–3

Ginsburg, F., Abu-Lughod, L. and Larkin, B. 11, 209
Ginsburg, Faye 11, 146, 148, 151, 184–5
global Bollywood 188
Global E-Waste Monitor 219, 222
global economic crisis and downturn (1970s) 157
Global Financial Crisis (GFC, 2008) 216–17
global internet access 184, 186
global media audiences, development of 65–6
Global North 3, 40, 95, 117, 130, 131, 144
Global Partnership for Education (GPE) 242–3
Global South 1, 21–2, 40, 47, 94, 96, 97, 184, 186, 243; ICT4D in new media worlds 197, 217, 222, 229; media empowerment 112, 114, 118, 121–2, 125, 128, 130, 131–2, 133, 139, 153
globalization of media, structural-adjustment and 30, 157–91; African Development Bank 161; African Union (AU) 161; Afrobarometer 185; *Areopagitica* (Milton, J.) 170–71; automated teller machines (ATMs) 185; BBC (British Broadcasting Corporation) 165–6, 169; Bolivian Tin Workers' Union (FSTMB) 176; cathode ray tubes (CRTs) 166, 218–19; Chicago School 163; community media 175–80; Democratic Republic of Congo (DRC) 169, 216, 217–18, 226; digital divide 184–5; discussion questions 190; DStv (Digital Satellite television) 168, 170, 196; England, Bill of Rights (1689) 171; Farabundo Marti National Liberation Front (FMLN) 175; 4G networks 183, 186, 187, 210; France, Declaration of the Rights of Man and of the Citizen (1789) 171; Freedom of the Press Report 174; further reading, suggestions for 190–91; global Bollywood 188; global economic crisis and downturn (1970s) 157; global internet access 184,

186; globalization of media content 158, 164–70; Import Substitution Industrialization (ISI) 159; International Bureau for the Development of Communication (UNESCO) 173; International Monetary Fund (IMF) 162, 163, 187, 223; McBride Report (1980) 173; market-led mechanisms for growth 157–8; media development 170–75; 'Media for Development' ('M4D') 158; media globalization 164–70; media infrastructures, development of 158; media ownership, expansion of 158; Miners' Radio in Bolivia 176–7; mobile phone revolution 180–87; modernization, adherence to central ideas and practices of 157; MTN Group (formerly M-Cell), South Africa 182; multimedia sources 191; 'neo-liberal turn,' economic crises (1970s) and 158–64; structural-adjustment programmes (SAPs) 162, 168, 173; summary 189–90; telephony, access to 189; 3G networks 183, 186, 187, 205; transnational companies (TNCs) 160; UN Educational, Scientific, and Cultural Organization (UNESCO) 166, 178, 184, 186; United States, Bill of Rights (1789) 171; US Civil Rights Movement 174; US National Telecommunications and Information Administration (NTIA) 184; Vivo Participacoes (VP), Brazil 182; 'Washington Consensus' 158; World Bank 161, 162, 163, 187; *World CultureReports* (UNESCO) 178; Zimbabwe Broadcasting Corporation (ZBC) 170
Goetz, N. 72
Goggin, G. and Clark, J. 211
Goodwill Ambassadors (UNICEF) 252, 256–7
Gourevitch, P. 73
Graham, Aubrey 96
Grant, A. and Wilkinson, J. 183
Gregory, S. 213–14

Grindle, M. 160
gross domestic product (GDP) 116, 160, 202–3
Grossman, L. 186
Group of Eight (G8) 244–5, 246
GROW campaign (Oxfam) 27, 103–4
GSMA Intelligence 3, 182–5, 187, 202–3
Guiltinan, J. 219
Guiyi in China 220–21
Gumucio-Dagron, A. 136, 140–41
Gunkel, D. 184–5
Gupta, A. 132
Gursel, Z. 29

Habimana, Kantano 224
Habyarimana, Juvenal 224
Hagen, Erica 214–15
Haiti earthquake disaster (2010) 95; GIS and 212–13
Halkin, Alexandra 17, 146–8
Hall, Stuart 8–9, 41, 52
Hall's Theory (1973) 194
Haney, E. 165
al Haq, Mahbub 124–5
Harris, Alice and John 69, 70
Harrison, G. 246, 255
Hattori, M. 26, 101
Heeks, R. 3
Heffelfinger, E. and Wright, L. 99
Herman, Edward 122, 199
Highly-Indebted Poor Countries (HIPC) Initiative 239–40, 246
Hill, A. 251
HIV/AIDS pandemic: *Communications Framework for HIV/AIDS* (UNAIDS, 1999) 143; 'Media for Development' ('M4D') 47, 55–6, 57, 58, 141, 142, 248–9
Hjarvard, S. 8
Hobbs, R. 22
Honduras, social marketing and infant mortality in 47–8
Hooper, Captain Willoughby Wallace 24, 69, 78
Hornik, R. 119

Howard, P., Agarwal, S. and Hussain, M. 206, 207
Howden, D. 255
Howley, K. 178, 179
Huesca, R. 142, 176–7
Hughes, N. and Lonie, S. 185
Hugo, P. 194, 220
Hulme, David 237, 239, 244
Human Development Index (HDI) 241
Human Poverty Index (HPI) 124–5
humanitarianism: histories of 66–77; humanitarian imagery, overexposure to 94–5; international development and, elision in media imagery of 64–5

iconographic imagery 65; 'Iconography of Suffering' 93–4
'ICT4D' 35, 158, 186, 189, 236, 257; media and development, relationship between 5, 6
'ICT4D' in new media worlds 30, 192–232; *Africa: The Impact of Mobile Phones* (Vodafone) 202; africasacountry.com 208–9; Anti-homosexuality Act (2014) 227; Arab Spring, media and 206–7; Bottom of the Pyramid (BoP) approach 203–4; challenges and detriments 215–28; challenges in new environments for ICT4D 215–28; Consultative Group to Assist the Poor (CGAP) 205; 'cross-platform' approaches 194; 'crowded' media environments 193–4; CTCnet 199; discussion questions 230–31; electrical and electronic equipment (EEE) 218–19; English Premier League (EPL) football 195–6, 216–17; e-waste 218–19; e-waste generation 194; FBI Internet Crime Complaint Center 229; further reading, suggestions for 231; Gateway TV (GTV) 195–6, 216–17; genre and reception, complexities of 193–4; geographic information systems (GIS): Haiti earthquake disaster (2010) and 212–13; KONY 2012 campaign and 213–14; Map Kibera Project (MKP) and 214–15; Global E-Waste Monitor 219, 222; Global Financial Crisis (GFC, 2008) 216–17; Global South 197, 217, 222, 229; Guiyi in China 220–21; Haiti earthquake disaster (2010), GIS and 212–13; Hall's Theory (1973) 194; ICT4D 2.0 193; International Criminal Tribunal for Rwanda (ICTR) 225; international development, emergence of 'new orthodoxy' in 192; International Telecommunications Union (ITU) 200; internet, responses to developments of 198–202; internet scams 229–30; iPhone5S 219; *Kanugura* (Hutu extremist newspaper) 226; KONY 2012 campaign, social media and 213–14; liquid crystal display (LCD) televisions 218–19; Map Kibera Project (MKP) 214–15; media activism 205–10; media content, exposure to 195; media environments, opportunities and challenges of innovations in 193; 'Media for Development' ('M4D') 193, 226; media infrastructures, expansion of 216–17; media ownership, expansion of 217–18; mobile money 203–5; mobile phone revolution, responses to 198–203; multimedia resources 232; non-governmental organizations (NGOs) 193, 195–6, 200–201, 205, 210, 213, 215, 217, 221–2, 226; opportunities and potential 195–215; outcomes detrimental to development goals 194; Panos Institute 197; Parallel Vote Tabulation (PVT) 208; participatory GIS 210–15; print media, responses to globalization of 195–8; radio, responses to globalization of 195–8; Radio Bentiu FM 226; Radio for Peacebuilding (R4P) network 226; Radio-Television Libre des Milles Collines (RTLM) 223–6; Resolve LRA Crisis Initiative 213–14; SMS text

messaging 206, 207, 208, 210, 211–12, 215; social media, responses to developments in 198–203; socio-economic development, effect of media shifts on 192; Solving The E-Waste Problem (STEP) initiative 222; structural-adjustment programmes (SAPs) 223; summary 230; *Telecentre Cookbook for Africa* (UNESCO, 2001) 201; television, responses to globalization of 195–8; 3D spatial models 211; toxic media content 222–8; UN Educational, Scientific, and Cultural Organization (UNESCO) 200, 201; UN Stabilization Mission in the Democratic Republic of Congo (MONUSCO) *226*; UN World Summits on the Information Society (WSIS) 200; Web 2.0 211; World Bank 205, 206, 223; World Bank World Development Report (2016) 199
'identifiable victim effect' 88
The Image, or, What Happened to the American Dream? (Boorstin, D.) 167
Import Substitution Industrialization (ISI) 159
Indian Famine Relief Committees 24–5
indigenous environmental (or ecological) knowledge (IEK) 16
indigenous knowledge (IK) 130
indigenous media (IM): criticisms of 149–52; media empowerment and 144–5, 146–8, 153
industrialization 40, 128, 162; growth of 124; state-led industrialization 158–9
inequalities: digital divide and 184–5; economic imbalances and 122–3
Infant Formula Action Coalition (INFACT) 52
information-communication technologies (ICTs) 3, 4
'information poverty,' concept of 236
Ingold, T. 13
Interactive Voice Response (IVR) surveys 243

International Bureau for the Development of Communication (UNESCO) 173
International Committee of the Red Cross (ICRC) 25
International Criminal Tribunal for Rwanda (ICTR) 225
international development: agencies of, increase in numbers of 66; emergence of 'new orthodoxy' in 192; humanitarianism and, elision in media imagery of 64–5; outcomes detrimental to goals of 194; practice of development, orientation towards 113–14; as transitive process for modernization 40
International Development, UK Department for (DfID) 142, 204–5
International Development Association (IDA) 34
International Finance Corporation (IFC) 34
international intellectual property (IP) laws 16
International Journal of Cultural Studies 102
International Monetary Fund (IMF): celebrity, development and 238, 239–40, 246; globalization of media, structural-adjustment and 162, 163, 187, 223; media and development, relationship between 2, 18, 19
International Research and Exchanges Board Media Sustainability Index (MSI) 22
International Telecommunications Union (ITU) 200
internet: internet scams 229–30; responses to developments of 198–202
Inuit Broadcasting Corporation (IBC) 150–51
Invisible Children 28, 213–14
iPhone5S 219
Islamic State (ISIS) 29, 227

Jacobs, Sean 100
James, Wendy 179

Jana Sanskriti and TFD in India 139
Japan International Cooperation Agency (JICA) 36
Jayasuriya, Kanishka 237
Jensen, Mike 8, 201
Jhala, A. 166
Johnson, Douglas 255–6
Johnson, Lyndon B. 72–3
Joint Church Aid (JCA) 72, 73, 95
Jones, Quincy 244
Jones, W. 209, 210

Kahn, Alta 145
Kakwani, N. and Pernia, E. 240
Kamlongera, C. 138, 140
Kangalawe, R. 133
Kanugura (Hutu extremist newspaper) 226
Kapoor, I. 248, 253
Karlyn, A. 57
Kato, David 227
Katz, Elihu 39
Kavoori, A. and Punathambekar, A. 188
Keele University 244
Kendall, C., Foote, D. and Martorell, R. 47–8
Kenny, C. 4, 199
Khan, S. and Christiansen, J. 19, 158
Khan, Salman 188
Kharas, H. 246
Khondker, H. 207
Kidd, Ross 138, 139, 142
Kiir, Salva 255
Kimber, Captain John (slave trader) 68
Kitimana, Noel ('Noheli') 224
knowledge transfers, communication of 35, 112–13
Koczberski, G. 126
Kony, Joseph 142, 213–14
KONY 2012 campaign 28; social media and 213–14
Kotler, P. 43
Kovarik, B. 1, 4
Krieg, Peter 49
Kroo Bay 'slum' area in Freetown, Sierra Leone 96

Kuper, A. 13
Kurdi, Aylan, tragic death of 105–7

La Guardia, Fiorello 174
La Pastina, A., Rego, C. and Straubhaar, J. 54–5
Lanctot, B. 165
Lazarsfeld, Paul 39
Lennie, J. and Tacchi, J. 137, 143
Lennie, June 151
Leopold II, King of the Belgians 67
Lerner, Daniel 5, 37–8, 39, 40, 41; media empowerment 119, 120, 124
Leveson Report (2012) 23
Levy, S. 186
Lewis, D. and Kanji, N. 136
Lewis, D., Rodgers, D. and Woolcock, M. 24
Leys, C. 13, 15, 115, 117
LGBTI desires, articulation of 188
Lipson, C. 161
liquid crystal display (LCD) televisions 218–19
Lissner, J. 25, 74
Live Aid 25, 76–7, 168, 236, 244, 246
Lizarzaburu, J. 54–5
Lorber, H. and Cornelius, M. 52
Lord's Resistance Army (LRA) 142, 213–14
Losifidis, P. and Wheeler, M. 227
Lousley, C. 26, 76–7, 78, 88
Lovelock, James 128
Lumiere, Auguste and Louis 165
Lynch, M., Freelon, D. and Aday, S. 29
Lyons, T. and Mandaville, P. 209

McBride, Sean 121
McBride Report (1980) 173
McCall, M. and Minang, P. 211
McCarthy, N. 188
McCombs, M. 197
McGregor, J. and Primorac, R. 209
McKemey, K., Scott, N., Souter, D., Afullo, T., Kibombo, R. and Sakyi-Dawson, O. 204

McLuhan, Marshall 167, 227
McPhail, T. 10, 57, 120
McQuail, D. 12
Madonna 246, 257
'Madonna and Child' image 88–9
Maina, Betty 243
Mano, W. 166, 168, 183
Manufacturing Consent (Herman, E. and Chomsky, N.) 122
Map Kibera Project (MKP) 214–15
Marconi, Guglielmo 165
Mariam, Mengistu Haile 75
market activities, guiding beneficial outcomes from 234
market-led mechanisms for growth 157–8
Maron, Mikel 214–15
Marshall Plan 33
Martens, Renzo 97–8
Martin, J., Abbas, D. and Martins, R. 174
Marxist scholarship 116, 118, 123
Masaccio, Tommaso 91, 92
Mass Media and National Development (Schramm, W.) 39–40
Massachusetts Institute of Technology (MIT) 37
Maurer, B. 205
Mawarire, Pastor Evan 209
Meadows, M. and Molnar, H. 151
Médecins sans Frontières (MSF) 72
media activism 205–10
media and development, relationship between 1–32; British Colonial Film Unit (BCFU) 9–10, 52; 'development,' definition of 12–20; discussion questions 32; foreign direct investment (FDI) 18, 164; Freedom House *Freedom of the Press* Reports 22, 173–4; further reading, suggestions for 32; geographic information systems (GIS) 17, 29, 143, 211–12; GROW campaign (Oxfam) 27, 103–4; indigenous environmental (or ecological) knowledge (IEK) 16; 'Information and Communication Technologies for Development' ('ICT4D') 5, 6;
information-communication technologies (ICTs) 3, 4; International Committee of the Red Cross (ICRC) 25; international intellectual property (IP) laws 16; International Monetary Fund (IMF) 2, 18, 19; Invisible Children 28, 213–14; ISIS (Islamic State) 29, 227; KONY 2012 campaign 28; Leveson Report (2012) 23; 'media,' definition of 6–12; media development 20–24; media representations of development 24–9; non-governmental organizations (NGOs) 1, 14, 15, 16–17, 19 20; Press Freedom Index (PFI, Reporters Sans Frontières) 22, 23; SMS (short message service) 17; structural-adjustment programmes (SAPs) 2, 4, 18, 19; summary 31; UN Conference on Trade and Development (UNCTAD) 3; UNICEF Press Centre 25; United Nations (UN) 2, 57, 72; 'Uses and Gratification Theory' (UGT) 12; World Bank 2, 16, 18, 19, 34; World Summits on the Information Society (WSIS) 3, 200
media content, exposure to 195
media defined 6–12
media development: globalization of media, structural-adjustment and 170–75; media and development, relationship between 20–24
media empowerment 30, 112–56; Americas Media Initiative (AMI) 147–8; Bretton-Woods Institution 140; Canadian Broadcasting Corporation (CBC) 150–51; Canadian Radio-Television and Telecommunications Commission (CRTC) 150–51; 'C4D' (communication for development) 136, 138, 143, 151; Chiapas Media Project in Mexico 147–8; communication of knowledge transfers 112–13; *Communications Framework for HIV/AIDS* (UNAIDS, 1999) 143; Cultural Imperialism School 121; dependency

theory 115–22; development potential 113–14; discussion questions 154; *Dramas of Nationhood* (Abu-Lughod, L.) 128; environmental critique of modernization theory 128–30; feminist critiques of modernization theory 122–8; further reading, suggestions for 154–5; Gaia Theory 128; Gender and Development (GAD) 125; Global South 112, 114, 118, 121–2, 125, 128, 130, 131–2, 133, 139, 153; gross domestic product (GDP) 116, 160, 202–3; Human Poverty Index (HPI) 124–5; indigenous knowledge (IK) 130; indigenous media (IM) 144–5, 146–8, 153; indigenous media (IM), criticisms of 149–52; International Development, UK Department for (DfID) 142, 204–5; Inuit Broadcasting Corporation (IBC) 150–51; Jana Sanskriti and TFD in India 139; Lord's Resistance Army (LRA) 142, 213–14; *Manufacturing Consent* (Herman, E. and Chomsky, N.) 122; 'Media for Development' ('M4D') 113, 118–19, 120, 125–6, 130, 136–7, 143, 149–50, 153; Media Imperialism Debate 120, 121, 166; media role, recasting of 114; media sources 155–6; 'modernization,' paradigm of 112; modernization theory, critiques of 114; modernization theory, 'M4D' and 113; Multi-dimensional Poverty Index (MPI) 125, 241–2; New World Information and Communication Order (NWICO) 121, 178; non-governmental organizations (NGOs) 135, 140, 147–8, 149, 152; North American Free Trade Agreement (NAFTA) 147; *Our Common Future* ('Brundtland Report,' 1987) 129; participatory action research (PAR) 132–3, 136, 137–8, 140, 144, 145; participatory communication 132–43; participatory communication, criticisms of 149; participatory rural appraisal (PRA) 134; *Pedagogy of the Oppressed* (Freire, P.) 132–3; post-colonial development and 131–2; practice of development, orientation towards 113–14; Promedios (NGO) 147–8; rapid rural appraisal (RRA) 134; *Rural Development* (Chambers, R.) 134; summary 153; 'technology transfer' 112; Theatre in Education (TIE) Movement 138, 139; traditional environmental knowledge (TEK) 130; UN Conference on the Human Environment (Stockholm, 1972) 129; UN 'Decade for the Advancement for Women' 125; UN Earth Summit, Rio de Janeiro (1992) 129–30; UN Educational, Scientific, and Cultural Organization (UNESCO) 121; UN Food and Agriculture Organization (FAO) 143; UN Inter-Agency Round Tables on Communication for Development 143, 151; UN Joint Program on HIV/AIDS (UNAIDS) 143; UN World Commission on Environment and Development (WCED) 129; UN World Summit on Sustainable Development (Johannesburg, 2002) 130; USAID 129, 136, 163; Wan Smolbag and TFD in Vanuatu 140–41; *Woman's Role in Economic Development* (Boserup, E.) 123–4; Women in Development (WID) 125, 129; World Bank 129, 133, 136, 140, 143, 146; World Congress on Communication for Development (WCCD) 143; Zapatista National Liberation Army (EZLN) 147–8; *see also* globalization of media, structural-adjustment and

'Media for Development' ('M4D') 5, 6, 29, 33–63; Academy for Educational Development 43; baby milk, investigation on use of 49–51, 52; development communication, models of 36–40; Development Media International (DMI) 60; *Diffusion of Innovations* (Rogers, E.) 38–9, 182,

204; discussion questions 61; DKT International 43; entertainment-education 52–9; Entertainment-Education Network Africa 58; European Recovery Programme (ERP) 33; further reading, suggestions for 62; Futures Group 43; genesis of media for development 33–6; globalization of media, structural-adjustment and 158; HIV/AIDS pandemic 47, 55–6, 57, 58, 141, 142, 248–9; Honduras, social marketing and infant mortality in 47–8; ICT4D in new media worlds 193, 226; Infant Formula Action Coalition (INFACT) 52; international development as transitive process for modernization 40; International Development Association (IDA) 34; International Finance Corporation (IFC) 34; Japan International Cooperation Agency (JICA) 36; Marshall Plan 33; *Mass Media and National Development* (Schramm, W.) 39–40; media empowerment and 113, 118–19, 120, 125–6, 130, 136–7, 143, 149–50, 153; modernization, international development as transitive process for 40; *Modernization Among Peasants; The Impact of Communication* (Rogers, E. and Svenning, L.) 39; multimedia sources 62–3; multiple and concurrent sexual partnerships (MCPs) 56; non-governmental organizations (NGOs) 49, 55, 60, 72; North Atlantic Treaty Organization (NATO) 33; Overseas Development Assistance (ODA) 35, 159, 246; *The Passing of Traditional Society: Modernizing the Middle East* (Lerner, D.) 37–8; PCI Media Impact 57–9, 60; Plymouth Report (1937) 37; Population Services International 43; public health campaigns 45–52; social marketing 41–5; social marketing and infant mortality in Honduras 47–8; Soul City, South Africa 55–6; Soul City Institute 55, 56, 58–9; summary 61; Technical Cooperation Program Unit (, US, TCPU) 34, 35; Telenovelas 54–5; *Tinka Tinka Sukh* ('Happiness Lies in Small Things') in India 57–8; UN Children's Fund (UNICEF) 47; UN Development Programme (UNDP) 34; UN Partnership on Measuring ICT for Development 36; USAID 34, 43, 47; War on Want 49–50; World Health Organization (WHO) 47; *see also* 'ICT4D'

media globalization 164–70; structural-adjustment and 158, 163–4, 168–9, 170, 175, 178, 179, 180
Media Imperialism Debate 120, 121, 166
media infrastructures: development of 158; expansion of 216–17
media ownership, expansion of 158, 217–18
media sources, empowerment and 155–6
Media Sustainability Index (MSI, International Research and Exchanges Board) 22
Melkote, S. and Steeves, H. 17, 120, 137
Melkote, Srivinas 137, 151
Messi, Lionel 256
Michaelangelo 90, 91
Mill, John Stuart 21
Millennium Development Goals (UNDESA, 2008) 236, 241–3, 246, 249
Miller, Lee 80
Mills, S. 139
Milton, John 21, 170–71, 172
Minderhoud, A.-M. 19, 198
Miners' Radio in Bolivia 176–7
mobile money 203–5
mobile phone revolution 180–87; responses to 198–203
modernization: adherence to central ideas and practices of 157; international

development as transitive process for 40; paradigm of 112
Modernization Among Peasants; The Impact of Communication (Rogers, E. and Svenning, L.) 39
modernization theory 15, 16, 26, 30, 59, 61, 101, 152–3, 185, 233; critiques of 114, 115–16, 117–18, 119–20, 122–8, 128–30; dependency theory undermining logic of 117–18, 119–20; environmental critique of 128–30; feminist critiques of 122–8; interventionist logics of 115–16, 117; 'M4D' and 113
Moeller, Susan 26, 95, 174
Mohanty, Chandra Talpade 127
Montague, D. 218
Moon, J. 249
The Theory of Moral Sentiments (Smith, A,) 163
Mottaz, L. 21, 173
MTN Group (formerly M-Cell), South Africa 182
Mugabe, Robert 170, 209
Muller, Max 49, 51
Multi-dimensional Poverty Index (MPI) 125, 241–2
multimedia resources: celebrity, development and 259–60; development, representations of 111; globalization of media, structural-adjustment and 191; ICT4D in new media worlds 232; 'Media for Development' ('M4D') 62–3
multiple and concurrent sexual partnerships (MCPs) 56
Mulvey, Laura 126
Myers, M. 22, 57, 168–9, 198
Mytton, Graham 36, 166

Naess, Arne 128
Nahimana, Ferdinand 224, 225–6
Naim, M. 17
national media environments, liberalization of 175, 178
N'dour, Youssou 244

negative imagery, ethical implications of 97
Nelson, Johnny 145
Nelson, N. and Wright, S. 149
neo-liberalism 19, 234; community media and 179; 'neo-liberal turn,' economic crises (1970s) and 158–64
New Internationalist 49
New World Information and Communication Order (NWICO) 121, 178
New York Review of Books 95
newly industrialized countries (NICs) 237
News of the World 23
Ngeze, Hassan 226
Ngugi, B., Pelowski, M. and Ogembo, J. 204
Nielinger, O. 4
Nielsen, N. 98
Nissinen, S. 26, 96
Nogueira, M. 138
non-governmental organizations (NGOs): celebrity, development and 244, 257; media and development, relationship between 1, 14, 15, 16–17, 19 20; media empowerment 135, 140, 147–8, 149, 152; 'Media for Development' ('M4D') 49, 55–6, 60, 72
Nordenstreng, K. and Varis, T. 118
North American Free Trade Agreement (NAFTA) 147
North Atlantic Treaty Organization (NATO) 33
Nzima, Sam 82

Ocampo, J. and Ros, J. 159, 161
O'Connor, A. 176–7
Okolloh, O. 211
On Photography (Sontag, S.) 95
Orientalism (Said, E.) 121
Orjuela, C. 210
Ostergaard-Nielsen, E. 209
Otim, P. 17, 142
Ott, B. and Mack, R. 5, 12
Ouedraogo, Idrissa 99

Our Common Future ('Brundtland Report,' 1987) 129
Overseas Development Assistance (ODA) 35, 159, 246
Overseas Development Institute (ODI) 105
Oxfam: GROW campaign 103–4; suffering mother and child poster 81
Oxford University 125

Pack, S. 145
Palecanda, M. 28
Panos Institute 197
Parallel Vote Tabulation (PVT) 208
Parpart, J. 125
participatory communication 17, 30, 158, 175, 193, 226, 236, 243; criticisms of 149, 150; focus of, call for shift in 152; media empowerment and 114, 132–43, 144, 147, 151, 153; participatory action research (PAR) and 132–3, 136, 137–8, 140, 144, 145; participatory GIS 210–15; participatory rural appraisal (PRA) and 134
Parvez, Nazia 96
The Passing of Traditional Society: Modernizing the Middle East (Lerner, D.) 37–8
PCI Media Impact 57–9, 60
Pedagogy of the Oppressed (Freire, P.) 132–3
Peet, R. and Hartwick, E. 14
Perez de Cuellar, Javier 129
Perry, Katy 256
Peters, William 244
Pettifor, A. 244
Pettit, J., Salazar, J. and Gumucio-Dagron, A. 210
Pfau, M., Haigh, M., Logsdon, L., Perrine, C., Baldwin, J., Breitenfeldt, *et al.* 25
Philo, G. 25, 75, 76–7
Pieterson, Hector 82
Pink Floyd 246
Pitketty, T. 235
Plastow, J. 138
Plymouth Report (1937) 37

Poindexter, David 56, 57
The Political Economy of Growth (Baran, P.A.) 116
Pollack, Sydney 99
Polman, Paul 243
Ponte, S. and Richey, L. 247
Population Services International 43
Porter, D. and Craig, D. 238
post-colonial development 131–2
post-humanitarian communication 99–107
'post-Washington Consensus': development of 233–4; emergence of 235, 236, 244, 256; encouragement of private aid and PPPs 235–6; media celebrities and 236–7; metrics and targets focus of 236
Pottier, J., Bicker, A. and Sillitoe, P. 16
Poverty Reduction Strategy Papers (PRSPs) 16, 240, 242
Prahalad, C. and Hammond, A. 173
Prahalad, Coimbatore 203–4, 234
Prahalad and Hammond 21
Prebisch, Raoul 115, 116
Press Freedom Index (PFI, Reporters Sans Frontières) 22, 23
print media, responses to globalization of 195–8
Promedios (NGO) 147–8
Prunier, G. 223
public health campaigns 45–52
public-private partnerships (PPPs) 234, 247
purchasing power parity (PPP) 241, 242, 243
Pype, K. 216

Qvortrup, Lars 199

radio, responses to globalization of 195–8
Radio Bentiu FM 226
Radio for Peacebuilding (R4P) network 226
Radio-Television Libre des Milles Collines (RTLM) 223–6
Radio Venceremos 175
Rahnema, M. and Bawtree, V. 15, 131, 132
Rahnema, Majod 131–2

Ramiro Beltran, Luis 120
Rapaport, R. 184–5
rapid rural appraisal (RRA) 134
Reagan, Ronald 162
Redford, Robert 99
Reeves, H. and Baden, S. 125
Rennie, E. 14, 152, 179
Reporters Sans Frontières Press Freedom Index (PFI). 22, 23
Resolve LRA Crisis Initiative 213–14
Revue Noire 99
Rheingold, Howard 206
Rhodes, Cecil John 208
Rice, R. 9
Rice, R. and Paisley, W. 47–8
Richey, L. 25, 28, 254
Richey, L. and Ponte, S. 248–9
Rist, G. 13, 14, 133
Roberto, E. 43
Rodenbeck, M. 29
Rodney, W. 15, 255
Rogers, E. and Antola, L. 54–5
Rogers, E. and Svenning, L. 39
Rogers, Everett 5, 7, 38–9, 41–2, 57, 60; ICT4D in new media worlds 204, 207; media empowerment 119, 120, 126; media globalization, structural-adjustment and 180, 182
Rolling Stone 227–8
Rony, F. 150
Roosevelt, Eleanor 174
Rosenberg, E. 229–30
Rosselli, Cosimo 91
Rosser, Andrew 237
Roth, L. 150, 151
Rousseau, Jean-Jacques 171–2
Rowe, D. 167
Ruggiero, T. 12
Ruggiu, Georges 224
Rural Development (Chambers, R.) 134
Russell, Jason 214
Russomanno, J. 171

Sabido, Miguel 54, 55, 56, 57
Sachs, Wolfgang 15, 131–2
Sadgrove, J., Vanderbeck, R., Andersson, J., Valentine, G. and Ward, K. 227
'safety nets,' provision of 234
Sahn, D., Dorosh, P. and Younger, S. 18
Said, Edward 121
Salgado, Sebastiao 80, 86, 93, 257
San Francisco State University 144
Sanskriti, Jana 139
Saunders, K. 126
Schelling, Thomas 88
Schneider, J. 166
Schramm, Wilbur 5, 8, 39–40, 120
Scott, M. 21, 27, 173, 175, 180, 251
Sellers, William 9
Sembène, Ousmane 99
Sen, Amartya 124–5
Serra, N. and Stiglitz, J. 19, 158, 234, 239
Servaes, Jan 137, 143, 149
Shawcross, W. and Hodgson, F. 93
Sheffer, G. 209
Shriver, Bobby 248–9
Sillitoe, P. 16
Singer, Hans 115, 116
Singer-Prebisch hypothesis 115–16, 117
Singhal, A. and Rogers, E. 58
Singhal, Arvind 58
Sireau, N. 246
Sissako, Abderrahmane 140
Skuse, A. 57
Sliwinski, S. 68, 80
Slocum, N. 16, 133
Smith, Adam 162–3
Smith, W. 47–8
Smolbag, Wan 140–41
SMS (short message service) 17; surveys 243; text messaging 206, 207, 208, 210, 211–12, 215
Snoop Dogg 246
social change, community management of 179–80
social marketing 41–5; infant mortality in Honduras and 47–8
social media, responses to developments in 198–203
Social Research 115

Society for Effecting the Abolition of the Slave Trade (SAST) 67–8, 93
socio-economic development, effect of media shifts on 192
soldier-protector image 88, 90, 91
Solving The E-Waste Problem (STEP) initiative 222
Sontag, Susan 26, 88, 95–6
Soul City, South Africa 55–6; Soul City Institute 55, 56, 58–9
southern societies, systematic exploitation of 117
Stabilization Mission in the Democratic Republic of Congo (MONUSCO) *226*
Stevie Wonder 246
Sting 244
Stottlemyre, S. and Stottlemyre, S. 212
Strand, C. 227
Straus, Scott 225
Streep, Meryl 99
structural-adjustment programmes (SAPs): globalization of media, structural-adjustment and 162, 168, 173; ICT4D in new media worlds 223; media and development, relationship between 2, 4, 18, 19
Struk, J. 84
suffering, Christian iconography of 87–8, 89–93, 93–4
summaries: celebrity, development and 258; development, representations of 109–10; globalization of media, structural-adjustment and 189–90; ICT4D in new media worlds 230; media and development, relationship between 31; media empowerment 153; 'Media for Development' ('M4D') 61
Sumner, A. and Mallett, R. 235

Tacchi, Jo 151
Taylor, R. and Gaskell, I. 140–41
Technical Cooperation Program Unit (US, TCPU) 34, 35
technological disadvantage, dependency theory and 118
'technology transfer,' empowerment and 112
Telecentre Cookbook for Africa (UNESCO, 2001) 201
Telenovelas 54–5
telephony, access to 189
television, responses to globalization of 195–8
Tettey, W. 173
Thatcher, Margaret 162
Theatre for Development (TFD) 17, 138, 139, 140–41, 142, 146, 153
Theatre in Education (TIE) Movement 138, 139
'third way' in development 233
'Third World' 1; *see also* Global South
Thompson, K. 166
3D spatial models 211
3G networks 183, 186, 187, 205
Through Navajo Eyes (Worth, S. and Adair, J.) 145
Thussu, D. 178
Time Magazine 80
Tinka Tinka Sukh ('Happiness Lies in Small Things') in India 57–8
Tomlinson, J. 121
toxic media content 222–8
traditional environmental knowledge (TEK) 130
transnational companies (TNCs) 160
'trickle-down' process 234
Truman, Harry S. 33–5, 36–7, 113, 115, 131
Tsosie, Mary Jane 145
Tsosie, Maxine 145
Tufte, T. 56
Tufte, T. and Mefalopulos, P. 149
Turner, Terence 146
Twomey, C. 25, 67, 70

UN Children's Fund (UNICEF): celebrity, development and 252; 'Media for Development' ('M4D') 47; Press Centre 25
UN Educational, Scientific, and Cultural Organization (UNESCO): celebrity,

development and 236; globalization of media, structural-adjustment and 166, 184, 186; ICT4D in new media worlds 200; International Bureau for the Development of Communication 173; media empowerment 121
UN Food and Agriculture Organization (FAO): development, representations of 76; media empowerment 143
'Under Western Eyes: Feminist Scholarship and Colonial Discourses' (Mohanty, C.T.) 127–8
underdevelopment, dependency theory and 116–17
United Nations (UN): Conference on the Human Environment (Stockholm, 1972) 129; Conference on Trade and Development (UNCTAD) 3; 'Decade for the Advancement for Women' 125; Department for Economic and Social Affairs (UNDESA) 236, 241–3, 246, 249; Development Programme (UNDP) 34, 241; Earth Summit, Rio de Janeiro (1992) 129–30; Educational, Scientific, and Cultural Organization (UNESCO) 21, 35, 36, 39; High Commission for Refugees (UNHCR) 251; High Level Plenary Meeting (2010) 243; Human Development Reports (UNDP) 241; Information and Communication Technologies Task Force (UNICTTF) 236; Inter-Agency Round Tables on Communication for Development 143, 151; International Bureau for the Development of Communication (IBDC) 21; International Criminal Tribunal for Rwanda (ICTR) 225; Joint Program on HIV/AIDS (UNAIDS) 143; media and development, relationship between 2, 58, 72; Millennium Summit (New York, 2000) 241; Partnership on Measuring ICT for Development 36; Stabilization Mission in the Democratic Republic of Congo (MONUSCO) *226*; System Task Team 243; Universal Declaration of Human Rights (UNGA, 1948). 21, 172; World Commission on Environment and Development (WCED) 129; World Summit on Sustainable Development (Johannesburg, 2002) 130; World Summits on the Information Society (WSIS) 200
United States: Agency for International Development (USAID) 34, 43, 47; Bill of Rights (1789) 171; Civil Rights Movement 174; National Telecommunications and Information Administration (NTIA) 184; Technical Cooperation Program Unit (US, TCPU) 34, 35; USAID 34, 43, 47, 129, 136, 163
University of Cape Town (UCT) 208
University of Manchester 247
University of Pennsylvania 144
Unwin, T. 3
urbanization 37, 40, 128, 160; growth of 124
'Uses and Gratification Theory' (UGT) 12
Uvin, P. 223

Van der Gaag, N. and Nash, C. 76, 102
Van Dijk, J. 184–5
Vandevoordt, R. 28
Vaughan, Peter 57
Vernet, Horace 165
Vestergaard, A. 26, 93
Vigil, J. 175
'visual memory' 80, 93
Vivo Participacoes (VP), Brazil 182
Vodafone 202
Vokes, Richard 7, 19, 24, 28, 71, 99, 142; ICT4D in new media worlds 196, 198, 210, 213–14, 216–17, 223, 225

Waisbord, S. 10, 48, 137
Wakefield, A. 56
Walker, Peter 140–41
Wan Smolbag and TFD in Vanuatu 140–41
War on Want 49–50
Washington Consensus 17–18, 19, 195, 197, 203, 234, 238, 239; globalization of

media, structural-adjustment and 158; media globalization, structural-adjustment and 163–4, 168–9, 170, 175, 178–80; poorest people and policies of 235; post-Washington Consensus 19, 233–4, 235, 236–7, 238–9, 244, 246–7, 256
Wasserman, H. 22
Wealth of Nations (Smith, A,) 163
Web 2.0 211
Welch, D. 172
Wilberforce, William 68
Wilke, J. 172
Wilkie, Wendell 174
Wilkins, K. and Enghel, F. 247
Williams, Serena 256
Williamson, John 17, 163
Wilson, P. and Stewart, M. 152
Winfrey, Oprah 188
Woman's Role in Economic Development (Boserup, E.) 123–4
Women in Development (WID) 125, 129
Wood, D. 165
Woodward, H. 140–41
World Bank: celebrity, development and 238, 239–40, 243, 246; global poverty line, development of 240, 241; globalization of media, structural-adjustment and 161, 162, 163, 187; ICT4D in new media worlds 205, 206, 223; media and development, relationship between 2, 16, 18, 19, 34; media empowerment 129, 133, 136, 140, 143, 146; World Development Report (2016) 199
World Congress on Communication for Development (WCCD) 143
World CultureReports (UNESCO) 178
World Food Programme (WFP) 102
World Health Organization (WHO) 47
World Lutheran Foundation 94–5
World Summits on the Information Society (WSIS) 3, 200
worldwewant2030.org 243
Worth, Sol 144, 145, 151
Wortham, E. 147–8

Young, R. 15, 132
Yousafzai, Malala 257–8
Yrjola, Rinna 254

Zapatista National Liberation Army (EZLN) 147–8
Zimbabwe Broadcasting Corporation (ZBC) 170
Zook, M., Graham, M., Shelton, T. and Gorman, S. 211, 212–13